Wetlands

LAW AND POLICY

Understanding Section 404

Susan L. Stephens, Kim D. Connolly, and Sarah P. Jarboe

ABA AMERICAN BAR ASSOCIATION
Environment Energy and Resources Section

Cover design by Sara Wadford/ABA Design

Printed in the United States of America.

28 27 26 25 24   5 4 3 2 1

ISBN 978-1-63905-474-9

TABLE OF CONTENTS

ABOUT THE AUTHORS

Susan L. Stephens has more than 30 years of experience practicing environmental & natural resource and administrative law, including rulemaking practice and procedure and administrative litigation. Her practice focuses on balancing property and resource use with competing private, governmental, and citizen interests.

Susan is board certified by the Florida Bar in State & Federal Government & Administrative Practice. She represents clients before various federal, state, regional, and local environmental agencies in connection with the obtainment, interpretation, compliance, and enforcement of environmental permits for regulated industrial, commercial, and development activities. This representation includes matters related to resource extraction, wetlands and mitigation banks, agritourism, wastewater, submerged lands, and state- and federal-listed wildlife. This has included significant experience working with agencies to obtain Section 404 wetland permits.

Susan graduated from Florida State University College of Law in 1993 with highest honors. She has been heavily involved with the American Bar Association Section of Environment, Energy, and Resources since graduation, including serving on the Council, Special Committee on Sponsorship, Special Committee on Marketing & Communications, and the *Trends* newsletter Editorial Board, as well as several substantive committees. She writes and presents on a variety of environmental law topics. She and her husband Richard have two grown sons and enjoy hiking, biking, and exploring together.

Kim D. Connolly is a law professor teaching environmental, clinic, and experiential courses, focusing scholarship on resources/environmental law and access to justice. Professor Connolly has focused her academic career on how best to educate future lawyers, as well as how best to use laws and policies to protect the planet and its inhabitants. She serves as the Vice Dean for Advocacy and Experiential Learning for the University at Buffalo School of Law, and directs the Clinical Legal Education Program. Professor Connolly often presents and participates in collective endeavors that focus on experiential legal education, and has served in national leadership positions (including president of the Clinical Legal Education Association) for many years. Professor Connolly also studies, writes, and speaks about environmental and animal law policies, creatively examining and sharing ideas as to how to move toward a sustainable future. She teaches two clinics at the School of Law: the Environmental Advocacy Clinic and the Animal Law Pro Bono Clinic. She also teaches substantive courses in the area of environmental law, and experiential classes in the area of ethics. Before joining the law faculty at School of Law, Professor Connolly taught at the University of South Carolina School of Law, where she was associated faculty at the School of the Environment. Before teaching, she practiced law with a number of Washington, D.C., law firms, including Beveridge & Diamond and Hunton & Williams. She received her JD, magna cum laude, from Georgetown University Law Center and her LLM with highest honors from George Washington University Law School.

Sarah P. Jarboe is an experienced environmental attorney practicing at English Lucas Priest & Owsley, LLP. She represents clients on environmental matters, including Clean Water Act Section 404, NPDES permitting, the Resource Conservation and Recovery Act, the Clean Air Act, and Superfund. Her practice includes environmental permitting, enforcement matters, regulatory interpretation, environmental litigation, and negotiations with federal and state agencies. Ms. Jarboe has worked on many "waters of the U.S." (WOTUS) matters, often joining consultants in the field to collaborate on the legal aspects of wetlands delineations and jurisdictional determinations. She currently serves as co-counsel in litigation challenging EPA's WOTUS rule, and she co-authored Chapter 22, Wetlands Considerations in Real Estate Transactions, in the American Bar Association's (ABA) fifth edition of *Environmental Aspects of Real Estate and Commercial Transactions: Acquisition, Development, and Liability Management.* Ms. Jarboe is an active ABA member, participating in the Section of Environment, Energy, and Resources' (SEER's) Leadership Development Program (2014–2015) and serving on SEER's 2016, 2017, 2020, 2022, and 2024 Fall Conference Planning Committees. Ms. Jarboe graduated from Vanderbilt University Law School, where she was managing editor of the Environmental Law and Policy Annual Review Journal. Before joining ELPO, she served as a law clerk for Kentucky's Supreme Court Chief Justice.

Lajuana S. Wilcher is a partner at English, Lucas, Priest & Owsley, LLP in Bowling Green, Kentucky. Ms. Wilcher was confirmed by the U.S. Senate in 1989 as EPA's Assistant Administrator for Water (including wetlands). As the senior manager for EPA's water programs nationwide, she was the decision official for seminal Clean Water Act Section 404 policy decisions and Section 404 permit vetoes. She was a partner at Winston & Strawn (1993–1996) and LeBoeuf, Lamb, Greene & MacRae (1996–2002) before becoming Secretary of Kentucky's Environmental and Public Protection Cabinet (2003–2006). Ms. Wilcher advises individual and corporate landowners throughout the country on Section 404 issues, among other aspects of environmental law. Ms. Wilcher has testified about wetland issues before Congress and has presented on wetlands issues nationally and internationally. She currently serves as co-counsel in litigation challenging EPA's WOTUS rule and is a fellow of the American College of Environmental Lawyers.

PREFACE AND ACKNOWLEDGMENTS

This book primarily focuses on the regulatory regime created by Section 404 of the federal Clean Water Act, known in ordinary parlance as the "dredge and fill" permitting program, with a particular focus on wetlands regulation. It also touches on state, local, and international laws touching on wetlands. This book provides a succinct yet complete overview of the legal landscape governing activities in and development of wetlands and other surface waters and contains important tips to and resources for practitioners for navigating that landscape.

The first edition of this book was published in 2005 by Kim D. Connolly, Stephen M. Johnson, and Douglas P. Williams. Work on the second edition of this book was initiated by Professor Connolly and completed by Susan Stephens, who reorganized the chapter list, rewrote chapters, and applied updates to reflect the current legal landscape of Section 404.

Chapters 1 and 3 through 10 in the first edition were originally written by Kim D. Connolly and subsequently rewritten and updated by Susan L. Stephens.

Chapter 2 was originally written by Kim D. Connolly, subsequently rewritten by Sara P. Jarboe and LaJuana S. Wilcher, and edited by Susan L. Stephens.

Susan is grateful to the following law students for their editorial assistance:

- Anna Maresa Semper, Florida State University 2024
- Kimberly Hutchinson, Stetson University 2023
- Selina Nadeau, Stetson University 2023
- Maria Schaible, George Washington University 2023

EXECUTIVE SUMMARY

The word "wetlands" refers to a variety of important ecosystems found throughout the world characterized by hydric soil, wetland vegetation, and a particular category of hydrology. A complex web of local, state, federal, and international law regulates activities in and near wetlands because of the value those systems provide to the ecosystem and in particular to downstream water quality. This book focuses primarily on the federal regulations governing wetlands: the Clean Water Act's Section 404 program. The U.S. Army Corps of Engineers, U.S. Environmental Protection Agency, and the states all play a role in implementing the Section 404 program, and these overlapping authorities create complexity and, in some cases, conflict, that are important for an environmental practitioner to understand. Implementation of the program often brings private and public development projects into conflict with groups that seek to protect wetlands from impact. In fact, disputes continue to rage in our court systems over the scope of the Section 404 program, which wetlands can be regulated by it, and the states' role in that process.

This book proceeds in logical and sequential fashion, starting with an overview of the history and scope of the Section 404 program and following with chapters explaining when a wetland is (or is not) subject to regulation under the program and which activities are subject to regulation. For regulated activities in jurisdictional wetlands, Chapters 4 and 5 explain how to navigate through the permit process and when abbreviated permits like general permits might be available. Chapters 6 and 7 expand on the permitting process for issuing individual permits, including a chapter on mitigation to offset wetland impacts and a discussion of the interagency coordination requirements intertwined with the program. Chapter 8 explains the various avenues available for a disappointed applicant or a third party to challenge the agency decision in issuing or denying a permit, as well as agency enforcement actions. Finally, Chapter 9 provides a general overview of local, state, and international wetland policies and regulations and attempts to forecast what the regulatory future may hold.

1 CHAPTER

Regulating Wetlands: A Historical Introduction and Overview of the Process

I. Introduction

The word "wetlands" refers to a variety of important ecosystems found throughout the world.[1] While wetlands across the United States differ in some important ways, they all share general characteristics of hydric soil, distinguishing vegetation, and a particular category of hydrology.[2] Wetlands include marshes, swamps, fens, bogs, tundra, and similar ecosystems and include both estuarine and freshwater systems.[3] Wetlands

---

1. *See generally* STEPHEN M. JOHNSON, WETLANDS LAW: A COURSE SOURCE (2015), https://open.umn.edu/opentextbooks/textbooks/wetlands-law-a-course-source. Since 1981, Springer has published the peer-reviewed scientific journal WETLANDS, which has distributed top-notch wetlands science to the world. *See Wetlands*, SPRINGER LINK, http://link.springer.com/journal/13157. The premier resource for wetland scientists, the Society of Wetlands Scientists, may also be of interest to those examining the policy of wetlands as it relates to wetlands science. SOCIETY OF WETLAND SCIENTISTS, http://www.sws.org/.

2. 40 C.F.R. § 232.2 (wetland definition).

3. *See* U.S. ARMY CORPS OF ENG'RS, RECOGNIZING WETLANDS: AN INFORMATIONAL PAMPHLET, https://www.nae.usace.army.mil/Portals/74/docs/regulatory/Forms/Recognizing_Wetlands.pdf.

are not just pretty places: they provide many services, including supporting clean drinking water, reducing flood events, and providing habitat for myriad fish and animal species, both vertebrate and invertebrate. They also support food crops such as rice and cranberries and trap and filter water pollutants, as well as offering opportunities for leisure and amusement.[4] While in their natural state they provide many vital services to both nature and humans,[5] conflicts often arise when wetlands lie in the path of development or other uses.

A complex web of local, state,[6] and federal laws currently regulate wetlands throughout the United States, typically in an attempt to balance some use of these areas by humans with needed protection for the services they provide.[7] Although multiple governmental programs impact wetlands in various ways, this book focuses on the heart of wetland regulation: the Clean Water Act (CWA)'s Section 404 program.[8] Over the years, wetlands regulation has become a controversial

4. *See generally* Nat'l Acad. of Sciences, Nat'l Rsch. Council, Wetlands: Characteristics and Boundaries (1995), https://nap.nationalacademies.org/catalog/4766/wetlands-characteristics-and-boundaries; U.S. Env't Prot. Agency, Economic Benefits of Wetlands, https://nepis.epa.gov/Exe/ZyPDF.cgi/2000D2PF.PDF?Dockey=2000D2PF.PDF. *See also* Brief of Ecological Society of America, Society of Wetland Scientists, American Society of Limnology and Oceanography, and Estuarine Research Federation as Amici Curiae in Support of Respondents, Rapanos v. United States, Carabell v. U.S. Army Corps of Eng'rs, 547 U.S. 715 (2006), https://www.justice.gov/sites/default/files/osg/briefs/2005/01/01/2004-1384.mer.aa.pdf, https://www.law.cornell.edu/supct/cert/04-1034.

5. The international treaty protecting wetlands, the Ramsar Convention on Wetlands, hosts a website with helpful documents and fact sheets on wetland ecosystem services. *See* The Ramsar Convention on Wetlands, *Ramsar Fact Sheets Reference Sources*, https://www.ramsar.org/document/ramsar-fact-sheets-reference-sources (last visited Apr. 10, 2024).

6. For a listing of state wetlands programs, *see* Ass'n of State Wetland Managers, Status and Trends Report on State Wetland Programs in the United States (2015).

7. The home page for the Corps Regulatory Program states "The Regulatory Program is committed to protecting the Nation's aquatic resources, while allowing reasonable development through fair, flexible and balanced permit decisions." U.S. Army Corps of Eng'rs, *Regulatory (Permits)*, http://www.usace.army.mil/Missions/CivilWorks/RegulatoryProgramandPermits.aspx (last visited Mar. 22, 2024).

8. 33 U.S.C. § 1344 (2023); *see* Kim Diana Connolly, Stephen M. Johnson & Douglas R. Williams, Wetlands Law and Policy: Understanding Section 404 (Am. Bar Ass'n 2005).

area,[9] garnering the interest of diverse stakeholders.[10] The attempts to define the wetlands and surface waters subject to CWA jurisdiction—known as "waters of the United States," or WOTUS—over the past three presidential administrations highlight this controversy, as all three definitions have been challenged in court by a variety of stakeholders.[11] As a result, implementation of these laws receives regular and intense scrutiny.[12] This makes writing about wetlands law both important and challenging.

---

9. Claudia Copeland, *Wetlands: An Overview of Issues,* CONG. RSCH. SERV. (Dec. 5, 2013), https://nationalaglawcenter.org/wp-content/uploads/assets/crs/RL33483.pdf ("Wetland protection efforts engender intense controversy over issues of science and policy. Controversial topics include the rate and pattern of loss, whether all wetlands should be protected in a single fashion, the ways in which federal laws currently protect them, and the fact that 75% of remaining U.S. wetlands are located on private lands.").

10. *See, e.g.*, MARK S. DENNISON & JAMES F. BERRY, WETLANDS: GUIDE TO SCIENCE, LAW, AND TECHNOLOGY 12 (William Andrew Inc., 1993) ("Today, regulation of wetlands is one of the most controversial areas of environmental protection law and policy. Private property owners, government regulators and wetland scientists are engaged in ongoing and vigorous debate concerning which wetlands should be regulated, how they should be regulated, and to what degree they should be regulated. Much of the controversy is driven by the conflicting economic demands of private property rights proponents and land developers who want to use wetlands, and the environmental protectionist goals of various public interest groups who want to preserve them."); *see also* Kim Diana Connolly, *Any Hope for Happily Ever After? Reflections on Rapanos and the Future of the Clean Water Act Section 404 Program, in* THE SUPREME COURT AND THE CLEAN WATER ACT: FIVE ESSAYS 43–44 (VT. J. ENV'T L. 2006), https://papers.ssrn.com/sol3/papers.cfm?abstract_id=1495166.

11. For a detailed history of the controversy surrounding the definition, *see* the regulatory tracker maintained by the Harvard Law School, *Defining Waters of the United States (WOTUS)*, https://eelp.law.harvard.edu/2017/09/defining-waters-of-the-united-states-clean-water-rule/ (last visited Mar. 1, 2024).

12. *See, e.g.*, Sackett v. U.S. Env't Prot. Agency, 598 U.S. 651 (2023) (narrowing the definition of WOTUS and casting doubt upon the WOTUS definition of the Biden administration); Pascua Yaqui Tribe v. U.S. Env't Prot. Agency, 557 F. Supp. 3d 949 (D. Ariz. 2021) (vacating and remanding the WOTUS definition of the Trump administration); *In re* E.P.A., 803 F.3d. 804 (6th Cir. 2015) (stay of the Obama administration "Clean Water Rule" WOTUS definition pending litigation); *see also* Alyson C. Flournoy, *Section 404 at Thirty-Something: A Program in Search of a Policy*, 55 ALA. L. REV. 607, 608 (2004) ("Over the years, both governmental and non-governmental reports have highlighted the persistent gaps in knowledge, enforcement, monitoring, funding, and interagency coordination under section 404, and the attendant disappointing results. . . . A review of the section 404 program's evolution under successive administrations reveals a program (and agency) perpetually in flux with a poorly-defined goal. A broad look at section 404's first thirty years highlights important

Based on congressional action in the 1970s and 1980s, subsequent regulatory developments and jurisprudence authorize the U.S. Army Corps of Engineers (Corps) and the U.S. Environmental Protection Agency (EPA) to assert federal jurisdiction over wetlands if they qualify as "waters of the United States" pursuant to CWA Section 404.[13] There have been other developments as well. Though not mandated by the CWA, the Carter administration established a parallel national goal "to minimize the destruction, loss or degradation of wetlands, and to preserve and enhance the natural and beneficial values of wetlands" in 1977.[14] President George H.W. Bush then campaigned on—and

---

tensions that have beset the section 404 program from its inception."); Hope Babcock, *Federal Wetlands Regulatory Policy: Up to Its Ears in Alligators*, 8 PACE ENV'T L. REV. 307 (1991) ("An examination of the federal wetlands permitting program reveals significant problems. These problems, combined with ingrained attitudes about the sanctity of private property, lack of public appreciation of wetland values, and insufficient political will to protect them, make it easy to see why wetlands continue to disappear and why the federal wetlands regulatory program is one of the most controversial of the country's environmental programs."); Michael C. Blumm & D. Bernard Zaleha, *Federal Wetlands Protection under the Clean Water Act: Regulatory Ambivalence, Intergovernmental Tension, and a Call for Reform*, 60 U. COLO. L. REV. 695 (1989); Oliver A. Houck, *Hard Choices: The Analysis of Alternatives under Section 404 of the Clean Water Act and Similar Environmental Laws*, 60 U. COLO. L. REV. 773 (1989) (declaring that Section 404 of the Clean Water Act "lies like an open wound across the body of environmental law, one of the simplest statutes to describe and one of the most painful to apply").

13. *Sackett*, 598 U.S. 651 at Part II.A. (discussing the history of the CWA's applicability to wetlands). *See* Chapter 2 concerning what constitutes a WOTUS subject to CWA Section 404.

14. 42 Fed. Reg. 26961 (Exec. Order 11990 of May 24, 1977); *see also* James Salzman & J.B. Ruhl, *"No Net Loss"—Instrument Choice in Wetlands Protection, in* MOVING TO MARKETS IN ENVIRONMENTAL REGULATION: LESSONS FROM TWENTY YEARS OF EXPERIENCE (Jody Freeman & Charles D. Kolstad eds., 2006), http://scholarship.law.duke.edu/cgi/viewcontent.cgi?article=2025&context=faculty_scholarship. For detailed tracking of wetlands losses, *see* U.S. FISH & WILDLIFE SERV., STATUS AND TRENDS OF WETLANDS IN THE CONTERMINOUS UNITED STATES 2009 TO 2019 (2024), https://www.fws.gov/media/status-and-trends-wetlands-conterminous-united-states-2009-2019; *see also* U.S. ARMY CORPS OF ENG'RS, REGULATORY GUIDANCE LETTER 02-02, GUIDANCE ON COMPENSATORY MITIGATION PROJECTS FOR AQUATIC RESOURCE IMPACTS UNDER THE CORPS REGULATORY PROGRAM PURSUANT TO SECTION 404 OF THE CLEAN WATER ACT AND SECTION 10 OF THE RIVERS AND HARBORS ACT OF 1899, at 1 (Dec. 24, 2002), https://www.usace.army.mil/Missions/Civil-Works/Regulatory-Program-and-Permits/Guidance-Letters/.

implemented—a "no net loss" wetlands policy,[15] and various administrations, since then, have recommitted to this goal; some have gone as far as seeking to achieve a net gain in wetland resources throughout the United States.[16] In addition to the CWA Section 404 regulatory program, other federal programs encourage preservation of wetlands through direct regulation, financial incentives, outright acquisition, or other management techniques.[17] At least 36 federal agencies have been identified as being involved in wetland-related activities.[18]

The federal government itself has acknowledged in the past that "[f]ederal policy is neither comprehensive nor consistent with respect to wetland use."[19] Wetland regulation acknowledges a past that has seen significant loss of wetlands acres and functions,[20] coupled with increasing awareness of the essential ecological services that wetlands

---

15. *George HW Bush-No Net Loss 1988*, C-SPAN, https://www.c-span.org/video/?c4907470/user-clip-george-hw-bush-net-loss-1988 (last visited Mar. 1, 2024).

16. *See* The White House, *Fact Sheet: President Announces Wetlands Initiative on Earth Day* (Apr. 22, 2004), http://georgewbush-whitehouse.archives.gov/news/releases/2004/04/20040422-1.html (setting forth information about President George W. Bush's announcement that his administration was "moving beyond a policy of 'no net loss' of wetlands to have an overall increase of wetlands in America each year"). During his presidential campaign in 2008, Barack Obama stated his intent to support "full funding for the North American Wetlands Conservation Act and fulfilling the goal of 'no net loss'; extending the swamp buster provisions of the Farm Bill, and amending the Clean Water Act to clarify that it protects isolated wetlands." *The Obameter—Support wetlands protection,* POLITIFACT.COM, http://www.politifact.com/truth-o-meter/promises/obameter/promise/282/support-wetlands-protection/.

17. "Compensatory mitigation on public lands may require multiple tools beyond land use plan designations, including right-of-way grants, withdrawals, disposal or lease of land for conservation, conservation easements, cooperative agreements, and agreements with third parties so that assurances of durability, including financial assurances, are in place to support the development, maintenance, and long-term effectiveness of the mitigation measures." U.S. Fish & Wildlife Serv. Mitigation Policy (May 10, 2023), https://www.fws.gov/policy-library/A1501fw2.

18. U.S. GOV'T ACCOUNTABILITY OFFICE, GAO/RCED-98-150, WETLANDS OVERVIEW—PROBLEMS WITH ACREAGE DATA PERSIST (1998), http://www.gpo.gov/fdsys/pkg/GAOREPORTS-RCED-98-150/pdf/GAOREPORTS-RCED-98-150.pdf.

19. R. Kramer et al., The Impact of Federal Programs on Wetlands, Volume 2: The Everglades, Coastal Louisiana, Galveston Bay, Puerto Rico, California's Central Valley, Western Riparian Areas, Southeastern and Western Alaska, The Delmarva Peninsula, North Carolina, Northeastern New Jersey, Michigan, and Nebraska: A Report to Congress by the Secretary of the Interior (Mar. 1994), https://tamug-ir.tdl.org/handle/1969.3/22747.

20. *See* STATUS AND TRENDS OF WETLANDS IN THE CONTERMINOUS UNITED STATES 2009 TO 2019, *supra* note 14. For the library collection of the U.S. Fish &

provide.[21] The vital functions performed by wetlands include maintaining and enhancing water quality, preventing or minimizing damage from floods and storms, protecting shorelines against erosion, providing habitat to a variety of species of fish and wildlife (including endangered or threatened species), and enhancing aesthetic and recreational experiences.[22] Since colonial times, experts estimate that nearly half of the wetlands in the contiguous United States—some 117 million acres—have been lost to development or otherwise destroyed.[23] Some states have lost more than 75 percent of their wetlands.[24] Furthermore,

---

Wildlife Service's Wetlands Status and Trends Reports from the 1780s through 2019, see https://www.fws.gov/library/collections/wetlands-status-and-trends-national.

21. Status and Trends of Wetlands in the Conterminous United States 2009 to 2019, *supra* note 14, Executive Summary ("Net wetland loss increased substantially (>50%) since the last Wetlands Status and Trends study period (2004–2009), resulting in the loss of 221K ac [89K ha] of wetlands, primarily to uplands, between 2009 and 2019."). *See also* U.S. Fish & Wildlife Serv., Status and Trends of Wetlands in the Conterminous United States 1986 to 1997, Executive Summary, https://www.fws.gov/media/status-and-trends-wetlands-conterminous-united-states-1986-1997 ("At the time of European settlement, the area that is now the conterminous United States contained an estimated 221 million acres (89.5 million ha) of wetlands. Over time, wetlands have been drained, dredged, filled, leveled, and flooded to the extent that less than half of the original wetland acreage remains (Dahl 1990)."). For an excellent history of wetlands in America, *see* Ann Vileisis, Discovering the Unknown Landscape: A History of America's Wetlands (1997).

22. *See* 33 C.F.R. § 320.4(b); EPA, America's Wetlands: Our Vital Link between Land and Water, Wetlands and People, https://www.epa.gov/sites/default/files/2021-01/documents/wetlands_our_vital_link_between_land_water.pdf. For an excellent overview of the value of wetlands, see Rudolf de Groot, Mishka Stuip, Max Finlayson & Nick Davidson, *Ramsar Technical Report No. 3 CBD Technical Series No. 27, Valuing Wetlands: Guidance for Valuing the Benefits Derived from Wetland Ecosystem Services,* Ramsar Tech. Reports (Nov. 2006), https://www.ramsar.org/sites/default/files/documents/pdf/lib/lib_rtr03.pdf; *see also* Millennium Ecosystem Assessment, Ecosystems and Human Well-Being: Wetlands and Water (2005), https://www.millenniumassessment.org/documents/document.358.aspx.pdf.

23. *See* Vileisis, *supra* note 21, at 2–4. For other estimates of wetland losses, *see* Kremer et al., *supra* note 19; U.S. Fish & Wildlife Serv., Wetland Status and Trends in the Coterminous United States, Mid-1970s to Mid-1980s (1991); U.S. Fish & Wildlife Serv., Wetlands of the U.S.: Current Status and Recent Trends (1984); U.S. Fish & Wildlife Serv., Wetland Losses in the United States, 1780s to 1980s (1990); Nat'l Wildlife Fed., Status Report on Our Nation's Wetlands (1987); U.S. Congress, Office of Technology Assessment, Wetlands: Their Use and Regulation (1984). For a discussion of problems associated with inventorying the nation's remaining wetlands, *see* U.S. Gov't Accountability Office, GAO/RCED-98-150, *supra* note 18.

24. Carolyn Wilke, *Mapping Wetland Loss Across Three Centuries,* Eos Sci. News (Mar. 10, 2023), https://eos.org/articles/mapping-wetland-loss-across-three-centuries.

despite programs to restrict development in wetlands, experts concluded that more than 58,000 acres of wetlands were lost annually in the conterminous United States between 1985 and 1995.[25] While that annual loss has slowed in recent years, the net loss of wetlands is still substantial. Between 2009 and 2019, there was a net loss of 221,000 acres, representing an average of 22,100 acres lost a year.[26]

This introductory chapter is designed to provide a brief history of federal wetlands regulation, as well as a snapshot of the CWA's Section 404 program (and a few other key laws). The chapter includes a checklist to help lawyers and others involved in law and policy regarding wetlands to determine whether a proposed project is subject to federal regulation and, if it is, what that regulation generally requires. Subsequent chapters help the reader delve deeper into each regulatory or policy area.

II. A Brief History of Federal Regulation of Wetlands

The Corps[27] has had responsibility to regulate waters in our nation for well over a century.[28] In passing the Rivers and Harbors Act[29] at the

25. Status and Trends of Wetlands in the Conterminous United States 1986 to 1997, *supra* note 21, at 9.

26. Status and Trends of Wetlands in the Conterminous United States 2009 to 2019, *supra* note 14. There is growing concern that replacement mitigation can't keep pace with the loss. Darryl Fears, *Study Says U.S. Can't Keep Up with Loss of Wetlands*, Wash. Post (Dec. 8, 2013), https://www.washingtonpost.com/national/health-science/study-says-us-cant-keep-up-with-loss-of-wetlands/2013/12/08/c4801be8-5d2e-11e3-95c2-13623eb2b0e1_story.html.

27. U.S. Army Corps of Eng'rs, The U.S. Army Corps of Engineers: A Brief History, http://www.usace.army.mil/About/History/BriefHistoryoftheCorps.aspx (last visited Apr. 2, 2024).

28. This authority came from the Rivers and Harbors Act of 1899 and its precursors. Rivers and Harbors Act of 1899, ch. 425, 30 Stat. 1121 (1899) (codified as amended at 33 U.S.C. §§ 401–418 (2000)). *See also* Rivers and Harbors Appropriations Act of 1886, ch. 929, 24 Stat. 310, 329 (1886); Rivers and Harbors Appropriations Act of 1890, ch. 907, 26 Stat. 426 (1890); River and Harbor Act of 1894, ch. 299, 28 Stat. 338, 363 (1894); River and Harbor Appropriations Act of 1896, ch. 314, 29 Stat. 202, 234 (1896); *see also* Gibbons v. Ogden, 22 U.S. 1, 6 (1824); The Daniel Ball, 77 U.S. 557 (1870); United States v. The Montello, 87 U.S. 430 (1874).

29. The full text of Section 10 of the Rivers and Harbors Act reads:

> That the creation of any obstruction not affirmatively authorized by Congress, to the navigable capacity of any of the waters of the United States is hereby prohibited; and it shall not be lawful to build or commence the building of any wharf, pier, dolphin, boom, weir, breakwater, bulkhead, jetty, or other structures in any port, roadstead, haven, harbor, canal, navigable river,

end of the 19th century, Congress made it unlawful "to excavate or fill, or in any manner to alter or modify the course, location, condition, or capacity of, any port, roadstead, haven, harbor, canal, lake, harbor of refuge, or inclosure [sic] within the limits of any breakwater, or of the channel of any navigable water" without a Corps permit.[30] Although litigation ensued,[31] generally the Corps' regulation of waters was considered vital to both development and national defense throughout the early and middle parts of the 20th century.[32] In the latter part of that century, as environmental consciousness made its way into policy and then law,[33] the Corps took on a new and expanded role.[34] This

---

> or other water of the United States, outside established harbor lines, or where no harbor lines have been established, except on plans recommended by the Chief of Engineers and authorized by the Secretary of War; and it shall not be lawful to excavate or fill, or in any manner to alter or modify the course, location, condition, or capacity of, any port, roadstead, haven, harbor, canal, lake, harbor of refuge, or inclosure [sic] within the limits of any breakwater, or of the channel of any navigable water of the United States, unless the work has been recommended by the Chief of Engineers and authorized by the Secretary of War prior to beginning the same.

33 U.S.C. § 403 (2000). The Corps' current regulations state in relevant part that "[t]he U.S. Army Corps of Engineers has been involved in regulating certain activities in the nation's waters since 1890." 33 C.F.R. § 320.1(a)(1) (2023).

30. 33 U.S.C. § 403.

31. *See generally* William Andreen, The Evolution of Water Pollution Control in the United States: State, Local and Federal Efforts, 1789–1972: Part II, 22 Stan. Env't L.J. 215, 215–49 (2003); William Andreen, The Evolution of Water Pollution Control in the United States: State, Local and Federal Efforts, 1789–1972: Part I, 22 Stan. Env't L.J. 145 (2003). *See also* Beatrice Hort Holmes, A History of Federal Water Resources Programs, 1800–1960 (1972).

32. U.S. Army Corps of Eng'rs, *supra* note 27.

33. *See generally* Senator Gaylord Nelson, *How the First Earth Day Came About*, Environlink, https://learn.saylor.org/mod/page/view.php?id=8453 (last updated Jan. 12, 2021) (noting that during the early and mid-1960s in giving nationwide speeches, Nelson determined that "[a]ll across the country, evidence of environmental degradation was appearing everywhere, and everyone noticed except the political establishment. The environmental issue simply was not to be found on the nation's political agenda. The people were concerned, but the politicians were not."). *See also* U.S. Env't Prot. Agency, Earth Day and EPA History, https://www.epa.gov/history/epa-history-earth-day (last updated July 17, 2023); John and Mildred Teal, Life and Death of the Salt Marsh (1969); Robert W. Adler, Jessica C. Landman & Diane M. Cameron, The Clean Water Act 20 Years Later 5–7 (1993).

34. *See* U.S. Army Corps of Eng'rs, *supra* note 27, at Environmental Activities, http://www.usace.army.mil/About/History/BriefHistoryoftheCorps/EnvironmentalActivities.aspx.

expansion was part of the 1960's conservation ethos[35] that led to the passage of the modern panoply of environmental laws.[36]

Through the passage of what quickly came to be known as the Clean Water Act,[37] the Corps was given significant responsibility in terms of regulating activities in wetlands and other waters of the United States.[38] This responsibility was shared with the newly created EPA.[39] Together, the Corps and EPA[40] created a permit process for discharges of dredged or fill materials into newly defined "navigable

35. *See* Library of Congress, Today in History: April 22—Earth Day, http://memory.loc.gov/ammem/today/apr22.html (last visited Apr. 2, 2024). One scholar reported that "[o]n August 31, [1970] Senator Ted Stevens of Alaska complained: 'Suddenly out of the woodwork come thousands of people talking about ecology.'" Jack Lewis, *The Birth of EPA*, EPA J., Nov. 1985, https://www.epa.gov/archive/epa/aboutepa/birth-epa.html. For a fascinating blog on the history of environmental law, see Sarah Milov & David Schorr, *Environment, Law, and History,* http://environmentlawhistory.blogspot.com.

36. *See generally* Richard J. Lazarus, The Making of Environmental Law (Univ. Chicago 2004). *See also* Patrick Rogers, *The Man Behind the Mission*, Natural Res. Def. Council (Apr. 19, 2016), https://www.nrdc.org/stories/man-behind-mission; William Andreen, *The Evolving Law of Environmental Protection in the United States*: *1970–1991*, 9 Env't & Plan. L.J. 96 (1992).

37. Pub. L. No. 92-500, 86 Stat. 816 (1972), *as codified in* 33 U.S.C. §§ 1251–1387 (2000), further amended in Pub. L. No. 95-217, 91 Stat. 1567 (1977); Pub. L. No. 100-4, 101 Stat. 45 (1987).

38. Specifically, Section 404 provided permitting authority to Secretary of the Army to "issue permits, after notice and opportunity for public hearings for the discharge of dredged or fill material into the navigable waters at specified disposal sites." 33 U.S.C. § 1344.

39. The National Archives, *Records of the Environmental Protection Agency [EPA]*, http://www.archives.gov/research/guide-fed-records/groups/412.html#412.1 (last visited Apr. 2, 2024).

40. EPA summarizes its role in Section 404 permitting as follows: "Develops and interprets policy, guidance and environmental criteria used in evaluating permit applications; Determines scope of geographic jurisdiction and applicability of exemptions; Approves and oversees State and Tribal assumption; Reviews and comments on individual permit applications; Has authority to prohibit, deny, or restrict the use of any defined area as a disposal site (Section 404(c)); Can elevate specific cases (Section 404(q)); Enforces Section 404 provisions." U.S. Env't Prot. Agency, *Wetland Regulatory Authority*, https://www.epa.gov/sites/default/files/2016-02/documents/regulatoryauthority.pdf (last visited Apr. 2, 2024).

waters."[41] Despite legal challenges,[42] the Corps quickly built a regulatory program.[43]

Notwithstanding decades of policy-level[44] and scholarly criticism,[45] wetlands in the United States are regulated under a system that has operated, on many levels, much the same for 50 years,[46] notwithstanding the controversy surrounding the WOTUS definition in recent years. While the statutory language has not changed in any substantive way in almost five decades, many important judicial and agency developments altered the parameters in ways important to lawyers and other stakeholders. Wetlands law and policy is the subject of mostly negative public discourse as well.[47] This book explores the parameters of the existing

41. *See* Chapter 2 for a detailed discussion of the controversies surrounding the debate over which waters are jurisdictional under the Clean Water Act.

42. *See, e.g.*, Leslie Salt Co. v. Froehlke 578 F.2d 742 (9th Cir. 1978); Minnehaha Creek Watershed Dist. v. Hoffman, 597 F.2d 617 (8th Cir. 1979); Avoyelles Sportsmen's League, Inc. v. Alexander, 511 F. Supp. 278 (W.D. La. 1981), *aff'd in part and rev'd in part on other grounds*, 715 F.2d 897 (5th Cir. 1983); Alma v. United States, 744 F. Supp. 1546 (S.D. Ga. 1990).

43. For some interesting scholarly insights into the early days of the Corps regulatory program, see Jon Kusler & Teresa Opheim, Our National Wetland Heritage: A Protection Guide 1 (2d ed. 1996); Office of Energy and Env't Law, Univ. of Ala. Law Ctr., A Survey of Wetlands Law: Monograph 3 (1980); Walter P. Stepien Jr. & Segundo J. Fernandez, Univ. of Miami Sea Grant, *Wetlands-Related Legislation in the United States* (Special Report #11, May 1977); Bernard N. Goode, *The Geographic Expansion of Section 404, in* Wetlands Law and Regulation 31, 31 (ALI-ABA Course of Study Materials, June 11–13, 1997, Washington, D.C.).

44. The Conservation Found., *Protecting America's Wetlands: An Action Agenda, The Final Report of the National Wetlands Policy Forum* (1988). This report opens with the observation that "[t]he United States urgently needs a better system for protecting and managing its wetlands." *Id.* at 1.

45. Pointing out the failures of the permitting process has been well done by scholars who have come before. *See, e.g.*, Blumm & Zaleha, *supra* note 12; Houck, *supra* note 12; Babcock, *supra* note 12; Timothy D. Searchinger, *Wetlands Issues 1993: Challenges and a New Approach,* 4 MD. J. CONTEMP. LEGAL ISSUES 13 (1993), Michael C. Blumm, *The Clinton Wetlands Plan: No Net Gain in Wetlands Protection,* 9 J. LAND USE & ENV'T L. 203 (1994); Flournoy, *supra* note 12.

46. The Clean Water Act was last amended in 1987 to increase criminal and noncriminal violations of the CWA and to add administrative penalties. 101 Stat. 45. For reflections on the 50th Anniversary of the CWA, *see* THE WHITE HOUSE, A PROCLAMATION ON THE 50TH ANNIVERSARY OF THE CLEAN WATER ACT (Oct. 17, 2022); U.S. GAO, *50 Years After the Clean Water Act—Gauging Progress* (Oct. 17, 2022), https://www.gao.gov/blog/50-years-after-clean-water-act-gauging-progress.

47. For various criticisms of the Section 404 program, *see* https://pacificlegal.org/case/sackett-v-environmental-protection-agency/; https://pacificlegal.org/clean-water-act-criminals/; https://pacificlegal.org/case/united-states-v-lapant/; http://www.epw

regulatory system. To help orient readers to the coming chapters, the next section provides a brief overview of the entire system.

III. The Section 404 Program Overview and Checklist

To assist in navigating this book, as well as the Section 404 program in general, this section provides a "checklist" overview to determine whether federal regulation might be triggered by proposed activities in a wetland and, if so, how that regulation might apply. Of course, each situation differs, sometimes significantly, and thus all proposals to undertake activities in wetlands require individual analysis and competent advice.

A few fundamentals can make the following checklist more useful. First, the core basis for the Section 404 program is found in the following CWA language: "[t]he Secretary [of the Army] may issue permits, after notice and opportunity for public hearings for the discharge of dredged or fill material into the navigable waters at specified disposal sites."[48] This language does not clearly define federal regulatory jurisdiction or its mandates, and, as a consequence, it becomes vital to consult implementing regulations issued by the Corps and EPA, as well as judicial decisions. Even these sources will often fail to provide clear answers, because, through the years, there has been considerable discord among the agencies themselves, as well as between the agencies and the courts.[49]

Second, it is important to know the key players in the wetlands regulatory arena. The Corps has responsibility for issuing permits for

.senate.gov/public/index.cfm?FuseAction=Files.View&FileStore_id=c5687274-ac36-434f-988e-0335fd9fc9f6; https://www.globalenergyinstitute.org/us-house-witnesses-clash-over-spruce-mine-permit; and https://www.globalenergyinstitute.org/us-chamber-sues-epa-and-army-corps-over-water-regulatory-overreach.

48. 33 U.S.C. § 1344.

49. One scholar recently summarized the tensions related to Section 404 regulation as follows: "These tensions can be traced in large measure to four structural flaws in section 404's design: the lack of a clear goal, the conflicts inherent in the Corps-EPA-section 404 relationship, reliance on a water statute to protect wetlands, and the regulation of activities in wetlands under a pollution control approach." Flournoy, *supra* note 12, at 608. *See also* Michael C. Blumm, *The Clean Water Act's Section 404 Permit Program Enters Its Adolescence: An Institutional and Programmatic Perspective*, 8 Ecology L.Q. 409 (1980); Blumm & Zaleha, *supra* note 12; Houck, *supra* note 12; and Robin Kundis Craig, *Beyond SWANCC: The New Federalism and Clean Water Act Jurisdiction*, 33 Env't L. 113 (2003).

the discharge of dredged or fill material,[50] except where states have assumed responsibility pursuant to Section 404(g) of the CWA.[51] By statute, the Corps is also responsible for enforcing "any condition or limitation set forth in a permit issued by" the Corps under Section 404.[52] The Corps performs these responsibilities primarily through delegation to district engineers in Corps' district offices. These district offices are organized into eight divisions[53] that provide oversight and hear administrative appeals.[54] On rare occasions, the decisions of district engineers may be "elevated" for review by Corps headquarters.[55]

---

50. 33 U.S.C. § 1344(a)–(b), (e). The home page for the website for the Corps regulatory program Headquarters office can be found at U.S. Corp of Eng'rs, *Regulatory Program and Permits*, http://www.usace.army.mil/Missions/CivilWorks/RegulatoryProgramandPermits.aspx (last visited Apr. 2, 2024). Local Corps offices can be found at Army Corps of Eng'rs, *Office Locator*, http://www.usace.army.mil/Contact/OfficeLocator.aspx.

51. To date, only two states, Michigan and New Jersey, have successfully assumed regulatory jurisdiction over wetlands and surface waters within their borders that are not "presently used, or are susceptible to use in their natural condition or by reasonable improvement as a means to transport interstate or foreign commerce shoreward to their ordinary high water mark, including all waters which are subject to the ebb and flow of the tide shoreward to their mean high water mark, or mean higher high water mark on the west coast, including wetlands adjacent thereto." 33 U.S.C. § 1344(g); *see also* https://www.epa.gov/cwa404g/basic-information-about-assumption-under-cwa-section-404. For an interactive map showing the regulatory status of each state and tribe in the country, *see* https://www.epa.gov/cwa404g/us-interactive-map-state-and-tribal-assumption-under-cwa-section-404. EPA approved Florida's Section 404 program in December 2020, but on February 15, 2024, the D.C. Circuit Court vacated Florida's Section 404 program prospectively for failure to comply with the Endangered Species Act. Ctr. for Biological Diversity, et al., v. Regan, et al., Case No. 21-119(RDM) (D.C. Cir. Feb. 15, 2024). While the court invited the defendants and intervenors to seek a limited stay of the vacatur as to applications that would not affect listed species, on April 12, the court denied Florida's motion for limited stay. Memorandum Opinion, Case No. 21-119(RDM) (Apr. 12, 2024). Thus, the State of Florida issued Section 404 permits in "assumed waters" only between December 2020 and February 15, 2024. Florida is appealing the vacatur. Center for Biological Diversity, et al., v. Regan, et al., Civil Action No. 21-119 (RDM) (D.C. Cir. Apr. 15, 2024).

52. 33 U.S.C. § 1344(s).

53. A map identifying the boundaries of Corps division offices can be found at U.S. Army Corps of Eng'rs, *Where We Are—U.S. Army Corps of Engineers*, http://www.usace.army.mil/Locations.aspx (last visited Apr. 2, 2024).

54. 33 C.F.R. pt. 331. See Chapter 9 for an overview of the administrative appeals process.

55. Elevations are pursuant to 33 U.S.C. § 1344(q). *See generally* EPA, *Dispute Resolution under CWA Section 404(q)*, https://www.epa.gov/cwa-404/dispute-resolution-under-cwa-section-404q (last updated Mar. 26, 2024).

The Corps has promulgated regulations to implement its Section 404 program responsibilities.[56] To supplement and clarify these regulations, the Corps occasionally issues Regulatory Guidance Letters (RGLs), which may be accessed online.[57] In addition, other written guidance to district engineers sometimes may be provided from Corps headquarters.[58] Although directed at obligations of Corps employees, these informal sources of regulatory information often provide useful and important details about particular issues under the Section 404 program and are worth examining.

In addition to regulations and guidance issued by Corps headquarters, the Corps' district engineers also may issue general permits authorizing a variety of activities within particular regions, states, or localities.[59] Corps headquarters also issues general permits, typically every five years, to authorize activities on a regional or nationwide basis.[60]

EPA also plays a significant role in the Section 404 program. In issuing permits, the CWA requires the Corps to apply guidelines promulgated by EPA in conjunction with the Corps.[61] Commonly referred to as the 404(b)(1) Guidelines, these "guidelines" are actually formal, binding regulations.[62] Additionally, EPA may "veto" any Corps decision to issue a Section 404 permit.[63] EPA also has certain

56. 33 C.F.R. pts. 320–332 (2023).

57. *See* U.S. Army Corps of Eng'rs, *Regulatory Guidance Letters*, https://www.usace.army.mil/Missions/Civil-Works/Regulatory-Program-and-Permits/Guidance-Letters/ (last visited Apr. 2, 2024).

58. For an example of such a "memorandum to the field" see U.S. EPA Dep't of Defense & Army Corps of Eng'rs Memorandum to the Field, *Appropriate Level of Analysis Required for Evaluating Compliance with the Section 404(b)(1) Guidelines Alternatives Requirements*, https://www.epa.gov/cwa-404/memorandum-appropriate-level-analysis-required-evaluating-compliance-cwa-section-404b1 (last updated Mar. 26, 2024).

59. 33 U.S.C. § 1344(e).

60. *See* 33 C.F.R. pt. 330; *Nationwide Permit Information*, http://www.usace.army.mil/Missions/CivilWorks/RegulatoryProgramandPermits/NationwidePermits.aspx (last visited Apr. 2, 2024). *See* Chapter 5 for a detailed overview of the nationwide permit process.

61. 33 U.S.C. § 1344(b).

62. 40 C.F.R. pt. 230, http://www.nap.usace.army.mil/Portals/39/docs/regulatory/regs/40cfr230.pdf. *See* Chapter 4 for a detailed overview of the Section 404(b)(1) Guidelines.

63. 33 U.S.C. § 1344(c). *See* Chapter 7 for a detailed overview of the EPA veto process.

enforcement responsibilities for Section 404,[64] and is also granted authority to review and approve applications by states seeking to assume some of the Corps' permitting responsibilities within the respective states' geographic boundaries.[65] The statutory division of authority between EPA and the Corps has, in certain circumstances, generated confusion about program responsibilities, some of which has been clarified through memoranda of agreement between the agencies.[66]

Given this background with respect to the regulatory players, the following checklist should prove helpful in determining whether—and how—specific activities in particular wetlands might be regulated. The subsequent chapters then provide significant detail about each program's requirements.

---

64. *See* 33 U.S.C. § 1319; *see also* Memorandum between the Department of the Army and the Environmental Protection Agency concerning *Federal Enforcement for the Section 404 Program of the Clean Water Act* (1989), https://www.epa.gov/cwa-404/federal-enforcement-section-404-program-clean-water-act (last updated Jan. 11, 2024).

65. Provision for and criteria governing state assumption of permitting authority are found in Section 404(g) of the Clean Water Act, 33 U.S.C. § 1344(g).

66. *See* Memorandum of Agreement Concerning the Determination of the Geographic Jurisdiction of the Section 404 Program, *reprinted in* 58 Fed. Reg. 4995 (Jan. 19, 1993); Memorandum of Agreement between the Environmental Protection Agency and the Department of the Army Concerning the Determination of Mitigation under the Clean Water Act Section 404(b)(1) Guidelines, *reprinted in* 55 Fed. Reg. 9210 (Mar. 12, 1990); Clean Water Section 404(q) Memorandum of Agreement between the Environmental Protection Agency and the Department of the Army, https://www.epa.gov/cwa-404/cwa-section-404q-memorandum-agreement-between-epa-and-department-army-text (last updated Apr. 1, 2024); Memorandum of Agreement between the Department of the Army and the Environmental Protection Agency Concerning Federal Enforcement for the Section 404 Program of the Clean Water Act, https://nepis.epa.gov/Exe/ZyPDF.cgi/200053CG.PDF?Dockey=200053CG.PDF (last visited Apr. 2, 2024); 1986 Memorandum of Agreement between the Assistant Administrator for External Affairs and Water, U.S. Environmental Protection Agency, and the Assistant Secretary of the Army for Civil Works Concerning Regulation of Discharges of Solid Waste under the Clean Water Act, https://www.epa.gov/cwa-404/memorandum-agreement-between-epa-and-army-concerning-regulation-discharges-solid-waste (last updated May 4, 2023).

Additionally, the Corps and EPA have jointly issued field guidance concerning the Section 404 program. *See* EPA, Memorandum: Individual Permit Flexibility for Small Landowners, https://www.epa.gov/cwa-404/memorandum-individual-permit-flexibility-small-landowners-under-cwa-section-404 (last updated Mar. 26, 2024); Memorandum: *Appropriate Level of Analysis*, *supra* note 58.

Checklist to Determine Whether and How to Apply Federal Regulation to Wetlands in the United States

1. Does the federal government have geographic jurisdiction over the project you are proposing? (See Chapter 2.)
   a. May the project area properly be delineated as a wetland?
   b. Assuming the project area does include wetlands, are these wetlands "navigable waters"/"waters of the United States"?
2. Does the federal government have jurisdiction to regulate the activity you are proposing to undertake? (See Chapter 3.)
   a. Is the activity exempted by statute from federal regulation?
   b. Does the project contemplate any discharges?
   c. If discharges are contemplated, will dredged or fill material be included in the discharge?
3. If the government has jurisdiction over the project area and the proposed activities, do you qualify for
   a. A Section 404(e) permit (a nationwide permit, a state programmatic general permit, or a regional general permit) (See Chapter 5) or
   b. A letter of permission? (See Chapter 5.)
4. If you are required to obtain an individual permit, have the following conditions been met? (Generally, see Chapter 4.)
   a. Compliance with the Section 404(b)(1) Guidelines, including a practicable alternatives analysis and mitigation plan (See Chapter 6.)
   b. Satisfaction of the Public Interest Review (See Chapter 4.)
   c. Compliance with other applicable laws, such as the Endangered Species Act, the National Historic Preservation Act, and the National Environmental Policy Act (See Chapter 4.)
   d. Certification from the appropriate state(s) that you comply with applicable state laws, including state water quality standards (Section 401 of the Clean Water Act) and coastal zone management programs (Coastal Zone Management Act) (See Chapter 7.)
5. If the Corps district proposes to issue a permit, do EPA and other agencies concur with its analysis? (See Chapter 7.)
6. If you disagree with the District Office decision, will you choose to bring (See Chapter 8):
   a. An Administrative Appeal
   b. A Court challenge
   c. A Takings challenge
7. Have you undertaken something that should require a permit, or violated a permit, triggering an enforcement action? (See Chapter 8.)

A. Does the Federal Government Have Geographic Jurisdiction?

As discussed in detail in Chapter 2, Section 404 only applies if the federal government has jurisdiction over the area proposed for a project or development. Determining whether such jurisdiction exists requires answers to two questions. First, can the land be delineated as a wetland? Second, if wetlands are part of the project area, are these wetlands "navigable waters" (otherwise known as "waters of the United States")?

Wetland delineation is based on a scientific assessment of the particular property. Both EPA and the Corps have promulgated identical regulations defining wetlands as "those areas that are inundated or saturated by surface or ground water at a frequency and duration sufficient to support, and that under normal circumstances do support, a prevalence of vegetation typically adapted for life in saturated soil conditions."[67] To ascertain whether the three parameters in this definition (hydrophytic vegetation, hydric soil, and hydrology) are met, field personnel use a delineation manual.[68] In most cases, assistance from someone with wetland science expertise is helpful in the delineation process.[69] All three criteria must be met for an area to qualify as a wetland.[70]

The second question as to whether geographic jurisdiction can be claimed requires analysis of whether a delineated wetland may properly be treated as "navigable waters" as required by the statutory language in Section 404.[71] "Navigable waters" are defined in the CWA as "waters of the United States," or WOTUS.[72] The courts have concluded that this definition signaled Congress's intent to provide a

67. 33 C.F.R. § 328.3(b) (Corps); 40 C.F.R. § 230.3(t) (EPA).

68. U.S. Army Corps of Eng'rs, Wetlands Delineation Manual (1987), https://www.lrh.usace.army.mil/Portals/38/docs/USACE%2087%20Wetland%20Delineation%20Manual.pdf, Regional Supplements to the 1987 Delineation Manual are available at U.S. Army Corps of Eng'rs, *Regional Supplements to Corps Delineation Manual,* http://www.usace.army.mil/Missions/CivilWorks/RegulatoryProgramandPermits/reg_supp.aspx (last visited Apr. 2, 2024).

69. The Society of Wetland Scientists provides listings of wetland-related courses, including many about delineation. Society of Wetland Scientists, *Wetland-Related Training Courses and Workshops,* https://www.sws.org/education-outreach/.

70. EPA, *How Wetlands Are Defined and Identified under CWA Section 404*, https://www.epa.gov/cwa-404/how-wetlands-are-defined-and-identified-under-cwa-section-404 (last updated Apr. 1, 2024).

71. 33 U.S.C. § 1344(a).

72. *Id.* § 1362(7).

more expansive jurisdiction under Section 404 than is provided by the Corps' jurisdiction over activities in "navigable waters" under the Rivers and Harbors Act of 1899 (RHA).[73] On this basis, federal regulatory jurisdiction has evolved over the years to include areas that fall well beyond traditional views of what may be treated as "navigable waters."

The evolution of the Corps' jurisdiction shifted with three U.S. Supreme Court decisions: *Solid Waste Agency of Northern Cook County v. U.S. Army Corps of Engineers (SWANCC)*,[74] *Rapanos v. United States*,[75] and *Sackett v. EPA*.[76] Since these crucial decisions, many courts and scholars have considered the ramifications of these cases.[77] Three different presidential administrations have issued revised regulations defining WOTUS, with the most recent going into effect on March 20, 2023, was being promptly challenged, and then quickly amended on September 8, 2023, after *Sackett v. EPA* declared much of the rule invalid.[78] This subject is treated in detail in Chapter 2.

B. Does the Federal Government Have Jurisdiction to Regulate the Activity You Are Proposing to Undertake?

As discussed in detail in Chapter 3, even if an area is delineated as a wetland and is a "WOTUS," project activities in these wetlands may not be subject to regulation under Section 404. A number of determinations are involved in deciding whether a proposed activity is a regulated activity: Does an exemption apply? Is there a discharge? If so, is dredged or fill material being discharged?

Congress included statutory exemptions to Section 404 regulation through Section 404(f)(1).[79] The first, and most significant, Section 404(f)(1) exemption is for "normal farming, silviculture and ranching

73. *See, e.g.*, Nat. Res. Def. Council, Inc. v. Callaway, 392 F. Supp. 685 (D.C. Cir. 1975); United States v. Riverside Bayview Homes, 474 U.S. 121 (1985).

74. 531 U.S. 159 (2001).

75. 547 U.S. 715 (2006).

76. 598 U.S. 651 (2023).

77. *See* U.S. EPA, *History of "Waters of the United States,"* https://www.epa.gov/cwa-404/definition-waters-united-states-under-clean-water-act#history.

78. *See* 88 Fed. Reg. 3004 (Jan. 18, 2023), https://www.epa.gov/system/files/documents/2023-01/Revised%20Definition%20of%20Waters%20of%20the%20United%20States%20FRN%20January%202023.pdf; 88 Fed. Reg. 61964 (Sep. 8, 2023) .

79. 33 U.S.C. § 1344(f).

activities."[80] That exemption applies to certain continuous activities involving farming, timber harvesting, and related activities.[81] Section 404(f)(1) also includes other exemptions for maintenance (including emergency repair of recently damaged, currently serviceable structures), construction of temporary sedimentation basins, construction or maintenance of farm ponds, irrigation ditches, farm or forest roads, and temporary roads for moving mining equipment.[82] These exemptions do not apply, however, if the proposed activity has "as its purpose bringing an area of the navigable waters into a use to which it was not previously subject, where the flow or circulation of navigable waters may be impaired or the reach of such waters be reduced[.][83] More information about exemptions is provided in Chapter 3.

Assuming an exemption does not apply to a particular activity, Section 404 will not be triggered unless the proposed activity involves a "discharge." Discharges of dredged or fill material generally convert wet areas into sites suitable for agriculture, commercial, residential, or other forms of development, or to enhance the navigability of deep-water areas. CWA Section 301 generally prohibits the "discharge of any pollutant by any person" that does not comply with conditions set forth in a permit.[84] The term "discharge of a pollutant" is defined to include "any addition of any pollutant to navigable waters from any point source."[85] The term "pollutant" is defined expansively to include a variety of fill materials, such as rock and sand, as well as "dredged spoil."[86] Thus, the prohibition against the addition of pollutants from point sources includes a variety of activities that are routinely undertaken to develop wetlands for residential, commercial, or agricultural purposes.

The term "discharge" became the subject of serious litigation and administrative actions starting in the 1990s. Referred to as the "Tulloch Rule," following a tumultuous back-and forth, the Corps and EPA promulgated a direct final rule to amend the regulation that defines the term "discharge of dredged material" to conform with the decision by

80. *Id.* § 1344(f)(1)(A).
81. *Id.* § 323.4.
82. *Id.* § 1344(f)(1)(B)–(E).
83. *Id.* § 1344(f)(2).
84. *Id.* § 1311(a).
85. *Id.* § 1362(12).
86. *Id.* § 1362(6).

returning to an earlier regulation in 2008.[87] Chapter 3 provides further detail on the current interpretation of the scope of activities properly classified as a "discharge."

Assuming that there is no applicable exemption and that an activity involves a discharge, the last question is whether the discharge includes dredged or fill material. Dredged material is "material that is excavated or dredged from waters of the United States."[88] Fill material is defined by the Corps as including "material placed in waters of the United States where the material has the effect of: (1) Replacing any portion of a water of the United States with dry land; or (2) Changing the bottom elevation of any portion of a water of the United States."[89] Fill material can include rock, sand, soil, clay, plastics, construction debris, wood chips, overburden from mining or other excavation activities, and certain other materials.[90] Further details on what constitutes dredged and fill material for purposes of regulation can be found in Chapter 3.

C. If the Government Has Jurisdiction and Regulates the Activity You Are Undertaking, Do You Qualify for Expedited Review?

As explained earlier, Section 404 prohibits discharges of dredged or fill material into waters of the United States unless authorized by a permit issued by the Corps or expressly exempted by statute.[91] The Corps considers almost 100,000 permit applications per year.[92] However, most activities subject to Section 404 jurisdiction do not require

87. U.S. Army Corps of Eng'rs & U.S. Env't Prot. Agency, Revisions to the Clean Water Act Regulatory Definition of "Discharge of Dredged Material"; Final Rule, 73 Fed. Reg. 79,641 (Dec. 30, 2008), *see also* U.S. Env't Prot. Agency, *Further Revisions to the Clean Water Act Regulatory Definition of Discharge of Dredged Material*, http://water.epa.gov/lawsregs/lawsguidance/cwa/dredging/index_dredged.cfm (last updated Mar. 1, 2024).

88. 33 C.F.R. § 323.2(c).

89. *Id.* § 232.2(e)(1).

90. *Id.* § 232.2(e)(2).

91. Statutory exemptions are found at 33 U.S.C. § 1344(f). Regulations implementing these exemptions and promulgated by the Corps and EPA may be found, respectively, at 33 C.F.R. § 323.4 and 40 C.F.R. § 232.3.

92. Claudia Copeland, *The Army Corps of Engineers' Nationwide Permits Program: Issues and Regulatory Developments*, Cong. Rsch. Serv. (Jan. 30, 2012), http://www.fas.org/sgp/crs/natsec/97-223.pdf.

individual permits.[93] The majority of activities proceed under nationwide permits, state programmatic general permits, regional general permits, or letters of permission.[94]

CWA Section 404(e) authorizes the Corps to "issue general permits on a State, regional, or nationwide basis for any category of activities involving discharges of dredged or fill material" determined to be "similar in nature" and causing "only minimal adverse environmental effects," individually or cumulatively.[95] These general permits are essentially permits by rule, although many require the permittee to notify the Corps and obtain Corps sign-off before commencing activities involving jurisdictional discharges.[96] In addition, some require compensatory mitigation to offset the adverse impacts to wetlands caused by the activity.[97] More than 80 percent of the activities authorized by the Corps each year are authorized through Section 404(e) permits.[98] Expedited approval of proposed activity may also be obtained through letters of permission. These authorizations are available when a district engineer determines that the "proposed work would be minor, would not have significant individual or cumulative impacts on environmental values, and should encounter no appreciable opposition."[99] General permits, including nationwide permits, are discussed in detail in Chapter 5, and state programmatic permits are discussed in detail in Chapter 7.

D. If You Are Required to Obtain an Individual Permit, Have You Met Certain Required Conditions?

As set forth in detail in Chapters 4, 6, and 7, if a proposed activity needs an individual Section 404 permit, certain regulatory requirements will be triggered. These requirements include (1) satisfying the 404(b)(1)

93. 33 U.S.C. § 1344(e).

94. *See* Kim Diana Connolly, *Survey Says: Army Corps No Scalian Despot*, 37 Env't Law Rep. 10.317, n.6 (2007).

95. 33 U.S.C. § 1344(e).

96. *See generally Nationwide Permit Information*, *supra* note 60.

97. U.S. Army Corps of Eng'rs, *Compensatory Mitigation for Losses of Aquatic Resources*, 73 Fed. Reg. 19,594 (Apr. 10, 2008), https://www.govinfo.gov/content/pkg/FR-2008-04-10/pdf/E8-6918.pdf, *and codified at* 33 C.F.R. pt. 332 (2023) and 40 C.F.R. pt. 230, subpt. J (2023).

98. *Id.*

99. 33 C.F.R. § 325.2(e)(1).

Guidelines (including analyzing practicable alternatives, implementing appropriate and practicable minimization measures, and providing compensatory mitigation for unavoidable wetland impacts), (2) satisfying the public interest review,[100] and (3) ensuring compliance with other applicable federal and state laws.

The procedures for submitting and processing individual permit applications are discussed in detail in Chapter 4. The Corps cannot issue permits unless the proposed activity is in compliance with EPA's Section 404(b)(1) Guidelines.[101] These Guidelines prohibit discharges of dredged or fill material (1) if a practicable alternative with less adverse impact to the aquatic environment is available;[102] (2) if the discharge would cause or contribute to violations of various related laws including those addressing water quality standards, toxic effluent standards, or endangered or threatened species;[103] (3) if the discharge would "cause or contribute to significant degradation of the waters of the United States";[104] or (4) "unless appropriate and practicable steps have been taken which will minimize potential adverse impacts of the discharge on the aquatic ecosystem."[105] These Guidelines are discussed in detail in Chapter 4, with a focus on the required "practicable alternatives" analysis.

As part of Section 404(b)(1) compliance under existing mitigation regulations,[106] sequenced mitigation generally requires that (1) all adverse environmental impacts first be avoided to the maximum extent practicable, (2) any unavoidable impacts be minimized, and (3) compensatory mitigation be provided for any remaining adverse impacts.[107] A variety of mitigation methods may be available, including on-site mitigation, mitigation banks, and in-lieu fee arrangements.[108] Mitigation banks or in-lieu fee programs are preferred over

---

100. *Id.* § 320.4(a).
101. 40 C.F.R. pt. 230.
102. *Id.* § 230.10(a).
103. *Id.* § 230.10(b).
104. *Id.* § 230.10(c)
105. *Id.* § 230.10(d).
106. 33 C.F.R. pt. 332 and 40 C.F.R. pt. 230, subpt. J.
107. *See* Memorandum of Agreement between the Environmental Protection Agency and the Department of the Army Concerning the Determination of Mitigation under the Clean Water Act Section 404(b)(1) Guidelines, http://water.epa.gov/lawsregs/guidance/wetlands/mitigate.cfm (last update May 15, 2023).
108. *See generally* REGULATORY GUIDANCE LETTER 02-02, *supra* note 14; Federal Guidance for the Establishment, Use and Operation of Mitigation Banks, 60 Fed.

other types of mitigation. Mitigation requirements are discussed in detail in Chapter 6.

Even if a proposed activity complies with the Guidelines, the district engineer must also perform a "public interest" review.[109] Corps regulations provide that wetlands are "a productive and valuable public resource, the unnecessary alteration or destruction of which should be discouraged as contrary to the public interest."[110] To that end, the Corps evaluates probable impacts (including cumulative impacts) on the public interest of the proposed activity and its use.[111] The public interests factors considered by the Corps include conservation, economics, aesthetics, general environmental concerns, wetlands, historic properties, fish and wildlife values, floodplain values, land use, navigation, shore erosion and accretion, recreation, water supply and conservation, water quality, energy needs, safety, food and fiber production, mineral needs, considerations of property ownership, and the needs and welfare of the people.[112] The Corps will grant the permit unless the Corps determines that doing so would be contrary to the public interest.[113] Chapter 4 contains a more detailed discussion of the public interest review.

A variety of other statutes, such as the Endangered Species Act,[114] the National Environmental Policy Act,[115] and the National Historic Preservation Act,[116] may result in additional requirements and

Reg. 58,605 (Nov. 28, 1995); Federal Guidance on the Use of In-Lieu-Fee Arrangements for Compensatory Mitigation under Section 404 of the Clean Water Act and Section 10 of the Rivers and Harbors Act (2000), https://www.epa.gov/sites/default/files/2015-08/documents/in-lieu_fee_mitigation_guidance.pdf.

109. 33 C.F.R. § 320.4(a).

110. *Id.* § 320.4(b)(1).

111. *Id.* § 320.4(a)(1).

112. In every case, the Corps also considers (1) the relative extent of the public and private need for the proposed activity; (2) the practicability of using reasonable alternative locations and methods to achieve the objective of the proposed activity (if there are unresolved conflicts regarding resource use); and (3) the extent and permanence of the beneficial and/or detrimental effect that the activity is likely to have on the public and private uses to which the area is suited. *Id.* § 320.4(a)(2).

113. *Id.* § 320.4(a)(1).

114. 16 U.S.C. §§ 1531 *et seq.*

115. 42 U.S.C. §§ 4321 *et seq.*

116. 16 U.S.C. § 470.

conditions on a permit application.[117] Review requirements with respect to other federal laws are covered in Chapter 4.

Where applicable, certifications from state authorities also may be required. For example, an applicant must demonstrate that the activity will not violate state water quality standards. Section 401 of the CWA grants states authority to certify, condition, or deny licenses and permits issued by federal agencies, including Section 404 permits, depending on the effects that the licensed or permitted activity may have on state water resources and water quality.[118] Likewise, the Coastal Zone Management Act (CZMA) ensures that states retain authority to regulate the use of coastal wetlands by conditioning the issuance of federal permits on state determinations that the authorized activity is consistent with the state's coastal zone management programs.[119] More details about these state certifications are provided in Chapter 7.

E. If the Corps District Proposes to Issue a Permit, Do EPA and Other Agencies Concur with Its Analysis?

As discussed in detail in Chapter 7, EPA may play an important role throughout the permitting process, beyond enacting the Section 404(b)(1) Guidelines discussed earlier.[120] Pursuant to Section 404(q) mandates, the Corps has reached agreements with various federal agencies (including EPA) regarding efficient processing of permit applications.[121] Section 404(c) grants EPA the authority to "veto" Corps decisions to permit discharges of dredged or fill material in a defined area.[122] Such a veto requires a determination that the proposed discharge "will have an unacceptable adverse effect on municipal water supplies, shellfish beds and fishery areas (including spawning and breeding areas), wildlife, or recreational areas[.][123] As appropriate, other agencies must also be consulted during the permitting process,

117. *See generally* 33 C.F.R. § 320.3.

118. 33 U.S.C. § 1341; *see* 33 C.F.R. § 320.4(d).

119. 16 U.S.C. §§ 1451–1464.

120. *See* Chapter 7 in this book.

121. 33 U.S.C. § 1344(q); *see* Clean Water Act Section 404(q) Memorandum of Agreement between the Environmental Protection Agency and the Department of the Army, *supra* note 66.

122. 33 U.S.C. § 1344(c); 40 C.F.R. pt. 231.

123. 33 U.S.C. § 1344(c).

and necessary review procedures should be completed in a coordinated manner.[124]

F. If You Proceed through the Permitting Process but Disagree with the District Office, Will You Challenge the Decision?

If a Corps decides to issue a Section 404 permit, it will "proffer" a permit to the applicant, which the applicant must accept by signing and returning or raise objections to within the time specified in the proffer. Once the permit is countersigned by the Corps, it becomes final and effective. [125] If the Corps proposes to deny the permit or issue it with unacceptable conditions, applicants have various options to challenge the result. Applicants may bring an administrative appeal, mount a substantive challenge in federal court, or bring a challenge pursuant to the Takings Clause of the U.S. Constitution. See Chapter 8 for more details.

Pursuant to 33 C.F.R. Part 331, a Section 404 permit applicant that is dissatisfied with a Corps district decision on either a permit application or a jurisdictional determination may appeal[126] to one of eight regional Corps offices.[127] In some circumstances, such an appeal may be a necessary prerequisite to a legal challenge in federal court.[128] The appeals process is discussed in detail in Chapter 8.

---

124. 33 C.F.R. § 320.4(j)(1).

125. For a general discussion of the permit application processing steps, *see* https://www.lrl.usace.army.mil/Portals/64/docs/regulatory/Permitting/PermittingProcessInformation.pdf#.

126. The regulations define "appealable action" as "an approved [jurisdictional determination], a permit denial, or a declined permit." 33 C.F.R. § 331.1.

127. 33 C.F.R. pt. 331. For an interactive map of the Corps district offices, *see* https://www.usace.army.mil/Missions/Locations/.

128. 33 C.F.R. § 331.10. This regulation states that "[t]he final Corps decision on a permit application is the initial decision to issue or deny a permit, unless the applicant submits an RFA, and the division engineer accepts the RFA, pursuant to this Part." *Id.* If an action is appealed, the final Corps decision depends on the merit of the appeal: "(a) If the division engineer determines that the appeal is without merit, the final Corps decision is the district engineer's letter advising the applicant that the division engineer has decided that the appeal is without merit, confirming the district engineer's initial decision, and sending the permit denial or the proffered permit for signature to the appellant; or (b) If the division engineer determines that the appeal has merit, the final Corps decision is the district engineer's decision made pursuant to the division engineer's remand of the appealed action. These regulations provide that the Corps' initial decision to issue or deny a permit is the final decision on a permit

A dissatisfied permit applicant also may bring a suit in federal court challenging a final substantive decision of the Corps or EPA, provided that certain requirements are met. Final Corps decisions are defined as "the initial decision to issue or deny a permit," unless the applicant submits an accepted request for appeal under 33 C.F.R. Part 331.[129] For cases against the Corps or EPA, typical litigation requirements of standing, exhaustion of administrative remedies, ripeness, and mootness apply to such challenges.[130] The CWA does not provide a specific statute of limitations, but some courts have applied the six-year general statute of limitations for civil actions commenced against the United States.[131] Agency decisions challenged by permit applicants will be set aside only if they are found to be "arbitrary, capricious, an abuse of discretion, or otherwise not in accordance with law."[132] Court actions are discussed more fully in Chapter 8.

In certain cases, claims may be made that a Corps or EPA decision so restricts the use of private property that the agency action amounts to a "taking" in violation of the Fifth Amendment to the Constitution of the United States.[133] Because most of the nation's wetlands are in private ownership and because the Section 404 program can impose significant costs on landowners and developers, wetland protection measures often collide with the rights and economic expectations of property owners. Wetland cases have figured prominently in the development of takings jurisprudence in federal courts.[134] This issue

application. For an appealed action, where the division engineer determines that the appeal has merit, the final Corps permit decision is the district engineer's decision pursuant to the division engineer's remand." *Id. See* Ozark Soc'y v. Melcher, 229 F. Supp. 2d 896 (E.D. Ark. 2002); Bay-Houston Towing Co. v. United States, 58 Fed. Cl. 462, 471 (2003).

129. 33 C.F.R. § 331.10.

130. William L. Want, The Law of Wetlands Regulation §§ 9.3–9.8 (updated through 2023).

131. 28 U.S.C. § 2401 (2023).

132. 5 U.S.C. § 706(2); *see* Avoyelles Sportsmen's League v. Marsh, 715 F.2d 897, 904 (5th Cir. 1983).

133. U.S. Const. amend. V ("[N]or shall private property be taken for public use, without just compensation.").

134. Loveladies Harbor v. United States, 21 Cl. Ct. 153 (1990); Florida Rock Indus., Inc. v. United States, 21 Cl. Ct. 161 (1990); *see, e.g.*, Forest Properties, Inc. v. United States, 177 F.3d 1360 (Fed. Cir. 1999), *cert. denied*, 528 U.S. 951 (1999); Heck v. United States, 134 F.3d 1468 (Fed. Cir. 1998); Bayou des Familles v. United States, 130 F.3d 1034 (Fed. Cir. 1997); City Nat'l Bank v. United States, 33 Fed. Cl. 759 (1995).

became much more relevant in light of the 2013 Supreme Court decision in *Koontz v. St. Johns River Water Management District.*[135]

G. Have You Undertaken Something that Should Require a Permit, or Violated a Permit, Triggering an Enforcement Action?

The CWA includes an extensive array of measures to enforce the requirements of the Section 404 program. EPA, the Corps, and the Department of Justice share these enforcement responsibilities. EPA has civil and administrative enforcement power pursuant to Section 309 of the CWA,[136] while the Corps has enforcement authority pursuant to Section 309 and Section 404.[137] The Department of Justice, including its U.S. attorneys, represents the government in civil proceedings and is responsible for prosecuting persons who engage in activities prohibited and made criminal by Section 309(c).[138]

The government has several enforcement options. EPA and the Corps may issue administrative orders and cease and desist letters, respectively, requiring compliance with Section 404 program requirements.[139] Both may assess administrative penalties.[140] The government may initiate civil actions for injunctive relief, including restoration of damaged wetlands, and/or civil penalties.[141] EPA and the Corps may also refer particular violations to the Department of Justice for possible criminal prosecution.[142] In addition, Section 505 of the CWA provides for citizen suits.[143] Citizen suits may be brought (1) against "any person . . . who is alleged to be in violation of . . . an effluent standard or limitation under [the CWA]";[144] and (2) against EPA or the Corps

135. Koontz v. St. Johns River Water Mgmt. Dist., 570 U.S. 595 (June 25, 2013).

136. 33 U.S.C. § 1319. *See also* Memorandum of Agreement between the Department of the Army and the Environmental Protection Agency Concerning Federal Enforcement for the Section 404 Program of the Clean Water Act, *supra* note 66.

137. 33 U.S.C. § 1344(s).

138. *Id.* § 1319(c).

139. *Id.* § 1319(a) (EPA); *id.* § 1344(s)(1) (Corps).

140. *Id.* § 1319(g).

141. *Id.* § 1319(b), (d) (EPA); *id.* § 1344(s)(3)–(4) (Corps).

142. *Id.* § 1319(c).

143. *Id.* § 1365.

144. *Id.* § 1365(a)(1).

alleging that the agency has failed to perform a nondiscretionary act or duty.[145] Enforcement matters are discussed in detail in Chapter 8.

H. What Other Activities in Wetlands Might Be Regulated or Subject to Other Federal Programs?

The Section 404 program is the basic federal regulatory program relating to wetlands, but it is not the exclusive means through which the federal government influences the use and preservation of wetlands. A variety of "nonregulatory," incentive-based programs also exist, primarily relating to agricultural use of wetlands. In addition, the government has become very active in acquiring wetland resources, through either fee title acquisitions or the purchase of conservation easements. The full range of federal activities relating to wetlands is beyond the scope of this book. Additionally, many states have separate wetland regulation programs that can be more stringent than the federal program or encompass more wetlands;[146] these programs are beyond the scope of this book.

IV. Conclusion

This chapter offered both a historical overview of the federal government's role in protecting and regulating the uses of wetland resources, and a brief introduction to the modern regulatory program. The chapters that follow will provide readers an overview of current federal

145. *Id.* § 1365(a)(2).

146. *See, e.g.*, Nat'l Ass'n of Wetland Managers, *State Wetland Programs*, https://www.nawm.org/wetland-programs/state-wetland-programs, which summarizes the wetland programs in all 50 states. For example, the NAWM notes of the California's program "California relies primarily on CWA § 401 and the Porter-Cologne Water Quality Control Act to regulate wetlands statewide, but also has adopted laws and regulations directed at regional and/or coastal wetlands protection: the California Coastal Act, the McAteer-Petris Act, Wetlands Protection Act, and the Suisan Marsh Protection Act." *See* California State Wetland Program Summary, at 5, https://www.nawm.org/pdf_lib/state_summaries/california_state_wetland_program_summary_102615.pdf. NAWM notes that Florida's wetland program is more expansive than the federal program and is in addition to the federal 404 program, not in lieu thereof. Florida State Wetland Program Summary, at 2–3, https://www.nawm.org/pdf_lib/state_summaries/florida_state_wetland_program_summary_111615.pdf.

requirements, focusing on the CWA Section 404 program and what flows from the law that has developed around it.

Compliance with wetlands regulation has, in many cases, become routine for those who seek to undertake activities in regulated waters. In some cases, however, it can become reminiscent of a game of "swamp soccer"[147]—what has been called a "filthy and slippery"[148] game played in a muddy field or even in a fen—with various players exhausting themselves in a messy arena. For those who work in this arena, it is an active, messy area with only one certainty: wetlands regulation will continue to evolve.

147. *See* SWAMP SOCCER, https://swampsoccer.co.uk/.

148. *See Filthy and Slippery Swamp Soccer Comes to Scotland*, https://www.youtube.com/watch?v=CGFScQm6zvg (noting that the best thing to do in order to have a successful game is to keep the "ball in the air").

2 CHAPTER

When Is a (Wet) Land a Water of the United States?

I. Introduction

Whether a particular patch of ground is regulated under the federal Clean Water Act[1] (CWA) hinges on whether the land is a "water of the United States"[2] pursuant to the statute. Section 404 of the CWA prescribes a labyrinthine regulatory approach to discharges of dredged or fill materials placed into "navigable waters."[3] "Navigable waters" are defined as "waters of the United States" (sometimes referred to herein as WOTUS), including the territorial seas.[4] The U.S. Army Corps of Engineers (Corps) is charged with issuing permits for such discharges, but the Corps must follow U.S. Environmental Protection Agency (EPA) guidelines in doing so.[5] EPA also has the authority to

1. The Federal Water Pollution Control Act (FWPCA) is commonly referred to as the Clean Water Act following the 1977 amendments to the FWPCA. Pub. L. No. 95-217, 91 Stat. 1566 (1977) (codified at 33 U.S.C. §§ 1251–1388).

2. Waters that fall within the jurisdiction of the CWA commonly are referred to as "waters of the United States" or "WOTUS." This chapter will use the phrase "waters of the United States" or "WOTUS" when referring to jurisdictional waters.

3. 33 U.S.C. § 1344.

4. *Id.* § 1362(7).

5. *Id.* § 1344(a), (b)(1); *see also* 40 C.F.R. § 230 (containing the guidelines).

veto permits issued by the Corps.[6] The ultimate administrative authority to construe the jurisdictional reach of the term "navigable waters," including wetlands, rests with the EPA.[7]

Wetlands regulation under the CWA has been one of the most fractious publicly contested and legally vexing issues in the history of the EPA. Wetlands regulation is in the public eye largely because CWA Section 404 applies to individual landowners and homeowners, just as if they were the business entities typically regulated by EPA. Homeowners may lack the expertise, knowledge, or funds to determine whether a wetland is even on their property. Wetlands are considered by some to be merely *wet lands*; they don't understand how or why their property is subject to a federal *clean water act*. Wetlands, however, can be found in neighbors' backyards or low-lying farmland; they are parts of real estate tracts that are purchased, surveyed, conveyed by deed, and recorded in local courthouses throughout the country.[8] The responsibility of a landowner or operator to make or obtain a jurisdictional determination concerning whether or the extent to which real estate may be considered a WOTUS before engaging in mechanized land clearing, otherwise disturbing the land, or placing fill material is one of the few federal mandates imposed on both businesses and average Americans by federal environmental laws. And, even for the most sophisticated developer, compliance with CWA Section 404 can be complex, expensive, and time-consuming.

Debates concerning which wetlands should be regulated under the CWA have raged on the floor of Congress, the halls of state and federal agencies, in courtrooms, and in the White House itself for decades. The lack of clarity has left the regulated community in a quandary about when a CWA Section 404 permit is required and spurred scores of lawsuits. At the heart of the controversy over the federal regulation of wetlands is *which* wetlands are subject to the jurisdiction of

6. 33 U.S.C. § 1344(c).

7. Civiletti Memorandum, 43 Op. Att'y Gen. 197 (1979).

8. Although many well-known wetlands such as the Everglades and the Great Dismal Swamp are owned by government agencies, nearly 75 percent of wetlands in the United States are in private ownership. U.S. Env't Prot. Agency, EPA 843-F-01-002d, Threats to Wetlands (Sept. 2001), https://www.epa.gov/sites/default/files/2021-01/documents/threats_to_wetlands.pdf#:~:text=Nearly%2075%20percent%20of%20all%20wetlands%20are%20privately,the%20public%20participate%20in%20wetland%20management%20and%20protection, (last visited Mar. 1, 2024).

the federal CWA. Four U.S. Supreme Court cases have attempted to answer that central question, each of which will be discussed briefly herein. Indisputably, however, the May 25, 2023, U.S. Supreme Court decision in *Sackett v. Environmental Protection Agency*, provides the public and legal practitioners the most definitive explanation of the CWA's reach seen to date. As a result, many of the nuances of 50 years of previous rulemakings, guidelines, and interpretations largely are matters of interest rather than important legal precedent or current legal guidance.

This chapter first will describe wetlands, their functions, and values, and how they are defined by EPA and the Corps. It will then detail the May 2023 landmark opinion in *Sackett*, which interprets the reach of the CWA more narrowly than EPA and the Corps have in the past, and more specifically than any previous Supreme Court case. The chapter will next explain the August 2023 EPA and Corps' final rule conforming the agencies' January 2023 regulatory interpretation of WOTUS (including wetlands) to the holding in *Sackett*. Lastly, this chapter will address boundary delineation and wetlands characterization techniques used by the federal agencies and jurisdictional determinations issued by the Corps.

II. Wetlands Definitions and Functions

Wetlands are the link between open water and dry land, serving as important and dynamic functional and physical transition zones between aquatic and terrestrial ecosystems.[9] Some wetlands remain saturated year-round, while others are dry for most of the year.

The CWA does not explicitly define "wetlands." EPA and the Corps regulations, however, set out the following definition in 40 C.F.R. § 232.2 and 33 C.F.R. § 328.3(c)(1), respectively:

> Wetlands means those areas that are inundated or saturated by surface or ground water at a frequency and duration sufficient to support, and that under normal circumstances do support, a prevalence of vegetation typically adapted for life in saturated

9. U.S. ENV'T PROT. AGENCY, EPA 843-F-04-011a, WETLANDS OVERVIEW (Dec. 2004), https://nepis.epa.gov/Exe/ZyPDF.cgi/500025PY.PDF?Dockey=500025PY.PDF.

soil conditions. Wetlands generally include swamps, marshes, bogs, and similar areas.[10]

Wetlands play a vital role in the environment, offering significant benefits to wildlife habitats and the human ecosystem.[11] Vital wildlife habitat is provided within wetland ecosystems, supporting a diversity of species, including fish, birds, mammals, reptiles, and amphibians. It is estimated that more than one-third of the United States' threatened and endangered species live only in wetlands, and nearly half use wetlands at some point in their lives.[12] Wetlands serve as natural filters that improve water quality, removing pollutants and excess nutrients. They help prevent flooding by acting as sponges, absorbing and slowly releasing floodwaters to prevent damage. Wetlands also maintain surface water levels during dry spells when aquatic resources are scarce.

These critical services are made possible by the unique properties of wetlands, such as their inundated or saturated soils and aquatic vegetation. In addition, wetlands provide shoreline erosion control, opportunities for recreation and aesthetic appreciation, natural products for our use, and carbon sequestration.[13] In essence, wetlands are invaluable natural features that make critical contributions to the landscapes they inhabit. Wetlands are among the most biologically productive ecosystems in the world, and their preservation protects wildlife, safeguards water supplies, reduces flooding, and nourishes entire ecosystems.

---

10. The federal agencies' definition is analogous to the purely scientific definition of "wetlands," which is "an ecosystem that depends on constant or recurrent, shallow inundation or saturation at or near the surface of the substrate. The minimum essential characteristics of a wetland are recurrent, sustained inundation or saturation at or near the surface and the presence of physical, chemical, and biological features reflective of recurrent, sustained inundation or saturation. Common diagnostic features of wetlands are hydric soils and hydrophytic vegetation. These features will be present except where specific physicochemical, biotic, or anthropogenic factors have removed them or prevented their development." NAT'L RSCH. COUNCIL, WETLANDS: CHARACTERISTICS AND BOUNDARIES 3 (National Academy Press 1995), https://doi.org/10.17226/4766.

11. U.S. Env't Prot. Agency, *Why Are Wetlands Important?*, https://www.epa.gov/wetlands/why-are-wetlands-important (last updated Mar. 22, 2023).

12. *Id.*

13. *Id.*; Sara Ernst, *Learn How Wetlands Can Naturally Help with Climate Change Impacts*, U.S. GEOLOGICAL SURV. (May 12, 2023), https://www.usgs.gov/centers/whcmsc/news/learn-how-wetlands-can-naturally-help-climate-change-impacts#:~:text=Wetlands%20can%20capture%20large%20quantities,hundreds%20to%20thousands%20of%20years.

III. Wetlands Values and Public Perception

The vital functions of wetlands have not always been understood or valued. For many years, people considered them only to be habitat for mosquitos and vectors for disease, such as malaria. The federal Swamp Lands Acts of 1849, 1850, and 1860 granted approximately 64 million acres of federally owned swamps and wetlands, including much of the Everglades, to states, if they would agree to use the proceeds to drain and turn wetlands into arable lands or to construct flood control structures. For decades, people drained or filled wetlands for development or agricultural purposes. A recent study estimates wetlands losses of 40 percent in the United States since European settlement.[14]

As Americans became more aware of the values of wetlands, the political tides on wetlands protection and preservation began to shift. In 1977, President Jimmy Carter issued Executive Order 11990, aimed at avoiding "the long and short term adverse impacts associated with the destruction or modification of wetlands and to avoid direct or indirect support of new construction in wetlands wherever there is a practicable alternative. . . ."[15]

That same year, Congress amended the CWA and used the word "wetlands" for the first time in the statute.[16] This clarified congressional intent to include wetlands under Section 404.

In 1987, at the request of EPA, the National Wetlands Policy Forum was convened by the Conservation Foundation, a nonprofit environmental group headed by William K. Reilly, who later became the administrator of EPA from 1989–1993. The Forum was composed of an alliance of government officials, industry, agriculture, and environmental advocates. A 1988 report by the Forum, titled "Protecting America's Wetlands,"[17] estimated that 300,000 to 500,000 acres of wetlands were disappearing in the United States each year. The report advocated for a national goal of "no net loss of wetlands" by offsetting

---

14. Rob Jordan, *Stanford-Led Study Finds Global Wetlands Losses Overestimated Despite High Losses in Many Regions*, Stanford Univ. (Feb. 8, 2023), https://news.stanford.edu/2023/02/08/new-chance-protect-wetlands/.

15. Exec. Order No. 11990, 42 Fed. Reg. 26,961 (May 24, 1977).

16. 33 U.S.C. § 1344(g).

17. Thomas H. Kean, Nat'l Wetlands Policy F., Protecting America's Wetlands: An Action Agenda (Conservation Foundation 1988).

any wetland losses with new wetland restoration or creation.[18] This groundbreaking approach continues to influence wetland management efforts today.

No net loss of wetlands was promoted as a national goal by then Vice President and presidential candidate George H.W. Bush.[19] When he was elected President, he delivered on his campaign promise when EPA and the Corps adopted a memorandum of understanding in 1989 establishing that the goal of the United States is to achieve "no net loss of wetlands[,]"[20] requiring mitigation for wetlands losses that could not be avoided or minimized. Every President from 1989 to 2016 adopted the "no net loss of wetlands" policy, which has resulted in aggressive (some would say too aggressive) permitting and mitigation requirements imposed by EPA and the Corps. That approach was successful. EPA reported that "no net loss" of wetlands was achieved in fiscal years 2009 through 2011.[21]

IV. Which Wetlands Are Waters of the United States

Congress intended the CWA to "restore and maintain the chemical, physical and biological integrity of the Nation's waters."[22] To effectuate Congress's intent, the CWA prohibits the "discharge of any pollutant by any person" except in compliance with a permit issued under Sections 402 or 404 of the act.[23] Section 404 provides for the issuance of permits

---

18. Philip Shabecoff, *Coalition Urges Action to Save U.S. Wetlands*, N.Y. Times (Nov. 16, 1988), at A18.

19. *George HW Bush-No Net Loss 1988*, C-Span, https://www.c-span.org/video/?c4907470/user-clip-george-hw-bush-net-loss-1988 (last visited Mar. 1, 2024).

20. David J. Hayes & Nicole Gentile, *No Net Loss: How Mitigation Policy Can Spur Private Investment in Land and Wildlife Conservation*, Ctr. for Am. Progress 4 (Nov. 1, 2016), https://www.americanprogress.org/article/no-net-loss/#:~:text=How%20Mitigation%20Policy%20Can%20Spur,lands%2C%20waters%2C%20and%20wildlife; *see* Memorandum of Agreement between the Environmental Protection Agency and the Department of the Army Concerning the Determination of Mitigation Under the Clean Water Act Section 404(b)(1) Guidelines, https://www.epa.gov/sites/default/files/2019-05/documents/1990_army-epa_mitigation_moa.pdf.

21. Off. of Water, U.S. Env't Prot. Agency, National Water Program: Best Practices and End of Year Performance Report 52–54 (Mar. 2014), https://www.epa.gov/sites/default/files/2015-06/documents/2013_full_report_0.pdf.

22. 33 U.S.C. § 1251(a).

23. *Id.* § 1311.

for the discharge of dredged or fill material "into the navigable waters," and it is this section of the statute that generally controls activities in wetlands.[24] "Discharge of any pollutant" is defined as "any addition of any pollutant to navigable waters from any point source."[25] Congress defined "navigable waters" broadly to include "waters of the United States"[26] but failed to further provide a definition for the phrase "waters of the United States." Thus, the saga began.

That at least some wetlands are regulated WOTUS and subject to the CWA's jurisdiction is well established. Wetlands are explicitly included in Section 404(g) of the CWA and the legislative history of the 1977 CWA Amendments. Determining which wetlands are subject to Section 404 has been a moving target.

In the CWA's infancy, EPA and the Corps focused on permitting the most obvious waters and wettest wetlands. After discharges to the most significant waters and wetlands were addressed, the agencies' focus shifted to smaller bodies of water and wetlands that were not as recognizable as swamps, marshes, or bogs.

Court challenges ensued. In *U.S. v. Riverside Bayview Homes*,[27] the U.S. Supreme Court approved the agencies' regulation of wetlands that were adjacent to traditional navigable waters[28] or adjacent to tributaries of traditional navigable waters, even if those wetlands were on private property.

In 2001, the U.S. Supreme Court decided the next case determining whether certain wetlands were regulated under the CWA. In *Solid Waste Agency of Northern Cook County v. U.S. Army Corps of Engineers*, the Court held that the EPA and the Corps exceeded their regulatory authority under the CWA by regulating certain non-navigable, isolated, intrastate waters.[29] EPA and the Corps argued that waters in a former sand and gravel pit were regulated under the CWA because they were susceptible to use by migratory birds (the Migratory Bird Rule). The *SWANCC* Court ruled that the CWA did not cover all

24. *Id.* § 1344.
25. *Id.* § 1362(12).
26. *Id.* § 1362(7).
27. 474 U.S. 121 (1985).
28. Traditional navigable waters are those waters used or that have the capacity to be used by ships or boats, or even canoes, and include lakes, rivers, streams, and coastal areas used in commerce.
29. 531 U.S. 159 (2001).

isolated waters but, rather, required a significant nexus to traditional navigable waters for CWA jurisdiction to attach.

The next time that the U.S. Supreme Court spoke on the issue of WOTUS, the high court muddied the jurisdictional waters. *Rapanos v. United States* was a 4–1–4 decision in which five members of the court agreed on the outcome, based on different rationales.[30] Justice Scalia's plurality opinion, adopted by three other justices, opined that the CWA's jurisdiction extends only to "relatively permanent, standing, or continuously flowing bodies of water" and "those wetlands with a continuous surface connection to bodies that are 'waters of the United States' in their own right, so that there is no clear demarcation between 'water' and wetlands[.]"[31] Justice Kennedy, concurring in the result, outlined a broad "significant nexus test" for whether waters in the United States constituted WOTUS. He wrote that waters should be jurisdictional if, by themselves or in combination with similarly situated wetlands in the region, they significantly affect the physical, chemical, and biological integrity of downstream traditional navigable waters. If so, they would have a significant nexus on the traditional navigable waters and they should be considered jurisdictional.

EPA and the Corps embraced Justice Kennedy's sweeping and amorphous significant nexus test, issuing guidance documents in 2007 and 2008, developing a specific protocol for determining whether a water is a "relatively permanent water" with a continuance connection to a traditional navigable water (the plurality test).[32] This became their principal approach for determining jurisdiction. The agencies, however, "have had trouble deciding which wetlands should be analyzed under the significant nexus test" and "have struggled deciding how to apply it."[33]

---

30. 547 U.S. 715 (2006) (plurality opinion).

31. *Id.* at 739, 742.

32. The Rapanos guidance clarified that a wetland was "adjacent" if it had an unbroken hydrologic connection to jurisdictional waters, was separated from those waters only by a berm or similar feature, or was in reasonably close proximity to a jurisdictional water. The guidance did not provide a definition of "reasonably close proximity," and the significant nexus test was necessarily case specific. U.S. Env't Prot. Agency & U.S. Army Corps of Eng'rs, Clean Water Act Jurisdiction Following the U.S. Supreme Court's Decision in *Rapanos v. United States & Carabell v. United States*, https://www.epa.gov/sites/default/files/2016-02/documents/cwa_jurisdiction_following_rapanos120208.pdf.

33. Brief for the National Association of Home Builders of the United States as *Amici Curiae* Supporting Petitioners, Sackett v. Env't Prot. Agency, 598 U.S. 651 (2023) (No. 21-454).

As a result, jurisdictional decisions with significant environmental and economic implications were made on a case-by-case basis by federal agency field inspectors and delineators, who did not have the discretion nor framework to evaluate the intent of Congress or base their decisions on weighty constitutional issues of private property rights or the Interstate Commerce Clause. EPA and the Corps attempted for decades to provide consistency concerning the jurisdiction of the CWA by publishing multiple guidance documents and manuals and by promulgating federal rules that were, to the chagrin of the administration proposing them, stayed by federal courts with dizzying speed.[34] Congressional debate resulted in a legislative status quo with no forthcoming elucidation of the intended jurisdiction of the CWA.

The ultimate question upon which Section 404 wetland regulation rests—which wetlands are regulated under the CWA—was decided on May 25, 2023. On that date, the U.S. Supreme Court handed down a unanimous decision in *Sackett v. Environmental Protection Agency.*[35] The opinion of the Court described with notable clarity which wetlands would hereafter be subject to the CWA's jurisdiction.

A. Sackett v. Environmental Protection Agency

On May 25, 2023, the U.S. Supreme Court wrote a new chapter in the story of wetlands protection under the CWA. In a unanimous decision, the Supreme Court rejected the long-held and vigorously defended position of EPA and the Corps that the most tenuous links to traditional navigable waters were sufficient to confer regulatory jurisdiction over wetlands under the CWA.

First, the Court held that the term "waters" in the phrase "waters of the United States" means "only those relatively permanent, standing or continuously flowing bodies of water forming geographic[al] features' that are described in ordinary parlance as 'streams, oceans, rivers, and lakes.'"[36]

34. *See, e.g.*, Pascua Yaqui Tribe v. U.S. Env't Prot. Agency, 557 F. Supp. 3d 949 (D. Ariz. 2021) (vacating and remanding the Navigable Waters Protection Rule WOTUS definition of the Trump Administration); *In re* E.P.A., 803 F.3d. 804 (6th Cir. Feb. 22, 2016) (issuing nationwide stay of the Obama Administration "Clean Water Rule" WOTUS definition pending litigation).

35. 598 U.S. 651 (2023).

36. *Id.* at 671(citing *Rapanos*, 547 U.S. at 739).

Second, as to wetlands, only those wetlands that are essentially extensions of such "waters" can be jurisdictional. The Court held:

> In sum, we hold that the CWA extends to only those wetlands that are "as a practical matter indistinguishable from waters of the United States." This requires the party asserting jurisdiction over adjacent wetlands to establish "first, that the adjacent [body of water constitutes] . . . 'water[s] of the United States,' (i.e., a relatively permanent body of water connected to traditional interstate navigable waters); and second, that the wetland has a continuous surface connection with that water, making it difficult to determine where the 'water' ends and the 'wetland' begins."[37]

The *Sackett* decision represents a seismic shift in what wetlands are regulated under federal law by concluding that the *Rapanos* plurality was the appropriate test for defining WOTUS and soundly rejecting the significant nexus test. The Court also rejected the concept that a wetland can be grouped with 'similarly situated' waters to find a significant nexus and narrowed EPA's definition of the term "adjacent" to mean "continuously connected." Now, a landowner or legal practitioner may be able to determine whether a wetland is adjacent (has a continuous surface connection) to a traditional navigable water or other water body such as a river, stream, or lake, that in normal parlance would be considered a water of the United States.[38]

B. EPA and Corps' 2023 Revised Definition of WOTUS

The U.S. Supreme Court's interpretation of the CWA in *Sackett* invalidated significant portions of the EPA and Corps' most recent regulatory definition of "waters of the United States." On January 18, 2023, the agencies published the "Revised Definition of 'Waters of the

---

37. *Id.* at 684 (citing *Rapanos*, 547 U.S. at 755 (emphasis deleted)).

38. Although some sources praise the Sackett decision, Federal Statute: Clean Water Act "Waters of the United States" *Sackett v. EPA*, 137 HARV. L. REV. 390, 390; *A Clean Water Landmark for Liberty at the Supreme Court*, The Editorial Board, WALL ST. J. (May 25, 2023), EPA and many academicians condemn the Supreme Court's decision, *Article: Judicial Destruction of the Clean Water Act: Sackett v. EPA*, 91 U. CHI. L. REV. ONLINE 1, 20.

United States,'" yet another rule promulgated on the topic in the last eight years.[39]

The January 2023 rule attempted to further ingrain Justice Kennedy's significant nexus standard into the federal regulations.[40] Litigation challenging the January 2023 rule was filed in the Southern District of Texas, the District of North Dakota, and the Eastern District of Kentucky. At various stages of the litigation, preliminary injunctions were granted to enjoin the January 2023 rule in Idaho, Texas, Alabama, Alaska, Arkansas, Florida, Georgia, Iowa, Indiana, Kansas, Louisiana, Mississippi, Missouri, Montana, Nebraska, New Hampshire, North Dakota, Ohio, Oklahoma, South Carolina, South Dakota, Tennessee, Utah, Virginia, West Virginia, Wyoming, and Kentucky, in addition to enjoining application of the rule to specific plaintiffs-appellants and their members. During the pendency of the litigation and following issuance of the injunctions, the U.S. Supreme Court published the *Sackett* opinion.

In response to *Sackett*, EPA and the Corps issued a final rule amending the "Revised Definition of 'Waters of the United States'" on September 8, 2023 ("Conforming Rule").[41] The revised rule is intended to conform the agencies' January 18, 2023, definition of "waters of the United States" to the U.S. Supreme Court's interpretation of the CWA set forth in *Sackett*. The Conforming Rule simply removes those portions of the January 2023 rule that directly conflict with the decision in *Sackett*, by (1) finally banishing the significant nexus test, (2) eliminating automatic jurisdiction for interstate wetlands, and (3) revising the definition of "adjacent" to mean solely "having a continuous surface connection."[42]

At press time, the challenges to the January 2023 rule remain pending and the preliminary injunctions in 27 states and for certain parties

39. For a complete review of the federal rulemakings concerning WOTUS since 2015, see 88 Federal Register 3,004 (Jan. 18, 2023) and 88 Fed. Reg. 61,964 (Sept. 8, 2023).

40. Revised Definition of "Waters of the United States," 88 Fed. Reg. 3,004 (Jan. 18, 2023) (to be codified at 33 C.F.R. pt. 328, 40 C.F.R. pt. 120).

41. Revised Definition of "Waters of the United States"; conforming, 88 Fed. Reg. 61,964 (Sept. 8, 2023) (to be codified at 33 C.F.R. pt. 328, 40 C.F.R. pt. 120).

42. *Id.* at 61,966.

remain in place.[43] The Conforming Rule is effective in 23 states, the District of Columbia, and the U.S. Territories. In these jurisdictions and for these parties, pending resolution of the litigation, EPA and the Corps interpret WOTUS consistent with the pre-2015 regulatory regime to the extent it is not inconsistent with *Sackett*.[44] Figure 2.1 depicts the states where the Conforming Rule is in effect as well as those states subject to the pre-2015 rules and guidance. Practitioners should refer to the most recent EPA and Corps updates concerning the status of jurisdictional interpretations.

Operative Definition of "Waters of the United States"

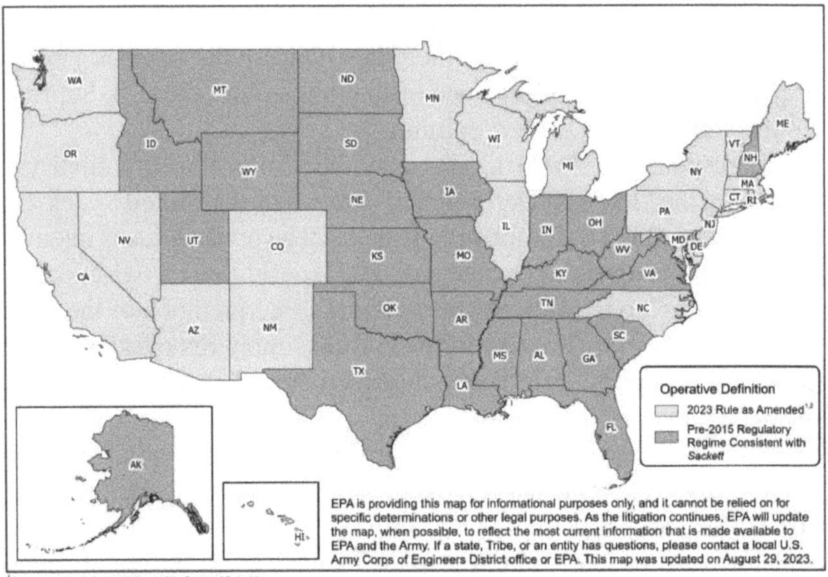

[1]Also operative in the U.S. territories and the District of Columbia
[2]The pre-2015 regulatory regime implemented consistent with *Sackett* is operative for the Commonwealth of Kentucky and Plaintiff-Appellants in Kentucky Chamber of Commerce, et al. v. EPA (No. 23-5345) and their members (Kentucky Chamber of Commerce, U.S. Chamber of Commerce, Associated General Contractors of Kentucky, Home Builders Association of Kentucky, Portland Cement Association, and Georgia Chamber of Commerce).

Figure 2.1 Operative definition of "waters of the United States"

43. U.S. Env't Prot. Agency, *Definition of "Waters of the United States": Rule Status and Litigation Update*, https://www.epa.gov/wotus/definition-waters-united-states-rule-status-and-litigation-update (last updated Sept. 8, 2023).

44. U.S. Env't Prot. Agency, *Pre-2015 Regulatory Regime*, https://www.epa.gov/wotus/pre-2015-regulatory-regime (last updated Oct. 10, 2023).

V. Wetlands Delineation and Classification

If a wetland meets the criteria set out in *Sackett*, such that it is a WOTUS and subject to the requirements of Section 404 of the CWA, a key issue is where the wetland begins and uplands end. In other words, what are the boundaries of a wetland that must be considered in wetland avoidance, minimization, and mitigation? That determination may be performed by a wetland delineator, the Corps, or both.

The following section discusses the delineation process for determining the existence and boundaries of wetlands. However, *Sackett* made clear that not all wetlands are regulated under the CWA. **Whether a particular wetland is subject to the CWA's jurisdiction must be decided as specified in *Sackett*.**

A. Wetlands Delineation

The determination of whether an area is considered a wetland depends on three interconnected criteria: vegetation, soil, and hydrology. The plants growing in an area are influenced by the soil conditions and the amount of water present in the soil. Most plants require oxygen circulated through the soil and cannot survive when the spaces between soil particles are saturated with water. Some plants, however, are adapted to thrive in these anaerobic, saturated soil conditions. Vegetation classified as hydrophytic (water loving) or facultative (water tolerant) plants were identified in the National Wetland Plant List compiled by the U.S. Fish and Wildlife Service and maintained by the Corps.[45] These types of plants are indicator species in determining the presence of wetlands. The list includes many common plant species that can grow equally well in both wetlands and uplands, such as red maple, Ohio buckeye, and Jack-in-the-Pulpit. The vegetation, soil characteristics, and hydrology of an area generally should all be considered together when evaluating wetlands.[46]

Soils that are saturated or flooded for extended periods develop distinctive hydric characteristics. The National Technical Committee for Hydric Soils defines a hydric soil as one that forms under saturated, flooded, or ponded conditions long enough during the growing season

45. U.S. Army Corps of Eng'rs, *National Wetland Plant List*, https://cwbi-app.sec.usace.army.mil/nwpl_static/v34/home/home.html (last visited Apr. 2, 2024).

46. *Id.*

to create anaerobic conditions in the upper layers.[47] In saturated soils, microbial activity depletes oxygen over time. Prolonged inundation can also prompt biogeochemical processes like the reduction, translocation, or accumulation of iron and other elements such as sulfur and manganese, resulting in specific soil colors or odors. Another feature of hydric soils is partially decomposed organic material. These identifying traits can persist even during dry periods. Thus, to determine whether an area was or is wetland, wetland delineators examine both the vegetation and these hydric soil indicators to determine whether an area has experienced previous flooding or saturation.[48]

Surprisingly, direct observation of standing water or saturated soils carries less weight in a wetland delineation than analysis of vegetation and soil characteristics. Regulators often view hydrophytic plant identification and hydric soil classification as more definitive indicators than visible water or saturation. This is because vegetation and distinctive soil features can persist even when other evidence of inundation or saturation is no longer apparent. While the presence of standing water or saturated soils is relevant, regulators emphasize evaluation of plant types and soil properties as primary criteria when delineating wetlands.

In fact, in disturbed areas that do not have standing water or saturated soils or hydrophytic vegetation, the presence of soils with hydric characteristics can be the sole ground upon which a delineator concludes that the land is a wetland if the delineator determines that the hydrology or vegetation would have been present under ordinary circumstances (prior to alteration of the area).[49]

---

47. *Hydric Soils*, Nat. Res. Conservation Serv., U.S. Dep't of Agric., https://www.nrcs.usda.gov/conservation-basics/natural-resource-concerns/soil/hydric-soils (last visited Oct. 9, 2023).

48. Nat. Res. Conservation Serv., U.S. Dep't of Agric., Field Indicators of Hydric Soils in the United States: A Guide for Identifying and Delineating Hydric Soils 1 (2017), https://www.nae.usace.army.mil/portals/74/docs/regulatory/JurisdictionalLimits/Hydric%20Soils%20in%20New%20England/Field_Indicators_of_Hydric_Soils_of_the_US_2017.pdf.

49. Memorandum of Agreement Concerning the Determination of the Geographic Jurisdiction of the Section 404 Program, 58 Fed. Reg. 4,995 (Jan. 19, 1993); Env't Lab'y, U.S. Army Corps of Eng'rs, Corps of Engineers Wetlands Delineation Manual 74 (1987), https://www.lrh.usace.army.mil/Portals/38/docs/USACE%2087%20Wetland%20Delineation%20Manual.pdf (hereinafter wetlands delineation manual).

The amount of observable water in wetlands can fluctuate over time based on seasons, weather, and other factors. Wetland indicators like saturated soils may be present along the "fringe" of a wetland during one site visit but not the next. This makes it challenging for delineators to draw precise wetland boundaries. Indeed, experienced wetland scientists can reasonably disagree on where to delineate the edge of a wetland because some of the scientific criteria involve subjective judgment.

Recognizing these complexities with delineating firm wetland boundaries, in 1993, EPA adopted the 1987 Army Corps Delineation Manual to provide guidance in drawing boundaries between uplands and wetlands.[50] However, the 1987 manual is just a starting point. Ten regional supplements have been published since 2007 (in final or draft form), covering different geographic areas. These should be consulted when delineating wetlands, with the caveat that, according to *Sackett*, not all wetlands are regulated.[51]

The National Wetlands Inventory (NWI) may also be consulted when delineating wetlands. The 1986 Emergency Wetlands Resources Act[52] directed the U.S. Fish and Wildlife Service to develop the NWI to classify and map wetlands nationwide.[53] The NWI serves various purposes, such as wetlands conservation efforts, emergency planning, and flooding disaster response. It does not, however, provide a legally definitive determination of whether a particular area is a wetland regulated under the CWA or in fact whether it is a wetland at all. Nor does the NWI represent an authoritative list of all CWA jurisdictional wetlands.

B. Wetlands Classification

Scientists' terminology used for wetlands can vary between agencies and contexts. Broadly, there are two major wetland categories: (1) coastal/tidal wetlands, which experience varying salinity and fluctuating water

50. *See generally* Wetlands Delineation Manual, *supra* note 49.

51. *Regional Supplements to Corps Delineation Manual*, U.S. Army Corps of Eng'rs, https://www.usace.army.mil/Missions/Civil-Works/Regulatory-Program-and-Permits/reg_supp/.

52. Emergency Wetlands Resources Act of 1985, 16 U.S.C. §§ 3901–3932 (2018).

53. *National Wetlands Inventory*, U.S. Fish & Wildlife Serv., https://www.fws.gov/program/national-wetlands-inventory (last visited Apr. 2, 2024).

levels; and (2) inland/non-tidal wetlands, which are most prevalent on floodplains, in isolated depressions surrounded by dry land, along lake/pond margins, or in other low-lying regions.[54] While the nomenclature may vary, this tidal/non-tidal dichotomy provides a basic framework for classifying wetland types.

The United States contains diverse wetland types, including but not limited to marshes, swamps, bogs, and fens,[55] which are described as follows:

- Marshes are frequently or continually flooded wetlands that are characterized by soft-stemmed herbaceous vegetation such as grasses, rushes, and sedges.[56] Non-tidal marshes are the most widespread and prevalent wetlands in North America, often found near lakes, ponds, rivers, and streams.[57]
- Swamps are characterized by woody plants and saturated soils during the growing season, with standing water at certain times of year.[58]
- Bogs are permanently saturated and characterized by the presence of peat, which is organic material deposited under inundated conditions due to incomplete decomposition,[59] acidic waters, and a floor of sphagnum moss.[60] Most of the water in bogs comes from precipitation rather than streams, groundwater, or runoff.[61]
- Fens are also permanently saturated wetlands characterized by the presence of peat. Contrary to bogs, however, fens receive water from sources other than precipitation, usually

54. *The Wetlands of the National Park Service*, Nat'l Park Serv., https://www.nps.gov/articles/wetlandsday17.htm#:~:text=Wetlands%20include%20areas%20where%20water,that%20occur%20in%20inland%20areas (last updated Fed. 2, 2017).

55. *Classification and Types of Wetlands*, U.S. Env't Prot. Agency, https://www.epa.gov/wetlands/classification-and-types-wetlands#undefined (last updated Apr. 13, 2023) (hereinafter *Classification and Types of Wetlands*).

56. *Wetlands, Marshes and Swamps*, Nat'l Park Serv., https://www.nps.gov/piro/learn/nature/wetlands.htm (last updated Sept. 22, 2021).

57. *Classification and Types of Wetlands*, *supra* note 55.

58. *Id.*

59. *Id.*

60. *Id.*

61. *Id.*

groundwater.[62] As a result, fens typically are less acidic and have higher nutrient levels than bogs.[63]

There are a variety of ways that wetlands can be classified. Different agencies classify wetlands using different classification systems for different purposes. The U.S. Fish and Wildlife Service often identifies differences among wetlands by using the Cowardin classification system, which classifies wetlands based on hydrologic regime, landscape location, and vegetation cover.[64] The Cowardin system has five major wetland types:[65]

- Marine—coastal wetlands influenced by ocean tides and salinity
- Estuarine (tidal)—coastal wetlands with variable salinity and tidal flooding
- Lacustrine—wetlands associated with lakes
- Palustrine[66]—inland, non-tidal wetlands with trees, shrubs, and emergent vegetation
- Riverine—wetlands and deepwater habitats within a river channel

The hydrogeomorphic (HGM) wetland classification system categorizes wetlands into five major types: riverine, slope, depressional, flat, and fringe.[67] Emphasizing hydrologic and geomorphic controls, the HGM approach groups wetlands with similar functions, which are the normal ecosystem activities occurring within a wetland.[68] This classification system assesses wetland functional capacity by examining the physical, chemical, and biological processes taking place within the wetland.[69]

---

62. *Id.*

63. *Id.*

64. *Id.*

65. Wetlands Subcomm., Fed. Geographic Data Comm., Classification of Wetlands and Deepwater Habitats of the United States 8–10 (Aug. 2013), https://www.fgdc.gov/standards/projects/wetlands/nwcs-2013.

66. Palustrine wetlands have often been the most troublesome for landowners because the ground may not have standing water on a regular basis.

67. Mark M. Brinson, U.S. Army Corps of Eng'rs, A Hydrogeomorphic Classification for Wetlands 1–3 (Aug. 1993), https://wetlands.el.erdc.dren.mil/pdfs/wrpde4.pdf.

68. *Hydrogeomorphic Approach for Assessing Wetlands Functions: Overview of the HGM Approach*, Eng'r Rsch. & Dev. Ctr., U.S. Army Corps of Eng'rs, https://wetlands.el.erdc.dren.mil/overview.html (last updated May 2010).

69. *Id.*

As discussed previously, identifying the presence, types, and boundaries of wetlands on a property typically requires specialized scientific and technical expertise. Consultants who specialize in wetland delineation can assist with this evaluation. Many Corps district offices provide online lists of independent delineation consultants, though the Corps does not endorse any particular professional. While there are no federally recognized licenses or certifications for wetland delineators, the Society of Wetland Scientists awards a Professional Wetland Scientist (PWS) Certification that is respected by many Corps officials.

In addition to delineating wetland boundaries, it is important that attorneys and consultants understand the difference between a wetland and a regulated wetland under the CWA. They should be prepared to engage with the Corps on whether a particular wetland falls under CWA jurisdiction, based on *Sackett* and the most recent EPA regulations and guidance. The wetland consultant typically submits her delineation and observations to the Corps to verify her result to obtain a preliminary or approved jurisdictional determination.

VI. Jurisdictional Determinations

Landowners or potential landowners seeking comfort about whether the CWA Section 404 requirements apply and the extent of wetland boundaries can request a jurisdictional determination (JD) from the Corps to gain their view on whether jurisdictional wetlands are located on a property. The Corps provides two JD types: preliminary and approved. A preliminary JD, while not definitive, offers written guidance "that there may be waters of the United States on a parcel of land or indications of the approximate location(s) of waters of the United States on a parcel of land."[70] Preliminary JDs are advisory only and cannot be appealed.

In contrast to preliminary JDs, approved jurisdictional determinations are more detailed and time-consuming. To issue an approved JD, the Corps district office will conduct a site visit and may need to consult with Corps headquarters and the EPA. The approved JD is a final decision by the Corps on whether jurisdictional waters of the United

70. 33 C.F.R. § 332.2.

States exist on a property and, if so, the physical boundaries. Since it is a final agency action, landowners can appeal an approved JD if they disagree with the Corp' determination.[71] Additionally, approved JDs generally remain effective for five years.

After the *Sackett* opinion was issued, the Corps implemented a nationwide "pause" on the issuance of approved jurisdictional determinations. At press time, the Corps lifted that pause following promulgation of the August 29, 2023, "Revised Definition of 'Waters of the United States'" discussed earlier.[72]

On September 27, 2023, the Corps and EPA issued a joint memorandum concerning the coordination of draft-approved JDs under the "pre-2015 regulatory regime."[73] Its purpose is to "establish a process by which the agencies will coordinate on CWA geographic jurisdictional matters to ensure accurate and consistent implementation of the pre-2015 regulatory regime where that regime is operative."[74]

This document clarifies that the agencies "will not assert jurisdiction based on the significant nexus standard, will not assert jurisdiction on interstate wetlands solely because they are interstate, will interpret 'adjacent' to mean 'having a continuous surface connection,'"[75] and will limit the scope of their jurisdiction over wetlands to those having a continuous surface connection to a traditional navigable water or a tributary of a traditional navigable water.

It is still unclear, however, how the agencies will actually implement their rules and guidance in the field in light of *Sackett*; nonetheless, the jurisdiction of the CWA is more clearly defined today than ever in the history of the law.

---

71. U.S. Army Corps of Eng'rs v. Hawkes Co., 578 U.S. 590, 595 (2016).

72. Press Release, U.S. Army Corps of Engineers, EPA and the Army Issue Final Rule to Amend 2023 Rule (Sept. 8, 2023), https://www.usace.army.mil/Media/Announcements/Article/3520843/8-september-2023-epa-and-the-army-issue-final-rule-to-amend-2023-rule/ ("Now that the conforming rule has become effective, the nationwide pause on issuance of certain approved jurisdictional determinations (AJDs) is now lifted in entirety. Effective immediately, USACE districts have resumed issuance of all AJDs nationwide under the applicable regulatory regime.").

73. Joint Coordination Memorandum to the Field between the U.S. Department of the Army, U.S. Army Corps of Engineers (Corps) and the U.S. Environmental Protection Agency (EPA) (Sept. 27, 2023), https://www.epa.gov/system/files/documents/2023-10/2023-joint-coordination-memo-pre-2015-regulatory-regime_508c.pdf.

74. *Id.*

75. *Id.*

VII. Conclusion

In conclusion, the most significant sea change in more than 50 years of the CWA's implementation occurred on May 25, 2023, when the U.S. Supreme Court issued *Sackett. Sackett* significantly restricted the federal agencies' interpretation of which wetlands and waters in the United States would be considered "waters of the United States" for purposes of regulation under the CWA. At press time, in some states, the EPA and the Corps' August 2023 conforming rule sets forth the operative definition of WOTUS. In other states, the pre-2015 regulatory regime is being implemented. At press time, Michigan and New Jersey, which implement the CWA 404 program in certain WOTUS,[76] follow the Conforming Rule promulgated by EPA and the Corps in September 2023.

76. Three states have assumed the program in state waters that are not presently used in or reasonably susceptible to use in navigation or their adjacent wetlands: Michigan (1984), New Jersey (1993), and Florida (2020). No tribes have yet assumed the program. An interactive map with links to the assumed Section 404 programs and showing the assumption efforts of all the states and tribes can be found here: https://www.epa.gov/cwa404g/us-interactive-map-state-and-tribal-assumption-under-cwa-section-404. Florida's approved Section 404 program was vacated by the D.C. Circuit Court on February 15, 2024. See note 51, *supra*.

3 CHAPTER

Identifying Activities That Fall under the Federal Wetland Regulatory Program

I. Introduction

The Corps regulates many—but not all—activities in wetlands and other waters. Such regulation proceeds, in most cases, via permit.[1] To determine whether a Corps permit is required for a specific activity, potential applicants or other stakeholders must assess whether the proposed activity falls under the broad jurisdiction of the Corps, and if it does, whether it qualifies as exempt. This chapter will help readers understand which activities are regulated and the parameters of the processes that have developed to govern any applicable regulation.

The chapter begins with a brief history of the Corps' regulation of activities and continues by providing details about which activities, in a broad sense, are regulated under law. It concludes by exploring the activities deemed exempt from regulation.

1. *See* Chapters 4 and 5 for information about individual and general permitting processes.

II. A Brief History of Federal Regulation[2]

The history of regulating activities in our nation's waters dates back to at least the Rivers and Harbors Act of 1899 (RHA).[3] While Section 10 of the RHA generally prohibits unpermitted "obstructions" to the "navigable capacity of any of the waters of the United States," it also more broadly makes it unlawful "to excavate or fill, or in any manner to alter or modify the course, location, condition, or capacity of, any port, roadstead, haven, harbor, canal, lake, harbor of refuge, or inclosure [sic] within the limits of any breakwater, or of the channel of any navigable water" without the appropriate permit.[4] For more than a century, the Corps[5] has used this latter provision to regulate activities in certain wetlands,[6] in a limited fashion. However, for many decades, federal law not only allowed but, in fact, dedicated resources to draining swamps and eliminating wetlands.[7] In fact, the Corps itself is responsible for constructing many of the canals and ditches that served to drain the Florida Everglades in order to convert it to

2. Please also see Chapter 1, Part II.

3. 33 U.S.C. §§ 401–418 (2023).

4. *Id.* § 403. The full text of Section 10 of the Rivers and Harbors Act is set forth in note 25 in Chapter 1, of this book and hasn't changed since 1947. The Corps' current regulations state in relevant part that "[t]he U.S. Army Corps of Engineers has been involved in regulating certain activities in the nation's waters since 1890," with a focus until 1968 on protection of navigation per the RHA. 33 C.F.R. § 320.1(a)(1).

5. *See* U.S. Army Corps of Eng'rs, *Regulatory Program*, http://www.usace.army.mil/Missions/CivilWorks/RegulatoryProgramandPermits.aspx. Congress created the United States Army Corps of Engineers in 1802. Act of Mar. 16, 1802, ch. 9, § 26, 2 Stat. 132, 137. Its duties eventually expanded to include regulatory functions. *See generally* Garrett Power, *The Fox in the Chicken Coop: The Regulatory Program of the U.S. Army Corps of Engineers*, 63 Va. L. Rev. 503 (1977).

6. *See* U.S. Army Corps of Eng'rs, *U.S. Army Corps of Engineers, A Brief History*, https://www.usace.army.mil/About/History/Brief-History-of-the-Corps/ (last visited Apr. 2, 2024).

7. "Prior to the mid-1980s, federal laws and policies to protect wetlands were generally limited to providing habitat for migratory waterfowl, especially ducks and geese. Some laws encouraged destruction of wetland areas, including selected provisions in the federal tax code, public works legislation, and farm programs. Since the mid-1980s, the values of wetlands have been recognized in different ways in numerous national policies, and federal laws either encourage wetland protection, or prohibit or do not support their destruction. These laws, however, do not add up to a fully consistent or comprehensive national approach." Cong. Rsch. Serv., Resources, Science, & Industry Division, *Wetlands: An Overview of Issues*, https://crsreports.congress.gov/product/pdf/rl/rl33483 (last updated Jan. 5, 2017).

agricultural use beginning in the latter part of the 19th century.[8] The passage of the Federal Water Pollution Control Act,[9] and its significant amendments in the 1970s,[10] which came to be known as the Clean Water Act,[11] added new and specific requirements to the regulatory arena that brought us to the modern age of regulating most activities in jurisdictional[12] wetlands.[13]

The Clean Water Act (CWA) Section 404[14] program was one of a number of new laws evolving in the late 1960s through the early 1980s.[15] Through the CWA, Congress sought to "restore and maintain the chemical, physical and biological integrity of our nation's waters."[16] Section 404 of the CWA is entitled "Permits for dredged or fill material."[17] As set forth herein, this law has been interpreted for more than 40 years to require federal permits for tens of thousands of actions annually.[18]

---

8. Christopher Meindl, et al., On the Importance of Claims-Making: The Role of James O. Wright in Promoting the Drainage of Florida's Everglades in the Early Twentieth Century, 92(4) ANNALS OF THE ASS'N OF AM. GEOGRAPHERS 682–701 (Dec. 2002).

9. Pub. L. No. 92-500, 86 Stat. 816 (1972).

10. Pub. L. No. 95-217, 91 Stat. 1567 (1977); Pub. L. No. 100-4, 101 Stat. 45 (1987).

11. Currently *codified in* 33 U.S.C. §§ 1251–1387 (2023).

12. For an explanation of which wetlands are subject to federal jurisdiction and which are not, see Chapter 2.

13. See generally William Andreen, The Evolution of Water Pollution Control in the United States: State, Local and Federal Efforts, 1789–1972: Part II, 21 STAN. ENV'T L.J. 215–94 (2003); William Andreen, The Evolution of Water Pollution Control in the United States: State, Local and Federal Efforts, 1789–1972: Part I, 21 STAN. ENV'T L.J. 145–200 (2003).

14. 33 U.S.C. § 1344 (2023).

15. *See generally* Richard J. Lazarus, The Making of Environmental Law (Univ. Chicago 2004).

16. 33 U.S.C. § 1251(a) (2023). To achieve this objective, Congress listed seven goals, each of which indicates concern for values other than navigability. *Id.* § 1251(a)(1)–(6). These broad goals of the law include "protection and propagation of fish, shellfish, and wildlife," "recreation in and on the water," elimination of "the discharge of toxic pollutants in toxic amounts," and "programs for the control of non-point source pollution." *Id.*

17. *Id.* § 1344.

18. *See* Cong. Rsch. Serv., *The Army Corps of Engineers' Nationwide Permits Program: Issues and Regulatory Developments* (Jan. 30, 2012, updated Jan. 12, 2017), https://crsreports.congress.gov/product/pdf/RL/97-223.

III. Regulated Activities

A. Statutory Authorities and Definitions

The CWA[19] establishes the basic structure for regulating discharges of pollutants into waters of the United States and regulating quality standards for surface waters. Section 301 of the CWA[20] prohibits all discharges of pollutants from a point source without a permit. Other sections of the CWA authorize certain discharges,[21] while Section 404 of the Clean Water Act specifically addresses permits "for the discharge of dredged or fill material into the navigable waters at specified disposal sites."[22] Thus, for a permit to be required under Section 404, there must be a (1) discharge (2) of dredged or fill material (3) into navigable waters (4) at a specified location. Chapter 2 examines the phrase "navigable waters." This chapter examines what constitutes a "discharge" and what is meant by "dredged or fill material."

1. What Is a Discharge?

The CWA provides that "[t]he term 'discharge' when used without qualification includes a discharge of a pollutant, and a discharge of pollutants."[23] It also defines discharge as: "(A) any addition of any pollutant to navigable waters from any point source, (B) any addition of any pollutant to the waters of the contiguous zone or the ocean from any point source other than a vessel or other floating craft."[24] The term "pollution" in its turn means "the man-made or man-induced alteration of the chemical, physical, biological, and radiological integrity of

---

19. 33 U.S.C. §§ 1251–1387 (2023).

20. 33 U.S.C. § 13111251–1387 (2023) is commonly referred to as the Clean Water Act following the 1977 amendments to the FWPCA. Pub. L. No. 95-217, 91 Stat. 1566 (1977) ("Sec. 518. This Act may be cited as the 'Federal Water Pollution Control Act' commonly referred to as the Clean Water Act.").

21. *E.g.*, section 311 (33 U.S.C. § 1321) regulates the discharges of oil and other hazardous substances; section 402 (33 U.S.C. § 1342) creates a permitting system for discharges of pollutants known as the National Pollutant Discharge Elimination System (NPDES). Except where states have assumed the permitting program, the Corps has primary responsibility for issuing Section 404 permits, while EPA has primary responsibility over NPDES permits, although EPA retains ultimate oversight of both programs. *See* Chapter 1.

22. 33 U.S.C. § 1344 (2023).

23. *Id.* § 1362(16) (definition of "discharge").

24. *Id.* § 1362(12).

water."[25] Section 404 regulates discharges "of dredged or fill material." Therefore, Section 404 regulation is triggered when a discharge involves (1) the addition to "navigable waters"[26] of (2) dredged or fill material that is a (3) pollutant (4) from a point source. As discussed later, Congress defined two of these terms (point source and pollutant) in the statute itself, and the Corps later defined the terms "dredged material" and "fill material" via regulation. The discharge must, first and foremost, add a pollutant to navigable waters.

It is important to note, before moving on, that, because it is not a "discharge," the draining of wetlands is not explicitly regulated under Section 404,[27] although many drainage activities, such as constructing a ditch in a wetland, may involve discharges of dredged or fill material requiring a Section 404 permit. Excavation and/or clearing wetland vegetation may or may not be regulated, depending on the particular situation.[28] The extent to which specific activities in jurisdictional waters[29] are regulated is, in fact, a tumultuous subject. The Congressional Research Service explained in 2017:

---

25. *Id.* § 1362(19).

26. *See* Chapter 2 for a discussion of how this term has been interpreted.

27. Save Our Cmty. v. U.S. Env't Prot. Agency, 971 F.2d 1155 (5th Cir. 1992); Great Basin Mine Watch v. Hankins, 456 F.3d 955 (9th Cir. 2006). Several states that have their own wetland regulatory programs do regulate beyond discharge. *See, e.g.*, Protected Waters and Wetlands Permit Program, MINN. STAT. ANN. § 103G.333(1)(a) ("Wetlands must not be drained, excavated, or filled wholly or partially unless replaced by restoring or creating wetland areas of at least equal public value."), https://www.revisor.mn.gov/statutes/cite/103G.222 (Minnesota); Dredge in Wetlands, N.H REV. STAT. ANN. §§ 482-A:1–482-A:27 ("No person shall excavate, remove, fill, dredge or construct any structures in or on any bank, flat, marsh, or swamp in and adjacent to any waters of the state without a permit from the department." *Id.* § 482-A3) (New Hampshire), https://law.justia.com/codes/new-hampshire/2022/title-l/title-482-a/section-482-a-3/; and Environmental Resource Permitting, FLA. ADMIN. CODE Ch. 62-330 (". . . a permit is required prior to the construction, alteration, operation, maintenance, removal, or abandonment of . . . (a) any project in, on, or over wetlands or other surface waters." *Id.* r. 62-330.020(2)), https://www.flrules.org/gateway/ruleno.asp?id=62-330.020 (Florida). The National Association of Wetland Managers, State Wetland Programs, https://www.nawm.org/wetland-programs/state-wetland-programs, summarizes the wetland programs in all 50 states: *See* note 146 of Ch. 1 of this book.

28. Excavation is an activity that is specifically regulated under the more limited jurisdictional reach of Section 10 of the Rivers and Harbors Act of 1899. 33 U.S.C. § 403 (2023).

29. *See* Chapter 2.

> Wetland protection efforts continue to engender controversy over issues of science and policy. Topics include the rate and pattern of loss, whether all wetlands should be protected in a single fashion, the effectiveness of the current suite of laws in protecting them, and the fact that 75 percent of remaining U.S. wetlands are located on private lands.[30]

While not expressly referenced in Section 404 of the CWA, the definition of "discharge," as noted earlier," requires there to be a discernable point source. But what does that mean in the context of a Section 404 discharge? Congress defined "point source" as "any discernible, confined and discrete conveyance, including but not limited to any pipe, ditch, channel, tunnel, conduit, well, discrete fissure, container, rolling stock, concentrated animal feeding operation, or vessel . . . from which pollutants are or may be discharged."[31] In the context of wetlands and other waters, equipment routinely used to clear or alter wetlands (such as backhoes, bulldozers, and dump trucks) has been held to be a "point source" when used to place or move pollutants.[32]

The U.S. Supreme Court has held in the Section 402 context that the movement of water and pollutants through dams, pump stations,

30. Laura Gatz & Megan Stubbs, Cong. Rsch. Serv., *Wetlands: An Overview of Issues* (Jan. 6, 2017), https://www.everycrsreport.com/files/20170105_RL33483_740bd446f7ec4e3db28c47e468ee392cc2e00b93.pdf; *see also* Warren E. Leary, *In Wetlands Debate, Acres and Dollars Hinge on Definitions*, N.Y. Times, C4 (Oct. 15, 1991), https://www.nytimes.com/1991/10/15/news/in-wetlands-debate-acres-and-dollars-hinge-on-definitions.html; Kim Diana Connolly, *Keeping Wetlands Wet: Are Existing Protections Enough?*, 6 Vt. J. Env't L. 169 (2004), https://digitalcommons.law.buffalo.edu/cgi/viewcontent.cgi?article=1370&context=journal_articles.

31. 33 U.S.C. § 1362(14).

32. *See, e.g.*, Borden Ranch P'ship v. U.S. Army Corps of Eng'rs., 261 F.3d 810, 815 (9th Cir. 2001), *aff'd by an equally divided court*, 537 U.S. 99 (2002); United States v. Pozsgai, 999 F.2d 719, 726 n.6 (3d Cir. 1993); Avoyelles Sportsmen's League v. Marsh, 715 F.2d 897, 922 (5th Cir. 1983); Matter of Alameda Cnty. Assessor's Parcel, 672 F. Supp. 1278, 1284–85 (N.D. Cal. 1987); United States v. Tull, 615 F. Supp. 610, 622 (E.D. Va. 1983), *aff'd*, 769 F.2d 182 (4th Cir. 1985), *rev'd on other grounds*, 481 U.S. 412 (1987); United States v. Weisman, 489 F. Supp. 1331, 1337 (M.D. Fla. 1980). *See also* Oregon Nat. Desert Ass'n v. U.S. Forest Serv., 550 F.3d 778 (9th Cir. 2008) (holding the term discharge for purposes of water quality certification was limited to effluents from point sources rather than from living stock as non-point sources); Ecological Rights Found. v. Pac. Gas & Elec. Co., 713 F.3d 502 (9th Cir. 2013) (holding ERF failed to state a claim under the CWA because discharges of stormwater from the utility poles are neither a "point source discharge" nor "associated with industrial activity").

and other drainages between two parts of a waterbody does not result in the "addition" of a "pollutant" into waters of the United States."[33] However, that does not preclude regulation. In a 1990 challenge to National Pollutant Discharge Elimination System (NPDES) regulations governing placer mines, the Ninth Circuit in *Rybachek v. E.P.A.* did not disturb EPA's interpretation that "addition" includes "resuspension" of rocks and sand from a placer mining sluice box to a stream, even when the rocks and sand came from the streambed and not from some other location.[34] In 2021, relying on the Ninth Circuit's decision in *Rybachek*, the District Court for Idaho ruled that the process material discharged from a suction dredge mine to navigable waters is "addition of a pollutant," but not "the discharge of dredged or fill material" and thus requires a Section 402 NPDES permit, not a Section 404 permit.[35] The district court subsequently awarded the plaintiffs injunctive

33. Los Angeles Cnty. Flood Control Dist. v. Nat. Res. Def. Council, Inc., 568 U.S. 78, 80–82 (2013) (transferring water from an improved portion of a navigable waterway to an unimproved portion is not the addition of a pollutant); S. Fla. Water Mgmt. Dist. v. Miccosukee Tribe, 541 U.S. 95, 109–12 (2004) (pumping water within parts of the same waterbody is not an "addition" of pollutants). *See also* S. Side Quarry, LLC v. Louisville & Jefferson Cnty. Metro. Sewer Dist., 28 F.4th 684 (6th Cir. 2022) (holding that flow of creek into quarry and then back into creek pursuant to sewer district's flood control plan was not a "discharge" which required Kentucky Pollution Discharge Elimination System (KPDES) permit; and diversion channel into quarry area fell within Environmental Protection Agency's definition of a "water transfer" such that sewer district did not need a Kentucky Pollution Discharge Elimination System (KPDES) permit to use quarry as a detention basin); ONRC Action v. U.S. Bureau of Reclamation, 798 F.3d 933 (9th Cir. 2015) (holding that the waters of channel were not meaningfully distinct from waters of the river, and thus Bureau was not required to obtain a permit for discharge of pollutants from the channel to the river).

34. Rybachek v. E.P.A., 904 F.2d 1276 (9th Cir. 1990) (dismissing challenge to rulemaking to create performance standards for NPDES permits for placer mines under Section 402, upholding EPA finding that placer mining discharges pollutants within meaning of the act whether the rocks and sand come from the adjacent stream bank or the streambed itself). *Rybachek* did not address the issue of incidental fallback, but whether EPA had the authority to promulgate regulations under Section 402 that governed placer mining. As such, the case was distinguished by the D.C. Circuit in Nat'l Mining Ass'n v. U.S. Army Corps, *see infra* note 70, on the ground that *Rybachek* did not address the issue of exclusion as incidental fallback, but whether or not the material was a "pollutant" and whether resuspension in the stream was the "additional of a pollutant." *See also* Nw. Env't Def. Ctr. v. Env't Quality Comm'n, 223 P.3d 1071 (Or. Ct. App. 2009).

35. Idaho Conservation League v. Poe, 2021 WL 2316158 (Dist. Idaho 2021). Mr. Poe had obtained the required permits from the state of Idaho for his suction dredge

relief and assessed civil penalties against Mr. Poe of $150,000.[36] The Pacific Legal Foundation appealed the decision on behalf of Poe, arguing that instream suction dredge mining was analogous to the transfer of water upheld in the *L.A. County* and *Miccosukee Tribe* cases and distinguishable from the Rybacheck case because the action does not add in new material from the outside world.[37] On November 20, 2023, the Ninth Circuit affirmed the district court ruling, holding that the return of the discarded mine materials to the water constituted the "addition" of a "pollutant" and required an NPDES permit rather than a Section 404 permit.[38] The Pacific Legal Foundation continues to fight on, however, and at press-time, a petition for certiorari review of the Ninth Circuit's decision was pending before the U.S. Supreme Court.[39] Given the decidedly conservative leaning of the current Supreme Court on environmental cases, this petition bears watching.

2. What Is "Dredged or Fill Material"?

Congress defined "pollutant" (in the definitions section applicable to the entire CWA) to include a wide array of materials, including "dredged spoil," "sewage," "biological material," "rock," and "sand."[40] In the context of Section 404, courts have construed the definition of "pollutant" broadly to include a wide range of diverse materials, including "fill material";[41] "dredged materials, including native soils excavated by ditching activities";[42] "rock fill, dirt, organic debris, and

mining activity in the South Fork Clearwater River in Idaho, but had not obtained an NPDES permit under Section 402 of the CWA. The Idaho Conservation League filed a citizen's suit against Poe, alleging the activity constituted the addition of a pollutant without a NPDES permit, and the court agreed.

36. Idaho Conservation League v. Poe, 2022 WL 4536465 (Dist. Idaho 2022)

37. Idaho Conservation League v. Poe, 86 F.4th 1243, (9th Cir. 2023).

38. *Id.*

39. Poe v. Idaho Conservation League, Case No. 23-1028 (U.S. Mar.19, 2024).

40. 33 U.S.C. § 1362(6) (2023). The definition reads "dredged spoil, solid waste, incinerator residue, sewage, garbage, sewage, sludge, munitions, chemical wastes, biological materials, radioactive materials, heat, wrecked or discarded equipment, rock, sand, cellar dirt and industrial, municipal, and agricultural waste discharged into water." *Id.*

41. United States v. Zanger, 767 F. Supp. 1030, 1034 (N.D. Cal. 1991); *see also* Swinomish Indian Tribal Cmty. v. Skagit Cnty. Dike Dist. No. 22, 618 F. Supp. 2d 1262 (W.D. Wash. 2008) (holding CWA applied to district's discharge of dredged and fill materials in course of tidegate replacements).

42. *See, e.g.*, United States v. Wilson, 133 F.3d 251 (4th Cir. 1997).

biological materials,"[43] and other matter.[44] Although they limit the scope of Section 404, the terms "dredged material" and "fill material" are not defined in the CWA. Rather, these terms are defined by the EPA and Corps in their rules. Because these terms were not defined by Congress, what constitutes a Section 404 discharge has been the subject of a number of court cases.

3. What Is Fill Material?

Regulation of discharges of fill material[45] is relatively straightforward in terms of interpreting "addition of a pollutant." In the past, the Corps defined "fill" based on a so-called "primary purpose test" through which it only regulated materials "used for the primary purpose of replacing aquatic area with dry land or changing the bottom elevation of a water body."[46] By contrast, the EPA historically used an "effects" test rather than a purpose test, regulating materials that had the effect of replacing "waters of the United States" with dry land or changing

43. *See, e.g.*, United States v. Sweeney, 483 F. Supp. 3d 871, 911–13 (E.D. Cal. 2020) (applying the CWA definition of "discharge of a pollutant" to include "any addition of any pollutants," 33 U.S.C. § 1362(12) (A), and "pollutant" to include constituents such as "dredged spoil," "solid waste," "biological materials," "wrecked or discarded equipment," "rock," "sand," and "cellar dirt"); United States v. Banks, 873 F. Supp. 650, 657 (S.D. Fla. 1995), *citing* United States v. Carter, 18 Env't Rep. Cas. (BNA) 1804, 1807 (S.D. Fla. 1982); United States v. Huebner, 752 F.2d 1235, 1242 (7th Cir. 1985), *cert. denied*, 474 U.S. 817 (1985); N. Carolina Shellfish Growers Ass'n v. Holly Ridge Associates, LLC, 357 N.C. 1429, 676–77 (E.D.N.C. 2003) (sediment).

44. *See* Borden Ranch P'ship v. U.S. Army Corps of Eng'rs., 261 F.3d 810, 815 (9th Cir. 2001), *aff'd*, 537 U.S. 99 (2002) (finding "Soil [that] was wrenched up, moved around, and redeposited somewhere else" was a pollutant); United States v. Pozsgai, 999 F.2d 719, 725 (3d Cir. 1993), *cert. denied*, 510 U.S. 1110 (concrete rubble and cinder block); Hanson v. United States, 710 F. Supp. 1105, 1107 (E.D. Tex. 1989) (bricks and sheet metal); Minnehaha Creek Watershed Dist. v. Hoffman, 597 F.2d 617, 626–27 (8th Cir. 1979) (dams and riprap); Avoyelles Sportsmen's League v. Alexander, 473 F. Supp. 525, 532 (W.D. La. 1979) ("sheared trees and vegetation and scraped soil and leaf litter"); Avoyelles Sportsmen's League v. Marsh, 715 F.2d. at 924–25 (burying and discing of land-clearing debris is "discharge of fill material"). Water itself, however, has been found not to be a pollutant under the definition. Orleans Audubon Soc'y v. Lee, 742 F.2d 901, 910–11 (5th Cir. 1984).

45. *See generally* U.S. Army Corps of Eng'rs, *Information Relation to the "Fill" Rule*, http://www.usace.army.mil/Missions/CivilWorks/RegulatoryProgramandPermits/RelatedResources/fill_info.aspx.

46. 33 C.F.R. § 323.3(e) (2001) (superseded).

the bottom elevation of a water body for any purpose.[47] In 2002, the Corps and EPA reconciled their previously differing "fill material" definitions by amending both Corps and EPA regulations to provide a single consistent definition following EPA's original approach, defining "fill material" as discharges that have the effect of changing the elevation of a water body rather than examining the purpose of the discharge.[48] Therefore, adding fill material[49] is regulated under Section

47. 40 C.F.R. § 232.2 (2001) (superseded).

48. Final Revisions to the Clean Water Act Regulatory Definitions of "Fill Material" and "Discharge of Fill Material," 67 Fed. Reg. 31,129 (May 9, 2002). This rule reconciled an issue raised in a U.S. District Court for the Southern District of West Virginia case holding mountaintop coal mining operations (in which tons of rock and earth are disposed of into valley streams) required a Section 404 permit to discharge material. Bragg v. Robertson, 72 F. Supp. 2d 642 (S.D. W. Va. 1999), *affirmed in part, vacated in part and remanded with instructions*, Bragg v. W. Va. Coal Ass'n, 248 F.3d 275 (4th Cir. 2001), *cert. denied*, 534 U.S. 1113 (2002); *see also* Kentuckians for the Commonwealth v. Rivenburgh, 204 F. Supp. 2d 927, 941 (S.D. W. Va. 2002), *rev'd*, 317 F.3d 425 (4th Cir. 2003) (lower court holding that "[w]hen overburden is dumped into valleys and streams to get rid of it, the disposal has the effect of creating dry land, but not the purpose. Because land creation or elevation is not a principal purpose of overburden disposal in streams, such a discharge would not meet the Corps' definition of "fill material" . . . nor be permittable under § 404" (reversed by the Fourth Circuit)).

49. Fill material is now defined as "(1) Except as specified in paragraph (3) of this definition, the term fill material means material placed in waters of the United States where the material has the effect of: (i) Replacing any portion of a water of the United States with dry land; or (ii) Changing the bottom elevation of any portion of a water of the United States. (2) Examples of such fill material include, but are not limited to: rock, sand, soil, clay, plastics, construction debris, wood chips, overburden from mining or other excavation activities, and materials used to create any structure or infrastructure in the waters of the United States. (3) The term fill material does not include trash or garbage." 33 C.F.R. § 323.2(e). "Discharge of fill material" is defined in current Corps regulations to include the following activities: "[p]lacement of fill that is necessary for the construction of any structure or infrastructure in a water of the United States; the building of any structure, infrastructure, or impoundment requiring rock, sand, dirt, or other material for its construction; site-development fills for recreational, industrial, commercial, residential, or other uses; causeways or road fills; dams and dikes; artificial islands; property protection and/or reclamation devices such as riprap, groins, seawalls, breakwaters, and revetments; beach nourishment; levees; fill for structures such as sewage treatment facilities, intake and outfall pipes associated with power plants and subaqueous utility lines; placement of fill material for construction or maintenance of any liner, berm, or other infrastructure associated with solid waste landfills; placement of overburden, slurry, or tailings or similar mining-related materials; and artificial reefs. The term does not include plowing, cultivating, seeding and harvesting for the production of food, fiber, and forest products

404, unless an exemption applies, whether or not filling the wetland is the goal.[50]

As noted, both Section 402 and Section 404 require a permit for certain discharges of pollutants. Determining which of these sections governs the discharge of "fill" became an issue in a 2009 U.S. Supreme Court case. In *Coeur Alaska, Inc. v. Southeast Alaska Conservation Council*, the Court addressed for the first time the issue of which activities are regulated under CWA Section 404[51] rather than Section 402.[52] There, the Court reviewed the Ninth Circuit's decision in *Southeast Alaska Conservation Council v. U.S. Army Corps of Engineers*, which rejected as inappropriate a Corps-issued permit allowing a froth-flotation mill related to gold mining to discharge what it designated as "fill material."[53] At issue was whether Section 404 or Section 402 of the Clean Water Act governed such releases into a navigable water. The releases for which the permit was sought would indisputably "kill all [of the lake's] fish and nearly all the aquatic life."[54] The Ninth Circuit rejected the Corps' reasoning that the discharge was subject to Section 404 rather than Section 402 permitting standards; the Court held, "Even though the discharge in this case facially qualifies for the permitting scheme under § 404 of the Clean Water Act because it will change the bottom elevation of Lower Slate Lake, the discharge is nevertheless prohibited by the clearly applicable and specific performance standard" promulgated for froth-flotation mills pursuant to Section 301 and Section 306 of the CWA.[55] The Ninth Circuit held that "[t]he plain language and structure of the Clean Water Act demonstrate that EPA's performance standard governs in

---

(See Section 323.4 for the definition of these terms). See Section 323.3(c) concerning the regulation of the placement of pilings in waters of the United States." 33 C.F.R. § 323.2(f).

50. *See* 33 C.F.R. § 323.3(a) ("Except as provided in Section 323.4 of this Part, DA permits will be required for the discharge of dredged or fill material into waters of the United States. . . .").

51. 33 U.S.C. § 1344 (2023).

52. *Id.* § 1342; Coeur Alaska, Inc. v. Se. Alaska Conservation Council, 557 U.S. 261 (2009).

53. Se. Alaska Conservation Council v. U.S. Army Corps of Eng'rs, 486 F.3d. 638 (9th Cir. 2007).

54. *Id.* at 642.

55. *Id.* at 655.

this case," and remanded to the district court to vacate the Section 404 permits.[56]

In an opinion by Justice Kennedy, joined by Chief Justice Roberts, as well as Justices Thomas, Breyer, and Alito, and joined in part by Justice Scalia, the Supreme Court reversed and ruled that the Corps, not the EPA, has authority to permit the slurry discharge.[57] The opinion noted that by specifying that, "[e]xcept as provided in . . . [§ 404,]" the EPA "may . . . issue permit[s] for the discharge of any pollutant," Section 402(a) precludes EPA-issued permits for fill materials falling under the Corps' Section 404 authority.[58] The Court pointed further to EPA's own rule, which provides that discharges of fill material regulated under Section 404 "do not require [EPA § 402] permits."[59] The Court concluded that, because Section 404(a) empowers the Corps to "issue permits . . . for the discharge of . . . fill material," and the agencies' joint regulation defines "fill material" to include "slurry . . . or similar mining-related materials" having the "effect of . . . [c]hanging the bottom elevation" of water, the slurry Coeur Alaska wished to discharge falls well within the Corps' Section 404 permitting authority, rather than the EPA's Section 402 authority.[60]

The dissent asserted that "Section 404 neither mentions § 306 nor states a contrary requirement. The Act can be home to both provisions, with no words added or omitted, so long as the category of 'dredged or fill material' eligible for a § 404 permit is read in harmony with § 306. Doing so yields a simple rule: Discharges governed by EPA performance standards are subject to EPA's administration and receive permits under the NPDES, not § 404."[61] The dissent warned that the reading by the majority means that "[w]hole categories of

56. *Id.*

57. *Coeur Alaska Inc.*, 557 U.S. at 291.

58. *Id.* at 273.

59. *Id.*

60. *Id.* at 262. Justice Breyer issued a concurring opinion, in which he acknowledged dangers noted by the dissent but stated that "there are safeguards against that occurring. . . . The EPA has never suggested that it would interpret the regulations so as to turn § 404 into a loophole, permitting evasion of a 'performance standard' simply because a polluter discharges enough pollutant to raise the bottom elevation of the body of water." Justice Breyer also noted that Corps regulation under § 404 includes "the EPA . . . retain[ing] an important role in the permitting process," namely the veto. Justice Scalia's concurrence agrees in the outcome, but raised issues with respect to Chevron/Mead deference granted to the agencies. *Id.* at 291–95.

61. *Id.* at 301.

regulated industries can thereby gain immunity from a variety of pollution-control standards."[62]

Thus, any pollutant that has the effect of replacing the bottom of a water of the United States or changing the bottom elevation is "fill material," and the discharge of such material into that water is subject to Section 404 permitting, not Section 402, even if the purpose of the discharge is disposal, not fill.

4. What Is Dredged Material?

Significantly more controversial, however, is regulation of "dredged" material when it involves analyzing whether—and the extent to which—the redeposit of materials into the same waters from which they were removed, excavated, cleared, or otherwise disturbed can properly be regarded as a regulated "addition" of a pollutant or, specific to Section 404, "dredged material." The formal definition of "dredged material" is straightforward: it is material "excavated or dredged from waters of the United States."[63] When that dredged material is then discharged to a navigable water, it is subject to Section 404 of the CWA. The issue becomes trickier to conceptualize, however, when the dredged material is not moved to another location to be discharged (e.g., discharging the material excavated from dredging a shipping channel into near-shore shallower waters as a means of disposing of the material) but rather is discharged or "redeposited" in the same general area from which it was removed. Is it truly the "addition of a pollutant" to pick up material and put it down again in the same place?

The Fourth Circuit explained the redeposit phenomenon as follows:

> [T]he statute does not prohibit the addition of material; it prohibits "the addition of any pollutant." The idea that there could be an addition of a pollutant without an addition of material seems to us entirely unremarkable, at least when an activity transforms some material from a nonpollutant into a pollutant, as occurred here. In the course of digging a ditch across the [particular] property, the contractor removed earth and vegetable matter from the wetland. Once it was removed, that

62. *Id.* at 302.

63. 33 C.F.R. § 323.2(c) (2023). *See* United States v. Hummel, No. 00-C-5184, 2003 WL 1845365 (N.D. Ill. 2003) (redeposit of dredged material); United States v. Sweeney, 483 F. Supp. 3d. 871 (E.D. Cal. 2020) (redeposit of dredged material).

> material became "dredged spoil," a statutory pollutant and a type of material that up until then was not present on the [] property. It is of no consequence that what is now dredged spoil was previously present on the same property in the less threatening form of dirt and vegetation in an undisturbed state. What is important is that once that material was excavated from the wetland, its redeposit in that same wetland added a pollutant where none had been before.[64]

This debate about discharge and excavated material became more heated in the late 1990s with respect to so-called "incidental fallback." In 1986, Corps and EPA promulgated rules defining the "discharge of dredged material" to exclude "de minimis, incidental soil movement occurring during normal dredging operations."[65] As of 1993, as a result of litigation, the definition of "discharge of dredged material" had been revised to *include* "any addition, including any redeposit,

64. United States v. Deaton, 209 F.3d 331, 335 (4th Cir. 2000), *cert. denied*, 541 U.S. 972 (2004) (holding that "sidecasting" dredged material in a jurisdictional wetland is the "discharge of a pollutant" under the CWA); *accord* Avoyelles Sportsmen's League v. Marsh, 715 F.2d 897 (5th Cir. 1983) ("[t]he word 'addition,' as used in the definition of 'discharge,' may reasonably be understood to include 'redeposit,'" where such "redepositing activities would significantly alter the character of the wetlands and limit the ecological functions served by the tract." Furthermore, because "'dredged' material is by definition material that comes from the water itself," construing the term "addition" to impose a requirement that the pollutant come from outside sources "would effectively remove the dredge-and-fill provisions from the statute." *Id.* at 923–24); United States v. M.C.C. of Florida, Inc., 772 F.2d 1501, 1506 (11th Cir. 1985), *vacated and remanded on other grounds*, 481 U.S. 1034 (1987), *readopted in part and remanded on other grounds*, 848 F.2d 1133 (11th Cir. 1988), *reh'g granted in other part*, 863 F.2d 802 (11th Cir. 1989) (redepositing sediment and vegetation dredged by tugboat propellers onto adjacent sea grass beds was an "addition" of a pollutant that impacted the physical and biological integrity of the waters in question).

65. 33 C.F.R. § 323.2(d) (1987) (superseded). In 1986, the Corps modified the definition of "discharge of dredged material" through a new regulation, effective in January 1987. Final Rule for Regulatory Programs of the Corps of Engineers, 51 Fed. Reg. 41,206 (Nov. 13, 1986). This rule stated that dredging was not regulated if the dredged material was not redeposited within the "waters of the United States." *See* 33 C.F.R. § 323.2 (1987); Reid v. Marsh, 20 Env't Rep. Cas. (BNA) 1336, 1341–42 (N.D. Ohio 1984). To deal with the issue of not regulating dredging but regulating any redeposit, the 1986 regulation directed that the "discharge of dredged material" "does not include *de minimis*, incidental soil movement occurring during normal dredging operations." Final Rule for Regulatory Programs of the Corps of Engineers, 51 Fed. Reg. at 41,232; 33 C.F.R. § 323.2 (1987).

of dredged material, including excavated material, into waters of the United States which is incidental to any activity,"[66] unless it "does not have or would not have the effect of destroying or degrading an area of waters of the United States."[67]

This 1993 rule came to be called the "Excavation Rule" or the "Tulloch Rule," after Corps District Engineer Colonel Tulloch.[68] The Tulloch Rule narrowed the redeposit concept significantly: "[t]he term ('discharge of dredged material') does not include de minimis incidental soil movement occurring during normal dredging operations."[69] The Tulloch Rule[70] resulted from a settlement agreement reached with environmental interest groups in *North Carolina Wildlife Federation, et al. v. Tulloch.*[71]

The 1993 Tulloch Rule was itself the subject of a facial challenge not long after its promulgation. In *National Mining Association v. U.S. Army Corps of Engineers*, the Circuit Court for the District of Columbia held that Congress did not intend to regulate purely incidental fallback under Section 404.[72] The court invalidated the Tulloch Rule, concluding that incidental fallback during excavation activities cannot properly be regarded as the "addition of a pollutant."[73] The court distinguished earlier "redeposit" cases, concluding that none of those decisions specifically addressed whether incidental fallback from excavation activities constitutes a discharge.[74] On that question, the

66. 33 C.F.R. § 323.2(d)(1)(iii) (1994) (superseded).

67. *Id.* § 323.2(d)(3)(i) (1994) (superseded).

68. *See* Bradford C. Mank, American Mining Congress v. Army Corps of Engineers: Ignoring Chevron and The Clean Water Act's Broad Purposes, 25 N. Ky. L. Rev. 51 (1997).

69. 33 C.F.R. § 323.2(d) (1994) (superseded).

70. 58 Fed. Reg. 45,008 (Aug. 25, 1993).

71. Civil No. C90-713-CIV-5-BO (E.D. N.C. 1996).

72. Nat'l Mining Ass'n v. U.S. Army Corps of Eng'rs, 145 F.3d 1399 (D.C. Cir. 1998). While both *Rybachek* and *National Mining* address the discharge of rocks and sediment from mining operations, the court in *National Mining* distinguished *Rybachek*; "Rybachek would help the agencies if the court had held that imperfect extraction, i.e., extraction accompanied by incidental fallback of dirt and gravel, constituted 'addition of a pollutant,' but instead it identified the regulable discharge as the discrete act of dumping leftover material into the stream after it had been processed." The parties in *Rybachek* simply did not raise the question of incidental fallback. The appeal of the *Poe* case does not reference the *National Mining* case but does attack the District Court's reliance on *Rybachek. See supra* note 35 and accompanying text.

73. *Nat'l Mining Ass'n*, 145 F.3d at 1405.

74. *Id.* at 1406.

court concluded that the "term 'addition' cannot reasonably be said to encompass the situation in which material is removed from the waters of the United States and a small portion of it happens to fall back."[75]

The *National Mining Association* opinion indicated that the Corps would not be precluded from regulating "some forms of redeposit"[76] and acknowledged that requiring all regulated pollutants to "come from outside sources would effectively remove the dredge-and-fill provision from the statute."[77] Accordingly, it limited its holding to the Corps' attempt, under the Tulloch Rule, to regulate "a wide range of activities that cannot remotely be said to 'add' anything to the waters of the United States."[78]

Subsequent to that decision, "addition" was explored in the context of "deep ripping."[79] In *Borden Ranch Partnership v. U.S. Army Corps of Engineers*,[80] the Ninth Circuit held, and the Supreme Court affirmed,[81] that this practice was subject to the Corps jurisdiction under Section 404.[82]

In response to *National Mining Association*, in 1999 the Corps and EPA again amended the definition of "discharge of dredged material" to clarify that not all redeposits of dredged material are "discharges" subject to Section 404 regulation and to exclude "incidental fallback" from the definition of "discharge of dredged materials."[83] The 1999 Rule

75. *Id.* at 1404.

76. *Id.* at 1405.

77. *Id.* (quoting *Avoyelles Sportsmen's League*, 715 F.2d at 924 n.43).

78. *Id.*

79. Regulatory Guidance Letter 96-2, *Applicability of Exemptions under Section 404(f) to "Deep-Ripping" Activities in Wetlands*, 62 Fed. Reg. 31,504 (June 9, 1997) ("the mechanical manipulation of the soil to break up or pierce highly compacted, impermeable or slowly permeable subsurface soil layers, or other similar kinds of restrictive soil layers. These practices are typically used to break up these subsoil layers (e.g., impermeable soil layer, hardpan) as part of the initial preparation of the soil to establish an agricultural or silvicultural operation.").

80. 261 F.3d 810 (9th Cir. 2001).

81. Borden Ranch P'ship v. U.S. Army Corps of Eng'rs, 537 U.S. 99 (2002). This affirmance was per curiam by an equally divided Court (4–4); Justice Kennedy did not participate in the consideration or decision. *Id.*

82. *See Borden Ranch*, 261 F.3d at 816 (attempt to convert, into a vineyard, property that had been used primarily as rangeland for cattle that included vernal pools, swales, and intermittent drainage areas, all of which depended on a dense layer of "clay pan" to maintain their hydrologic features).

83. 64 Fed. Reg. 25,120, 25,121 (May 10, 1999). A reviewing court upheld that rule, but cautioned the agencies not to adopt "an unduly narrow" definition of

was only intended to be an interim rule to comply with the injunction issued by the Court in *National Mining Association* until the agencies "undertake notice and comment rulemaking that will make a reasoned attempt to more clearly delineate the scope of CWA jurisdiction over redeposits of dredged material in waters of the U.S."[84] In January 2001, the agencies promulgated the replacement rule—issuing a new final rule redefining "discharge of dredged material."[85] Dubbed "Tulloch II," the 2001 rule provided, in pertinent part:

> (d)(1) Except as provided below in paragraph (d)(2), the term discharge of dredged material means any addition of dredged material into, including any redeposit of dredged material other than incidental fallback within, the waters of the United States. The term includes, but is not limited to, the following:
>
> (i) The addition of dredged material to a specified discharge site located in waters of the United States;
>
> (ii) The runoff or overflow from a contained land or water disposal area; and
>
> (iii) Any addition, including redeposit other than incidental fallback, of dredged material, including excavated material, into waters of the United States which is incidental to any activity, including mechanized landclearing, ditching, channelization, or other excavation.[86]

The rule also defined "incidental fallback" as "the redeposit of small volumes of dredged material that is incidental to excavation activity in waters of the United States when such material falls back to substantially the same place as the initial removal."[87] Finally, it created a rebuttable presumption: "[t]he Corps and EPA regard the use of mechanized earth-moving equipment to conduct land-clearing, ditching, channelization, in-stream mining or other earth-moving activity

---

"incidental fallback." Am. Mining Congress v. U.S. Army Corps of Eng'rs, 120 F. Supp. 2d 23, 30 (D.D.C. 2000).

84. 64 Fed. Reg. at 25,121.

85. Fed. Reg. 4550 (Jan. 17, 2001).

86. 33 C.F.R. § 323.3(d)(1) (2001) (superseded).

87. 66 Fed. Reg. at 4575 (codified at 33 C.F.R. § 323.2(d)(2)(ii) and 40 C.F.R. § 232.2(2)(ii)) (superseded). ("Examples of incidental fallback include soil that is disturbed when dirt is shoveled and the back-spill that comes off a bucket when such small volume of soil or dirt falls into substantially the same place from which it was initially removed.").

in waters of the United States as resulting in a discharge of dredged material unless project-specific evidence shows that the activity results in only incidental fallback."[88]

Shortly after the Corps finalized the 2001 rule amendments redefining "discharge of dredged materials," the National Association of Home Builders filed a facial challenge to the revised definition.[89] Initially dismissed by the District Court as not ripe for review,[90] the D.C. Circuit Court ruled in 2006 that the lawsuit could proceed.[91] Reconsideration by the D.C. District Court resulted in a 2007 summary judgment ruling holding that the "Tulloch II" rule was invalid.[92] The 2007 holding concluded that the definition of "incidental fallback" erroneously included a volume requirement.[93] The court indicated that incidental fallback instead should be distinguished from regulable redeposit by (1) the time the material is held before being dropped to earth, and (2) the distance between the place where material is collected and the place where it is dropped.[94] The D.C. District Court also directed the agencies to reconsider the rebuttable presumption that the use of mechanized earthmoving equipment in waters of the United States resulted in a discharge of dredged material unless project-specific evidence shows otherwise, noting that the agencies cannot require project-specific evidence from projects over which they have no regulatory authority.[95]

In December 2008, the Corps and EPA amended the definition of "discharge of dredged material" yet again, by returning to the 1999 regulation that the court in *American Mining Congress* upheld.[96] Accordingly, the definition of "discharge of dredged material" now provides in part as follows:

---

88. *Id.* (codified at 33 C.F.R. §323.2(d)(2)(i) and 40 C.F.R. § 232.2(i)) (superseded).

89. Nat'l Ass'n of Home Builders v. U.S. Army Corps of Eng'rs, 311 F. Supp. 2d 91 (D.C. 2004).

90. *Id.* at 93.

91. Nat'l Ass'n of Home Builders v. U.S. Army Corps of Eng'rs, 440 F.3d 459 (D.C. Cir. 2006).

92. Nat'l Ass'n of Home Builders v. U.S. Army Corps of Eng'rs, 2007 U.S. Dist. LEXIS 6366 (D.D.C., Jan. 30, 2007).

93. *Id.*

94. *Id.*

95. *Id.*

96. American Mining Congress v. U.S. Army Corps of Eng'rs, 120 F. Supp. 2d 23 (D.C. 2000).

(d)(1) Except as provided below in paragraph (d)(2), the term *discharge of dredged material* means any addition of dredged material into, including redeposit of dredged material other than incidental fallback within, the waters of the United States. The term includes, but is not limited to, the following:

(i) The addition of dredged material to a specified discharge site located in waters of the United States;

(ii) The runoff or overflow from a contained land or water disposal area; and

(iii) Any addition, including redeposit other than incidental fallback, of dredged material, including excavated material, into waters of the United States which is incidental to any activity, including mechanized landclearing, ditching, channelization, or other excavation.

(2) The term *discharge of dredged material* does not include the following:

(i) Discharges of pollutants into waters of the United States resulting from the onshore subsequent processing of dredged material that is extracted for any commercial use (other than fill). These discharges are subject to section 402 of the Clean Water Act even though the extraction and deposit of such material may require a permit from the Corps or applicable State section 404 program.

(ii) Activities that involve only the cutting or removing of vegetation above the ground (e.g., mowing, rotary cutting, and chainsawing) where the activity neither substantially disturbs the root system nor involves mechanized pushing, dragging, or other similar activities that redeposit excavated soil material.

(iii) Incidental fallback.

(3) Section 404 authorization is not required for the following:

(i) *Any incidental addition, including redeposit, of dredged material* associated with any activity that does not have or would not have the effect of destroying or degrading an area of waters of the United States as defined in paragraphs (d)(4) and (d)(5) of this section; *however, this exception does not apply to any person preparing to undertake mechanized landclearing, ditching, channelization and other excavation activity in a water of the United States, which would result in a*

> *redeposit of dredged material, unless the person demonstrates to the satisfaction of the Corps, or EPA as appropriate, prior to commencing the activity involving the discharge, that the activity would not have the effect of destroying or degrading any area of waters of the United States*, as defined in paragraphs (d)(4) and (d)(5) of this section. *The person proposing to undertake mechanized landclearing, ditching, channelization or other excavation activity bears the burden of demonstrating that such activity would not destroy or degrade any area of waters of the United States.*[97]

Thus, while the person undertaking activity that will cause incidental fallback/redeposit still bears the burden of demonstrating that the fallback will not destroy or degrade jurisdictional waters, there is no rebuttable presumption that the activity is the discharge of dredged material.

IV. Exempt Activities

Even if there is a discharge, a permit may not always be required. Congress exempted certain activities[98] from regulation under CWA Section 404(f).[99] That section exempts the following activities:

> (A) normal farming, silviculture and ranching activities such as plowing, seeding, cultivating, minor drainage, harvesting for the production of food, fiber, and forest products, or upland soil and water conservation projects;

97. 33 C.F.R. § 323.2(d) (emphasis added): *see also* 40 C.F.R. § 232.2.

98. U.S. Env't Prot. Agency, *Exemptions to Permit Requirements under CWA Section 404*, https://www.epa.gov/cwa-404/exemptions-permit-requirements-under-cwa-section-404 (last updated Mar. 26, 2024) ("In general, Section 404 of the Clean Water Act requires permits for the discharge of dredged or fill material into waters of the United States, including wetlands. However, certain activities are exempt from permit requirements under Section 404(f)(1).").

99. 33 U.S.C. § 1344(f) (2023). The Corps' implementing regulations are found at 33 C.F.R. § 323.4, and EPA's implementing regulations are found at 40 C.F.R. § 232.3. *See* United States v. Cumberland Farms of Conn., Inc., 647 F. Supp. 1166 (D. Mass. 1986) (discussing the addition of the exemptions to Section 404 in 1977. *Id.* at 1175.); *see also* Margaret Spring, *The Clean Water Act Section 404(f) Exceptions: A Call to End the Open Door Policy*, 1 Duke Env't L. & Pol'y Forum 57 (1991), http://scholarship.law.duke.edu/delpf/vol1/iss1/6/.

> (B) maintenance, including emergency reconstruction of recently damaged parts, of currently serviceable structures such as dikes, dams, levees, groins, riprap, breakwaters, causeways, and bridge abutments or approaches, and transportation structures;
>
> (C) construction or maintenance of farm or stock ponds or irrigation ditches, or the maintenance of drainage ditches;
>
> (D) construction of temporary sedimentation basins on a construction site which does not include placement of fill material into the navigable waters;
>
> (E) construction or maintenance of farm roads or forest roads, or temporary roads for mining equipment, where such roads are constructed in accordance with best management practices, to assure that flow and circulation patterns and chemical and biological characteristics of the navigable waters is not reduced, and that any adverse effect on the aquatic environment will be otherwise minimized;
>
> (F) activities where a State has an approved nonpoint source management program.[100]

Various statutory and regulatory conditions limit these exemptions,[101] which have been interpreted narrowly by the courts.[102] The legislative history shows an intent to exempt "narrowly defined activities that cause little or no adverse effects either individual or cumulatively."[103] These exemptions are also restricted by Section 404(f)(2)'s "recapture" provision, which directs that:

> Any discharge of dredged or fill material into the navigable waters incidental to any activity having as its purpose bringing

---

100. 33 U.S.C. § 1344(f)(1)(A)–(F) (2023). Listed exempt activities are not subject to regulation under Section 404, Section 301, *id.* § 1311 (governing effluent limitations), or Section 402, *id.* § 1342 (governing the National Pollutant Discharge Elimination System), but are subject to the effluent standards and prohibitions of Section 1317 governing toxic and pretreatment standards. *Id.* § 1344(f)(1).

101. 33 C.F.R. § 323.4.

102. *See, e.g.*, U.S. v. Akers, 785 F.2d 814, 819 (9th Cir. 1986); Greenfield Mills, Inc. v. Macklin, 361 F.3d 934, 949 (7th Cir. 2004); Borden Ranch P'ship v. U.S. Army Corps of Eng'rs, 261 F.3d 810, 815–16 (9th Cir. 2001), *aff'd by an equally divided court*, 537 U.S. 99 (2002); U.S. v. Larkins, 852 F.2d 189, 192 (6th Cir. 1988).

103. 123 Cong. Rec. S39, 188 (daily ed. Dec. 15, 1977) (statement of Rep. Muskie).

an area of the navigable waters into a use to which it was not previously subject, where the flow or circulation of navigable waters may be impaired or the reach of such waters be reduced, shall be required to have a permit under this section.[104]

In 2009, the U.S. Court of Appeals for the Second Circuit deferred to the agency and lower court (and concurred with other courts' interpretations in similar situations)[105] in upholding the application of the exemption in Section 404(f)(1)(C) to construction of a new stock pond on an existing farm; the court found that the "recapture" provision of 404(f)(2) did not subject the pond to regulation.[106]

The first 404(f) exemption, for "normal farming, silviculture and ranching activities," has been narrowly construed by Corps' regulations and regulatory guidance.[107] The exemption does not "provide a total automatic exemption for all activities related to agricultural silvicultural or ranching practices. Rather, Section 404(f)(1) exempts only those activities specifically identified in paragraphs (A) through (F), and 'other activities of essentially the same character as named.'"[108] Importantly, Section 404(f)(1)(A) is limited to activities that are part

104. 33 U.S.C. § 1344(f)(2) (2023). To be "recaptured" an activity must meet both a "purpose" and an "effects" test. *See Greenfield Mills, Inc.*, 361 F.3d at 955, *citing Borden Ranch P'ship*, 261 F.3d at 815; *Avoyelles Sportsmens League*, 715 F.2d at 926.

105. Coon v. Willet Dairy Ltd. P'ship, 536 F.3d 171 (2d Cir. 2008), *citing* Conant v. United States, 786 F.2d 1008, 1010 (11th Cir. 1986) (per curiam) ("The plain purpose of the statute and regulations is to allow people to build ponds in connection with a previously established farming operation."); *In re Carsten*, 211 B.R. 719, 736 (Bankr. D. Mont. 1997) ("Consequently, as applied to such construction the 'new use' provision of § 1344(f)(2) cannot mean . . . that if a farm pond did not in the past exist, then the construction of such constitute a new use sufficient to invoke the recapture provision. Again, such an interpretation would impermissibly render the pond construction exemption a mere superfluity.").

106. *Coon*, 536 F.3d at 175.

107. 33 C.F.R. § 323.4(a)(1)(iii); *accord* United States v. Huebner, 752 F.2d 1235, 1240 (7th Cir. 1985) (exemption applies only to "'narrowly defined activities . . . that cause little or no adverse effects either individually or cumulatively [and that do not] convert more extensive areas of water to dry land or impede circulation or reduce the reach and size of the water body").

108. Corps Regulatory Guidance Letter 96-02 at ¶ 2.

of an "established (i.e., ongoing) farming, silviculture, or ranching operation."[109]

Likewise, the exemption for maintenance of currently serviceable structures does not include activities that "change[ ] the character, scope, or size of the original fill design."[110] Exempted emergency reconstructions of recently damaged structures must proceed "within a reasonable time after the damage occurs."[111] Farm or stock pond construction should consider "the relative size of a proposed pond in relation to the size of the farming/ranching operation"[112] and "must actually be used in [established] farming/ranching operations" to qualify for an exemption.[113] For purposes of the exemption for construction of temporary sedimentation basins on construction sites,[114] "construction site" is defined as "any site involving the erection of buildings, roads, and other discrete structures and the installation of support facilities necessary for [the] construction and utilization of such structures" as well as "any other land areas which involve land-disturbing excavation activities . . . where an increase in the runoff of sediment is controlled through the use of sedimentation basins."[115] While construction and maintenance of farm roads, forest roads, and temporary mining roads are exempt, the exemption applies only if best management practices (BMPs) are used that meet certain "baseline provisions" set out in the rule; the rule sets out 15 requirements for the

---

109. 33 C.F.R. § 323.4(a(1)(ii) (noting that "Activities on areas lying fallow as part of a conventional rotational cycle are part of an established operation. Activities which bring an area into farming, silviculture, or ranching use are not part of an established operation. An operation ceases to be established when the area on which it was conducted has been converted to another use or has lain idle so long that modifications to the hydrological regime are necessary to resume operations.").

110. 33 C.F.R. § 323.4(a)(2) (2023).

111. *Id.*

112. Regulatory Guidance Letter 87-9, *Section 404(f)(1)(C) Exemption for Construction or Maintenance of Farm or Stock Ponds* 1 (Aug. 27, 1987) (expired), https://cdm16021.contentdm.oclc.org/digital/collection/p16021coll9/id/1351/rec/1.

113. *Id.* The requirement that the farm pond be constructed only at an established farming operation does not appear in the exemption language, and this guidance letter has expired. The exemption may still apply if the pond was constructed, in part, for "secondary recreational use." *In re Carsten*, 211 Bankr. 719, 734 (D. Mont. 1997).

114. 33 C.F.R. § 323.4(a)(4).

115. *Id.*

exemption to apply, such as minimum feasible widths and locational restrictions.[116]

V. Conclusion

Since the *National Home Builders* case, the definition of "discharged of dredged or fill material" has seemed relatively "settled" in the wetlands regulatory world. In fact, the 2008 revised definition of discharge[117] elicited almost no commentary,[118] except for descriptive articles.[119] Likewise, there has been little litigation over the scope of the CWA exemptions; the relevant rules have not been amended since 1986, so there seems to be little discontent with the current statutory exemptions and the manner in which they are interpreted. However, given the move of the U.S. Supreme Court away from the *Chevron* deference that served to underpin many of the judicial decisions in this arena, it is unclear whether stakeholders will remain content with the permitting decisions being made under the existing definitions. With the U.S. Supreme Court's decision in *Sackett v. E.P.A.*,[120] the intense attention that has been devoted to the geographical jurisdiction issues[121] may be refocused to other agency rules such as mitigation

116. *Id.* § 323.4(a)(6).

117. Revisions to the Clean Water Act Regulat0ory Definition of "Discharge of Dredged Material," 73 Fed. Reg. 79,641 (Dec. 30, 2008) (codified at 33 C.F.R. pt. 323 and 40 C.F.R. pt. 232).

118. Cf. Rebecca Shawn Finley, Tulloch III or Congressional Solution?, Nat. Res. & Env't 63 (Winter 2008); Louis N. Smith, How Is the Corps of Engineers Reacting to the Decision in American Mining Congress v. U.S. Army Corps of Engineers, Which Struck Down the Tulloch Rule regarding Federal Regulation of Removal of Material from Wetlands? (Spring 1997) (criticizing the Corps' narrow reading of the January 1997 American Mining Congress decision), https://www.waterlaws.com/tulloch-rule.

119. Linda Roeder, Env't Prot. Agency, U.S. Army Corps of Engineers Revise Definition of "Discharge of Dredged Material," 249 BNA Daily Env't A-7 (Dec. 30, 2008).

120. 143 S. Ct. 1322 (2023).

121. The *Sackett* decision is discussed in detail in Chapter 2.

banking or nationwide permits.[122] As is true of all areas of wetlands law, there may be developments in either area in the coming years, so prudent practitioners and permit applicants will watch carefully.

If attention returns to the activities area, history shows that Section 404's language by itself is not entirely clear as to the breadth of intended federal jurisdiction with respect to regulated activities. Consequently, as explored earlier, understanding various implementing regulations and other guidance documents issued by the Corps and EPA, as well as myriad judicial decisions, is required for appropriate application of Section 404's requirements.[123] Yet, even these sources often fail to provide clear answers in all cases, because, through the years, there has been considerable discord among all stakeholders—including the agencies, the permitted community, the conservation community, and the courts—with respect to the program's coverage.[124]

---

122. *See, e.g.*, 2024 National Mitigation Banking—Environmental Markets Conference—Connecting Nature-Based Solutions, https://mitigationbankinginc.com/2024-national-mitigation-banking-environmental-markets-conference/ (annual conference focusing on the Compensatory Mitigation Rule, which is discussed in detail in Chapter 6); *see also* Cong. Rsch. Serv., *The Army Corps of Engineers' Nationwide Permits Program: Issues and Regulatory Developments, Summary* (Jan. 12, 2017) (regarding criticism of the nationwide permit program), https://www.everycrsreport.com/files/20170112_97-223_271c5b98b058e7b84bab465be90e05777cf735ea.pdf.

123. For a detailed overview of these requirements, see Kim Diana Connolly, Stephen M. Johnson & Douglas R. Williams, Wetlands Law and Policy: Understanding Section 404 (Am. Bar Ass'n 2005).

124. One recently summarized the tensions related to Section 404 regulation as follows: "These tensions can be traced in large measure to four structural flaws in section 404's design: the lack of a clear goal, the conflicts inherent in the Corps-EPA-section 404 relationship, reliance on a water statute to protect wetlands, and the regulation of activities in wetlands under a pollution control approach." Alyson C. Flournoy, *Section 404 at Thirty-Something: A Program in Search of a Policy*, 55 Ala. L. Rev. 607 (2004), http://scholarship.law.ufl.edu/facultypub/61, at 608; *see also* Michael C. Blumm, *The Clean Water Act's Section 404 Permit Program Enters Its Adolescence: An Institutional and Programmatic Perspective*, 8 Ecology L.Q. 409 (1980); Michael C. Blumm & D. Bernard Zaleha, *Federal Wetlands Protection under the Clean Water Act: Regulatory Ambivalence, Intergovernmental Tension, and a Call for Reform*, 60 U. Colo. L. Rev. 695 (1989); Oliver A. Houck, *Hard Choices: The Analysis of Alternatives under Section 404 of the Clean Water Act and Similar Environmental Laws*, 60 U. Colo. L. Rev. 773 (1989); Sam Kalen, *Commerce to*

Such discord could re-emerge given the right circumstances. Given the steady move of the U.S. Supreme Court away from agency deference, those circumstances are sure to arise in the future.[125]

Conservation: The Call for a National Water Policy and the Evolution of Federal Jurisdiction Over Wetlands, 69 N.D. L. Rev. 873 (1993).

125. In the 1984 case of Chevron, U.S.A., Inc. v. Nat. Res. Def. Council, Inc., 467 U.S. 837 (1984), the U.S. Supreme Court held that a federal agency must conform to any clear and unambiguous legislative statements when interpreting and applying a law, but courts should defer to the agency's interpretation when the statute is ambiguous, as long as the agency interpretation is reasonable. The so-called *Auer* doctrine took *Chevron* a step further, holding that an agency's interpretation of its own regulations is "controlling unless plainly erroneous or inconsistent with the regulation." Auer v. Robbins, 519 U.S. 452 (1997). In recent years, the U.S. Supreme Court has indicated a shift away from deference to agency interpretations reflected by the Chevron decision, narrowly upholding *Auer* in limited fashion in 2019. Kisor v. Wilkie, 139 S. Ct. 2400 (2019). The U.S. Supreme Court recently agreed to hear the related cases of Loper Bright Enters v. Raimondo, U.S. Case No. 22-451, and Relentless, Inc. v. Dep't of Commerce, U.S. Case No. 22-1219, squarely on the issue of the application of the Chevron doctrine in environmental cases. Oral argument was held in the consolidated cases on January 17, 2024, and a decision was pending as of publication. These cases involve challenges to the authority of the National Marine Fisheries Service (NMFS) under the Magnuson-Stevens Act (MSA) to require operators of domestic fishing vessels to pay the salaries of federal observers that are carried on board their vessels to observe compliance with NMFS regulations. While the MSA does expressly require vessels to pay the salaries of federal monitors in three narrow circumstances, the statute caps those salaries at 2–3 percent of the value of the vessel's catch. Petitioners unsuccessfully appealed the NMFS's requirement in fisheries management plans for vessels to pay federal observers' salaries in circumstances not expressly authorized by the MSA and without the protections of the statutory cap on those salaries. A divided panel of the U.S. Court of Appeals for the District of Columbia (D.C. Circuit) upheld the district court's grant of summary judgment in the *Loper Bright* case to NMFS, upholding NMFS's interpretation of its authority to require vessels to pay federal observer salaries on the basis of Chevron deference. Loper Bright Enters. v. Raimondo, 45 F.4th 359 (D.C. Cir. 2022). The First Circuit Court of Appeals reached a similar decision in Relentless, Inc., et al. v. United States Dep't of Com., 62 F.4th 621 (1st Cir. 2023).

4

CHAPTER

Navigating the Permitting Process

I. Introduction

This chapter focuses on the permitting process. CWA Section 404[1] authorizes the Corps to issue permits for the "discharge of dredged or fill material into the navigable waters."[2] Discharges into wetlands and other waters without such a permit almost always violates the statute.[3] Interpreting exactly when a permit is needed requires a case-by-case analysis.[4] If the wetland or water is subject to CWA jurisdiction[5] and

1. 33 U.S.C. § 1344 (2023). The Federal Water Pollution Control Act (FWPCA) is commonly referred to as the Clean Water Act following the 1977 amendments to the FWPCA. Pub. L. No. 95-217, 91 Stat. 1566 (1977) ("Sec. 518. This Act may be cited as the 'Federal Water Pollution Control Act' commonly referred to as the Clean Water Act.").

2. 33 U.S.C. § 1344(a) (2023).

3. *Id.* § 1311(a).

4. *See generally* Kim Diana Connolly, Stephen M. Johnson & Douglas R. Williams, Wetlands Law and Policy: Understanding Section 404 (Am. Bar Ass'n. 2005).

5. *See* Chapter 2 for a discussion of when a wetland is "Water of the United States" (WOTUS) subject to CWA jurisdiction.

no exemption applies,[6] a permit will be required. The Corps issues three types of general permits (nationwide permits, regional general permits, and programmatic general permits) and two types of individual permits (standard permits and letters of permission, issued under an abbreviated process for minor projects not meeting general permit criteria).[7] Chapter 5 of this book addresses when a discharge qualifies for a general, programmatic or nationwide permit, while this chapter focuses on situations where an individual permit is required. More than 97 percent of the Corps' regulatory workload is processed in the form of general permits.[8] Most individual permits and some general permits will require mitigation of some sort.[9]

This chapter explores the basic requirements to obtain an individual permit from the Corps. It opens with a brief discussion of the Corps Regulatory program, followed by a summary of the permitting process and regulatory criteria, and a discussion of the role EPA and other agencies play in the process. It briefly discusses the abbreviated permitting process for minor activities that do not qualify for a general permit (letters of permission). It closes with issues to watch and includes an "Application Checklist" in an appendix.

A word of caution to readers: given the many nuances associated with the permitting process, this chapter is intended only as an orientation and reference. Even if you read this book thoroughly and become very familiar with the Corps and EPA regulations, use guidance documents and other sources to help guide you; in almost every case, consulting with Corps personnel or other experts can increase the likelihood of navigating the individual permitting process much more efficiently and successfully.

The predecessor to the Corps started regulating activities in our nation's waters well over a century ago, under the Rivers and Harbors

6. *See* Chapter 3 for a discussion of which activities are subject to CWA Section 404 and which activities are exempt.

7. *See, e.g.*, U.S. Army Corps of Engineers, Savannah District website, Savannah District > Missions > Regulatory > Permitting (army.mil); Jacksonville District website, https://www.saj.usace.army.mil/Missions/Regulatory/Source-Book/.

8. *See* Cong. Rsch. Serv., *The Army Corps of Engineers' Nationwide Permits Program: Issues and Regulatory Developments* (Jan. 12, 2017), https://www.everycrsreport.com/reports/97-223.html.

9. *See* Chapter 6.

Act of 1899.[10] Pursuant to both Section 404[11] and the Rivers and Harbors Act, Corps project managers have considered hundreds of thousands of permit requests for many different projects involving aquatic resources such as wetlands.[12] In recent years, Corps personnel have reviewed close to 90,000 permit applications per year.[13] According to the Corps' regulatory website, the Corps denies less than 1 percent of submitted permit applications.[14] Furthermore, most permit applications proceed in an expedited manner[15] that does not involve the level of analysis required for standard individual permits, such as the project-specific Section 404(b)(1) Guidelines analysis or public interest review discussed in this chapter.

II. Permitting Process

Throughout the United States, Corps offices are divided into eight regional divisions and 38 districts.[16] Division and district boundaries, for the most part, are determined by watersheds,[17] and often cross state lines.[18] The districts[19] are the "operational level" of the Corps, implementing day-to-day activities in all of the mission areas, including

10. 33 U.S.C. §§ 401–418 (2023); *see* Chapter 1, Part II.

11. 33 U.S.C. § 1344 (2023).

12. The White House Archives, George W. Bush, *Detailed Information on the Corps of Engineers: Regulatory Program Assessment*, https://georgewbush-whitehouse.archives.gov/omb/expectmore/detail/10001130.2003.html.

13. *See* Cong. Rsch. Serv., *supra* note 8.

14. U.S. Army Corps of Eng'rs, Frequently Asked Questions, https://www.usace.army.mil/Missions/Civil-Works/Regulatory-Program-and-Permits/Frequently-Asked-Questions/ (stating that denials are usually where applicants "have refused to change the design, timing, or location of the proposed activities"). Note that at least one district office has put the nationwide permit denial rate at 3 percent: Philadelphia District & Marine Design Center > Missions > Regulatory > FAQs (army.mil) (last visited June 19, 2023).

15. Most permits processed by the U.S. Army Corps of Engineers are general permits issued pursuant to Section 404(e), 33 U.S.C. § 1344(e). *See* Chapter 5 for a discussion of the various types of general permits that can be issued under CWA Section 404.

16. *See* U.S. Army Corps of Eng'rs, *Where We Are*, http://www.usace.army.mil/Locations.aspx (last visited Apr. 2, 2024).

17. *See id.*

18. *See id.*

19. Direct links to Corps district offices can be found at U.S. Army Corps of Eng'rs Locations, http://www.usace.army.mil/Locations.aspx.

those considered regulatory.[20] Thus, the following discussion represents general principles and approaches that may vary in actual practice depending on the district in question. Each district typically has a website where additional permitting information specific to that district can be found.[21] Pursuant to Section 404(g)–(h), two states have Section 404 programs approved by EPA pursuant to Section 404(g) and its implementing rules.[22] In states with an EPA-approved program, state regulations govern implementation of the Section 404 program over wetlands and waters of their respective states, except for tidal waters and their adjacent wetlands and waters that are presently used or susceptible to use in interstate or foreign commerce and their adjacent wetlands, which remain under Corps administration subject to Corps rules.[23]

A. The Application

If an individual, or standard, permit is required, the Corps encourages, but does not require, a pre-application consultation, particularly for larger or more complex activities.[24] As one Corps district explains:

---

20. *See* U.S. Army Corps of Eng'rs, Regulatory Program & Permits—Find a Regulatory Office, https://www.usace.army.mil/Missions/Civil-Works/Regulatory-Program-and-Permits/Regulatory-Contacts/.

21. *See, e.g.*, Jacksonville District Regulatory Source Book, https://www.saj.usace.army.mil/Missions/Regulatory/Source-Book/ (last visited June 19, 2023); Savannah District Permitting, https://www.sas.usace.army.mil/Missions/Regulatory/Permitting.aspx (last visited June 19, 2023).

22. 40 C.F.R. pt. 124 (2023).

23. 33 U.S.C. § 1344(g)–(h) (2023). Subsection (g) allows states and tribes to assume administration of the Section 404 permitting program for discharges to navigable waters "other than those waters which are presently used, or are susceptible to use in their natural condition or by reasonable improvement as a means to transport interstate or foreign commerce shoreward to their ordinary high water mark, including all waters which are subject to the ebb and flow of the tide shoreward to their mean high water mark, or mean higher high water mark on the west coast, including wetlands adjacent thereto." The two states with active programs are Michigan (1984), and New Jersey (1993). Florida's program was approved in 2020, but was vacated in early 2024. See note 51 in Chapter 1 of this book, and Part II of Chapter 7, for more information on the status of Florida's 404 program. No tribes have yet assumed the program. An interactive map with links to the assumed Section 404 programs and showing the assumption efforts of all the states and tribes can be found here: https://www.epa.gov/cwa404g/us-interactive-map-state-and-tribal-assumption-under-cwa-section-404.

24. 33 C.F.R. § 325.1(b) (2023).

Pre-application consultation usually involves one or several meetings between an applicant, USACE staff, interested resource agencies (federal, state, or local), and sometimes the interested public. The basic purpose of such meetings is to provide for informal discussions about the pros and cons of a proposal relative to its effects on the aquatic environment while the applicant is still in the planning process. The process allows for a consideration of potentially less environmentally damaging alternatives available to accomplish the project purpose, to discuss measures for reducing the impacts of the project, and to inform the applicant of the factors the USACE must consider in its decision-making process.[25]

The application itself[26] requires a variety of relevant information, including a complete description of the proposed activity (including necessary drawings, sketches, or plans sufficient for public notice);[27] location, purpose, and need for the proposed activity; scheduling information regarding the proposed activity; the names and addresses of adjoining property owners and the location and dimensions of adjacent structures; and a list of authorizations required by other federal,

---

25. U.S. Army Corps of Eng'rs, Fort Worth District, Individual Permits, http://www.swf.usace.army.mil/Missions/Regulatory/Permitting/IndividualPermits.aspx. *See also* Jacksonville District Regulatory Division—Source Book, https://www.saj.usace.army.mil/Missions/Regulatory/Source-Book/ (Processing Steps) ("You are encouraged to contact the local Corps of Engineers field office in your area prior to making a permit application. Pre-application consultation usually involves one or more meetings between an applicant, Corps district staff, interested resource agencies (federal, state and/or local), and sometimes the interested public. The basic purpose of such meetings is to provide for informal discussions about the pros and cons of a proposal before an applicant makes irreversible commitments of resources (funds, detailed designs, etc.). The process is designed to provide the applicant with an assessment of the viability of some of the more obvious alternatives available to accomplish the project purpose, to discuss measures for reducing the impacts of the project, and to inform him of the factors the Corps must consider in its decision making process.") (last visited July 29, 2023).

By discussing the work prior to submitting an application, your application can be processed more efficiently.

26. A copy of the current application form for standard permits (ENG 4345) can be found at U.S. Army Corps of Eng'rs, Application for a Department of the Army Permit, https://www.usace.army.mil/Missions/Civil-Works/Regulatory-Program-and-Permits/Obtain-a-Permit/ (last visited July 29, 2023).

27. Detailed engineering plans and specifications are not required at this stage, but are recommended to facilitate faster review. 33 C.F.R. § 325.1(d)(1) (2023).

interstate, or local agencies for the work, including all approvals or denials already made.[28] An application checklist is included as an appendix to this chapter.

Individual permit applications must also describe the purpose of the discharge; explain the type, composition, and quantity of the material and the method of transportation and disposal of the material; and provide details about the location of the disposal site.[29] The permit application is a fillable form, but cannot currently be submitted online.[30] It can be either mailed to the local Regulatory Field Office or sent electronically to the district's designated general email mailbox.[31] The application must be accompanied by sufficient explanatory information, including a full set of clear plan drawings, and other scientific information as may be needed for the Corps to assess whether the proposed activity will meet the applicable regulatory requirements.[32] Information regarding all related activities, such as subsequent phases in a multiphase project, should be included.[33] The amount of information required will depend upon the complexity of the project.

The receiving Corps district office nominally has 15 days to review a submitted application and determine whether it is complete.[34] An application is complete when the Corps receives sufficient information to issue a public notice.[35] After the completeness determination, the Corps can request additional information if it is essential to make a public interest determination.[36] However, as a practical matter, there are few mechanisms to force the Corps reviewer to review the application within that timeframe, and larger projects will typically take more time and multiple information requests.[37] While the Corps states a goal of processing individual permit applications within 120 days

28. *Id.*

29. *Id.* § 325.1(d)(4).

30. *See* U.S. Army Corps of Eng'rs, Obtain a Permit, https://www.usace.army.mil/Missions/Civil-Works/Regulatory-Program-and-Permits/Obtain-a-Permit/.

31. *See* Jacksonville District Regulatory Division—Source Book (army.mil), https://www.saj.usace.army.mil/Missions/Regulatory/Source-Book/, Permitting, Standard Permit, Application Forms.

32. *Id.*, Permitting, Processing Steps.

33. *Id.*

34. 33 C.F.R. § 325.2(a) (2023).

35. *Id.* § 325.1(d)(9).

36. *Id.* § 325.1(d)(9), (e).

37. Under the federal Administrative Procedure Act, a court can compel an agency to take action that is "unlawfully withheld or unreasonably delayed," but normally,

from the date the application is deemed complete, where the project is large or controversial or will impact endangered species or historic properties, the processing time can be significantly longer.[38]

B. The Public Notice

Once an application is deemed complete, a public notice—including specifics about the applicant and the activity—must be issued.[39] Among other requirements, the public notice should identify the location of the activity, a brief description, and enough information concerning the nature of the activity to allow for meaningful public input.[40] The nature of any proposed in-water structures, the amount and type of materials to be discharged, and plans and elevation drawings should all be referenced in the public notice.[41] The notice must include summary statements regarding any known historic properties or endangered species and any other information needed to assist interested parties in assessing the effect of the activity on the public interest.[42] And of course, the notice must specify the deadline for submitting public comments and the process by which to do so.[43] Public notices must be distributed as specified in the Corps' rules to ensure appropriate public and local, state, and federal input.[44] Public notices are also posted in reverse chronological order on the official website of the district processing the application.[45] The sufficiency of the public notice must be judged based on the relevant information available to the Corps at the time the notice was issued, which is typically the information contained in the permit application. The Corps is not required to include detailed conclusions and findings

---

preliminary, procedural, or intermediate agency action is not directly reviewable. 5 U.S.C. § 704, § 706 (2023).

38. Jacksonville District Regulatory Division—Source Book (army.mil), https://www.saj.usace.army.mil/Missions/Regulatory/Source-Book/, Permitting, Processing Steps.

39. *Id.* §§ 325(c), 325.3(a).

40. *Id.* § 325.3.

41. *Id.*

42. *Id.*

43. *Id.*

44. *Id.* § 325.3(d).

45. *See, e.g.*, Baltimore District > Missions > Regulatory > Public Notices (army.mil); Detroit District > Missions > Regulatory Program and Permits > Public Notices (army.mil); Los Angeles District Public Notices (army.mil).

in the notice, provided the notice includes the relevant information and issues in the notice.[46]

The public notice is distributed to other federal agencies with statutory commenting authority, including the EPA,[47] the U.S. Fish and Wildlife Service (FWS),[48] the National Marine Fisheries Service (NMFS),[49] state and/or tribal historic preservation offices,[50] state environmental agencies with jurisdiction,[51] and other federal and state agencies.[52] More details are explored with respect to these

46. Great Salt Lake Minerals & Chemicals v. Marsh, 596 F. Supp. 548 (D. Utah 1984).

47. The CWA anticipates that EPA, FWS, NMFS, and other federal agencies will comment on wetland permit applications. *See* 33 U.S.C. § 1344(q) (2023).

48. The Fish and Wildlife Coordination Act, 16 U.S.C. §§ 661–666(c) (2023), requires the Corps to consult with the FWS or the NMFS, and with the head of the appropriate state agency exercising administration over the wildlife resources of the state when the Corps reviews a wetland permit application. 33 C.F.R. §§ 320.3(e), 320.4(c) (2023). In addition, the Endangered Species Act, 16 U.S.C. § 1531–1544 (2023) may also require the Corps to consult with the FWS and the NMFS when it issues certain permits.

49. In addition to the laws cited in the previous footnote, the Magnuson-Stevens Fishery Conservation and Management Act, 16 U.S.C. § 1855(b)(2) (2023) requires the Corps to consult with NMFS when a proposed federal activity may adversely affect identified Essential Fish Habitat (EFH). *See* 50 C.F.R. pt. 600 (2023). For general information about EFH, see National Oceanic and Atmospheric Administration Fisheries, *Essential Fish Habitat Consultations*, https://www.fisheries.noaa.gov/national/habitat-conservation/consultations-essential-fish-habitat; *see also* Kim Diana Connolly, *An Introduction to the Essential Fish Habitat (EFH) Consultation Process for the South Atlantic Area*, 11 Southeastern Env't L.J. 1 (2003); Kenyon C. Lindeman, Roger Pugliese, Gregg T. Waugh & Jerald S. Ault, *Developmental Patterns within a Multispecies Reef Fishery: Management Applications for Essential Fish Habitats and Protected Areas,* 66 Bull. Marine Sci. 929 (2000).

50. The National Historic Preservation Act of 1966, 54 U.S.C. § 306101, requires the Corps to consult with state/tribal historic preservation officers and the federal Advisory Council on Historic Preservation when it issues certain permits. *See also* 33 C.F.R. pt. 325, App. C (2023).

51. The Corps cannot issue a wetland permit unless the state in which the discharge will occur certifies that the discharge will not affect the quality of the water in the state in violation of any effluent limitations, water quality standards, or water quality requirements of that state. 33 U.S.C. § 1341; 33 C.F.R. §§ 320.3(a), 325.1(d)(4), 325.2(b)(1) (2023). Certification of consistency under the Coastal Zone Management Act is also required where a state has a coastal zone management program. 16 U.S.C. § 1456(c)(3)(A).

52. Federal agencies have entered into various memoranda of agreement (MOA) pursuant to Section 404(q) of the Clean Water Act, 33 U.S.C. § 1344(q), that governs the manner in which they will comment on proposed applications and resolve any

inter-coordination requirements later in this chapter. Section 404(c) of the CWA authorizes the EPA Administrator

> to prohibit the specification (including the withdrawal of specification) of any defined area as a disposal site, and he is authorized to deny or restrict the use of any defined area for specification (including the withdrawal of specification) as a disposal site, whenever he determines, after notice and opportunity for public hearings, that the discharge of such materials into such area will have an unacceptable adverse effect on municipal water supplies, shellfish beds and fishery areas (including spawning and breeding areas), wildlife, or recreational areas.[53]

This is known as EPA's "veto authority" over Corps permits.[54] EPA's special oversight role and its power to veto permit issuance are also discussed later in this chapter.[55] The public notice is the formal trigger to initiate these intergovernmental coordinations, but applicants with large or complex projects should initiate this coordination early. For example, applicants with projects with the reasonable potential to adversely affect species that are listed as endangered or threatened under the Endangered Species Act should begin early consultation with the FWS prior to undertaking wildlife surveys on the property to agree on appropriate survey protocols and consult with FWS regarding the results of a survey prior to preparing a biological assessment, which is required for permits for major construction activities.[56] This is an optional process but can ultimately reduce permitting timeframes.

The Corps must inform the applicant about substantive comments that the agency received and provide the applicant the opportunity to

---

disputes regarding applications. Copies of the MOAs may be found at U.S. Army Corps of Eng'rs, Memorandum of Understanding, http://www.usace.army.mil/Missions/CivilWorks/RegulatoryProgramandPermits/MOUMOAs.aspx.

53. 33 U.S.C. § 1344(c) (2023).

54. *See* https://www.epa.gov/cwa-404/clean-water-act-section-404c-veto-authority.

55. The CWA explicitly authorizes EPA to veto the Corps' issuance of a wetland permit. 33 U.S.C. § 1344(c).

56. 50 C.F.R. § 402.12 (2023); Final ESA Section 7 Consultation Handbook, ch. 7 (Mar. 1998), https://www.fws.gov/sites/default/files/documents/endangered-species-consultation-handbook.pdf.

supply additional information or supplement the application.[57] The Corps may also require the applicant to submit additional information to address specific issues raised during the public comment period.[58] The applicant must respond to any Corps' request for information within 30 days, unless a request for additional time is approved.[59] If the applicant does not respond to the Corps' request for additional information, the agency will consider the application withdrawn, or will make a final decision on the application as is.[60] The Corps may also hold a public hearing on any permit application prior to review unless the agency determines "that the issues raised are insubstantial or there is otherwise no valid interest to be served by a hearing."[61]

C. The Permitting Criteria

A Section 404 permit must be denied if it does not comply with the Section 404(b)(1) Guidelines EPA promulgated in consultation with the Corps.[62] These guidelines prohibit the Corps from issuing a wetland permit if there is a "practicable alternative" to the proposed activity that would have a less adverse impact on the aquatic ecosystem and if "appropriate and practicable steps to minimize potential adverse

57. 33 C.F.R. § 325.1(e) (2023). The regulations specify that "[a] summary of the comments, the actual letters or portions thereof, or representative comment letters may be furnished to the applicant." *Id.* § 325.2(a)(3). *See also* Mall Properties, Inc. v. Marsh, 672 F. Supp. 561, 574–75 (D. Mass. 1987) (holding that the Corps violated its regulations when it failed to inform the permit applicant that the state governor had objected to the proposed permit), *appeal dismissed* on finding that remand order was not appealable, 841 F.2d 440 (1st Cir. 1988).

58. 33 C.F.R. § 325.2(a)(3) (2023).

59. *Id.* § 325.2(d)(5). When an applicant requests additional time to respond to the Corps' request for information, the agency may grant the request, make a final decision on the permit, or consider the application withdrawn. *Id.*

60. *Id.*

61. *Id.* § 327.4(b). A hearing request must state with particularity the reasons for the hearing. Before the Corps grants a request for a hearing, it may attempt to resolve the issues raised by the requester informally. *Id.* Any hearing must comply with certain requirements. *Id.* § 327.11 (2023).

62. 33 U.S.C. § 1344(b)(1); *see also* 33 C.F.R. § 320.4(a)(1)(2023) ("[A] permit will be denied if the discharge authorized by such permit would not comply with the . . . 404(b)(1) Guidelines."); *id.* § 323.6(a). Although they are referred to as guidelines, the 404(b)(1) Guidelines are binding regulations. As the name implies, the 404(b)(1) Guidelines apply solely to Section 404 permits and therefore are inapplicable to permits issued solely under Section 10 of the Rivers and Harbors Act.

impacts" on the aquatic ecosystem have not been proposed.[63] In addition, the guidelines create a presumption that there are practicable alternatives to discharges of dredged or fill material into wetlands when the proposed activity is not water-dependent.[64]

The 404(b)(1) Guidelines also prohibit the issuance of a permit when the activity authorized by the permit causes or contributes to significant degradation of waters of the United States,[65] causes or contributes to a violation of state water quality standards, violates federal toxic pollution standards, jeopardizes endangered species or destroys or adversely modifies their critical habitat, or violates federal marine sanctuary protection requirements.[66] Further, the 404(b)(1) Guidelines form the basis for the mitigation requirements, which are discussed in Chapter 6.[67] Subpart J of the guidelines, known as the Compensatory Mitigation Rule, establishes the standards and criteria for allowing the use of compensatory mitigation to offset adverse impacts to waters of the United States that cannot be avoided or minimized and establishes a step-wise sequence of review: avoidance, minimization, then mitigation.[68]

---

63. 40 C.F.R. § 230.10(a), (d) (2023); *see generally* Oliver Houck, *Hard Choices: The Analysis of Alternatives under Section 404 of the Clean Water Act and Similar Environmental Laws*, 60 U. Colo. L. Rev. 773 (1989).

64. 40 C.F.R. § 230.10(a)(3) (2023). An example of a water-dependent activity is a marina or boat slip; a commercial development or industrial activity is generally not considered water-dependent. For example, the 11th Circuit Court of Appeals has held that a limestone mine is not considered "water-dependent" because the basic purpose of the activity is to mine limestone, which does not require the mine be located in a wetland, despite the fact that the limestone reserves are present only in limited quantities, including underneath wetlands, which must be disturbed to recover the resource. Sierra Club v. Van Antwerp, 362 Fed. Appx. 100.

65. *Id.* § 230.10(c). The guidelines identify effects deemed to be "significant," and establish tests to be used in determining significance. *Id.* In addition, the Corps has clarified that the term "significant" under the 404(b)(1) Guidelines does not have exactly the same meaning as the term "significant" under NEPA. Regulatory Guidance Letter 87-02, *Use of the Word "Significant" in Permit Documentation* (Mar. 30, 1987).

66. 40 C.F.R. § 230.10(b) (2023).

67. *See* Chapter 6.

68. 40 C.F.R. § 230.91(2023). While the Corps does not have parallel 404(b)(1) Guidelines, but instead applies the EPA rules in 40 C.F.R. pt. 230, it does have parallel compensatory mitigation rules, which can be found at 33 C.F.R. pt. 332 (2023).

The Corps also undertakes a "public interest" review of the proposed activity[69] that evaluates probable impacts, including cumulative impacts, on the public interest of the proposed activity and its use.[70] Contrary to when it was first created, the modern Corps public interest review standard is not whether a proposed activity is in the public interest, but whether granting the permit would be "contrary to" the public interest.[71] The required public interest review considers the following factors:

- Conservation
- Economics
- Aesthetics
- General environmental concerns
- Wetlands
- Historic properties
- Fish and wildlife values
- Flood hazards
- Floodplain values
- Land use
- Navigation
- Shore erosion and accretion
- Recreation
- Water supply and conservation
- Water quality
- Energy needs
- Safety
- Food and fiber production
- Mineral needs
- Considerations of property ownership
- In general, the needs and welfare of the people[72]

---

69. The Corps conducts a "public interest" review for all individual applications under the Rivers and Harbors Act, the Clean Water Act, and the Ocean Dumping Act. 33 C.F.R. § 320.4.

70. *Id.* § 320.4(a)(1).

71. *Id.* § 320.4(a)(1); *see* Kim Diana Connolly, *Shifting Interests: Rethinking the U.S. Army Corps of Engineers Permitting Process and Public Interest Review in Light of Hurricanes Katrina and Rita*, 32 T. MARSHALL L. REV. 109 (2006), Kim Diana Connolly, *Climate Change in Wetland Ecosystems: Meeting the Needs and Welfare of the People and the Planet*, *in* CLIMATE CHANGE: A READER (William Rodgers et al., eds. 2011).

72. 33 C.F.R. § 320.4(a)(1) (2023). In every case, the Corps considers (1) the relative extent of the public and private need for the proposed activity; (2) the

The decision to issue or deny a permit is based on this public interest review as well as the Section 404(b)(1) Guidelines analysis.[73] Multiple other laws can be triggered during the permit review process—many of these are discussed here or in other chapters.

The National Environmental Policy Act (NEPA)[74] requires federal agencies to consider environmental impacts for any and all federal "actions," and to prepare an environmental impact statement (EIS) if there is a "major federal action significantly affecting the quality of the human environment."[75] All federal agencies must follow the

---

practicability of using reasonable alternative locations and methods to achieve the objective of the proposed activity (if there are unresolved conflicts regarding resource use); and (3) the extent and permanence of the beneficial and/or detrimental effect that the activity is likely to have on the public and private uses to which the area is suited. *Id.* § 320.4(a)(2). Earlier versions of the Corps public interest review involved evaluation of fewer factors. *See* Regulatory Programs of the Corps of Engineers, 42 Fed. Reg. 37,122 (1977). Earlier versions also involved a test as to whether the issued permit would be in the public interest. *See* Interim Final Rule for Regulatory Programs of the Corps of Engineers, 47 Fed. Reg. 31,794 (1982).

73. *See* U.S. Army Corps of Engineers Permitting Process Information, https://www.lrl.usace.army.mil/Portals/64/docs/regulatory/Permitting/PermittingProcessInformation.pdf#:~:text=The%20public%20interest%20review%20involves%20an%20analysis%20of,and%20the%20needs%20and%20welfare%20of%20the%20people.

74. 42 U.S.C. §§ 4321, *et seq.* (2023). An excellent website with links to relevant materials, and access to background and historical materials regarding NEPA, is hosted by the Council on Environmental Quality. Council on Environmental Quality, National Environmental Policy Act, https://ceq.doe.gov/.

75. 89 Fed. Reg. 35442, 35575 (May 1, 2024), to be codified at 40 C.F.R. § 1508.1(i) (effective July 1, 2024): "Effects or impacts means changes to the human environment from the proposed action or alternatives that are reasonably foreseeable and include the following: (1) Direct effects, which are caused by the action and occur at the same time and place. (2) Indirect effects, which are caused by the action and are later in time or farther removed in distance, but are still reasonably foreseeable. Indirect effects may include growth-inducing effects and other effects related to induced changes in the pattern of land use, population density or growth rate, and related effects on air and water and other natural systems, including ecosystems. (3) Cumulative effects, which are effects on the environment that result from the incremental effects of the action when added to the effects of other past, present, and reasonably foreseeable actions regardless of what agency (Federal or non-Federal) or person undertakes such other actions. Cumulative effects can result from actions with individually minor but collectively significant effects taking place over a period of time. (4) Effects include ecological (such as the effects on natural resources and on the components, structures, and functioning of affected ecosystems), aesthetic, historic, cultural, economic, social, or health, such as disproportionate and adverse effects on communities with environmental justice concerns, whether direct, indirect,

Council on Environmental Quality (CEQ) NEPA regulations.[76] The Corps also has enacted its own regulations with procedures for review of wetland permit applications.[77]

---

or cumulative. Effects also include effects on Tribal resources and climate change-related effects, including the contribution of a proposed action and its alternatives to climate change, and the reasonably foreseeable effects of climate change on the proposed action and its alternatives. Effects may also include those resulting from actions which may have both beneficial and adverse effects, even if on balance the agency believes that the effects will be beneficial."

76. Codified at 40 C.F.R. Part 1500, et. seq., the original NEPA rules were enacted in 1978 and stayed virtually the same for decades, with only minor amendments in 1985 and 2005. 43 Fed. Reg. 55,978 (Nov. 29, 1978); 51 Fed. Reg. 15625 (Apr. 25, 1986); 70 Fed, Reg, 41148 (July 18, 2005). The principle means of interpreting the rules for years was the guidance document entitled "Forty Most Asked Questions Concerning CEQ's National Environmental Policy Act Regulations," https://www.energy.gov/nepa/downloads/forty-most-asked-questions-concerning-ceqs-national-environmental-policy-act (Mar. 23, 1981, as amended in 1986). The NEPA process has been cited as unduly cumbersome and time-consuming, and a 2020 CEQ study found that it takes an average of 4.5 years for an infrastructure project to complete the NEPA process. CEQ, Environmental Impact Statement Timelines (2010-2018), https://ceq.doe.gov/docs/nepa-practice/CEQ_EIS_Timeline_Report_2020-6-12.pdf. (June 12, 2020), p. 1.

With many in the regulated community complaining about the time and expense associated with the NEPA process and to conform to President Trump's Executive Order 13807, "Establishing Discipline and Accountability in the Environmental Review and Permitting Process for Infrastructure Projects," CEQ undertook the first major overhaul of the NEPA rules in July 2020. 85 Fed. Reg. 43304 (July 16, 2020). These overhauls went too far in the eyes of many states and environmental groups, who filed suit, and the CEQ immediately delayed implementation of the 2020 rule early during the Biden Administration. Tad Macfarlan et al., NEPA: The Old Becomes New, 14 Nat. L. Rev. 148 (Jan. 28, 2022). The CEQ then proposed a two-phased approach to updating and streamlining the NEPA rules, with Phase I largely restoring the NEPA rules to their pre-2020 interpretation in October 2021. 86 Fed. Reg. 55757 (Oct. 7, 2021). The Phase II rules were published on May 1, 2024, at 89 Fed. Reg. 35442 and will become effective July 1, 2024. The Phase II rules implement key policy priorities of the Biden Administration, namely climate change and environmental justice, expressly defining the "effects" of the action to include "disproportionate and adverse effects on communities with environmental justice concerns, whether direct, indirect, or cumulative," and specifically requiring consideration of the effects on Tribal resources and climate change-related effects. 89 Fed. Reg. at 35442-43, 35575. While the Phase II rules incorporate both time limits and page limits for the NEPA-required environmental documents, many do not think the streamlining will be particularly effective in reducing the time and expense of NEPA compliance. See, e.g., Josh Kaplowitz et al., Locke Lord QuickStudy: Trust the Process? CEQ's NEPA Phase II Regulations a Mixed Bad and a Missed Opportunity (May 14, 2024), https://www.lockelord.com/newsandevents/publications/2024/05/quickstudy-ceq-nepa-phase-ii#_ftn4.

77. *See* 33 C.F.R. pt. 325, App. B (2023); 33 C.F.R. pt. 230 (2023). 33 C.F.R. pt. 230 was adopted in 1988; 33 C.F.R. pt. 325, Appendix B was adopted in 1986; neither

When the Corps receives a permit application, it must decide on the appropriate level of review: the proposed activity might be deemed a major action that requires an EIS, or it might be considered an activity exempt from NEPA review.[78] Most applications will proceed, however, with an environmental assessment (EA) process that determines whether an EIS is warranted for the proposed activity.[79]

---

has been updated to reflect changes in the CEQ rules since 2020, and at press-time, no schedule had been announced for incorporating the Phase I and Phase II rules.

78. CEQ's regulations require agencies to establish categorical exclusions (CEs) for categories of actions that "normally do not have a significant effect on the human environment, individually or in the aggregate" and thus do not ordinarily require preparation of either an Environmental Impact State (EIS) or an Environmental Assessment (EA). 89 Fed. Reg. at 35557 (to be codified at 40 C.F.R. §1501.4(a)). If an agency proposes to take an action that does not qualify for a CE, the agency should prepare either an EA or an EIS, as appropriate. Id. (to be codified at 40 C.F.R. §1501.4(b)(2)). The Corps categorically excludes small private piers, small docks, boat houses, minor utility distribution and collection lines, boat launching ramps, applications that qualify as letters of permission, and several other minor activities from NEPA review. 33 C.F.R. § 325, App. B(6).

79. 33 C.F.R. §§ 230.10, 325, App. B(7). In lieu of preparing its own EA or EIS, the Corps sometimes relies on NEPA documents that have been prepared by other agencies for the project. *See, e.g.*, Town of Norfolk v. U.S. Army Corps of Eng'rs., 968 F.2d 1438, 1447–48 (1st Cir. 1992); Abenaki Nation of Mississquoi v. Hughes, 805 F. Supp. 234, 246 (D. Vt. 1992), *aff'd*, 990 F.2d 729 (2d Cir. 1993); Friends of Capital Crescent Trail v. U.S. Army Corps of Eng'rs., 453 F. Supp. 3d 804, 809 (D. Md. 2020), *aff'd*, 855 Fed. Appx. 121 (4th Cir. 2021); Sierra Club v. U.S. Army Corps of Eng'rs, 990 F. Supp. 2d 9, 33–36 (D.D.C. 2013) (FWS' issuance of a biological opinion did not trigger a duty to undertake a full NEPA review.); All. for Legal Action v. U.S. Army Corps of Eng'rs., 314 F. Supp. 2d 534, 551–52 (M.D.N.C. 2004) ("The Corps' determination that the FAA's alternatives analysis satisfied the Section 404(b)(1) Guidelines was not arbitrary or capricious."); Coeur D'Alene Lake v. Kiebert, 790 F. Supp. 998 (D. Idaho 1992); *see also* 33 C.F.R. § 230.21. Note that the Phase II NEPA rules place time limits for relying on prior programmatic NEPA documents; documents that are more than five years old must be reevaluated to determine whether they have continued validity, and that reevaluation must be contained in the agency's NEPA document. 89 Fed. Reg. at 35561-562 (to be codified at 40 C.F.R. §1501.11).

The EA process examines environmental effects of the proposed activity[80] and any alternatives to the proposal.[81] NEPA requires that anticipated mitigation measures, such as an applicant's proposal to restore wetlands or replace ecosystem services likely impacted by the proposed activity, be considered as part of the review.[82] The courts have allowed planned mitigation to reduce projected impacts of a

---

80. When an activity that requires a wetland permit is part of a larger project, the Corps' NEPA regulations specify that the agency should examine the impacts of the activity that requires the permit *and* any portions of the larger project over which the Corps has sufficient "control and responsibility" to warrant review. 33 C.F.R. § 325, App. B(7)(b); see California Trout v. Schaefer, 58 F.3d 469, 473–74 (9th Cir. 1995) (Corps appropriately examined the impacts of a discharge of fill material into 4.18 acres of wetlands, rather than the impacts of an entire water diversion project, because the Corps only had control or responsibility over the fill activity); Winnebago Tribe of Nebraska v. Ray, 621 F.2d 269, 271 (8th Cir. 1980) (Corps appropriately examined the impacts of a 1.25 mile segment of a proposed power line, rather than the entire 67-mile line, because the Corps did not have control over the remainder of the project); Save the Bay, Inc. v. U.S. Army Corps of Eng'rs, 610 F.2d 322, 327 (5th Cir. 1980), *modified and reh'g denied en banc*, 1980 U.S.App. Lexis 19594, 14 Env't Rep. Cas. (BNA) 1542; Sierra Club v. U.S. Army Corps of Eng'rs, 990 F. Supp. 2d 9, 33–36 (D.D.C. 2013) (holding that collective actions of multiple federal agencies undertaking inter-governmental coordination did not trigger a duty to review entire pipeline); City of Dania Beach, Fla. v. U.S. Army Corps of Eng'rs, 12-60989-CIV, 2012 WL 3731516, 5 (S.D. Fla. July 6, 2012) (Court agrees with the Corps that the scope of its environmental review was properly limited to the impact of the runway expansion on the nearby wetlands.). In contrast, if a permit applicant plans to undertake several activities that would require wetland permits, and the activities are related to a single project, the applicant must include all of those activities in a single application, 33 C.F.R. § 325.1(d)(2), and the Corps should evaluate the impacts of all of the activities in a single NEPA document. 89 Fed. Reg. at 35563 (to be codified at 40 C.F.R. §1502.4). The Corps cannot "'evade [its] responsibilities' under the National Environmental Policy Act by 'artificially dividing a major federal action into smaller components, each without a significant impact.'" Preserve Endangered Areas v. U.S. Army Corps of Eng'rs, 87 F.3d 1242, 1247 (11th Cir. 1996), *citing* Coalition on Sensible Transp., Inc. v. Dole, 826 F.2d 60, 68 (D.C. Cir. 1987); *cf* Ctr. for Biological Diversity v. U.S. Army Corps of Eng'rs, 2017 WL 4861457 (M.D. Fla. 2017), *per curiam aff'd*, 941 F.3d 1288 (11th Cir. 2019) (Corps decision not to consider environmental effects of phosphogypsum stacks at phosphate fertilizer plant in assessing the effects of a phosphate mine permit (which were to supply phosphate rock to the fertilizer plant) was not arbitrary and capricious.).

81. 33 C.F.R. §§ 230.10, 325, App. B(7).

82. 89 Fed. Reg. at 35565 (to be codified at 40 C.F.R. §1502.14(e)). The NEPA mitigation requirements are separate and distinct from the mitigation requirements of the Section 404(b)(1) Guidelines.

proposed activity such that no EIS is required.[83] The EA process triggers a public notice designed to elicit comments from the public and other agencies to be taken into account before the end of the application process.[84] In most wetlands permit applications, the EA process will result in a finding of no significant impact on the human environment, making an EIS unnecessary.[85] The Corps has enormous authority in determining whether to proceed to an EIS, even if other federal agencies disagree.[86]

In rare cases, the Corps may conclude that the impacts of a proposed activity are significant and that an EIS is necessary.[87] In such

---

83. *See* All. for the Wild Rockies v. Pena, 865 F.3d 1211, 1222–23 (9th Cir. 2017), citing Friends of the Payette v. Horseshoe Bend Hydroelectric Co., 988 F.2d 989 (9th Cir. 1993); Friends of the Payette v. Horseshoe Bend Hydroelectric Co., 988 F.2d 989 (9th Cir. 1993) (upholding the Corps' decision to not prepare an EIS because the proposed activity, including mitigation measures, would not have a significant impact on the human environment); *see also* Preserve Endangered Areas v. U.S. Army Corps of Eng'rs, 87 F.3d at 1248; Friends of the Earth v. Hintz, 800 F.2d 822, 837–38 (9th Cir. 1986); Forty Most Asked Questions Concerning CEQ's National Environmental Policy Act Regulations, 46 Fed. Reg. 18,026 (1981) (note that the continued validity of all of the Forty Most Asked Questions guidance document is in question in light of the 2024 NEPA rule amendments. As of press-time, however, the guidance remained valid). The NEPA mitigation analysis is different from the 404(b)(1) Guidelines mitigation analysis, in that the Corps may not consider proposed mitigation measures when it evaluates whether alternatives to a proposed development activity would have a less adverse impact on the environment under the guidelines. *See* Chapter 6 of this book for more information about satisfying mitigation requirements.

84. 33 C.F.R. § 325, App. B(7).

85. When the agency concludes that it is not necessary to prepare an EIS, it issues a Finding of No Significant Impact (FONSI) for the permit application. *Id.* The agency will normally combine the EA, FONSI, Statement of Findings for the permit, and any analyses that are required to comply with the Section 404(b)(1) Guidelines in a single document. *Id.*

86. *See* California Trout v. Schaefer, 58 F.3d 469; Roanoke River Basin Ass'n v. Hudson, 940 F.2d 58, 64 (4th Cir. 1991); Cent. Sierra Env't Res. Ctr. v. U.S. Forest Serv., 916 F. Supp. 2d 1078, 1091 (E.D. Cal. 2013), citing California Trout v. Schaefer, 58 F. 3d 469, 475 (9th Cir. 1995) (other agencies' concerns regarding U.S. Army Corps' environmental assessment insufficient to show NEPA violation, as Corps responded to concerns and there was no significant disagreement between the agencies); Hoosier Env't Council, Inc. v. U.S. Army Corps of Eng'rs, 105 F. Supp. 2d 953, 976 (S.D. Ind. 2000) (The fact that other agencies disagree with the Corps' decision about whether to require an EIS or to issue a permit does not mean the decision is wrong.).

87. The Corps prepared only 111 environmental impact statements in the period of time between 2010 and 2018, approximately 12 a year. CEQ, Environmental Impact Statement Timelines (2010–2018) (June 12, 2020).

cases, the Corps must prepare an EIS before it issues the permit.[88] The EIS process is time-consuming and expensive, and the Corps usually requires the permit applicant to pay for the EIS.[89] Before the agency begins to prepare an EIS, it must provide notice, through the Federal Register, that it plans to prepare an EIS,[90] and it must solicit input from the public regarding the scope of issues and alternatives to be considered in the EIS.[91] After the scoping process is completed, the agency

88. The EIS examines the environmental impact of the proposed action, including unavoidable adverse environmental effects, alternatives to the proposed action and their impacts, and any irretrievable commitment of resources that would be involved in the proposed action. 42 U.S.C. § 4332(2)(C) (2023). However, the EIS is not required to consider all "effects that are 'caused by' a change in the physical environment in the sense of 'but for' causation." Metropolitan Edison Co. v. People Against Nuclear Energy, 460 U.S. 766, 774, 103 S. Ct. 1556, 75 L. Ed. 2d 534 (1983). (NEPA did not require Nuclear Regulatory Commission to consider the psychological health damage from the risk of nuclear accident to residents near Three Mile Island). Instead, NEPA requires a "reasonably close causal relationship between a change in the physical environment and the effect at issue," akin to the "familiar doctrine of proximate cause." Agencies and courts must "look to the underlying policies or legislative intent in order to draw a manageable line between those causal changes that may make an actor responsible for an effect and those that do not." *Id.* at 774 n.7, Citing *Metro Edison,* the 11th Circuit Court of Appeals held that the Area-Wide Environmental Impact Statement prepared under NEPA for three pending phosphate mine projects in central Florida did not need to consider phosphogypsum-related effects, because phosphogypsum is a waste byproduct from the fertilizer manufacturing process, not mining of the phosphate ore, and any effects from phosphogypsum would be too attenuated to meet the *Metro Edison* test. Ctr. for Biological Diversity v. U.S. Army Corps of Eng'rs, 941 F.3d. 1288, 1295–98 (11th Cir. 2019).

89. 33 C.F.R. pt. 325, App. B(9)f; *see also* ICF International, Venner Consulting, CH2M Hill and the University of Florida, *Guide to Estimating Environmental Costs* (Oct. 2008), https://environment.transportation.org/wp-content/uploads/2022/03/nchrp25-25task%2039guidance.pdf.

90. 33 C.F.R. § 230.12; 89 Fed. Reg. at 35560 (to be codified at 40 C.F.R. §1501.9 (Public and governmental engagement)).

91. 33 C.F.R. § 230.12; 89 Fed. Reg. at 35560 (to be codified at 40 C.F.R. §1501.9. "Agencies shall: (1) Invite the participation of any likely affected Federal, State, Tribal, and local agencies and governments, as early as practicable, including, as appropriate, as cooperating agencies under §1501.8 of this subchapter; (2) Conduct, as appropriate, early engagement with likely affected or interested members of the public (including those who might not be in accord with the action), unless there is a limited exception under §1507.3(d)(3) of this subchapter; and (3) Consider what methods of outreach and notification are necessary and appropriate based on the likely affected entities and persons; the scope, scale, and complexity of the proposed action and alternatives; the degree of public interest; and other relevant factors. When selecting appropriate methods for providing public notification, agencies shall

prepares a draft EIS and makes it available for public comment.[92] If the Corps will have a public hearing on the permit application, the draft EIS must be made available to the public at least 15 days before the hearing, and the draft EIS may be discussed at that hearing.[93] The agency must respond to all of the comments that it receives on the draft EIS when it prepares the final EIS.[94] In addition, when the Corps decides to issue or deny the permit, the agency must prepare a "concise" record of decision (ROD). Among other things, the ROD details "whether all practicable means to avoid or minimize environmental harm from the alternative selected have been adopted, and if not, why they were not."[95]

The Endangered Species Act requires federal agencies to ensure any actions they take (including permit issuance) do not jeopardize the continued existence of an endangered or threatened species, or destroy or adversely modify their critical habitat.[96] This is separately reinforced in the 404(b)(1) Guidelines, which prohibit issuance of

---

consider the ability of affected persons and agencies to access electronic media and the primary languages of affected persons." 89 Fed. Reg. at 35560 (to be codified at 40 C.F.R. §1501.9(c)). "As part of the scoping process, the lead agency shall invite the participation of likely affected Federal, State, Tribal, and local agencies and governments, the proponent of the action, and other likely affected or interested persons." 40 C.F.R. § 1501.9(b).

92. *See* 33 C.F.R. pt. 325, App. B(9); 33 C.F.R. pt. 230, App. C (Notice of Intent to Prepare a Draft EIS); 89 Fed. Reg. at 35564 (to be codified at 40 C.F.R. §1502.9(b)). "After preparing a draft environmental impact statement and before preparing a final environmental impact statement the agency shall: (1) Obtain the comments of any Federal agency that has jurisdiction by law or special expertise with respect to any environmental impact involved or is authorized to develop and enforce environmental standards; and (2) Request the comments of: (i) Appropriate State, Tribal, and local agencies that are authorized to develop and enforce environmental standards; (ii) State, Tribal, or local governments that may be affected by the proposed action; (iii) Any agency that has requested it receive statements on actions of the kind proposed; (iv) The applicant, if any; and (v) The public, affirmatively soliciting comments in a manner designed to inform those persons or organizations who may be interested in or affected by the proposed action." 89 Fed. Reg. at 35567 (to be codified at 40 C.F.R. §1503.1(a)).

93. 33 C.F.R. pt. 325, App. B(11).

94. *Id.* at pt. 325, App. 89 Fed. Reg. at 35564 and 35567 (to be codified at 40 C.F.R. §1502.9(c) and §1503.4). Comments must be timely and substantive to require a response.

95. 89 Fed. Reg. at 35569 (to be codified at 40 C.F.R. § 1505.2).

96. 16 U.S.C. § 1536(a)(2) (2023); *see also* 33 C.F.R. § 320.3(i).

a 404 permit that has such an effect.[97] When the Corps receives a wetland permit application, it reviews the application to ensure those requirements are met.[98] Part of that evaluation includes a preliminary effects determination. The Corps uses species effect determination keys and other guidance documents developed jointly with the Fish and Wildlife Service or the National Marine Fisheries Service[99] under the Endangered Species Act to make a determination as to whether a species is likely to have an adverse effect on listed species or their designated critical habitat.[100] If the proposed dredge and fill activity is associated with a major construction project, the applicant will be required to submit a biological assessment to assist the Corps in this effort.[101] If the Corps concludes that the proposed activity will not affect endangered or threatened species or their critical habitat, it will include a statement to that effect in the public notice for the permit application.[102] If, on the other hand, the Corps concludes that the activity may adversely affect an endangered or threatened species, it will begin formal consultation procedures with the FWS or NMFS under the Endangered Species Act.[103] If the Corps ultimately concludes that the activity will jeopardize an endangered or threatened species or

97. 40 C.F.R. § 230.10(b)(3).

98. 33 C.F.R. § 320.4(c); § 325.2(b)(5).

99. The NMFS has jurisdiction over marine species under the Endangered Species Act. 50 C.F.R. § 402.01(b) (2023).

100. *See, e.g.*, U.S. Army Corps of Engineers, Jacksonville District Source Book, https://www.saj.usace.army.mil/Missions/Regulatory/Source-Book/ (last visited July 29, 2023), Endangered Species tab, which provides links to guidance materials and/or effect keys for nearly two dozen species.

101. 50 C.F.R. § 402.12.

102. 33 C.F.R. § 325.2(b)(5). The Corps is not required to consult with FWS or NMFS if it independently makes a determination that the dredge and fill activity is not reasonably likely to affect listed species or their critical habitat, which it typically will do by resorting to species effect keys, programmatic biological opinions, and other guidance promulgated by NMFS or FWS. If the Corps determines the proposed action may affect, but is not likely to adversely affect, listed species/habitat, then it engages in information consultation with the FWS or NMFS pursuant to 50 C.F.R. § 402.13. If the wildlife agency agrees with the "not likely to adversely affect" determination, consultation ends. If as a result of informal consultation, FWS or NMFS determines the project is reasonably likely to adversely affect listed species or critical habitat, informal consultation must become formal consultation. 50 C.F.R. §§ 402.13, 402.14.

103. The consultation procedures are codified in 50 C.F.R. pt. 402: 50 C.F.R. §§ 402.13 (informal consultation), 402.14 (formal consultation).

destroy or adversely affect its critical habitat, the Corps must deny the permit.[104] Compliance with the consultation requirements of the ESA and other wildlife statutes can be generally accomplished programmatically for nationwide permits, regional general permits, and programmatic general permits, although the presence of endangered or listed species on a given project site may require additional consultation, and incidental take cannot be authorized by the Corps through a general permit.[105]

Clean Water Act 401 Certification. Pursuant to Section 401 of the CWA, a federal agency cannot issue a permit to conduct an activity that may result in discharge into WOTUS unless a Section 401 water quality certification is issued, or certification is waived. States and authorized tribes where the discharge would originate are generally responsible for issuing water quality certifications, but where they do not have authority, EPA issues the certification.[106] Section 401 thus operates to require the Corps to obtain water quality certification from either the state or tribe (or in some cases EPA) before issuing a Section

---

104. During the consultation process, if the proposed activities are likely to adversely affect a threatened or endangered species or may adversely affect or destroy critical habitat, the FWS or the NMFS must prepare a "biological opinion" that evaluates whether the proposed activity will jeopardize the continued existence of a threatened or endangered species. 50 C.F.R. § 402.14. If the death or injury of an individual of the species is reasonably certain to result from the proposed activity (including by modifying essential habitat the species uses for nesting/denning, foraging, or breeding), the biological opinion will also include an incidental take statement, which specifies the amount and extent of incidental take (injury/death) of that species that is authorized by the opinion. The opinion may also suggest reasonable and prudent measures the Corps could place on the permit to ensure that the activity will not jeopardize such species or adversely affect or destroy designated critical habitat. *Id.* Even if the FWS or the NMFS concludes that the proposed activity will jeopardize a threatened or endangered species, the Corps retains the ultimate authority to determine whether the activity will jeopardize such species. Roosevelt Campobello Intern. Park v. U.S. Env't Prot. Agency, 684 F.2d 1041, 1049 (1st Cir. 1982); Sierra Club v. Froehlke, 534 F.2d 1289, 1303 (8th Cir. 1976). The Corps will also consider the impacts of proposed activities on endangered or threatened species or their critical habitat as part of the agency's "public interest" review. *See* Town of Norfolk v. U.S. Army Corps of Eng'rs, 968 F.2d at 1453; Red Lake Band of Chippewa Indians v. United States Army Corps of Engineers, CV 20-3817 (CKK), 2021 WL 430054, 3 (D.D.C. Feb. 7, 2021).

105. *See, e.g.*, Department of the Army, Corps of Engineers, Reissuance and Modification of Nationwide Permits, 86 Fed. Reg. 2744, Part III.D (Jan. 13, 2021). See Chapter 5 for more details.

106. 33 U.S.C. § 1341.

404 permit, which specifically authorizes discharge (of dredged or fill material) into WOTUS, meaning the state or tribe must confirm the proposed activity will not violate various state water quality laws.[107] States can, in essence, veto permits that do not comply with state water quality standards by denying 401 certification. States can also condition their certification with additional requirements to the permit.[108] The state issues, denies, or conditions a 401 certification through notice and comment procedures that are established by the state.[109] Permit applicants can challenge the state's action only in state court or administrative tribunals.[110]

If the permit applicant does not submit the state's 401 certification with the application, the Corps notifies the applicant that the certification is required.[111] In such cases, the Corps sends a copy of the notice to the state environmental agency that will provide the certification, and requests certification for the proposed activity, when the Corps issues the public notice for the permit application.[112] The Corps cannot issue the permit unless the state issues the 401 certification or waives

107. *Id.* § 1341(a)(1); *see also* 33 C.F.R. §§ 320.3(a), 325.1(d)(4). 401 certification may also be required from states other than the state where the polluting activity takes place. When the Corps receives a permit application, it must notify EPA that it has received the application (called a Section 401(a)(2) notice). 33 U.S.C. § 1341 (a)(2). If the EPA administrator determines that the activity that will be authorized by the permit may affect the water quality of any other state, the administrator notifies the other state, the Corps, and the permit applicant that the Corps has received a permit application for an activity that may affect the water quality of the state. *Id.*

108. 33 U.S.C. § 1341(a)(1).

109. *Id.*

110. Roosevelt Campobello Intern. Park v. U.S. Env't Prot. Agency, 684 F.2d at 1056.

111. 33 C.F.R. § 325.2(b)(1).

112. *Id.* §§ 325.2(b)(1), 325.3. The public notice is also sent to EPA, and serves as the notice required by Section 401(a)(2) of the Clean Water Act. *Id.* § 325.2(b)(1)(i). If EPA determines that the proposed activity will affect the water quality of any other state, the agency will notify the other state, the Corps, and the permit applicant. *Id.* EPA must make that determination within 30 days after receipt of the Corps notice. *Id.* If the other state determines that the proposed activity will violate any water quality requirements of that state, the state can object to the issuance of the permit within 60 days after EPA's notice. *Id.* If the objecting state requests a hearing, the Corps will hold a hearing to consider the water quality impacts of the permit on the objecting state. *Id.* Based on the comments of EPA, the objecting state, and any evidence presented at the hearing, the Corps will include conditions in the permit, if issued, that are necessary to ensure that the activity will comply with water quality requirements of the objecting state. *Id.*

its right to issue the certification.[113] Section 401 gives states and tribes a "reasonable period of time (which shall not exceed one year)" to act on a certification request.[114] Corps regulations provide that a state will waive its right to issue a 401 certification if the state does not act on the Corps' request for certification within 60 days.[115] Water quality certification by states and tribes can be accomplished programmatically for nationwide permits, regional general permits, and programmatic general permits.[116]

The Coastal Zone Management Act authorizes certain states to develop management plans to protect their coastal zone, and provides grants to states to administer coastal zone management programs.[117] If a state has adopted an approved coastal zone management program,[118] the Corps cannot issue a wetland permit for an activity that affects the coastal zone unless the state certifies that the proposed activity complies with the state's program.[119]

If the activity to be authorized by a wetland permit will affect the coastal zone of a state that has an approved coastal zone management program, the permit applicant must initially certify to the Corps that the activity complies with the state program.[120] The Corps includes that

113. *Id.* § 325.2(b)(1)(ii).

114. 33 U.S.C. § 1341(a)(1). EPA's 401 certification rules were amended in 2023. The amendments were published September 27, 2023, became effective November 27, 2023, and are codified at 40 C.F.R. pt. 121 (2023). *See* 88 Fed. Reg. 66,558 (Sept. 27, 2023), https://www.epa.gov/system/files/documents/2023-09/federal-register-version-of-2023-clean-water-act-section-401-water-quality-certification-improvement-rule.pdf. Chapter 7 contains more details about the water quality certification process.

115. 33 C.F.R. § 325.2(b)(1)(ii). The Corps can extend the time for the state to respond to a request for certification for as long as a year, consistent with the one-year limit in Section 401. *Id.* Normally, though, the Corps does not extend the time for the state's response.

116. *See, e.g.*, Dep't of the Army, Corps of Eng'rs, Reissuance and Modification of Nationwide Permits, 86 Fed. Reg. 2744 Part III.G (Jan. 13, 2021). See Chapter 5 for more details.

117. 16 U.S.C. § 1452.

118. Coastal zone management plans are reviewed and approved by the Secretary of Commerce. *Id.*

119. *Id.* § 1456(c)(3)(A). The act places additional constraints on federal agencies when they are the permit applicant. *See* 16 U.S.C. § 1456(c); 33 C.F.R. § 325.2(b)(2)(i).

120. *Id.* § 325.2(b)(2)(ii).

certification in the public notice for the permit application,[121] provides a copy of the notice to the state coastal zone agency, and asks the agency to concur with the applicant's certification.[122] The state agency can concur with the certification, object to the certification, or inform the Corps that the agency will review the issue further.[123] Coastal Zone Management Act concurrency from coastal states can be accomplished programmatically for nationwide permits and other types of CWA general permits.[124]

Some states have entered into operating agreements with the Corps regarding both coastal zone management and water quality certification, providing the procedures for obtaining both of those certifications for Section 404 permits.[125]

The National Historic Preservation Act (NHPA) requires federal agencies that undertake or license activities that may affect properties listed on the National Register of Historic Places to consider the effect of the project on those properties and to provide the Advisory Council on Historic Preservation (ACHP) an opportunity to comment on the project.[126] The Corps has established NHPA regulations[127] that set forth additional permit review procedures the agency must use when a permit applicant proposes to conduct an activity that would involve property listed or eligible for listing on the National Register of Historic Places (designated historic properties).[128]

When the Corps receives a complete wetland permit application, the agency's NHPA regulations require it to determine whether there are

121. *Id.* § 325.3(a)(16).

122. *Id.* § 325.2(ii).

123. *Id.*

124. *See, e.g.*, Dep't of the Army, *supra* note 16, at Part III.H. See Chapter 5 for more details.

125. Operating Agreement among the Jacksonville District of the U.S. Army Corps of Engineers, the State of Florida Department of Environmental Protection, the Northwest Florida Water Management District, the South Florida Water Management District, the St. Johns River Water Management District, the Southwest Florida Water Management District, and the Suwannee River Water Management District Concerning Regulatory Programs for Activities in Wetlands and Other Surface Waters, Including Waters of the United States (Sept. 4, 2012) at Part II (Water Quality Certification) and Part III (Coastal Zone Consistency Concurrence), https://floridadep.gov/ogc/ogc/content/operating-agreements#federal (last visited July 30, 2023).

126. 16 U.S.C. §§ 470, 470 (f). The ACHP has promulgated regulations that authorize state historic preservation officers (SHPOs) to consult with agencies and comment on projects in lieu of, or in addition to, the ACHP. 36 C.F.R. pt. 800.

127. 33 C.F.R. § 325, App. C.

128. *Id.* § 325.2(b)(3).

any designated historic properties or undesignated historic properties that may be affected by the proposed activity.[129] The Corps includes its determination in the public notice for the permit application, and sends a copy of the notice to the state historic preservation officer (SHPO), the ACHP, the regional office of the National Park Service, any affected tribal historic preservation officer (THPO), and other parties for their comments.[130] The Corps may also identify properties that could be eligible for listing on the National Register during its review of the application.[131] If the Corps discovers additional historic properties that may be affected by the proposed activity after the Corps issues the public notice, it will immediately inform the applicant, the SHPO, the local government, and the ACHP, and allow them 30 days after that notice to provide comments.[132] The regulations establish detailed procedures that the Corps must follow, in consultation with SHPOs, THPOs, the ACHP, and the Keeper of the National Register, in order to evaluate historic properties discovered during the permitting process to determine whether the properties are eligible for listing on the National Register.[133]

The regulations also require the Corps to consult with the SHPO and the ACHP to determine whether the proposed activity will adversely

129. 33 C.F.R. § 325, App. C(3)(a). The regulations encourage the Corps and applicants to consider the impacts of projects at the earliest practical time. If the Corps is aware, at the time of a pre-application consultation, that a proposed project will affect a designated historic property, the Corps should inform the applicant at that time that the Corps will review the permit application pursuant to the agency's NHPA regulations. *Id.* § 325, App. C(3)(c). In addition, the Corps should discuss measures or alternatives to avoid or minimize effects on historic properties at the earliest practical time. *Id.* § 325, App. C(3)(d). Under the NHPA regulations, the Corps examines the impacts of the discharge of the dredged or fill material into wetlands on historic properties. However, the agency also examines the impact of activities that occur outside of the waters of the United States on historic properties if (1) the activity would not occur but for the authorization of work or structures in the waters of the United States; (2) the activity is integrally related to the work or structures authorized within the waters of the United States; and (3) the activity must be directly associated with the work or structures to be authorized. *Id.* § 325, App. C(1)(g)(1). As a practical matter, cultural resource assessment surveys (CRAS) are conducted more and more frequently on greenfield sites and even on urban infill sites, given the frequency with which cultural resources or historical structures or sites are encountered. For a discussion of the typical cultural resource survey process, *see infra*, note 139.

130. *Id.* § 325, App. C(4)(a).

131. *Id.* § 325, App. C(4)(b).

132. *Id.*

133. *Id.* § 325, App. C(5)–(6).

affect designated historic properties.[134] The Corps cannot make a final decision on the permit until it consults with the SHPO and/or the ACHP.[135] Although the NHPA does not require the Corps to avoid or minimize the effects of a proposed activity on historic properties,[136] the Corps, through its "public interest" review, will add conditions to permits to minimize or avoid harm to historic properties if necessary to protect the public interest.[137] Finally, if the proposed activity would result in the irrevocable loss of important scientific, prehistoric, or archaeological data, the Corps must notify the National Park Service regarding the potential loss and any conditions that the Corps will place on the permit to mitigate the loss.[138] Increasingly, a permit applicant is wise to include a cultural resource assessment survey prepared by a cultural resource management company to expedite this review process, particularly if historic properties or archaeological finds are likely.[139]

Essential Fish Habitat. In some coastal areas, the Corps may have to do an essential fish habitat (EFH) consultation. Section 305(b) of the Sustainable Fisheries Act of 1996 (SFA), identifying the contribution of habitat loss and degradation on fishery declines, amended the Magnuson-Stevens Act to create a new program to protect "essential fish

134. *Id.* § 325, App. C(7)–(9).

135. *Id.*

136. Under the NHPA, as long as the Corps consults with the ACHP and considers the impact of a project on historic properties, the Corps can issue a permit for the project even though it will adversely affect historic properties. 36 C.F.R. § 800.6(b) (2023).

137. 33 C.F.R. § 325, App. C(10)(a).

138. *Id.* § 325, App. C(10)(b).

139. The first step in assessing cultural or historical resources is to conduct a Phase 1 cultural resources survey to identify and record all cultural resources within a project area. These could include areas like prehistoric Native American archaeological sites; historic homesteads or cemeteries; or other man-made features such as structures, midden heaps, or earthworks. This initial survey includes fieldwork, literature review, lab work if any resources are found, and a cultural resources assessment survey report, which also assesses the National Historic Registry listing criteria set forth in 36 C.F.R. 60.4. Phase 1 reports are generally submitted to the State Historic Preservation Officer (SHPO) and the Tribal Historic Preservation Officer (THPO) for review. Phase II involves further evaluation of any identified resources, while Phase III addresses remediation measures for resources that cannot be avoided or minimized. *See* State of California Native American Heritage Commission, *Understanding Cultural Resources*, https://nahc.ca.gov/resources/understanding-cultural-resources/#:~:text=There%20are%20three%20basic%20phases%20of%20concern%20to,should%20be%20implemented%20by%20a%20qualified%20professional%20archaeologist (last visited July 31, 2023).

habitat" that has been described and identified in fishery management plans adopted by any regional fishery management council.[140] Actions that are authorized, funded, or undertaken by a federal agency, including many approved by the Corps, require consultation with NMFS when those actions may adversely affect any EFH.[141] Consultation requirements may be fulfilled by one of five types of consultations: (1) existing procedures, (2) programmatic consultations, (3) general concurrences, (4) abbreviated consultations, and (5) expanded consultations.[142] Existing procedures are those that already occur independent of EFH requirements and may satisfy the EFH consultation requirement if so determined by NMFS.[143] Programmatic consultation is appropriate when there is adequate information available to "address all reasonably foreseeable adverse effects on EFH of an entire program."[144] A general concurrence may be given when NMFS determines that a type of action will likely have only a minimal adverse impact on EFH.[145] Abbreviated consultation procedures may be used for those actions that do not qualify for a general concurrence, but will not cause "substantial adverse effects on EFH."[146] For those actions that may result in substantial adverse effects, expanded consultations are required.[147]

Agencies must also provide NMFS with a written assessment of the effects of the action on EFH when the effects may be adverse.[148] NMFS

140. 16 U.S.C. § 1855(b) (2023). EFH is defined as "those waters and substrate necessary to fish for spawning, breeding, feeding, or growth to maturity. For the purpose of interpreting the definition of essential fish habitat: 'Waters' include aquatic areas and their associated physical, chemical, and biological properties that are used by fish and may include aquatic areas historically used by fish where appropriate; 'substrate' includes sediment, hard bottom, structures underlying the waters, and associated biological communities; 'necessary' means the habitat required to support a sustainable fishery and the managed species' contribution to a healthy ecosystem; and 'spawning, breeding, feeding, or growth to maturity' covers a species' full life cycle."). 50 C.F.R. § 600.10.

141. 16 U.S.C. § 1855(b)(2).

142. 50 C.F.R. § 600.920 (2023).

143. *Id.* § 600.920(f). Existing procedures include the consultation and coordination procedures required by the CWA, ESA, and NEPA. These procedures and the EFH requirements can be combined but NMFS must get timely notice of actions adversely affecting EFH.

144. *Id.* § 600.920(j).

145. *Id.* § 600.920(g).

146. *Id.* § 600.920(h).

147. *Id.* § 600.920(i).

148. *Id.* § 600.920(c).

then submits an EFH conservation recommendation to the agency, to which the agency must provide a written response.[149] The response must describe measures to avoid, mitigate, or offset the impact of the activity on the EFH.[150] If the agency ultimately acts in defiance of NMFS's recommendations, it must explain its reasons for doing so.[151] EFH consultation occurs on a programmatic basis as applicable during the approval process for nationwide permits, regional general permits, and programmatic general permits under the CWA that might affect EFH.[152]

The Corps' review of a wetland permit application generally proceeds concurrently with the review of relevant federal, state, and local agencies.[153] Accordingly, the Corps may establish joint review procedures with expert agencies on a state or local level.[154] The Corps must fully consider the comments of those agencies regarding their areas of expertise on relevant statutes, regulations, and policies.[155] This consideration of expert agency comments can come into play when the Corps determines whether issuance of the permit is contrary to the public interest.[156] Timing may vary as to whether the Corps or other agencies complete their reviews first.[157] However, the Corps retains full authority to decide whether to issue or deny a permit, or to include specific conditions.[158] While due consideration should be given to the official views of a state, regional, or local agency having jurisdiction, the permit decision will generally not be delayed pending action by another federal, state, or local agency.[159] Permits are sometimes issued pending final review by other expert agencies where the authorizations are not prerequisites to issuance and the other authorities can undertake their review without

149. *Id.* § 600.920(i), (k).

150. *Id.* § 600.920(k)(1).

151. *Id.* § 600.920(k)(2).

152. *See, e.g.*, Dep't of the Army, Corps of Eng'rs, Reissuance and Modification of Nationwide Permits, 86 Fed. Reg. 2744 Part III.E (Jan. 13, 2021). See Chapter 5 for more details.

153. 33 C.F.R. § 320.4(j)(1).

154. *Id.* §§ 320.4(j)(5), 325.2(e)(3).

155. *See id.* § 320.4(c), (h), (i), (j); Slagle v. United States By and Through Baldwin, 809 F. Supp. 704, 712 (D. Minn. 1992) (Corps must consider the comments of local agencies); Sierra Club v. Alexander, 484 F. Supp. 455 (N.D. N.Y. 1980), *aff'd*, 633 F.2d 206 (2d Cir. 1980).

156. 33 C.F.R. § 320.4.

157. *Id.* §§ 320.4(j)(1), 325.2(d)(4).

158. *Id.*

159. *Id.* § 320.4(j)(1).

the applicant biasing the review by undertaking substantial resources commitments on the basis of the Corps permit.[160]

The district engineer is charged with the final decision on permit applications,[161] which is either issuance or denial. The permit will be issued with general conditions[162] and usually also with those additional special conditions "necessary to satisfy legal requirements or to otherwise satisfy the public interest requirement. Permit conditions will be directly related to the impacts of the proposal, appropriate to the scope and degree of those impacts, and reasonably enforceable."[163] Permit issuance must be supported by a written statement of findings (SOF).[164] To accept a proffered permit, the applicant must sign the permit to indicate understanding of, and intent to comply with, conditions included in the permit.[165] The issuance of the permit does not convey any property rights or exclusive privileges to the applicant.[166]

Permits usually authorize that the discharged material can remain indefinitely.[167] However, permits also usually require that the per-

160. *Id.* § 325.2(d)(4). As an example, a wetland permit cannot be issued without completing formal consultation if the proposed activity will adversely affect endangered or listed species pursuant to 50 C.F.R. pt. 402. 33 C.F.R. § 325/2(b)(5). In contrast, while due consideration should be given to the official views of a state, regional, or local agency having jurisdiction, the permit decision will generally not be delayed pending action by another federal, state, or local agency. *See id.* § 320.4(j)(1).

161. 33 C.F.R. §§ 325.2(a)(6), 325.8. District engineers refer permit applications to the division engineer for decision when (1) a referral is required by a memorandum of agreement with other federal agencies; (2) the recommended decision is contrary to the written position of the governor of the state in which the permitted activity will take place; (3) there is substantial doubt as to authority, law, regulations, or policies applicable to the proposed activity; (4) a higher authority requests that the application be forwarded for decision; or (5) the district engineer is precluded by law or procedures from taking final action on the application. *Id.* § 325.8(b). The division engineer may refer the application to the chief of engineers in similar situations. *Id.* § 325.8(c).

162. *See* 33 C.F.R. pt. 325, app. A, ENG Form 1721, for the general conditions that will be included in all Section 404 permits.

163. 33 C.F.R. § 325.4 (2023). Examples of special conditions would include conditions necessary to ensure compliance with the 404(b)(1) Guidelines or the Endangered Species Act. *Id.* § 325.4(a)(1). This could include a special condition requiring the applicant to comply with the reasonable and prudent measures included in a biological opinion issued by FWS.

164. *Id.* § 325.2(a)(6). If an EIS was prepared for the decision, the Corps must prepare a record of decision for the decision instead of a statement of findings. *Id.*

165. *Id.*

166. *Id.* § 320.4(g).

167. *Id.* § 325.6(b). "Permits for the existence of a structure or other activity of a permanent nature are usually for an indefinite duration with no expiration date cited."

mittee start and finish construction work (or other work) associated with the permitted activity on specific dates.[168] Corps approval for the construction work (or other work) associated with the activity will automatically expire on the date specified in the permit, unless the permittee requests and receives an extension from the district engineer before that date,[169] which generally must comply with the normal permit issuance procedures.[170] Such extensions are generally granted unless the district engineer determines that an extension would be contrary to the public interest in the particular case.[171]

On its own or at the request of the permittee or a third party, the Corps has authority to reevaluate a valid permit and consider the circumstances or conditions of any permit.[172] Such a reevaluation may result in a Corps decision to modify, suspend, or revoke the permit as necessary, based on considerations of the public interest.[173] In deciding whether to modify, suspend, or revoke a permit, the Corps will consider factors such as (1) the permittee's compliance with the permit, (2) changes in circumstances relating to the permitted activity and whether the permit conditions are adequate to address those changes; (3) significant objections to the permitted activity that were not considered earlier; (4) changes in the law; and (5) whether modification, suspension, or revocation would adversely affect the permittee's reasonable plans and investments.[174] Such reevaluations are unusual.

If the final decision is to deny a permit, the Corps must advise the applicant in writing of the reason(s) for denial.[175] In the rare instance

---

Id. However, where the permit authorizes temporary fills, it will include a definite expiration date. *Id.*

168. *Id.* § 325.6(c). A typical construction period is five years, but if the Corps issues the Section 404 permit, can be issued for the period of time necessary to complete the proposed activity, even if that is substantially longer than five years, such as may be required for multi-phase development projects. Section 404 permits that are issued by states that have assumed administration of the Section 404 program can be issued only "for a fixed term not exceeding five years." 33 U.S.C. § 1344(h)(1)(A)(ii) (2023).

169. *Id.* § 325.6(d).

170. *Id.*

171. *Id.*

172. *Id.* § 325.7(a).

173. *Id.*

174. *Id.*

175. *Id.* § 325.2(a)(7).

that the Corps denies an application for an individual permit,[176] or, more commonly, includes terms and conditions in an individual permit that lead an applicant to decline the permit, the applicant can either redesign the project to address the bases for denial and submit a new application[177] or appeal the Corps' action through an administrative appeal.[178] There are also opportunities for judicial review of agency actions, which are further discussed in Chapter 8.

The Corps uses information management techniques to track permitting data. The Corps manages data related to the individual permitting program through the OROMBIL Regulatory Module (Operations & Maintenance Business Information Link), "ORM" for short.[179]

As this chapter demonstrates, the individual permitting process is complex. Navigating it successfully can be daunting. The EPA has developed a helpful "self-audit checklist" for 404 permit applicants,[180] as have several Corps districts.[181] But the best tool for the applicant almost always is contacting the staff at the relevant Corps district offices.

---

176. The Corps states on its website that on a national basis, "less than one percent of all requests for permits are denied. Those few applicants who have been denied permits usually have refused to change the design, timing, or location of the proposed activity." Regulatory Program Frequently Asked Questions (army.mil).

177. *Id.*

178. 33 C.F.R. § 320.1(a)(2).

179. ORM can be accessed at https://corpslakes.erdc.dren.mil/employees/ombil-rec/ombil.cfm. ("Within the Regulatory program, the Corps has used its OMBIL Regulatory Module 2 (ORM2) data base to document key information about regulatory permit activities. ORM2 is used by all 38 District offices data is shared electronically with U.S. EPA on a daily basis. Data on mitigation and conservation banks and in lieu fee mitigation programs, such as types and numbers of mitigation and conservation bank and in-lieu fee program sites, associated documents, mitigation credit availability, service areas, as well as information on national and local policies and procedures that affect mitigation and conservation bank and in-lieu fee program development and operation is housed on a dedicated website found at *RIBITS*, https://ribits.ops.usace.army.mil/ords/f?p=107:2. The site was developed by the Corps with support from the U.S. Fish and Wildlife Service and the U.S. Env't Prot. Agency, U.S. Army Corps of Eng'rs, U.S. Army Corps of Engineers (USACE) Improving Performance of Federal Permitting and Review of Infrastructure Projects Agency Plan (Sept. 2012), at 10.

180. U.S. Env't Prot. Agency, II. Dredge and Fill/Wetlands (Section 404) Self-Audit Checklist, https://archive.epa.gov/compliance/resources/publications/assistance/sectors/web/pdf/myer2_dredgeandfill.pdf.

181. *See, e.g.*, U.S. Army Corps of Eng'rs, Philadelphia District, Individual Permit Application Checklist, http://www.nap.usace.army.mil/Portals/39/docs/regulatory/ip/ip_app_check.pdf; U.S. Army Corps of Eng'rs, Savannah District, Individual Permit Checklist, https://www.dot.ga.gov/PartnerSmart/EnvironmentalProcedures

III. APPENDIX—Checklist for a Complete[182] Individual Permit Application Packet[183]

_____ Jurisdictional determination (JD) request or approved JD[184]

_____ Application submitted on ENG Form 4345[185]

_____ The name, email address, street address, and telephone number of the applicant

_____ Applicant's signature, and (if applicable) authorized agent's signature and proof of authorization

_____ The nature, purpose, and need for the proposed activity; this should include approximate dates to begin and complete all proposed work

---

/Ecology1/References/Individual%20Permit%20Application%20Checklist%20-%20USACE.pdf; U.S. Army Corps of Engineers, Fort Worth District, Regulatory Permitting: Individual Permits, http://www.swf.usace.army.mil/Missions/Regulatory/Permitting/IndividualPermits.aspx; U.S. Army Corps of Eng'rs, Albuquerque District, Checklist of Complete Application Information, https://www.spa.usace.army.mil/Missions/Regulatory-Program-and-Permits/IP/. Some district checklists incorporate state-specific requirements. *See, e.g.*, U.S. Army Corps of Eng'rs, Galveston District, TCEQ Checklist for Tier 1 projects, https://swfapps.usace.army.mil/pubdata/environ/regulatory/permitting/tceq/tierismallprojectschecklistattachment1.pdf; U.S. Army Corps of Eng'rs, Chicago District, Illinois App Checklist, http://www.lrc.usace.army.mil/Missions/Regulatory/Illinois/AppChecklist.aspx.

182. Note that in the course of the approval process many permit applicants will be required to provide additional information deemed necessary to make a public interest determination and a determination of compliance with Section 404(b)(1) Guidelines. Such additional information may include—but is not limited to—appropriate and practicable mitigation, alternatives, and impacts of the proposed activity on endangered species and cultural resources. *See* explanatory material elsewhere in this chapter. Current guidance also requires the Corps to consider additional factors like environmental justice as part of its NEPA review. *See* https://www.epa.gov/environmentaljustice/environmental-justice-and-national-environmental-policy-act (last checked May 28, 2024).

183. This is a general checklist—many districts have their own requirements, and applicants are advised to check with staff at their local district offices.

184. The U.S. Army Corps of Eng'rs, Approved JD Form can be found at https://permits.ops.usace.army.mil/orm-public. Examples of approved JDs can be found at https://watersgeo.epa.gov/cwa/CWA-JDs/.

185. *See* U.S. Army Corps of Eng'rs, Obtain a Permit, https://www.usace.army.mil/Missions/Civil-Works/Regulatory-Program-and-Permits/Obtain-a-Permit/, for the current form and instructions on how to complete the form.

_____ The location of the proposed activity, including latitude and longitude and directions to the site and the name of the waterbody that will be directly impacted

_____ A complete description of the proposed activity, its intended purpose and use, including drawings, sketches, or plans necessary for meaningful public notice on 8.5- × 11-inch sheets;[186] planning documents, including cross-section/elevation/profile drawings showing location and nature of all proposed activities, including the size relationship of the proposed structures to the size of the impacted waterway and depth of water in the area

_____ A complete description of all activities reasonably related to the project, full descriptions of any structure to be constructed, and descriptions (including quantity) of any material to be discharged

_____ If dredging is proposed, a description of the material, method, and plans for disposal

_____ If discharge is proposed, the source of the material; the purpose of the discharge; a description of the type, composition, and quantity of the material; the method of transportation of the material; and where it will occur

---

186. All maps should include a title block with the title, date, number scheme (sheet __ of __), and source; a north indicator; a scale or explicit dimensions, the map creator, the project or study area boundary, and a legend that clearly identifies features presented. Maps should be developed so that information presented is clearly marked and shown in relation to the nearest roads, water features, and cities and towns. All maps must be in black and white on 8.5- × 11-inch paper, and may be based on U. S. Geological Survey (USGS) maps, state, county, and city maps, soil survey maps, and floodplain maps.

Planning drawings should show existing and proposed plan views for each element of work, structure, fill and excavation proposed located with respect to a fixed point such as a plat line, set of UTM coordinates, set of latitude/longitude coordinates, or some fixed, immovable object. Plan-view drawings must clearly indicate the direction of water flow. Match-line drawings may be used for projects requiring a larger size than 8.5 × 11 inches, in order to be clear and legible. Match-line drawings must be labeled clearly. Plan view drawings must clearly show a delineation/determination of water features within the permit area that are potential waters of the United States.

Cross-section/elevation/profile must show existing and proposed water depths and land elevations relative to the ordinary high water mark when applicable. For reservoirs, normal pool, or conservation, elevation and any other established seasonal elevations, for example, recreational pool, power pool, and so on, must be shown elevations must be expressed relative to the National Geodetic Vertical Datum (NGVD).

_____ If an impoundment structure is proposed, documented compliance of established state dam safety criteria or proof that the structure has been designed (and in some cases reviewed) by qualified persons

_____ Description of avoidance, minimization, and compensatory mitigation measures (or, alternatively, a statement of why mitigation should not be required)

_____ Names and addresses of adjoining property owners

_____ Proposed schedule

_____ List of authorizations believed to be required by other federal, interstate, state, or local agencies for the work, indicating whether they have been applied for, and if so, were approved

_____ For major construction projects, a biological assessment meeting the requirements of 50 C.F.R. § 402.12 and a cultural resource assessment survey pursuant to Section 106 of the NHPA[187]

_____ Any other available and relevant information to assist interested parties in evaluating likely impacts of the proposed activity on factors affecting the public interest[188]

---

187. Large or complex projects will require substantially more detailed information in order to satisfy the 404(b)(1) Guidelines and Corps rules contained in 33 C.F.R. pts. 320 and 325. The prepared applicant will "frontload" the application to minimize additional information requests and shorten overall processing timelines.

188. If applicable, this information should include information evaluating the public interest factors in 33 C.F.R. § 320.4(a), effects on fish and wildlife per 33 C.F.R. § 320.4(c), or effects on resources like floodplain storage, water supplies, energy, or navigation (33 C.F.R. § 320.4(l)–(o)).

5
CHAPTER

General and Nationwide Permits: Proceeding through Streamlined Processes

I. Introduction

The federal Clean Water Act (CWA) requires permits for most activities in "waters of the United States."[1] As a result, throughout the United States, many people, corporations, local governments, and others seek to undertake actions that require approval by the Corps.[2] When Corps district offices[3] around the nation authorize the tens of thousands of regulatory actions undertaken annually, they approve the vast majority

1. 33 U.S.C. § 1344 (2023). For detailed information about individual permitting and regulatory requirements that apply to all proposed activities, see Chapter 4. *See also* 33 C.F.R. § 320.2 (2023) (discussing different authorities to issue permits).

2. "The Corps evaluates permit applications for essentially all construction activities that occur in the Nation's waters, including wetlands." U.S. Army Corps of Eng'rs, Section on Regulatory Programs and Permits, *Regulatory (Permits)*, http://www.usace.army.mil/Missions/CivilWorks/RegulatoryProgramandPermits.aspx.

3. Direct links to all district offices can be found at U.S. Army Corps of Eng'rs, *Where We Are—U.S. Army Corps of Engineers*, http://www.usace.army.mil/Locations.aspx.

in a streamlined manner, through various general permits.[4] These nationwide and other general permits are meant to minimize the burden and delay of the Corps' regulatory program by authorizing certain covered activities that have minimal environmental impact.[5] In 2022, the Corps estimated that, on average, 40,000 reported activities proceed annually through nationwide permits (NWPs), and 30,000 more activities that do not require pre-construction notice to the Corps proceed under those permits.[6] Programmatic general permits and regional general permits also provided authorization for many additional actions: a regional general permit is issued for a specific geographic area by an individual Corps district, with region-specific terms and conditions, while a programmatic general permit is based on existing state, local, or other federal program and designed to avoid duplication of that program. A state programmatic general permit (SPGP) is based on an existing state regulatory program that provides similar protection to aquatic resources and can be issued by the Corps or by the state regulatory agency.[7]

This chapter is designed to help readers understand the origins of, and basic requirements associated with, Section 404 nationwide and other general permits. It opens with a brief history of the program and a summary of the process. Toward the end, the chapter includes a chart of current general conditions that apply to all NWPs, as well as a summary table of the NWPs issued in 2021 as an Appendix.

---

4. *See generally* 33 C.F.R. § 330 (2023); 40 C.F.R. § 230.7 (2023); *see also Nationwide Permit Information,* U.S. Army Corps of Eng'rs, 2012, http://www.usace.army.mil/Missions/CivilWorks/RegulatoryProgramandPermits/NationwidePermits.aspx. For helpful background, see also Claudia Copeland, *The Army Corps of Engineers' Nationwide Permits Program: Issues and Regulatory Developments,* Cong. Rsch. Serv. (Jan. 30, 2012), http://www.fas.org/sgp/crs/natsec/97-223.pdf.

5. *The Army Corps of Engineers' Nationwide Permits Program: Issues and Regulatory Developments*, U.S. Army Cong. Rsch. serv. 4 (Jan. 12, 2017), https://www.everycrsreport.com/files/20170112_97-223_271c5b98b058e7b84bab465be90e05777cf735ea.pdf.

6. Nationwide Permit Reissuance, U.S. Army Corps of Eng'rs (Jan. 2022), https://usace.contentdm.oclc.org/utils/getfile/collection/p16021coll7/id/19764.

7. U.S. Army Corps of Eng'rs, Missions/Civil Works/Regulatory Program and Permits/Obtain a Permit/Regional and Programmatic General Permits, https://www.usace.army.mil/Missions/Civil-Works/Regulatory-Program-and-Permits/Obtain-a-Permit/. As an example, activities eligible for the SPGP in Florida are those designated activities like docks or boat ramps that qualify for state permitting exemptions or general permits. U.S. Army Corps of Eng'rs, Jacksonville District, State Programmatic General Permit (SPGP), https://www.saj.usace.army.mil/SPGP/.

Some words of caution to readers: given the many nuances associated with general permits and their accompanying conditions, this chapter is intended only as an orientation and reference. Although the Corps designed this part of the permitting process to proceed in a streamlined manner, in many cases, consulting with Corps personnel or other experts increases the likelihood of navigating the process efficiently. Further, remember that NWPs are valid for only a set five-year period and must be reissued or they expire. This chapter should not serve as the sole source of information about the NWP that might be applicable to a discharge. The NWPs currently in effect when this book was written became effective March 15, 2021, and expire unless reissued on March 15, 2026.

II. History of the General Permitting Program

Congress first authorized nationwide and other general permits through its 1977 amendments to the Clean Water Act to "reduce the administrative paperwork and delay otherwise caused by having the Corps review every proposed dredge or fill activity under the individual permitting scheme."[8] The early NWPs were very permissive.[9] Following an almost two-year proposal process, in 1982, the Corps issued the first full set of 26 NWPs and codified them in the regulations.[10] They were amended and reissued in 1986,[11] 1991,[12] and in 1996.[13] Historically, NWP 26

---

8. Sierra Club v. U.S. Army Corps of Eng'rs, 464 F. Supp. 2d 1171 (M.D. Fla. 2006), *aff'd per curiam*, 508 F.3d 1332 (11th Cir. 2007) (citing S. Rep. No. 95-370, at 80 (1977), *reprinted in* 1977 U.S.C.C.A.N. 4326, 4405; H.R. Conf. Rep. 95-830, at 98 (1977), *reprinted in* 1977 U.S.C.C.A.N. 4424, 4473).

9. A summary of the first set of NWPs is available in Office of Energy and Env't L., Univ. of Ala. L. Ctr., A Survey of Wetlands Law: Monograph 3, at 16–20 (1980).

10. *See* Interim Final Rule for Regulatory Programs of the Corps of Engineers, 47 Fed. Reg. 31794 (July 22, 1982) (codified at 33 C.F.R. pts. 320–330). The original proposal was Proposal to Amend Permit Regulations for Controlling Certain Activities in Waters of the United States, 45 Fed. Reg. 62732 (Sept. 19, 1980). Links to all issued Federal Register Notices of Nationwide Permits can be found at *General Permits*, U.S. Army Corps of Eng'rs, Fort Worth District, http://www.swf.usace.army.mil/Missions/Regulatory/Permitting/GeneralPermits.aspx.

11. Interim Final Rule for Regulatory Programs of the Corps of Engineers, 51 Fed. Reg. 41206 (Nov. 13, 1986) (codified at 33 C.F.R. pts. 320–325, 329, 330).

12. Final Rule for Nationwide Permit Program Regulations and Issue, Reissue and Modify Nationwide Permits, 56 Fed. Reg. 59110 (Nov. 22, 1991) (codified at 33 C.F.R. pt. 330).

13. Final Notice for Issuance, Reissuance, and Modification of Nationwide Permits, 61 Fed. Reg. 41206 (Dec. 13, 1996).

provided for general permits in isolated and headwaters wetlands and had no acreage limits.[14] However, in 1984, the Corps imposed a maximum project limit of ten acres and required notification to the Corps for any project over one acre.[15] Following increasing pressure from environmental interests and others, in 1996, the Corps reduced the acreage limits to three acres and the notification threshold to one-third of an acre.[16] During the 1996 reissuance, the Corps indicated that the NWPs would thereafter be issued "separately from the regulations governing their use" and according to new rules.[17] Reissued NWP 26 was particularly controversial. The National Home Builders Association challenged the 1996 reissuance of NWP 26 on three points: (1) the expiration of NWP 26 in only two years rather than five (on December 13, 1998); (2) the prohibition against filling or excavating more than 500 linear feet of stream bed under NWP 26; and (3) the prohibition against using other NWPs with NWP 26 to authorize the loss of more than three acres of waters of the United States. On October 27, 1997, a court order was issued remanding the action to the Corps to specifically solicit public comments on the three changes.[18] In 1998, in response to the public comments, the Corps published notice that it was not making any changes to the reissued NWP 26, with the exception that the expiration date for NWP 26 was changed to March 28, 1998.[19]

On March 9, 2000, a major shift occurred when the Corps issued the next round of NWPs.[20] Issuing so-called "replacement permits,"

14. *See* note 15, *supra*.

15. Final Rule for Issuance, Reissuance and Modification of Nationwide Permits, 65 Fed. Reg. 12818 (Mar. 9, 2000).

16. 61 Fed. Reg. 65874 (Sept. 13, 1996), *as amended by* Final Notice of Issuance and Modification of Nationwide Permits, 65 Fed. Reg. 12818 (Mar. 9, 2000).

17. Final Notice for Issuance, Reissuance, and Modification of Nationwide Permits, 61 Fed. Reg. 41206 (Dec. 13, 1996).

18. The notice soliciting additional public comments was published on November 26, 1997. 62 Fed. Reg. 63224, Comments were accepted until February 26, 1998.

19. 63 Fed. Reg. 39276 (July 22, 1998).

20. Final Notice of Issuance and Modification of Nationwide Permits, 65 Fed. Reg. 12818 (Mar. 9, 2000).

the Corps eliminated NWP 26, a general permit that regulated headwaters and isolated waters,[21] which had become very controversial.[22]

The 2000 NWP reissuance limited the use of the nationwide permits to projects in wetlands less than half an acre and up to two acres for most of the NWPs.[23] The new regulatory framework prohibited all permanent above-grade fills in the 100-year floodplain below the headwaters of any stream for the replacement NWPs that authorize residential, commercial, and institutional development activities, as well as mining and agriculture activities.[24] It prohibited permanent above-grade fills in headwaters within the regulatory "floodway," and required any above-grade fill in the "flood fringe" to meet standards set by the Federal Emergency Management Agency (FEMA).[25] It also prohibited using the new and modified NWPs in "critical resource" waters, such as state natural heritage sites, state-designated outstanding natural resource waters, habitats for endangered or threatened species, and waters designated by the Corps.[26] It also provided a 300 linear foot limit for filling and excavating in stream beds for development, agriculture, and mining activities under the NWPs.[27] It required "preconstruction notification" (PCN) to the Corps before most projects if they would impact more than one-tenth of an acre,[28] and lengthened the PCN review period to 45 days.[29] The Corps made some modifications to these "replacement" NWPs in 2002.[30]

In 2007, the Corps again amended the existing NWPs.[31] This round added new permits for emergency repair activities, discharges into

---

21. *See Nationwide Permits Chronology and Related Materials under CWA Section 404*, U.S. Env't Prot. Agency, https://www.epa.gov/cwa-404/nationwide-permits-chronology-and-related-materials-under-cwa-section-404 (going back to 1995).

22. *See* Jodi Finder & Steven M. Reiness, *General Permits under Wetlands Law: The Rise and Fall of Nationwide Permit 26*, 3 Env't L. 891 (1997); Julie Sibbing, Virginia S. Albrecht & Kim Diana Connolly, *Wise Replacements for NWP 26*? 20 Nat'l Wetlands Newsletter 7 (Sept.–Oct. 1998), https://digitalcommons.law.buffalo.edu/cgi/viewcontent.cgi?article=1656&context=journal_articles.

23. 65 Fed. Reg. at 12821 (2000).

24. *Id.* at 12859.

25. *Id.* at 12819.

26. *Id.* at 12873.

27. *Id.* at 12819.

28. *Id.*

29. *Id.*

30. Issuance of Nationwide Permits, 67 Fed. Reg. 2020 (Jan. 15, 2002).

31. Reissuance of Nationwide Permits, 72 Fed. Reg. 11092 (Mar. 12, 2007).

ditches and canals, pipeline safety program designated time-sensitive inspections and repairs, commercial shellfish aquaculture activities, coal remining activities, and underground coal mining activities.[32] The final issuance of the 2007 NWPs was delayed, and to make up time, the notice made clear that those NWPs were immediately effective, so long as any person wanting to act under their authority obtained a project-specific water quality certification under CWA Section 401,[33] or, where applicable, coastal zone management certification.[34] Thereafter, in the 60 days following issuance of the new NWPs, every state had the opportunity to issue, deny, or condition generic Section 401 certifications or Coastal Zone Management Act (CZMA)[35] concurrences, along with state conditions to the NWPs.[36] Corps division engineers also had (as always) the opportunity to add, after public review and consultation, regional conditions to protect local aquatic ecosystems such as fens or bottomland hardwoods, or to minimize adverse effects on fish or shellfish spawning, wildlife nesting, or other ecologically critical areas.[37]

New NWPs were issued on February 21, 2012.[38] Most of the comments following the draft issued by the Corps[39] concerned NWP 21,[40] a general permit regulating coal mining that had previously received considerable attention.[41] The Corps specifically solicited comments

32. *Id.* at 56273–56276.

33. 33 U.S.C. § 1341 (2023). For a discussion of the state water quality certification process, see Chapter 7.

34. 33 C.F.R. § 320.3(b) (2023). For a discussion of the state Coastal Zone Management certification process, *see* Chapter 7.

35. 16 U.S.C. 33, §§ 1451 *et seq.* (2023). *See generally* Coastal Zone Management Act, National Oceanic and Atmospheric Administration, Office for Coastal Management, https://coast.noaa.gov/czm/act/.

36. *See* 72 Fed. Reg. at 11092 (Mar. 12, 2007).

37. *See, e.g.*, 2020 Nationwide Permits and Regional Conditions, Request for Comments on Proposed Regional Conditions under Consideration by the South Pacific Division for Sacramento District in California, Nevada, and Utah, U.S. Army Corps of Eng'rs, Sacramento District, https://www.spk.usace.army.mil/Media/Regulatory-Public-Notices/Article/2355185/2020-nationwide-permits-and-regional-conditions-request-for-comments/.

38. Reissuance of Nationwide Permits, 77 Fed. Reg. 10184 (Feb. 21, 2012).

39. Proposal to Reissue and Modify Nationwide Permits, 76 Fed. Reg. 9174 (Feb. 21, 2012).

40. Reissuance of Nationwide Permits, 77 Fed. Reg. at 10185 (Feb. 21, 2012).

41. Thomas L. Casey & David W. Mitchell, *Has EPA's "War on Coal" Stalled?*, 27 Nat. Res. & Env't 3, at 20 (Winter 2013).

on three potential options regarding modifications to the 2007 NWP 21 for the 2012 update: (1) eliminate NWP 21, (2) reissue the permit with restrictions on the size of wetlands losses and a prohibition on the use of NWP 21 in association with valley fills; and (3) initiate the same size restrictions as in option 2, without language on valley fills.[42] Although most commenters urged the Corps to eliminate NWP 21 altogether, the Corps instead chose option 2 by reissuing NWP 21 in a form that restricted activity to a half-acre of non-tidal waters and 300 linear feet of stream bed,[43] and prohibited NWP 21 use for valley fills.[44] The Corps also issued two new NWPs[45] and three new general conditions.[46] Applicants for 2012 NWPs had to abide, as always, by general conditions that apply to all NWPs in addition to complying with the specific limitations of each NWP.[47]

The nationwide permit program has been the subject of a number of lawsuits over the years.[48] For example, in September 2006, the U.S. District Court for the District of Columbia issued a long-awaited ruling[49] regarding the 2000/2002 NWP issuance.[50] Members of the regu-

42. The Corps' preferred option was option 2. *See* Proposal to Reissue and Modify Nationwide Permits, 76 Fed. Reg. 9174, 9181 (Feb. 16, 2011).

43. The district engineer could waive the stream bed restriction for intermittent and ephemeral streams. Reissuance of Nationwide Permits, 77 Fed. Reg. at 10203.

44. Reissuance of Nationwide Permits, 77 Fed. Reg. at 10204–05 (Feb. 21, 2012).

45. NWPs 51 and 52 pertain to renewable energy. Reissuance of Nationwide Permits, 77 Fed. Reg. at 10235–41 (Feb. 21, 2012).

46. General conditions 19, 21, and 24 pertain to migratory birds, artifacts, and impoundment structures, respectively. Reissuance of Nationwide Permits, 77 Fed. Reg. at 10,249–52, 10,257 (Feb. 21, 2012).

47. U.S. Army Corps of Eng'rs, 2012 Nationwide Permits, Conditions, District Engineer's Decision, Further Information, and Definitions (with corrections), https://www.usace.army.mil/Missions/Civil-Works/Regulatory-Program-and-Permits/Nationwide-Permits/2012-Nationwide-Permits-Final-Decision-Documents/.

48. *See* Randall S. Guttery, Stephen L. Poe & C.F. Sirmans, Federal Wetlands Regulation: Restrictions on the Nationwide Permit Program and the Implications for Residential Property Owners, 37 Am. Bus. L.J. 299 (Winter 2000); James L. Conner II, Environmental Law—Nationwide Permits for Categories of Waters Issued by the Corps of Engineers under FWPCA Section 404: A Legitimate Administrative Interpretation Ratified by Congress?, 61 N.C.L. Rev. 904 (1983); John H. Cushman, Jr., U.S. Seeks Changes in Wetland Rules, but 2 Sides Criticize Plan, N.Y. Times (June 24, 1998), at A-20.

49. Nat'l Ass'n of Home Builders v. U.S. Army Corps of Eng'rs, 453 F. Supp. 2d 116 (D.D.C. 2006).

50. 65 Fed. Reg. 12818 (Mar. 9, 2000); 67 Fed. Reg. 2020 (Jan. 15, 2002).

lated community[51] had sued the Corps, asserting that the NWPs as issued exceeded the Corps' authority.[52] The court held that the Corps "adequately explained its reasoning behind its issuance of the NWPs and [general conditions] and clearly acted within its authority."[53]

A few days before the D.C. District Court decision, the Corps[54] released its Notice of Proposed Rulemaking regarding the proposed reissuance of NWPs.[55] One goal of the Corps in proposing these revisions to the NWPs was "to revise the text of the NWPs, general conditions, and definitions so that they are clearer, more concise, and can be more easily understood by the regulated public, government personnel, and interested parties, while retaining terms and conditions that protect the aquatic environment."[56]

A similar lawsuit was brought in 2012, when the Sierra Club and other plaintiffs sought a temporary restraining order and preliminary injunction in the Western District of Oklahoma to prevent construction of the Keystone XL pipeline.[57] One main argument in the plaintiffs' challenge was that the Corps violated the CWA by issuing NWP 12, which regulates utility lines. Plaintiffs argued that the permit violated the CWA in several ways: (1) its definition of "single and complete project," allowed impermissible piecemealing of projects and facilitated misleading calculations of total effects of those projects; (2) the NWP allowed conversion of one type of wetland to another; and (3) it did not require inter-agency coordination for each linear

51. Suits were originally filed by the National Association of Home Builders, the National Federation of Independent Business, and the National Stone, Sand and Gravel Association. *Supra* footnote 50.

52. National Ass'n of Home Builders, *supra* 453 F. Supp. 2d at 121. *See also* Amena H. Saiyid, *Corps Authority to Issue Nationwide Permits Upheld in Decision by U.S. District Court*, 190 BNA Daily Env't Report (Oct. 2, 2006), at A-7.

53. National Ass'n of Home Builders, 453 F. Supp. 2d at 136.

54. Because NWPs are considered permits, and not regulations, the EPA is not directly involved in the actual issuance of the proposed permits.

55. Proposal to Reissue and Modify Nationwide Permits, 71 Fed. Reg. 56258 (Sept. 26, 2006). *See also* Amena H. Saiyid, *Corps Proposes Six New Nationwide Permits Allowing Pipeline Repair, Mining in Wetlands*, 186 BNA Daily Env't Report (2006), at A-1.

56. Proposal to Reissue and Modify Nationwide Permits, 71 Fed. Reg. 56258 (Sept. 26, 2006).

57. Sierra Club, Inc. v. Bostick, 2012 W.L. 3230552 (2012). The plaintiffs also alleged the Corps' NWP 12 verifications issued to TransCanada were inappropriate. *Id.* at *7.

project.[58] Plaintiffs also raised a National Environmental Policy Act (NEPA)[59] argument that a blanket half-acre threshold was inappropriate without further discussion and that an environmental assessment (EA) was insufficient.[60] The court rejected those arguments[61] and also concluded that, for success, plaintiffs would have needed to show the Keystone XL project would have more than a minimal impact on the environment.[62] Six months after *Sierra Club v. Bostick* was decided, the District Court for the District of Columbia decided a similar case involving the construction of a pipeline in Arkansas,[63] likewise concluding that NWP 12 as issued in 2012 complied with both the CWA and NEPA.[64]

In 2016, Black Warrior Riverkeeper brought suit to challenge NWP 21, asserting that the reissued permit was arbitrary and capricious, because numeric limitations on new projects described as "necessary" to prevent more than minimal environmental harm were not imposed on existing projects.[65] The 11th Circuit found "that the Corps has provided a 'satisfactory explanation for its action' based on its findings in the Revised Decision Document, so we will (as we must) defer to its decision."[66]

More recently, a number of lawsuits were brought to challenge NWP 12,[67] which authorizes utility line activities involving pipes, cables, lines, and wires. Such lawsuits, brought before the permits were revised again in 2017, were largely unsuccessful.[68]

---

58. *Id.* at *3.

59. 42 U.S.C. §§ 4321 *et seq.* (2023), *see generally* Council on Env't Quality, NEPA.gov: National Environmental Policy Act, https://ceq.doe.gov/.

60. Sierra Club, Inc. v. Bostick, at *5–*6. The plaintiffs' claims can be found in the plaintiffs' complaint. Complaint for Declaratory and Injunctive Relief and Petition for Review of Agency Action at 92-141, Sierra Club, Inc. v. Bostick, 2012 WL 5199520 (W.D. Okla. 2012).

61. *See* Sierra Club v. Bostick, 2012 WL 3230552, at *3–*6.

62. *Id.* at *7.

63. *See* Ouachita Riverkeeper, Inc. v. Bostick, 938 F. Supp. 2d 32 (D.C. 2013).

64. *Id.* at 10–11.

65. Black Warrior v. U.S. Army Corps of Eng'rs, 833 F.3d 1274 (11th Cir. 2016).

66. *Id.* at 34.

67. While not the version of NWP 12 at issue in the litigation, NWP 12 as currently promulgated can be found at https://usace.contentdm.oclc.org/utils/getfile/collection/p16021coll7/id/16834.

68. *See, e.g.*, Mobile Baykeeper, Inc. v. U.S. Army Corps of Eng'rs, 2014 W.L. 5307850 (2014); and Sierra Club, Inc. v. Bostick, 787 F.3d 1043 (10th Cir. 2015).

In short, the NWP program remained controversial on multiple levels. The Congressional Research Service summarized the debate in a 2017 report by noting:

> Developers and other industry groups say that it is too complex and burdened with arbitrary restrictions that limit opportunities for an efficient permitting process and have little environmental benefit. Environmentalists say that it does not adequately protect aquatic resources, because the review procedures and permit requirements are less rigorous than those for individual permits and because the Corps fails to adequately track impacts on aquatic resources . . . at issue is whether the program has become so complex and expansive that it cannot either protect aquatic resources or provide for a fair regulatory system, which are its dual objectives. Controversies also exist about the use of specific nationwide permits for authorizing particular types of activities. . . .[69]

On January 13, 2021, the Corps reissued and modified 12 NWPs and issued four new ones,[70] for which the general conditions and definitions were also reissued and modified.[71] On December 27, 2021, a second final rule was issued in which the Corps reissued 40 existing NWPs and issued one new NWP,[72] to which the January general con-

69. Cong. Rsch. Serv., *The Army Corps of Engineers' Nationwide Permits Program: Issues and Regulatory Developments* (Jan. 12, 2017), Summary, https://www.everycrsreport.com/files/20170112_97-223_271c5b98b058e7b84bab465be90e05777cf735ea.pdf.

70. Reissuance and Modification of Nationwide Permits, 86 Fed. Reg. 2744 (Jan. 13, 2021), as corrected on May 20, 2021, 86 Fed. Reg. 27,274. The final rule replaced "12 of the existing NWPs that were published in the January 6, 2017, final rule (82 FR 1860), specifically: NWP 12 (oil or natural gas pipeline activities; NWP 21 (surface coal mining activities); NWP 29 (residential developments); NWP 39 (commercial and institutional developments); NWP 40 (agricultural activities); NWP 42 (recreational facilities); NWP 43 (stormwater management facilities); NWP 44 (mining activities); NWP 48 (commercial shellfish mariculture activities); NWP 50 (underground coal mining activities); NWP 51 (land-based renewable energy generation facilities); and NWP 52 (water-based renewable energy generation pilot projects). This final rule issues four new NWPs: NWP 55 (seaweed mariculture activities); NWP 56 (finfish mariculture activities); NWP 57 (electric utility line and telecommunications activities); and NWP 58 (utility line activities for water and other substances)." *Id.* at 2747.

71. *Id.* at 2744.

72. Reissuance and Modification of Nationwide Permits, 86 Fed. Reg. 73522 (Dec. 27, 2021).

ditions apply. Together, these "reissued NWPs have no major changes from 2017," but "will streamline the requirements of the Clean Water Act and the Rivers and Harbors Act of 1899."[73] Changes include modifications to NWPs 21, 29, 39, 40, 42, 43, 44, 50, 51, and 52, which were revised to remove the 300-linear-foot limit for losses of stream bed where the aggregate acreage limit for WOTUS loss is a half-acre.[74] New NWPs authorized in 2021 address structures in marine and estuarine waters, utility line activities, and dredge and fill discharges.[75]

This brief history of the permitting program will hopefully assist applicants in understanding the current program. The next section will help readers understand the parameters of the current NWP program.

III. Basics of General Permits

As discussed in the introduction and elsewhere in this book, Section 404 of the CWA mandates permits for many activities.[76] The streamlined process under CWA Section 404(e)[77] allows the Corps to issue general permits for categories of activities involving discharges of dredged or fill material into waters of the United States that are of a similar nature and cause only minimal adverse environmental effects when performed separately and considered cumulatively.[78]

Issued by the various Corps district and division offices, state and regional general permits vary in different areas of the country.[79] Determining which permits might be available in a particular area requires a potential applicant to contact district or regional offices of the Corps.[80] Similarly, programmatic permits "founded on an existing

73. Nationwide Permit Reissuance, U.S. Army Corps of Eng'rs (Jan. 2022), https://usace.contentdm.oclc.org/utils/getfile/collection/p16021coll7/id/19764.

74. *Id.* For a summary of all changes made, *see id.*

75. *Id.*

76. *See* U.S. Env't Prot. Agency, *Section 404 Permitting*, http://water.epa.gov/lawsregs/guidance/cwa/dredgdis/.

77. 33 U.S.C. § 1344(e) (2023).

78. *Id. See* Alaska Ctr. for the Env't v. West, 157 F.3d 680 (9th Cir. 1998).

79. For examples of these geographic differences, see U.S. Army Corps of Eng'rs, Jacksonville District. https://www.saj.usace.army.mil/Missions/Regulatory; U.S. Army Corps of Eng'rs, Portland District, Regulatory Branch http://www.nwwp.usace.army.mil/Missions/Regulatory.

80. Contact information for the various district offices can be found at U.S. Army Corps of Eng'rs, *Regulatory Contact Information*, https://www.usace.army.mil/Missions/Civil-Works/Regulatory-Program-and-Permits/Regulatory-Contacts/.

state, local or other Federal agency program [are] designed to avoid duplication with that program"[81] and vary across the country.[82] More information and examples of state and regional general permits are provided in a later section.

General permits undergo a programmatic review as a whole when they are issued, meaning that a practicable alternatives analysis,[83] public interest review,[84] compliance with the NEPA,[85] and analysis of other matters are not undertaken on a permit-by-permit basis, because these matters have been addressed programmatically.[86] As a result, the processing time for such permits is significantly reduced.[87] General permits include state, regional, programmatic, and nationwide general permits.[88]

---

81. 33 C.F.R. § 325.5(c)(3) (2023).

82. As an example, the State Programmatic General Permit (SPGP VI) State of Florida authorize five types of activities that "qualify for are authorized by the specific State of Florida Exemptions and General Permits cited below, as adopted by reference in Chapter 62-330, Florida Administrative Code (F.A.C.) and meet the activity description provided in" the SPGP VI Conditions. https://www.saj.usace.army.mil/SPGP/ (effective July 27, 2021).

83. 40 C.F.R. § 230.10(a) (2023). "Despite the fact that many NWPs authorize discharges of dredged or fill material into special aquatic sites, they are still in compliance with the 404(b)(1) Guidelines. Section 230.7 of the 404(b)(1) Guidelines does not prohibit the use of NWPs to authorize discharges of dredged or fill material into special aquatic sites. Many NWPs contain additional provisions to protect special aquatic sites." 77 Fed. Reg. at 10187 (Feb. 21, 2012).

84. 33 C.F.R. § 320.4(a) (2023).

85. "In order to address the requirements of the National Environmental Policy Act, the Corps prepares a decision document for each NWP along with a 404(b)(1) Guidelines analysis." 72 Fed. Reg. at 11117 (Mar. 12, 2007).

86. *See* U.S. Army Corps of Eng'rs, *2021 Nationwide Permits Final Decision Documents,* https://www.usace.army.mil/Missions/Civil-Works/Regulatory-Program-and-Permits/Nationwide-Permits/. Each decision document includes a discussion of compliance with applicable laws, consideration of public comments, an alternatives analysis, and a general assessment of individual and cumulative impacts, including the general potential effects on public interest factors.

87. In reporting on the new NWPs, the National Law Review reported that, in fiscal year 2018, the average time to process a standard individual permit application was 264 days, while the average time to process a NWP authorization was 45 days. Andrew J. Turner & Brian R. Levey, *Army Corps Finalizes Nationwide Permit Renewal for Expedited Clean Water Act Permitting* Nat'l Law Rev. (Jan. 7, 2022), Clean Water Act Permit Rule Finalized by Army Corps (natlawreview.com).

88. See a detailed overview of general permits at Theda Braddock & Lisa Bernstein, Wetlands: An Introduction to Ecology, the Law, and Permitting 46–84 (2d ed. 2007).

As is true of individual permits, the relevant state(s) must certify that any discharge associated with an NWP will meet applicable requirements under CWA Section 401.[89] Accordingly, when the Corps proposes a nationwide (or regional) permit, a state may say that, as a whole, the permit does not meet CWA state requirements, thereby "denying" the blanket certification within that state.[90]

The Corps issued revised NWPs in 2021 (which it must do every five years).[91] The 2021 issuances included 57 total NWPs, which comprised 52 reissued NWPs and five new NWPs. The complete list of current NWPs is as follows:

1. Aids to Navigation
2. Structures in Artificial Canals
3. Maintenance
4. Fish and Wildlife Harvesting, Enhancement, and Attraction Devices and Activities
5. Scientific Measurement Devices
6. Survey Activities
7. Outfall Structures and Associated Intake Structures
8. Oil and Gas Structures on the Outer Continental Shelf
9. Structures in Fleeting and Anchorage Areas
10. Mooring Buoys
11. Temporary Recreational Structures
12. Oil or Natural Gas Pipeline Activities[92]
13. Bank Stabilization
14. Linear Transportation Projects
15. U.S. Coast Guard Approved Bridges

---

89. 33 U.S.C. §1341 (2023); 33 C.F.R. § 330 (2023).

90. *See, e.g.*, U.S. Army Corps of Eng'rs, Walla Walla District, *Water Quality Certification*, https://media.defense.gov/2021/Feb/28/2002590309/-1/-1/1/IDEQ_FINAL%20401%20WQC_2021%20NWPS.PDF (listing which 2021 NWPs the Idaho Department of Environmental Quality (IDEQ) certified and which NWPs they denied).

91. 33 C.F.R. § 330.5 (2023).

92. Oil and natural gas pipelines where originally included with other types of utility line activities; in light of the NWP 12 litigation just noted (*see supra* notes 58–65), it was recognized that oil and gas pipelines were often different in effect and nature than other types of utility line activities. Therefore, NWP 12 is now restricted to oil and natural gas pipelines meeting the NWP thresholds, while new NWP 57 addresses Electric Utility Line and Telecommunications Activities and NWP 58 governs Utility Line Activities for Water and Other Substances.

16. Return Water From Upland Contained Disposal Areas
17. Hydropower Projects
18. Minor Discharges
19. Minor Dredging
20. Response Operations for Oil and Hazardous Substances
21. Surface Coal Mining Operations
22. Removal of Vessels
23. Approved Categorical Exclusions
24. Indian Tribe or State Administered Section 404 Programs
25. Structural Discharges
26. [Reserved]
27. Aquatic Habitat Restoration, Establishment, and Enhancement Activities
28. Modifications of Existing Marinas
29. Residential Developments
30. Moist Soil Management for Wildlife
31. Maintenance of Existing Flood Control Facilities
32. Completed Enforcement Actions
33. Temporary Construction, Access, and Dewatering
34. Cranberry Production Activities
35. Maintenance Dredging of Existing Basins
36. Boat Ramps
37. Emergency Watershed Protection and Rehabilitation
38. Cleanup of Hazardous and Toxic Waste
39. Commercial and Institutional Developments
40. Agricultural Activities
41. Reshaping Existing Drainage Ditches
42. Recreational Facilities
43. Stormwater Management Facilities
44. Mining Activities
45. Repair of Uplands Damaged by Discrete Events
46. Discharges in Ditches
47. [Reserved][93]

93. Previously, NWP 47 authorized Pipeline Safety Program Designated Time Sensitive Inspections and Repairs; this NWP 47 authorized inspection, repair, rehabilitation, or replacement of any currently serviceable structure or fill for pipelines that have been identified by the U.S. Department of Transportation (DOT) Pipeline and Hazardous Materials Safety Administration's (PHMSA) Pipeline Safety Program as time-sensitive. This NWP was allowed to expire in 2012 because activities it

48. Commercial Shellfish Mariculture Activities
49. Coal Remining Activities
50. Underground Coal Mining Activities
51. Land-Based Renewable Energy Generation Facilities
52. Water-Based Renewable Energy Generation Pilot Projects
53. Removal of Low-Head Dams
54. Living Shorelines
55. Seaweed Mariculture Activities
56. Finfish Mariculture Activities
57. Electric Utility Line and Telecommunications Activities
58. Utility Line Activities for Water and Other Substances
59. Water Reclamation and Reuse Facilities

As can be seen from this list, the types of activities governed by NWPs vary, but include a variety of minor development, maintenance, and other activities. Certain districts post information on their websites about particular general permit applications,[94] but some do not. Most NWPs have acreage and linear feet limitations as well as other conditions, which should be carefully reviewed; many also require pre-construction notification to the Corps before activities under the permit can begin.[95] See the Appendix to this chapter for a summary of basic requirements associated with each current NWP.[96] A summary of the limits follows.

A. Limits on NWPs

Division Engineers may, after opportunity for public comment, modify, suspend, or revoke NWPs for specific geographic areas, classes of activities, or classes of waters.[97] Many Corps Districts and Divisions

authorized can be accomplished under other NWPs, such as NWP 3 or NWP 12. *See* 76 Fed. Reg. at 9180.

94. *See, e.g.*, U.S. Army Corps of Eng'rs, Albuquerque District, *Regional Conditions to the 2021 Nationwide Permits in the State of Colorado*, https://www.spa.usace.army.mil/Portals/16/docs/civilworks/regulatory/Regional%20Conditions/2021%20Regional%20Conditions/Appendix%204%20Colorado%20Regional%20Conditions%202021_Final_2022_02_17.pdf?ver=mRqAwqb7_kDxH5FJZcquHA%3d%3d.

95. The general conditions are discussed in Part III.B of this chapter.

96. For complete information about the 2021 NWPs, *see* https://www.usace.army.mil/Missions/Civil-Works/Regulatory-Program-and-Permits/Nationwide-Permits/.

97. 33 C.F.R. § 330.4 (2023).

have such regional conditions in place.[98] States may veto or condition NWPs in their jurisdiction either by denying or conditioning a Section 401 certification[99] or by denying or conditioning a CZMA consistency determination (where coastal zone consistency is required).[100]

The NWPs themselves state the specific conditions an activity must meet in order for the activity to be eligible for the NWP. First, the activity must be within the category of activity covered by the NWP.[101] In addition to being within the correct category, however, the activity must also stay below the designated impact thresholds for the NWP, which vary based on the NWP. Common—although not uniform—thresholds include limiting impacts to no more than one-half acre of non-tidal WOTUS.[102] A number of the NWPs require the applicant to submit a pre-construction notification (PCN) to the Corps prior to commencing the work; sometimes the PCN is required only if certain thresholds will be exceeded.[103] In additional to the conditions specific to the NWP, each activity eligible for an NWP must also comply with the general conditions applicable to all of the NWPs.

---

98. Because there is no centralized collection of these conditions, a search online or a call to the relevant office(s) is the best course of action in terms of finding applicable conditions.

99. EPA's rules at 40 C.F.R. pt. 121, effective July 1, 2021, address Section 401 certification generally.

100. RGL 92-04, *Section 401 Water Quality Certification and Coastal Zone Management Act Conditions for Nationwide Permits*, discusses the relationship between Section 401 certifications, CZMA determinations, and NWPs. RGL 92-04 expired in 1997.

101. For example, a solar project would by the type of activity potentially qualified to use NWP 51, Land-Based Renewable Energy Generation Facilities, which covers "Discharges of dredged or fill material into non-tidal waters of the United States for the construction, expansion, or modification of land-based renewable energy production facilities, including attendant features. Such facilities include infrastructure to collect solar (concentrating solar power and photovoltaic), wind, biomass, or geothermal energy. Attendant features may include, but are not limited to roads, parking lots, and stormwater management facilities within the land-based renewable energy generation facility." 86 Fed. Reg. at 2863.

102. *Id.* NWP 51 also prohibits use of the NWP in wetlands that are adjacent to tidal waters.

103. *Id.* NWP 51 requires a PCN be submitted if the discharge will result in the loss of more than 1/10th an acre of WOTUS.

B. General Conditions

General conditions apply to all NWPs. As set forth in the 2021 NWP note to the general conditions, the Corps specifies that NWP qualification requires a prospective permittee to "comply with the following general conditions, as applicable, in addition to any regional or case-specific conditions imposed by the division engineer or district engineer. Prospective permittees should contact the appropriate Corps district office to determine if regional conditions have been imposed on an NWP."[104] In short, on top of specifications set forth in each NWP, mandated conditions apply to each action that proceeds pursuant to an NWP.[105] General conditions are modified and their numbers expanded each time NWPs are reissued.[106]

The following table is a summary table of the 2021 general conditions. However, most general permits are nuanced and very explicit, and should therefore be reviewed with each particular proposed activity in mind. Some conditions may preclude certain activities from proceeding under an NWP, such as projects that would jeopardize an endangered species,[107] violate FEMA requirements,[108] impair tribal rights such as reserved water rights or treaty fishing and hunting rights,[109] or otherwise violate the conditions summarized briefly in the table on the following pages.

104. *2021 Nationwide Permit General Conditions*, https://usace.contentdm.oclc.org/utils/getfile/collection/p16021coll7/id/20099.

105. 33 C.F.R. § 330.4(c) (2023).

106. Margaret "Peggy" Strand & Lowell M. Rothschild, Wetlands Deskbook 69 (3d ed. 2009).

107. 86 Fed. Reg. at 2868–69 (General Condition 18).

108. *Id.* at 2868 (General Condition 10).

109. *Id.* (General Condition 17).

2021 Nationwide Permit General Conditions[110]

	General Condition	Summary of Prospective Permittee Responsibilities
1	Navigation	Projects must have no more than a minimal effect on navigation, lights and signals must comply with Coast Guard rules, and the Corps may require changes to and removal of completed structures.
2	Aquatic Life Movements	Projects must have no substantial impact on life cycle movements of species indigenous to the site, including migratory species, with some exceptions.
3	Spawning Areas	Activities in spawning areas should be avoided to the maximum extent practicable, and physical destruction is not allowed.
4	Migratory Bird Breeding Areas	Activities in migratory bird breeding areas should be avoided to the maximum extent practicable.
5	Shellfish Beds	Other than activities authorized by NWPs 4, 27, or 48, projects are not allowed in shellfish habitat.
6	Suitable Material	Activities must use both suitable and nontoxic material.
7	Water Supply Intakes	Activities are not allowed near public water intakes, unless for maintenance of those intakes or adjacent bank stabilization.
8	Adverse Effects from Impoundments	Impoundment effects should be minimized to the maximum extent practicable.
9	Management of Water Flows	Activities must have the smallest possible effect on the flow and location of open waters, with some exceptions.
10	Fills within 100-Year Floodplains	FEMA requirements must be followed in 100-year floodplains.
11	Equipment	Soil disturbance by equipment must be minimized.

110. The official description of current general conditions in a combined format can be found on the U.S. Army Corps of Engineers website. U.S. Army Corps of Eng'rs, *The 2021 Nationwide Permits, General Conditions, District Engineer's Decision, Further Information, and Definitions,* https://usace.contentdm.oclc.org/utils/getfile/collection/p16021coll7/id/20099. The Federal Register Notice details the general conditions as well. 86 Fed. Reg. at 2867-74.

	General Condition	**Summary of Prospective Permittee Responsibilities**
12	Soil Erosion and Sediment Controls	Appropriate steps must be taken to prevent erosion and control sediment, including soil stabilization. Preference is for work to take place during low-flow or dry seasons.
13	Removal of Temporary Fills	Following removal of temporary fills, the site must be returned to its pre-construction characteristics, including elevation.
14	Proper Maintenance	Maintenance shall be performed to ensure public safety and continued compliance with general conditions and any applicable specific conditions from the district.
15	Single and Complete Project	No NWP may be used for more than one single and complete project.
16	Wild and Scenic Rivers	NWPs may not be used for activities in national wild and scenic rivers, or rivers being studied for inclusion on that list, unless the relevant federal agency acknowledges in writing that the project will not impact the river's status.
17	Tribal Rights	Activities must not adversely impact reserved tribal rights, including water, treaty fishing, and hunting rights.
18	Endangered Species	Activities must not imperil the existence of endangered or threatened species. PCNs are required for any potential impacts to a listed species by nonfederal permittees, and federal agencies must follow ESA requirements.
19	Migratory Birds and Bald and Golden Eagles	Activities must comply with permitting requirements of the Migratory Bird Treaty Act and the Bald and Golden Eagle Protection Act, and "incidental take" permits may be required.
20	Historic Properties	Activities affecting sites in the National Register of Historic Places, as well as those eligible for inclusion in that list, must comply with the requirements of Section 106 of the National Historic Preservation Act as well as additional requirements.

	General Condition	Summary of Prospective Permittee Responsibilities
21	Discovery of Previously Unknown Remains and Artifacts	If any remains and artifacts are found during completion of the activity, the Corps must be notified and those remains or artifacts must be avoided until it is determined whether the site warrants inclusion in the National Register of Historic Places.
22	Designated Critical Resource Waters	Activities in waters designated as critical resources by federal or state governments will receive additional scrutiny, and some permits will not apply.
23	Mitigation	The Corps determines necessary mitigation to ensure impacts are no more than minimal. Compensatory mitigation is required for total wetland losses greater than 1/10 acre; other requirements may be triggered depending on the impacted waters.
24	Safety of Impoundment Structures	The Corps may require documentation showing the safety of impoundment structures.
25	Water Quality	Activities must be certified to be in compliance with CWA Section 401, either programmatically or individually.
26	Coastal Zone Management	For activities in coastal zones, state coastal zone management consistency, concurrence, or a presumption of same is required.
27	Regional and Case-by-Case Conditions	Activities must comply with Corps regional conditions, as well as any applicable federal, state, or tribal conditions.
28	Use of Multiple Nationwide Permits	Activities involving a single and complete project must only use one NWP, except when acreage of lost wetlands is less than the highest acreage limit for the NWPs used.
29	Transfer of Nationwide Permit Verifications	Permit verification may be transferred when the project site is sold, if the Corps is notified.
30	Compliance Certification	The Corps must receive signed notification of activity completion confirming compliance with the NWP as well as mitigation completion.

	General Condition	Summary of Prospective Permittee Responsibilities
31	Activities Affecting Structures or Works Built by the United States	Pre-construction notification is required if the activity will alter or temporarily or permanently occupy or use a Corps federally authorized civil works project.
32	Pre-Construction Notification (PCN)	The PCN should be submitted as early as possible, meet specific guidelines, and must be in writing. The PCN must include (1) the prospective permittee's contact information, (2) activity location, (3) state in which NWP(s) are being sought, (4) activity description, (5) delineation of wetlands and other waters on the project site, (6) proposed mitigation (if required), (7) name of endangered or threatened species that might be affected, (8) impact on historic properties, (9) identify wild and scenic rivers if applicable, and (10) comply with certain requirements if an authorized civil works project will be impacted. Coordination with other agencies may be required.

IV. Other General Permits

As explained in the introduction to this chapter, Congress approved so-called "general" permits to streamline the permitting process.[111] The majority of the general permits used today are NWPs, discussed in the previous section. But courts have supported the Corps' general permitting authority through general regional and state permits as well.[112]

Authorized by Section 404(e) and issued by the various Corps district and division offices, state and regional general permits vary in different areas of the country.[113] Pursuant to Section 404(e), they must authorize only activities that are both similar in nature and cause

111. Legislative History of the Clean Water Act of 1977, Cong. Rsch. Serv., 95th Cong., 2d Sess. 902, 903 (No. 95-14, Oct. 1978), at 349. 3 U.S.C. Cong. & Admin. News 4326, 4405, Pub. L. No 95-217, 91 Stat. 1566, 95th Cong., 1st Sess. (1977). *See also* 33 C.F.R. § 320.1(c).

112. *See, e.g.*, Alaska Ctr. for the Env't v. West, 157 F.3d 680 (9th Cir. 1998).

113. *See* Nat'l Ass'n of Wetland Managers, *State Programmatic General Permits*, https://www.nawm.org/wetland-programs/regulation/programmatic-general-permits.

only minimal adverse environmental effects when performed separately and considered cumulatively.[114] The Corps has issued general regulatory parameters for such permits.[115] To determine what permits might be available in a particular area, applicants should contact district or regional offices of the Corps. Likewise, programmatic permits "founded on an existing state, local or other Federal agency program [are] designed to avoid duplication with that program"[116] and vary across the country.

A. Regional General Permit Examples

Regional general permits usually cover common approvals sought in particular geographic areas. Potential permit applicants should check relevant district websites or call district or division offices to ascertain what might be available. Following are a few examples of permits available only in specific regions.

The Wilmington District has multiple regional general permits, including for marsh sills and a local coastal management act.[117] The Portland District has multiple general permits, including for aquatic habitat restoration in Oregon and discharges into vernal pools in a particular county.[118] The Jacksonville District also has multiple general permits, many of which are limited to certain geographic areas of the state.[119] More examples can be found on various district websites or by calling the district or division.

B. State Programmatic General Permits

State programmatic general permits (SPGPs) are time-limited authorizations for a state agency, designed to eliminate duplication of effort

114. 33 U.S.C. § 1344(e) (2023).

115. 33 C.F.R. §§ 322.2(f), 323.2(h), 325.2(e)(2) (2023).

116. *Id.* § 325.5(c)(3).

117. U.S. Army Corps of Eng'rs, Wilmington District, *Regional General Permits*, https://www.saw.usace.army.mil/Missions/Regulatory-Permit-Program/Permits/Regional-General-Permits/.

118. U.S. Army Corps of Eng'rs, *About Nationwide and Regional General Permits*, https://www.nwp.usace.army.mil/Missions/Regulatory/Nationwide/.

119. U.S. Army Corps of Eng'rs, Jacksonville District, *Source Book, General Permits*, https://www.saj.usace.army.mil/Missions/Regulatory/Source-Book/.

and allow for flexibility in particular geographic areas. In some districts, NWPs may be suspended in recognition of SPGPs.[120]

An SPGP "is the written vehicle identifying the terms, limitations, and conditions under which specific projects regulated by [an existing state, local, or federal authority] may be authorized under the Corps Regulatory Program with a much more efficient and abbreviated review by the Corps."[121]

SPGPs are developed in recognition of existing or planned state regulatory programs that, although not federally approved for full assumption pursuant to Section 404(g), are as protective or more protective of some or all of the waters regulated by the Corps pursuant to Section 404 of the Clean Water Act. More detail about the state assumption process can be found in Chapter 7.[122]

In the absence of an SPGP, a person seeking authority to fill wetlands might need to obtain separate state and federal individual permits invoking duplicative regulatory measures. While the SPGP does not completely eliminate Corps involvement over such activities, it can substantially reduce requirements and procedures for permit applicants, promoting more effective and efficient use of Corps regulatory resources.[123]

Under Section 404(e), not only must SPGPs be reviewed and reissued every five years for all permits,[124] but the Corps must also conduct periodic reviews of SPGPs to ensure that the state program is continuing to provide environmental protection at least equivalent to that which would otherwise be provided by the overall Corps Section 404 program.[125]

SPGP programs can be implemented gradually by, for example, instituting a program for a single watershed. The Corps has emphasized

120. *See* U.S. Army Corps of Eng'rs, Philadelphia District, *State Programmatic General Permits*, http://www.nap.usace.army.mil/Missions/Regulatory/Permits/SPGP.aspx.

121. *Id.*

122. *See* Chapter 7.

123. Proposed Regulatory Guidance Letter on Programmatic General Permits, 61 Fed. Reg. 18,575, 18,575 (Apr. 26, 1996), https://www.govinfo.gov/content/pkg/FR-1996-04-26/pdf/96-10334.pdf#page=1.

124. 33 U.S.C. § 1344(e).

125. 61 Fed. Reg. at 18,578. The frequency of review is discretionary. ("The Corps may conduct an annual review of the [SPGP], may require annual reporting by the [State] . . . or may conduct an overall review prior to expiration of the [SPGP] for consideration in the reevaluation of the [SPGP] for reissuance."). *Id.*

that "[o]ne of the key benefits of [SPGPs] is the flexibility they afford [states] in terms of the projects regulated and the geographic scope of regulation."[126] Likewise, SPGPs can apply to waters that would be excluded from assumption authority under Section 404(g), and can be flexibly tailored for a particular activity.[127] Furthermore, because SPGPs apply only to de minimis activities, federal oversight is limited. In many cases, states are likely to have a more thorough understanding of local issues and wetland areas than the federal government does.

Following are a few examples of permits available only in specific states.

Pennsylvania has developed an SPGP covering private residential construction in wetlands.[128] The permit authorizes the placement and maintenance of fill in, or the excavation of, non-tidal wetlands for the construction or expansion of single-family homes for the personal residence of the permittee, including reasonable and necessary features such as a driveway, storage shed, and utilities on a residential lot purchased by the permittee prior to November 22, 1991, where activities do not impact more than a half-acre of non-tidal wetland.[129]

---

126. *Id.* at 18,576. For an example of a limited SPGP, see Dep't of the Army Gen. Permit New Jersey-SPGP-17, https://www.nap.usace.army.mil/Portals/39/docs/regulatory/publicnotices/SPGP-17-NJ-Jan-2018.pdf (This general permit authorizes the construction of structures; performance of work and the discharge of dredged and fill material in substantially developed artificial tidal lagoons and their access channel).

127. For example, the SPGP for Florida covers work in marine waters that would be exempt from state permitting if certain thresholds are maintained. U.S. Army Corps of Eng'rs, Jacksonville District, *State Programmatic General Permit (SPGP)*, https://www.saj.usace.army.mil/SPGP/. Regulation of marine waters cannot be assumed by states pursuant to Section 404(g). 33 U.S.C. § 1344(g)(1) ("The Governor of any State desiring to administer its own individual and general permit program for the discharge of dredged or fill material into the navigable waters (other than those waters which are presently used, or are susceptible to use in their natural condition or by reasonable improvement as a means to transport interstate or foreign commerce shoreward to their ordinary high water mark, including all waters which are subject to the ebb and flow of the tide shoreward to their mean high water mark, or mean higher high water mark on the west coast, including wetlands adjacent thereto) within its jurisdiction may submit to the Administrator a full and complete description of the program it proposes to establish and administer under State law or under an interstate compact.").

128. Pa. Dep't of Env't Prot., *Chapter 105 General Permits*, https://www.dep.pa.gov/Business/Water/Waterways/Encroachments/PermittingAndAuthorizations/Pages/Chapter-105-General-Permits.aspx.

129. *Id.*

Wisconsin has an SPGP for "small wetland impacts" associated with commercial, residential, and industrial activities.[130] This general permit expedites projects resulting in the unavoidable filling of less than 10,000 square feet of wetlands if the project meets certain specifications and conditions, including specific location, design, and construction standards to ensure that minimal environmental effects occur.[131]

Utah has issued a statewide general permit for certain activities that have been authorized under the state's "Stream Alteration Program."[132] The permit applies to activities that minimally impact natural streams in Utah, including, but not limited to, culvert installation and replacement, bridges, low-water crossings, utility crossings, bank stabilization, linear transportation projects, maintenance of previously permitted activities, diversion structures, outfall structures, boat ramps, docks, commercial and residential construction, and flood control facilities.[133]

Florida has issued a statewide programmatic general permit for five types of activities that also qualify for specific state of Florida exemptions or general permits: shoreline stabilization (such as seawalls or riprap), boat ramps, docks, derelict vessel removal, and scientific devices.[134]

Those who may not qualify for a general permit of any kind may nevertheless be able to get a streamlined individual permitting process through a "letter of permission" (LOP), which the Corps defines as "a type of permit issued through an abbreviated processing procedure which includes coordination with Federal and state fish and wildlife agencies . . . and a public interest evaluation, but without the publishing of an individual public notice."[135] Certain dredging, in-water

130. Wis. Dep't of Nat. Res., *Wetland General Permit for Commercial, Residential, and Industrial Activities*, https://dnr.wisconsin.gov/sites/default/files/topic/Wetlands/DNR_General_Permit_01_2023_Wetland_Commercial_Residential_Industrial.pdf.

131. *Id.*

132. U.S. Army Corps of Eng'rs, *Programmatic General Permit 40: Minimal Impact Activities under the Stream Alteration Program in the State of Utah*, http://www.waterrights.utah.gov/strmalt/whitepapers/PGP40.pdf.

133. *Id.*

134. U.S. Army Corps of Eng'rs, Jacksonville District, *State Programmatic General Permit (SPGP)*, https://www.saj.usace.army.mil/SPGP/.

135. 33 C.F.R. § 325. 2(e)(1) (2023). Letters of permission require that (1) the activity must fall under a district engineer-created "list of categories of activities proposed for authorization under [letters of permission] procedures"; (2) the proposed

structures, and small marinas or multifamily piers are some of the types of activities that can qualify to use an LOP.[136] The LOP evaluation includes a 15-day comment period with state and federal agencies and adjacent property owners, rather than the full public notice process. A final decision is typically reached within 120 days from the date a complete application is received.[137]

Activities that do not qualify for any streamlined permitting procedure must proceed through the individual permitting process.[138]

V. Conclusion

The particulars of the Corps' Nationwide Permit Program are unpopular with many. Yet, the overall regulatory program could not function without such streamlining absent a significant investment of resources. Debates will continue, resulting in lawsuits and lengthy comments every five years on each new set of nationwide permits. Nevertheless, the vast majority of permitting actions will continue through such general permits, and familiarity with them is essential to those who are regulated by or practice in this area.

---

list is subject to public notice and comment and an opportunity for public hearing; and (3) state certification pursuant to Section 401 of the CWA has been issued or waived and applicable Coastal Zone Management consistency determinations have been made and concurred in by affected states. 33 C.F.R. § 325.2(e)(1)(ii)(A)–(C) (2023). *See also* U.S. Army Corps of Eng'rs, Jacksonville District, *Letter of Permission*, https://www.saj.usace.army.mil/Missions/Regulatory/Source-Book/.

136. *See* Public Notice, LOP categories of work - Project Management Reports (May 21, 1996), https://usace.contentdm.oclc.org/digital/collection/p16021coll7/id/17867.

137. *See* U.S. Army Corps of Eng'rs, Jacksonville District, *Letter of Permission*, https://www.saj.usace.army.mil/Missions/Regulatory/Source-Book/.

138. "Those activities that do not qualify for NWP authorization may be authorized by . . . individual permits." 72 Fed. Reg. at 11094 (Sept. 20, 2007).

6
CHAPTER

Satisfying Section 404 Mitigation Requirements

I. Introduction and Summary

The so-called 404(b)(1) Guidelines[1] mandate that an applicant for an individual permit for a Clean Water Act (CWA) Section 404[2] permit must first avoid impacts to wetlands (and other aquatic areas) to the extent practicable.[3] Then, following this avoidance step, the applicant must take "appropriate and practicable steps" to minimize potential adverse impacts of the discharge on these aquatic resources.[4] For any adverse impacts to the aquatic ecosystem that cannot be avoided and minimized, compensatory mitigation must be provided to offset all

1. 40 C.F.R. pt. 230 (2023).

2. 33 U.S.C. § 1344 (2018). The Federal Water Pollution Control Act (FWPCA) is commonly referred to as the Clean Water Act following the 1977 amendments to the FWPCA. Pub. L. No. 95-217, 91 Stat. 1566 (1977) ("Sec. 518. This Act may be cited as the 'Federal Water Pollution Control Act' commonly referred to as the Clean Water Act.").

3. As explained in Chapter 4, pursuant to the 404(b)(1) Guidelines, the U.S. Army Corps of Engineers (Corps) cannot issue the permit "if there is a practicable alternative to the proposed discharge which would have less adverse impact on the aquatic ecosystem so long as the alternative does not have other significant adverse environmental consequences." 40 C.F.R. § 230.10(a).

4. 40 C.F.R. § 230.10(d). *See* Chapter 4.

unavoidable impacts. Assuming that the United States has jurisdiction over a particular wetland or other water,[5] as well as jurisdiction over the proposed activity,[6] virtually all individual permits and many general permits require compensatory mitigation.[7] This "central premise of Federal wetland regulatory programs"[8] thus creates what is referred to as the three key steps that are generally applied sequentially in the following order in the "mitigation sequence": (1) avoidance, (2) minimization, and (3) compensation.[9] Avoid, minimize, then compensate sounds straightforward, but in many cases, compliance with mitigation obligations can become a multilevel and complex determination.

An additional underlying policy triggered by mitigation requirements is the attempt to achieve a goal of "no net loss" of wetland functions and values.[10] Talked about often, this is sometimes mislead-

5. *See* Chapter 2.

6. *See* Chapter 3.

7. *See generally* 33 C.F.R. § 320.4(r) (2023). Nationwide permits that require pre-construction notice and other types of general permits may also require compensatory mitigation, in the discretion of the Corps. *Reissuance and Modification of Nationwide Permits*, 86 Fed. Reg. 2744, 2870-72 (Jan. 13, 2021), as corrected on May 20, 2021, 86 Fed. Reg. 27274 ("The district engineer will consider the following factors when determining appropriate and practicable mitigation necessary to ensure that the individual and cumulative adverse environmental effects [of discharges qualifying for the use of nationwide permits requiring pre-construction notice to the Corps] are no more than minimal.") *See* Chapter 5 for a discussion of nationwide permits. For a chronology of the mitigation rule and links to regulatory guidance letters on the mitigation program, *see* U.S. Army Corps of Eng'rs Headquarters website, *Mitigation Information*, http://www.usace.army.mil/Missions/CivilWorks/RegulatoryProgramandPermits/mitig_info.aspx; *see also* Royal C. Gardner et al., *Compensating for Wetland Losses under the Clean Water Act (Redux): Evaluating the Federal Compensatory Mitigation Regulation*, 38 STETSON L. REV. 213 (2009).

8. White House Office on Env't Policy, *Protecting America's Wetlands: A Fair, Flexible, and Effective Approach* (Aug. 24, 1993), https://www.saj.usace.army.mil/Portals/44/docs/regulatory/sourcebook/regulations_policies/wetland_policy1995.pdf#:~:text=After%20hearing%20from%20States%2C%20developers%2C%20farmers%2C%20environmental%20interests%2C,Administration%20Wetlands%20Plan%20was%20issued%20in%20August%201993.

9. *See* Env't Prot. Agency, *Types of Mitigation under CWA Section 404: Avoidance, Minimization and Compensatory Mitigation*, https://www.epa.gov/cwa-404/types-mitigation-under-cwa-section-404-avoidance-minimization-and-compensatory-mitigation#:~:text=Clean%20Water%20Act-,Types%20of%20Mitigation%20under%20CWA%20Section,Avoidance%2C%20Minimization%20and%20Compensatory%20Mitigation (last visited August 19, 2023).

10. *See* Env't Prot. Agency; the U.S. Army Corps of Eng'rs; and the U.S. Dep'ts of Agric., Commerce, Interior, and Transp., *National Wetlands Mitigation Action Plan*

ing because the U.S. Environmental Protection Agency (EPA) and the Corps believe compensatory mitigation may not be practicable and appropriate for every permit action.[11] Accordingly, the "no net loss" goal has never been translated into mandatory limits on each permit decision.

The current regulations for compensatory mitigation were issued in April 2008, following tumultuous decades in the wetlands mitigation arena. That year concluded an extended process through which the Corps and EPA issued long-awaited new regulations.[12] These regulations set forth revised and detailed parameters for appropriate "actions taken to offset unavoidable adverse impacts to wetlands, streams, and other aquatic resources authorized by CWA section 404."[13] This chapter provides readers with a brief history of compensatory mitigation, current regulatory requirements, and tips for complying with those requirements.

II. Overview of the Compensatory Mitigation Rules

The Corps and ERP Compensatory Mitigation Rules regulations supersede all previous mitigation requirements,[14] including Regulatory Guidance Letter 02-2[15] and parts of the 1990 Memorandum of

1 (Dec. 24, 2002), https://www.spl.usace.army.mil/Portals/17/docs/regulatory/Mitigation/UsefulLinks/Nat%27l_Wetland_Mit_Action_Plan.pdf (last visited August 19, 2023). Although the current regulatory language does not use the actual term "no net loss," it does state that the "fundamental objective of compensatory mitigation is to offset environmental losses resulting from unavoidable impacts to waters of the United States." Compensatory Mitigation for Losses of Aquatic Resources, 73 Fed. Reg. 19,594, 19,672 (Apr. 10, 2008) (codified at 33 C.F.R. pts. 325, 332 and 40 C.F.R. pt. 230).

11. Memorandum of Agreement between the Environmental Protection Agency and the Department of the Army Concerning the Determination of Mitigation under the Clean Water Act Section 404(b)(1) Guidelines, 55 Fed. Reg. 9210, 9212 (1990), http://water.epa.gov/lawsregs/guidance/wetlands/mitigate.cfm (portions of this MOA concerning the type and location of compensatory mitigation were superseded by the 2008 compensatory mitigation rulemaking).

12. Compensatory Mitigation for Losses of Aquatic Resources, 73 Fed. Reg. at 19,594, codified at 33 C.F.R. pts. 325 and 332 as well as 40 C.F.R. pt. 230.

13. *Id.* at 19,594.

14. 40 C.F.R. § 230.91(e)(1).

15. 2002 Mitigation Regulatory Guidance Letter 02-2, https://www.epa.gov/cwa-404/2002-mitigation-regulatory-guidance-letter-rgl-02-2.

Agreement between the Environmental Protection Agency and the Department of the Army Concerning the Determination of Mitigation Under the CWA Section 404(b)(1) Guidelines.[16] That MOA no longer controls with respect to any provisions "relating to the amount, type, and location of compensatory mitigation projects," though all other provisions of the MOA remain in effect.[17]

The purpose of the Compensatory Mitigation Rules is "to establish standards and criteria for the use of all types of compensatory mitigation, including on-site and off-site permittee-responsible mitigation, mitigation banks, and in-lieu fee mitigation to offset unavoidable impacts to waters of the United States."[18] The mitigation rules create a strong preference for the use of mitigation banks and in-lieu fee programs, particularly for general permits,[19] although permittee-responsible compensatory mitigation is acceptable if there are no available bank or in-lieu fee credits or if permittee-responsible mitigation will result in greater ecological benefits, for example, because of the watershed scale of the proposed project.[20] The goal is "timely, high-quality mitigation"[21] that fully offsets environmental losses resulting from unavoidable wetland impacts.[22] Mitigation banks and in-lieu fee programs are preferred because "they usually involve consolidating compensatory mitigation projects [at a single location] where ecologically appropriate, consolidating resources, providing financial planning and scientific expertise (which often is not practical for permittee-responsible compensatory mitigation projects), reducing temporal losses of functions [because the mitigation is already in place prior to the impacts], and reducing uncertainty over project success."[23]

16. 55 Fed. Reg. 9210 (Mar. 12, 1990).
17. *See* 40 C.F.R. § 230.91(e)(2).
18. 33 C.F.R. § 332.1(a)(1).
19. *Id.* § 332.1(b).
20. *Id.* § 332.3(b).
21. Env't Prot. Agency & U.S. Army Corps of Eng'rs, Compensatory Mitigation Rule: Improving, Restoring, and Protecting the Nation's Wetlands and Streams Questions and Answers 3, http://water.epa.gov/lawsregs/guidance/wetlands/upload/2006_03_27_wetlands_pdf_CompMitRuleQA.pdf.
22. 33 C.F.R. § 332.3(a)(1).
23. *Id.*

III. History of Compensatory Mitigation

Compensatory mitigation for loss of wetland ecosystem services (sometimes referred to by the historic term "functions and values"[24]) has been required (and controversial) for many decades.[25] There is natural tension between maintaining undisturbed wetlands and the economic reality of impacting them for development.[26] One scholar summarized the tensions quite succinctly: "From an environmental perspective, it would be best if permits were not granted for activities that degrade and destroy wetlands. From a political perspective, this is simply not possible, given the amount of wetlands that are privately owned."[27]

Mitigation requirements pre-dated the Clean Water Act.[28] Through the Fish and Wildlife Coordination Act[29] and the NEPA,[30] the Corps required various compensations when issuing permits for many activities. The Council on Environmental Quality then adopted regulations defining mitigation (in a broader context) in 1978,[31] and

24. *See* Env't Prot. Agency, *How Do Wetlands Function and Why Are They Valuable?*, https://www.epa.gov/wetlands/how-do-wetlands-function-and-why-are-they-valuable (last visited Aug. 19, 2023).

25. *See*, e.g., Royal C. Gardner, No Net Loss: Lies, Damned Lies, and Statistics, in LAWYERS, SWAMPS AND MONEY—U.S. WETLAND LAW, POLICY, AND POLITICS 93, 93 (2011); Oliver A. Houck, More Net Loss of Wetlands: The Army-EPA Memorandum of Agreement on Mitigation under the 404 Program, 20 ENV'T L. REP. 10,212 (June 1990); William W. Sapp, The Supply-Side and Demand-Side of Wetlands Mitigation Banking, 74 OR. L. REV. 951 (1995).

26. Stephen M. Johnson, *Avoid, Minimize, Mitigate: The Continuing Constitutionality of Wetlands Mitigation After Dolan v. City of Tigard*, 6 FORDHAM ENV'T L.J. 689 ("[a]lthough wetlands provide a vast array of economic and environmental benefits, those benefits have often been ignored in the interest of the short-term economic gains provided by the housing developments and shopping malls built in their place").

27. Royal C. Gardner, *Beyond Jurisdiction: A Compensatory Mitigation Report from Florida*, *in* BEYOND JURISDICTION: WETLANDS LAW AND POLICY FOR THE NEXT DECADE (2014).

28. An excellent history of wetland mitigation was published almost four decades ago. *See* Edward T. LaRoe, *Wetland Habitat Mitigation: An Historical Overview*, 8(5) NAT'L WETLANDS NEWSL. 8 (Env't L. Inst. Sept.–Oct. 1986).

29. 16 U.S.C. § 661.

30. 42 U.S.C. §§ 4321–4347.

31. 40 C.F.R. § 1508.20.

in 1981 the U.S. Fish and Wildlife Service published a comprehensive mitigation policy.[32]

On a parallel track, the concept of "no net loss" was emerging. It was a creature of the presidential campaign and subsequent administration of President George H.W. Bush,[33] where by the end of the 1980s, one national refrain about the nation's wetlands became "no net loss."[34] The "no net loss" concept was codified into guidance and later regulation.[35] Keeping the national "no net loss" promise relies on compensatory mitigation[36] by seeking to assure that when wetlands are filled in one place, the services (and in many cases, acreage) of those wetlands are replaced in another. Actually achieving this goal, however, has proven challenging.[37]

---

32. U.S. Fish and Wildlife Service Mitigation Policy; Notice of Final Policy, 46 Fed. Reg. 7644 (Jan. 23, 1981).

33. *See* Craig Pittman & Matthew Waite, *The Promise, Plus*, *in* PAVING PARADISE: FLORIDA'S VANISHING WETLANDS AND THE FAILURE OF NO NET LOSS 90, 90–100 (2009).

34. As one example, see Interpreting the Rapanos/Carabell Supreme Court Decision: Hearing before the Subcomm. on Fisheries, Wildlife, and Water of the S. Comm. on Environment and Public Works, 109th Cong. 18-60 (2006) (statements of Benjamin H. Grumbles, Assistant Administrator for Water, U.S. Env't Prot. Agency, and John Paul Woodley, Jr., Assistant Secretary of The Army for Civil Works, Dep't of The Army) ("President Bush established, on Earth Day 2004, a national goal to move beyond 'no net loss' of wetlands and to attain an overall increase in the quantity and quality of wetlands in America. Specifically, the President established a goal to increase, improve, and protect three million acres of wetlands by 2009. Since the President announced this objective, EPA, the Corps, the U.S. Department of Agriculture (USDA), and the Department of Interior (DOI) have restored, created, protected or improved 1,797,000 acres of wetlands. We now have 588,000 acres of wetlands that did not exist in 2004, we have improved the quality of 563,000 wetland acres that already existed, and we have protected the high quality of 646,000 acres of existing wetlands.").

35. Memorandum of Agreement between the Environmental Protection Agency and the Department of the Army, *supra* note 11, at 9210.

36. Thomas H. Kean et al., Protecting America's Wetlands: An Action Agenda, the Final Report of the National Wetlands Policy Forum 42 (1988).

37. One recent study concluded ". . . that the regulatory responses recently adopted to deal with the risks associated with [mitigation banking] seem to be more effective than is often claimed in the literature, although there is still much to be improved. In the US, the USACE and the Environmental Protection Agency (EPA) have created a hybrid system that blends market characteristics and regulatory constraints, which may improve their ability to deal with the challenges of compensating wetland destruction. However, a second, more worrying, conclusion is that the question is still pending whether or not there is real achievement of No Net Loss of wetlands. . . ." Harold

At the same time, by the late 1980s, clashes about differing concepts and regulatory realities of mitigation between the Corps and EPA reached the courts. In a case often referred to as "Sweedens Swamp,"[38] a proponent sought a permit for activities that would have impacted 32 of 50 acres of wetlands. The permit included on-site mitigation of nine replacement and thirteen enhanced acres of wetlands, as well as off-site mitigation creating 36 acres.[39] EPA "vetoed"[40] issuance of the permit on the basis of EPA's different views on the Section 404(b)(1) Guidelines and mitigation policy, expressing skepticism about wetland creation as mitigation.[41] That led to new negotiations between the Corps and EPA as to the future of mitigation.

In November 1989, the Corps and EPA entered into a Memorandum of Agreement (MOA) on Mitigation.[42] The Mitigation MOA adopted EPA's approach of not considering mitigation as a factor favoring a permit, but rather requiring mitigation independently, after the application was deemed to meet permit criteria. Mitigation was to proceed via "sequencing,"[43] in which the Corps "first makes a determination that potential impacts have been avoided to the maximum extent practicable; remaining unavoidable impacts will then be mitigated

---

Levrel, Pierre Scemam & Anne-Charlotte Vaissière, *Should We Be Wary of Mitigation Banking? Evidence Regarding the Risks Associated with This Wetland Offset Arrangement in Florida*, 135 Ecological Econ. 136, 146 (2017), https://www.sciencedirect.com/science/article/pii/S0921800916304402; *see also* Karl Blankenship, *"No Net Loss" Proves to Be an Elusive Wetlands Goal*, Bay J. (Apr. 1, 1994), http://www.bayjournal.com/article/no_net_loss_proves_to_be_an_elusive_wetlands_goal.

38. William L. Want, Law of Wetlands Regulation § 6.40 (2013). *See also* Env't Prot. Agency, *Federal Register Notice of Proposed Determination regarding Sweedens Swamp, MA under CWA Section 404* (Aug. 21, 1985), https://www.epa.gov/cwa-404/federal-register-notice-proposed-determination-regarding-sweedens-swamp-ma-under-cwa-section.

39. Bersani v. U.S. Env't Prot. Agency, 674 F. Supp. 405 (N.D.N.Y. 1987); *aff'd*, 850 F.2d 36 (2d Cir. 1988).

40. Env't Prot. Agency, *Clean Water Act Section 404(c), Veto Authority*, https://www.epa.gov/cwa-404/clean-water-act-section-404c-veto-authority (last updated Jan. 25, 2024).

41. *Id.* at 411.

42. Memorandum of Agreement between the Environmental Protection Agency and the Department of the Army, 55 Fed. Reg. at 9212, *supra* note 11. Because it was a Memorandum of Agreement and not a regulation, some courts raise issues about whether it was binding. *See, e.g.*, Coeur D'Alene Lake v. Kiebert, 790 F. Supp. 998 (D. Idaho 1992).

43. *See generally* Want, *supra* note 38, at § 6.41.

to the extent appropriate and practicable by requiring steps to minimize impacts and, finally, compensate for aquatic resource values."[44] The Mitigation MOA also set forth a standard for the "amount" of mitigation, stating that it was not acreage-based, but rather required that, consistent with the policy of no net loss, functional value must be replaced.[45] At the same time, it acknowledged that "no net loss" was a programmatic rather than a permit-specific goal.[46] The Mitigation MOA was explicit in recognizing the importance of scientific analysis and expertise in the mitigation planning process.[47] The Mitigation MOA established preferences at the time for in-kind over out-of-kind compensatory mitigation, wetlands restoration over wetlands creation, and on-site (e.g., adjacent or contiguous to the discharge site) over off-site mitigation.[48] It did, however, also discuss the concepts (as they existed at the time) of both mitigation monitoring and mitigation banking.[49] For a few years, the Mitigation MOA was the sole guidance in place, while additional formal guidance subsequently emerged in terms of mitigation banking and in-lieu fees.

EPA and the Corps issued formal guidance on Mitigation Banks in 1995,[50] authorizing approved banks to provide compensatory mitigation

44. Memorandum of Agreement between the Environmental Protection Agency and the Department of the Army, *supra* note 11. The MOA likewise states that compensatory mitigation "may not be used as a method to reduce environmental impacts in the evaluation of the least environmentally damaging practicable alternatives for the purposes of requirements under § 230.10(a)." *Id.* at 9212.

45. "[F]or wetlands, such mitigation should provide, at a minimum, one for one functional replacement (i.e., no net loss of values), with an adequate margin of safety to reflect the expected degree of success associated with the mitigation plan." *Id.* at 9212–13.

46. Mitigation was not required where it was determined that "the mitigation measures necessary to meet this goal are not feasible, not practicable, or would accomplish only inconsequential reductions in impacts. Consequently, it is recognized that [the goal of] no net loss of wetlands functions and values may not be achieved in each and every permit action." *Id.* at 9211.

47. "Functional values should be assessed by applying aquatic site assessment techniques generally recognized by experts in the field and/or the best professional judgment of federal and state agency representatives." *Id.* at 9212.

48. *Id.*

49. *Id.* at 9213.

50. Federal Guidance for the Establishment, Use, and Operation of Mitigation Banks, 60 Fed. Reg. 58,605 (Nov. 29, 1995).

options for some permit applicants.[51] The guidance defined a mitigation bank as "a site where wetlands and/or other aquatic resources are restored, created, enhanced, or in exceptional circumstances, preserved expressly for the purpose of providing compensatory mitigation in advance of authorized impacts to similar resources."[52] Both public and private mitigation bank sponsors were authorized,[53] and mitigation activities to offset wetland impacts caused by the sponsor's own development projects were allowed, as was selling mitigation credits to others.[54] The Guidance concluded that because banks often preexisted the activities involved in the permit, and were thus functioning in advance of project impacts,[55] such credits could reduce the temporal loss of wetland functions and could reduce necessary time and other resources (by both applicant and agencies) that needed to be dedicated in terms of review.[56]

Under the guidance, mitigation banking instruments[57] were required, and those instruments had to be approved by a Mitigation Bank Review Team (MBRT). The MBRT was made up of representatives from the Corps; EPA; U.S. Fish and Wildlife Service (FWS); National Marine Fisheries Service (NMFS); Natural Resource Conservation Service (NRCS); and state, tribal, and local regulatory and resource agencies working together and "striv[ing] to obtain consensus on its actions."[58] Under the guidance, each bank's geographic service area was limited to a range that "can reasonably be expected to provide appropriate compensation" for wetland impacts,[59] such as a county or a watershed.[60] The guide made management of a mitigation bank during its operational life, and thereafter, the responsibility of the

---

51. *See generally* Env't Prot. Agency, *Mitigation Banks under CWA Section 404*, https://www.epa.gov/cwa-404/mitigation-banks-under-cwa-section-404 (last updated Oct. 31, 2023).

52. Federal Guidance for the Establishment, Use and Operation of Mitigation Banks, 60 Fed. Reg. at 58,614,

53. *Id.* at 58,613.

54. *Id.* at 58,607.

55. *Id.* at 58,612.

56. *Id.*

57. *Id.* at 58,610.

58. *Id.*

59. *Id.*

60. *Id.*

sponsor,[61] directing both protections (such as conservation easements and restrictive deeds) and formal financial assurances specified in the banking instrument to secure the longevity of replaced functions and values.[62]

Five years later, federal agencies issued Guidance on compensatory mitigation through in-lieu fees[63] designed to provide "funds to an in-lieu-fee sponsor instead of completing project-specific mitigation."[64] Several limits were placed on the use of money to mitigate, starting with detailed consultation with the other federal natural resource agencies and an opportunity for public notice and comment.[65] The guidance also directed that in-lieu-fee arrangements be developed to address the specific resource needs of a particular watershed and be self-sustaining, and that funds be used for replacing wetlands functions and values rather than financing non-mitigation programs such as education projects and research.[66] It directed that the amount of funds required should be based on a reasonable estimate of all funds needed to compensate for the impacts to wetlands or other waters of the particular activity authorized.[67]

Even with the Mitigation MOA and the two guidance documents, concerns continued to mount from many stakeholders on multiple levels about mitigation.[68] In 1999, the National Academy of Sciences through its National Research Council (NRC) was called upon to study the success of the nation's mitigation program. The NRC assembled a panel of experts who spent two years examining data, reviewing scientific findings, consulting experts and stakeholders, and conducting

---

61. *Id.* at 58,613. Sometimes a conservation organization or governmental agency can assume later management authority.

62. *Id.* at 58,612.

63. Federal Guidance on the Use of In-Lieu-Fee Arrangements for Compensatory Mitigation under Section 404 of the Clean Water Act and Section 10 of the Rivers and Harbors Act, 65 Fed. Reg. 66,914 (Dec. 28, 2000); *see* Royal C. Gardner, *Money for Nothing? The Rise of Fee Mitigation*, 19 VA. ENV'T L.J. 1, 18–33 (2000).

64. 65 Fed. Reg. at 66,915.

65. *Id.* at 66,916.

66. *Id.*

67. *Id.*

68. *See generally* Craig Pittman & Matthew Waite, *The Myth of Mitigation*, *in* PAVING PARADISE: FLORIDA'S VANISHING WETLANDS AND THE FAILURE OF NO NET LOSS, ch. 9 (2009).

site visits, culminating in a report that raised serious concerns about compensatory mitigation.[69]

The NRC committee found that, despite some progress in the past 20 years, the "goal of no net loss of wetlands is not being met for wetland functions by the [Clean Water Act section 404] mitigation program."[70] They examined claims that issued permits resulted in a paper "gain" in acreage of almost 2:1,[71] and emerged with questions about the true replication of lost functions and ecosystem services.[72] Simultaneously, the NRC concluded that many mitigation projects failed, either because they were not implemented at all, or, if they were implemented, they did not achieve the agreed-upon goals. The NRC concluded that successful wetland mitigation required resources and technical expertise.[73] Further, the NRC concluded that because the then-existing permitting process did not contemplate long-term oversight, data showed the "presumption that once mitigation sites meet their permit criteria they will be self-sustaining in the absence of any management or care is flawed."[74] Yet, the report was not

69. Compensatory Mitigation for Losses of Aquatic Resources, 73 Fed. Reg. 19,594, 19,670 (Apr. 10, 2008) (codified at 33 C.F.R. pts. 325, 332 and 40 C.F.R. pt. 230) ("[I]n 2001 the National Research Council (NRC) released a comprehensive evaluation of the effectiveness of wetlands compensatory mitigation required under section 404 of the Clean Water Act. This report noted concerns with some past wetland compensatory mitigation and provided recommendations for the federal agencies, states, and other parties to improve compensatory mitigation. This report was an important resource in the development of today's rule.").

70. NAT'L RSCH. COUNCIL, COMPENSATING FOR WETLAND LOSSES UNDER THE CLEAN WATER ACT 2 (2001), http://www.nap.edu/books/0309074320/html/; *see also* Fla. Dep't of Env't Regulation, Report on the Effectiveness of Permitted Mitigation (1991).

71. COMPENSATING FOR WETLAND LOSSES UNDER THE CLEAN WATER ACT, *supra* note 70, at 3.

72. Memorandum of Agreement between the Environmental Protection Agency and the Department of the Army, *supra* note 11, at 9212–13.

73. COMPENSATING FOR WETLAND LOSSES UNDER THE CLEAN WATER ACT, *supra* note 70, at 152. *See generally* J. B. Ruhl, James Salzman & Iris Goodman, *Implementing the New Ecosystem Services Mandate of the Section 404 Compensatory Mitigation Program: A Catalyst for Advancing Science and Policy*, 38 STETSON L. REV. 251 (2009).

74. COMPENSATING FOR WETLAND LOSSES UNDER THE CLEAN WATER ACT, *supra* note 70, at 152.

entirely negative: it also concluded that mitigation banks and in-lieu fee programs offered "some advantages over permittee-responsible mitigation."[75]

Ultimately, the NRC committee's report did not endorse a particular mechanism, but instead emphasized the importance of interagency review of mitigation projects, recommended earlier timing of the mitigation action, and noted that long-term stewardship of mitigation sites was necessary.[76] Later in 2001, the U.S. General Accounting Office issued a negative report on the in-lieu fee program, opining that "[t]he extent to which the in-lieu-fee option has achieved its purpose of mitigating adverse impacts to wetlands is uncertain."[77]

For a number of years thereafter, there was increased attention on mitigation bank and in-lieu fee programs. Still, an Environmental Law Institute study published in 2006 showed almost 60 percent of mitigation was still being performed by a permittee rather than these other options.[78] Meanwhile, through the National Defense Authorization Act for Fiscal Year 2004, Congress directed the Corps and EPA to issue a regulation that established standards for all forms of compensatory mitigation.[79] The statutory language mandating new regulations directed establishment of a "level playing field" for all methods of mitigation.[80]

---

75. *Id.* at 9. For a critique of that assessment, *see* Env't Law Inst., *Banks and Fees: The Status of Off-Site Wetland Mitigation in the United States* (2002), https://www.eli.org/research-report/banks-and-fees-status-site-wetland-mitigation-united-states and Jessica Wilkinson & Jared Thompson, *2005 Status Report on Compensatory Mitigation in the United States*, Env't Law Inst. (Apr. 2006), https://www.eli.org/research-report/2005-status-report-compensatory-mitigation-united-states.

76. Compensating for Wetland Losses under the Clean Water Act, *supra* note 70, at 9.

77. U.S. Gen. Accounting Office, GAO-01-325, Wetlands Protection: Assessments Needed to Determine Effectiveness of In-Lieu-Fee Mitigation, Report to Congressional Requesters (May 2001), http://www.gao.gov/new.items/d01325.pdf.

78. Wilkinson & Thompson, *supra* note 75, at 27.

79. National Defense Authorization Act for Fiscal Year 2004, Pub. L. No. 108-136, § 314, 117 Stat. 1392, 1430–31 (Nov. 24, 2003) (codified as amended at 10 U.S.C. § 2694b (2004)).

80. *Id.*

After a lengthy rulemaking process (a proposed rule was issued in 2006,[81] eliciting more than 12,000 comments,[82] many of them highly critical[83]), the Corps and EPA published revised compensatory mitigation regulations in April 2008 with a new and specific hierarchy for mitigation.[84] The details of that hierarchy are covered in the next section, as the Compensatory Mitigation Rule has been unchanged since 2008. Information materials were shared by the Corps and EPA shortly after the rule was published through Compensatory Mitigation Rule Familiarization Workshops under CWA Section 404[85] that are still available and provide valuable guidance for those new to the area.

One of the most significant changes in the nearly 15 years since the Compensatory Mitigation Rule was enacted in 2008 is the explosive growth of wetland mitigation banks and the creation of an entire industry around such banks. "In June 2008, a total of 706 mitigation banks with §404 credits had been approved. Between June 2008 and July 2018, an additional 873 mitigation banks with §404 credits were approved—more than a 120 percent increase. In the 10 years prior to the 2008 rule, the rate of approvals averaged about 56 banks per year (1998–2007). For the first 10 years since the 2008 rule, the rate of approvals has averaged about 86 banks per year (2008–2017), a more than 50 percent increase from the decade before."[86] The distribution of mitigation banks across the states also increased during the time period, as has the number and distribution of in-lieu fee (ILF)

---

81. Compensatory Mitigation for Losses of Aquatic Resources, 71 Fed. Reg. 15,520, 15,520 (proposed Mar. 28, 2006) (codified at 33 C.F.R. pts. 325, 332 and 40 C.F.R. pt. 230).

82. Compensatory Mitigation for Losses of Aquatic Resources, 73 Fed. Reg. 19,594, 19,595 (Apr. 10, 2008) (codified at 33 C.F.R. pts. 325, 332 and 40 C.F.R. pt. 230).

83. See James Murphy, Jan Goldman-Carter & Julie Sibbing, New Mitigation Rule Promises More of the Same: Why the New Corps and EPA Mitigation Rule Will Fail to Protect Our Aquatic Resources Adequately, 38 STETSON L. REV. 311 (2009).

84. Compensatory Mitigation for Losses of Aquatic Resources, 73 Fed. Reg. at 19,594 (Nov. 14, 2008). The Corps' compensatory mitigation rules at 33 C.F.R. part 332 mirror those of EPA at 40 C.F.R. part 230, subpart J.

85. U.S. Environmental Protection Agency, https://www.epa.gov/cwa-404/compensatory-mitigation-rule-familiarization-workshops-under-cwa-section-404.

86. Palmer Hough & Rachel Harrington, *Ten Years of the Compensatory Mitigation Rule: Reflections on Progress and Opportunities*, ENV'T LAW INST. (Jan. 2019), https://www.eli.org/sites/default/files/elr/featuredarticles/Jan19FA.pdf.

programs.[87] According to the Corps Regulatory In-Lieu Fee & Bank Tracking System database, as of February 2024, there were 2,572 active approved mitigation banks and ILF programs nationwide and 582 pending banks and ILF programs.[88] The length of time it takes to permit a mitigation bank has created issues, as is discussed later in this chapter.

IV. Basic Mitigation Requirements

Although the statutory language in Section 404[89] does not expressly require mitigation for every authorized permit, the authority granted to EPA in Section 404(b)(1)[90] has been interpreted to support the modern mitigation framework.[91] Thus EPA's Section 404(b)(1) Guidelines[92] support a robust regulatory framework requiring permit applicants to avoid, minimize, and compensate for most adverse impacts to waters of the United States.[93]

---

87. *Id.*

88. U.S. Army Corps of Engineers, Regulatory In-Lieu Fee & Bank Tracking System (RIBITS), *Banks & Sites,* https://ribits.ops.usace.army.mil/ords/f?p=107:158.

89. 33 U.S.C. § 1344.

90. *Id.* § 1344(b)(1).

91. Congress directed that regulations pursuant to Section 404(b)(1) "be based on criteria comparable to the criteria applicable" to ocean dumping permits and listed in CWA Section 403(c),. 33 U.S.C. § 1343(c). Those criteria mandate that permits for marine discharges be issued only after considering "other possible locations and methods of disposal . . . including land-based alternatives," *id.* § 1343(c)(1)(F), and "the effect of the disposal at varying rates, of particular volumes and concentrations of pollutants," *id.* § 1343(c)(1)(E). These congressional mandates implicitly require that permits be issued only after the practicability of avoiding and minimizing wetland impacts is considered.

92. Section 404(b)(1) Guidelines for Specific of Disposal Sites for Dredge or Fill Material, 40 C.F.R. pt. 230 (2018).

93. *Id.* § 230.10(a) (discussing avoidance and the alternatives analysis); *id.* § 230.10(d) (requiring minimization of potential impacts); *id.* §§ 230.70–.77 (further explaining measures that can minimize impacts); *id.* § 230.75(d) (providing that applicants may be required to develop or restore habitat to compensate for damage from their proposed activities). In a report summarizing the progress made in implementing the Compensatory Mitigation Rule, the Corps analyzed mitigation data from 2010 to 2014 and discovered that the majority of permitted impacts to jurisdictional wetlands and waters had been avoided and minimized to less than 1/10-acre, with only 10 percent of the written authorizations still requiring compensatory mitigation after avoidance and minimization measures had been employed. U.S. Army

A. Mitigation Sequencing: Avoidance

Mitigation must proceed in the "sequence" just described: avoid, minimize, and compensate. The Compensatory Mitigation Rule requires that all permit applicants "take all appropriate and practicable steps to avoid and minimize adverse impacts to waters of the United States."[94] The first step in mitigation is thus avoidance—searching for another alternative other than discharge in WOTUS.[95] In the case of an individual permit, this step is often coupled with the requirement through the Section 404(b)(1) Guidelines that permit applicants demonstrate there is no "practicable alternative to the proposed discharge which woud have less adverse impact on the aquatic ecosystem."[96] An applicant must therefore demonstrate that, considering the purpose of the project, the proposed discharge of dredged and fill material into WOTUS represents the "least damaging practicable alternative," commonly known as the "LEDPA."[97] The Corps must evaluate alternatives that are "practicable and reasonable" that would have a lesser adverse impact, but unless a project is water-dependent (like a marina or dock), it is the applicant's responsibility to rebut the presumption that there are sites available for the proposed activity that would not require WOTUS impacts.[98]

Corps of Eng'rs, The Mitigation Rule Retrospective: A Review of the 2008 Regulations Governing Compensatory Mitigation for Losses of Aquatic Resources, https://www.iwr.usace.army.mil/Portals/70/docs/regulatory/2015-R-03_Factsheet.pdf#:~:text=Over%20the%20past%20five%20years%2C%20the%20Corps%20issued,authorities%2C%20approximately%2010%25%20of%20which%20required%20compensatory%20mitigation.

94. 40 C.F.R. § 230.91(c).

95. Memorandum of Agreement between the Environmental Protection Agency and the Department of the Army, *supra* note 11 (Portions of this MOA that concern the type and location of compensatory mitigation are superseded by the 2008 Compensatory Mitigation Rule.).

96. 40 C.F.R. § 230.10(a). For more on navigating the practicable alternatives analysis, see Chapter 4.

97. *See* U.S. Army Corps of Eng'rs, Fort Worth District—Regulatory Division, Preparing an Alternatives Analysis under Section 404 of the Clean Water Act (Nov. 2014).

98. *Id. See also* Chapter 4, Part II.3 in this book.

B. Mitigation Sequencing: Minimization

The second step in the sequence is minimization; a permit applicant must take appropriate and practicable steps to minimize unavoidable adverse impacts to the aquatic ecosystems.[99] As described in the Section 404(b)(1) Guidelines, minimization can occur through a variety of means, including location choice for the discharge (such as using a space that is confined or has been previously used);[100] actions that affect the discharged material itself[101] or control the material after discharge (such as using cover vegetation to prevent erosion or using lined containment areas to prevent leaching);[102] actions that affect the method of dispersion (such as silt screens)[103] or technology to limit impacts (such as mats under heavy equipment to reduce wetland surface compaction and rutting);[104] or actions that limit impacts to plant and animal populations (such as timing discharges to avoid spawning, migration, or nesting seasons).[105] Again, the burden is on the applicant to demonstrate that all appropriate and practicable minimization measures have been taken, but the level of analysis required to satisfy the Section 404(b)(1) Guidelines depends on the scope, scale, and cost of the project.[106]

C. Mitigation Sequencing: Compensatory Mitigation

As the last step of the mitigation sequence, compensatory mitigation "may be required to ensure that an activity requiring a section 404 permit complies with the Section 404(b)(1) Guidelines."[107] Further, the Corps may determine that a permit must be denied if appropriate and practicable compensatory mitigation options are not available.[108]

---

99. 40 C.F.R. § 230.10 (d).
100. *Id.* § 230.70.
101. *Id.* § 230.71.
102. *Id.* § 230.72.
103. *Id.* § 230.73.
104. *Id.* § 230.74.
105. *Id.* § 230.75.
106. Env't Prot. Agency, Memorandum: Appropriate Level of Analysis Required for Evaluating Compliance with the CWA Section 404(b)(1) Guidelines Alternatives Requirements, https://www.epa.gov/cwa-404/memorandum-appropriate-level-analysis-required-evaluating-compliance-cwa-section-404b1.
107. 40 C.F.R § 230.91(c)(3).
108. *Id.*

Compensatory mitigation is only permissible to offset potential adverse impacts to the aquatic ecosystem that cannot be avoided and minimized.[109] This is the part of the sequence that can be complex.[110]

Compensatory mitigation involves efforts designed to restore, enhance, create, or preserve wetland functions in a manner that fully offsets the wetland functions that will be adversely impacted by the activity to be permitted. The Compensatory Mitigation Rule adopted a watershed approach to mitigation, which focuses on entire water systems and their constituent parts rather than just the specific site at issue.[111]

D. Mitigation Hierarchy

The Compensatory Mitigation Rule mandates a mitigation hierarchy[112] that requires the Corps to consider compensatory mitigation options in the following order (but does allow for deviation when the alternative mitigation would be environmentally preferable):

1. Mitigation bank credits
2. In-lieu fee program credits
3. Permittee-responsible mitigation under a watershed approach
4. On-site and in-kind permittee responsible mitigation
5. Off-site and/or out-of-kind permittee-responsible mitigation[113]

In addition to allowing deviation when another type of mitigation is environmentally preferable, such as a large-scale permittee-responsible

---

109. Memorandum of Agreement between the Environmental Protection Agency and the Department of the Army, *supra* note 11, at 9212.

110. The Federal Register notice governing compensatory mitigation is 113 pages long. Compensatory Mitigation for Losses of Aquatic Resources, 73 Fed. Reg. 19,594, 19,594 (Apr. 10, 2008) (codified at 33 C.F.R. pts. 325, 332 and 40 C.F.R. pt. 230).

111. 40 C.F.R. § 230.93(c) ("The district engineer must use a watershed approach to establish compensatory mitigation requirements in DA permits to the extent appropriate and practicable.").

112. *Id.* § 230.93(b)(1); 33 C.F.R. § 332.3(b)(1); Compensatory Mitigation for Losses of Aquatic Resources, 73 Fed. Reg. at 19,614 (Nov. 14, 2008) ("[A] secured site, an approved mitigation plan and other assurances must be in place before an initial allocation of credits can be sold or transferred to permittees. Before additional credits can be sold, the mitigation bank must achieve appropriate ecological milestones set out in its credit release schedule. Therefore, mitigation bank credits are generally more likely to be fulfilled sooner (or to be already fulfilled), than in-lieu fee program credits [or permittee-responsible mitigation]").

113. 33 C.F.R. § 332.3(b)(1).

project that will provide regional benefits to the watershed, deviation is also allowed when there are no or insufficient mitigation credits available in the watershed for the resource type being impacted. If permitted impacts are not located in the service area of an approved mitigation bank, or the approved mitigation bank does not have the appropriate number and resource type of credits available to offset those impacts, in-lieu fee mitigation, if available, is generally preferable to permittee-responsible mitigation, unless the applicant demonstrates otherwise.[114]

E. Mitigation for General Permits

Although much of what this chapter focuses on is individual permits, it is important to note that streamlined general permits may also require mitigation.[115] And, even though the permits are streamlined, sequencing is still required.[116] Some nationwide permits, for example, include the requirement to submit a pre-construction notification (PCN) requirements. These notices

> give the Corps the opportunity to evaluate certain proposed NWP activities on a case-by-case basis to ensure that they will cause no more than minimal adverse environmental effects, individually and cumulatively. . . . This case-by-case review of PCNs often results in district engineers adding activity-specific conditions to NWP authorizations to ensure that the adverse environmental effects are no more than minimal. These can include . . . compensatory mitigation requirements to offset authorized losses of jurisdictional waters and wetlands so that the net adverse environmental effects caused by the authorized activity are no more than minimal.[117]

---

114. *See* U.S. Corps of Eng'rs, Chicago District Website, *Regulatory—Compensatory Mitigation*, https://www.lrc.usace.army.mil/Missions/Regulatory/Compensatory-Mitigation/#:~:text=Compensatory%20mitigation%20is%20typically%20accomplished%20through%20either%20Mitigation,the%20appropriate%20resource%20type%20and%20within%20the%20watershed (last visited Apr. 11, 2024).

115. Issuance and Reissuance of Nationwide Permits: Notice, 86 Fed. Reg. 2744, 2831 (Jan. 13, 2021).

116. *Id.* at 2831 ("... the purpose of compensatory mitigation is to offset unavoidable adverse impacts which remain after all appropriate and practicable avoidance and minimization has been achieved").

117. *Id.* at 2745.

Any compensatory mitigation must comply with the Corps' Compensatory Mitigation Rule, and the amount of mitigation required is established on a case-by-case basis.[118] For NWPs, the preferred mitigation mechanism is mitigation bank credits or in-lieu fee programs., although the district engineer has the discretion to approve the use of permittee-responsible mitigation if the appropriate number and type of bank or in-lieu fee credits are not available at the time the PCN is submitted.[119] In no event can compensatory mitigation be used to increase the acreage losses allowed by the NWP at issue.[120]

F. The Compensatory Mitigation Plan

Mitigation can be performed using restoration, enhancement, establishment, and sometimes preservation. Restoration (defined as returning the natural or historic functions of a former or degraded wetland) is preferred given the increase in aquatic functions compared to enhancement or preservation and greater likelihood of success is greater compared to establishment (construction of a wetland in an upland area). When considering mitigation options, "[i]n general, the required compensatory mitigation should be located within the same watershed as the impact site, and should be located where it is most likely to successfully replace lost functions and services, taking into account such watershed scale features as aquatic habitat diversity, habitat connectivity, relationships to hydrologic sources (including the availability of water rights), trends in land use, ecological benefits, and compatibility with adjacent land uses."[121]

The first step in developing a compensatory mitigation is to determine the appropriate type and amount of mitigation required based on the unavoidable adverse impacts that are expected.

> Consistent with the Corps' regulations at 33 CFR Part 332, concerning compensatory mitigation for aquatic resource impacts, one objective is to provide a minimum one-to-one functional replacement for wetland loss. To do this, the functions of a

118. *Id.* at 2745, 2798.

119. *Id.* at 2871 (NWP Condition 23 governs compensatory mitigation for projects that quality to use a NWP. See Chapter 5 for more information about NWPs.).

120. *Id.* Most NWPs have an acreage limit of one-half acre of impacts to waters of the United States.

121. 33 C.F.R. § 332.3(b).

> wetland can be identified and evaluated through a numeric functional assessment methodology. While the Corps neither prescribes nor prohibits any specific numeric functional assessment, the Corps desires to be responsive to the needs of the public by accepting the same methodology required by state and local levels, when appropriate.[122]

The amount of the mitigation must be sufficient to replace the lost functions. If a suitable metric is not available to measure the function or condition of both the impact area and the mitigation area, a minimum one-to-one compensation ratio must be used.[123]

When permitted impacts are within the service area of an approved mitigation bank or in-lieu fee program and the bank or program has the same type of the same type of aquatic resources in a sufficient amount to offset the functional loss, the process is relatively straightforward: an applicant provides proof that sufficient credits are available and have been set aside for the applicant's use, and a specific permit condition requires the purchase of the required number of credits before wetland impacts can occur.[124]

If the bank or program does not have a sufficient number of credits, or if the applicant proposes permittee-responsible mitigation, a complex evaluation of a number of factors must be undertaken, such as the current condition of the impact area and the mitigation, their location and significance in the landscape, the timing of implementation of the mitigation compared to the time of the impacts, and whether the proposed mitigation is adequately buffered and protected against secondary and long-term impacts.[125]

An application requiring compensatory mitigation to offset wetland impacts must include a mitigation plan.[126] However, for permittees intending to use approved mitigation banks or in-lieu fee programs, their mitigation plans need only include certain basic information identifying the number and type of resource credits to be purchased and the specific bank or program to be used.[127] All other mitigation plans must

---

122. U.S. Army Corps of Eng'r, Jacksonville District Regulatory Division, *Source Book*, https://www.saj.usace.army.mil/Missions/Regulatory/Source-Book/.

123. 33 C.F.R. § 332.3(f).

124. 40 C.F.R. § 230.93(b)(2)–(3), (k)(4).

125. *Id.* § 230.93.

126. 33 C.F.R. § 332.4(c).

127. *Id.*

include the following same fundamental components: objectives,[128] site selection criteria,[129] site protection instruments (e.g., conservation easements),[130] baseline information (for impact and compensation sites),[131] credit determination methodology,[132] a mitigation work plan,[133] a maintenance plan,[134] ecological performance standards,[135] monitoring requirements,[136] a long-term management plan,[137] an adaptive management plan,[138] and financial assurances.[139] The regulations encourage a results-focused approach and, as such, expanded attention on mitigation banking.[140] By establishing enforceable standards and requirements in relation to compensation projects, the agencies stated an intent to establish sound structure to encourage public participation through increased transparency and greater accountability.[141] Additionally, the regulations hold all mitigation providers to the same standards in an attempt to ensure that providers of high-quality wetland replacement projects are not at a competitive disadvantage to others being held to lower standards.[142] The regulations also clearly affirm the requirement to adhere to the "mitigation sequence."[143]

More than a decade after the "new" mitigation rule,[144] while there have been some debates, there has not been the level of struggle or hostility that is seen in other areas of the CWA Section 404 regulatory arena. Mitigation appears to have become, for the most part, an accepted a part of the permitting process. The most pressing problem

128. *Id.* § 332.4(c)(2).
129. *Id.* § 332.4(c)(3).
130. *Id.* § 332.7(a).
131. *Id.* § 332.4(c)(4).
132. *Id.* § 332.5.
133. *Id.* § 332.4(c)(7).
134. *Id.* § 332.4(c)(8).
135. *Id.* § 332.5.
136. *Id.* § 332.6.
137. *Id.* § 332.7(d).
138. *Id.* § 332.7(c).
139. *Id.* § 332.3(n).
140. 73 Fed. Reg. at 19,620.
141. *Id.* at 19,640.
142. *Id.* at 19,594.
143. *Id.*
144. *See generally* Env't Law Inst., *Background on Compensatory Mitigation*, https://www.eli.org/compensatory-mitigation/background-compensatory-mitigation; Nat. Assn. of Wetland Managers, *Compensatory Mitigation*, https://www.nawm.org/wetland-programs/regulation/mitigation.html.

for the area of compensatory mitigation appears to be the availability of mitigation banks and in-lieu fee programs in the watersheds in which they are needed and the incredibly slow pace in permitting new mitigation banks.[145] There are simply not enough mitigation banks in the watersheds where impacts are occurring. The time it takes to approve mitigation banks is a critical factor in this shortage. A 2023 report presents data that indicates it now takes more than 1,000 days to fully approve the average mitigation bank, 50 percent longer than the 225 days specified in the 2008 Rule.[146] In the Jacksonville District, the District is in the process of developing a Proximity Factor Tool to address the bank shortfall.[147] The rules currently require the district engineer to require a mitigation ratio greater than one-to-one as needed to account for the distance between the impacts and the mitigation.[148] The draft Proximity Factor Tool purports to allow more flexibility to mitigate outside the watershed by quantifying the amount of additional mitigation that would be required if a mitigation bank outside of the impact watershed were offered as compensatory mitigation.

---

145. Federal mitigation banks are currently taking more than 1,000 days on average to approve, and in some jurisdictions even longer. Steve Martin & Becca Madsen, *The Time It Takes for Restoration: An Analysis of Mitigation Bank Instrument Timelines*, Env't Pol'y Innovation Ctr. & Ecological Restoration Business Assoc., Washington D.C. (2023), https://www.policyinnovation.org/blog/new-research-finds-that-wetland-and-stream-mitigation-banks-take-over-1000-days-to-approve (report reveals "persistent delays in the approval of a class of wetland and stream restoration projects called 'mitigation banks.'").

146. Martin & Madsen, *supra* note 146.

147. U.S. Army Corps of Eng'rs, Jacksonville District Regulatory Division, Public Notice Archive, Proximity Factor Tool Tool (Aug. 12, 2022), https://www.saj.usace.army.mil/Missions/Regulatory/Public-Notices/Article/3125671/proximity-factor-tool/. ("The proximity factor tool could be used to determine the amount of compensatory mitigation required to offset unavoidable impacts to waters of the United States in areas outside the impact 8-digit Hydrologic Unit Code (HUC), ecoregion, or approved mitigation bank and in-lieu fee service areas, etc. . . . The Corps Jacksonville District recognizes that the relevance of a compensatory mitigation project is diminished as the locations of the compensatory mitigation project site and impact site become further removed. Diminishing relevance expresses the relationship of the location of the compensatory mitigation project site and its relationship to the impact site. We also need to evaluate the relative importance of the suite of functions provided by the impacted aquatic resources and those at the compensatory mitigation project site.").

148. 33 C.F.R. § 332.3(f)(2).

7 CHAPTER

The Environmental Protection Agency, the Role of States, and Further Obligations

I. The Environmental Protection Agency and Other Federal Regulators, States, and Further Obligations

A. Introduction and Summary

Prior to 1970, there was no good mechanism at the federal level to address environmental protection.[1] Therefore, in 1970, upon the recommendation of a Presidential Advisory Council, President Nixon

1. "Our National Government is neither structured nor oriented to sustain a well-articulated attack on the practices which debase the air we breathe, the water we drink and the land that grows our food" and "the present departmental structure for dealing with environmental protection defies effective and concerted action," Memorandum for the President from the Exec. Office of the President, President's Advisory Council on Exec. Org., *Federal Organization for Environmental Protection* (Apr. 29, 1970) (known as the "Ash Council Memo"), https://www.epa.gov/archive/epa/aboutepa/ash-council-memo.html. *See also* Alexis C. Madrigal, *Gallery: Why Nixon Created EPA*, The Atlantic (Dec. 2, 2010), http://www.theatlantic.com/technology/archive/2010/12/gallery-why-nixon-created-the-epa/67351/.

created the EPA.[2] Two years later, when passing major amendments to the Federal Water Pollution Control Act,[3] this new agency was given major authority over clean water in the nation, including co-authority over the regulation of wetlands and other waters involving discharge with the Corps.[4]

In the decades that followed, there have been skirmishes about the parameters of the shared regulatory structure in this part of the statute,[5] but a typical apportionment of responsibilities has developed over time. Section 404 directs the following division of authority: (1) Section 404(a) authorizes the Corps to issue permits for the discharge of dredged or fill material;[6] (2) Section 404(b)(1) grants EPA authority ("in conjunction with" the Corps) to develop "Guidelines" to be applied to permit decisions;[7] (3) Section 404(q) sets forth a process for elevating issues to Corps Headquarters by various federal agencies, including EPA, regarding efficient permit processing;[8] and (4) Section 404(c) authorizes EPA to proscribe discharges of dredged or fill material in defined areas.[9] EPA's website identifies the relative roles as follows:

---

2. *See* U.S. Env't Prot. Agency, *The Origins of EPA* (Feb. 27, 2013) https://www.epa.gov/history/origins-epa.

3. Federal Water Pollution Control Act Amendments, Pub. L. No. 92-500, § 101, 86 Stat. 816 (1972), codified at 33 U.S.C. §§ 1251–1376. *See generally* Charles W. Smith, *Highlights of the Federal Water Pollution Control Act of 1972*, 77 Dick. L. Rev. 459 (1973); Kenneth M. Murchison, *Learning from More Than Five-and-a-Half Decades of Federal Water Pollution Control Legislation: Twenty Lessons for the Future*, 32 B.C. Env't Aff. L. Rev. 527 (2005).

4. See Sam Kalen, Commerce To Conservation: The Call For a National Water Policy and The Evolution of Federal Jurisdiction Over Wetlands, 69 N.D. L. Rev. 873, 887–97 (1993).

5. *Id. See also* Alyson C. Flournoy, *Section 404 at Thirty-Something: A Program in Search of a Policy*, 55 Ala. L. Rev. 607, 616–17 (2004) ("Congress's commitment of the section 404 program to the joint custody of the Corps and EPA is the second structural element that set us on a path fraught with tension, further clouding the policy waters. The decision to charge the Corps with implementing section 404 has been labeled 'ironic' by one leading authority, and 'a recipe for endless conflict' by another. (Citations omitted)").

6. 33 U.S.C. § 1344(a).

7. *Id.* § 1344(b)(1).

8. *Id.* § 1344(q).

9. *Id.* § 1344(c).

U.S. Army Corps of Engineers:

- Administers day-to-day Section 404 program, including individual and general permit decisions;
- Conducts or verifies jurisdictional determinations;
- Develops policy and guidance; and
- Enforces Section 404 provisions.

U.S. Environmental Protection Agency:

- Develops and interprets policy, guidance, and environmental criteria used in evaluating permit applications;
- Determines scope of geographic jurisdiction and applicability of exemptions;
- Approves and oversees State and Tribal assumption;
- Reviews and comments on individual permit applications;
- Has authority to prohibit, deny, or restrict the use of any defined area as a disposal site (Section 404(c));
- Can elevate specific cases (Section 404(q));
- Enforces Section 404 provisions.[10]

This section explores the primary roles of EPA in wetlands regulation. It begins with the Section 404(q) elevation process, continues by discussing EPA's "veto" authority under Section 404(c), and concludes with a brief examination of the Section 404(b)(1) Guidelines and enforcement. Note that there may be some procedural differences among regional offices of EPA,[11] and practitioners and other stakeholders would be well served by contacting their regional office[12] directly with specific inquiries regarding EPA and wetland regulation.

---

10. U.S. Env't Prot. Agency, *Permit Program under CWA Section 404,* https://www.epa.gov/cwa-404/permit-program-under-cwa-section-404 (last updated Mar. 11, 2024).

11. See, e.g., U.S. Env't Prot. Agency and U.S. Army Corps of Eng'rs, Interagency Understanding between the U.S. Environmental Protection Agency, Region 8 and The Department of The Army, Corps of Engineers, Albuquerque, Sacramento and Omaha Districts: Local Procedures for Individual Permit Decisions under Section 404 of The Clean Water Act and Section 10 of the Rivers and Harbors Act of 1899 in Accordance with the 1992 Section 404(Q) Memorandum of Agreement between the U.S. Environmental Protection Agency and the Department of the Army, Corps of Engineers (2011), http://www.spk.usace.army.mil/Portals/12/documents/regulatory/pdf/agreements/Interagency_Understanding_404q_local_procedures_14-April-2011.pdf.

12. For Section 404 contact information for the EPA Regional Offices around the country, *see* https://www.epa.gov/wetlands/forms/contact-us-about-wetlands#regional (last updated Mar. 11, 2024).

B. Section 404(q) Elevations

If EPA and the Corps seriously disagree about a particular Section 404 permit, EPA may attempt resolution through the Section 404(q) "elevation" process.[13] Section 404(q) requires agreements between the Corps and various federal resource agencies, including EPA, "to minimize, to the maximum extent practicable, duplication, needless paperwork, and delays in the issuance of permits under this section."[14] Congress passed Section 404(q) in an attempt to ensure that "a decision with respect to an application for a permit . . . will be made not later than the ninetieth day after the date the notice for such application is published."[15]

The Memorandum of Agreement[16] between EPA and the Corps implementing Section 404(q) (MOA) sets forth the procedures the agencies will follow when an EPA regional office is concerned that a particular proposed permit may warrant higher-level scrutiny. This process starts when EPA requests "elevation" of a Corps permit decision from the Corps' District Engineer to the Assistant Secretary of the Army for Civil Works.[17] The present MOA between the Corps and EPA establishes the following step-wise procedures.

First, EPA must provide project-specific comments on the proposal within the public comment period, which may be extended at EPA's request to a maximum of 60 days (or longer if the applicant requests).[18] In order to preserve the ability to further elevate the permit decision, during the public comment period, the EPA regional administrator (or designee) must notify the district engineer "that in the opinion of EPA the project *may* result in substantial and unacceptable impacts to aquatic resources of national importance. . . ."[19] Cases that do not meet

---

13. *See generally* U.S. Env't Prot. Agency, *Clean Water Act Section 404(q) Dispute Resolution Process*, https://www.epa.gov/sites/default/files/2016-03/documents/404q_factsheet.pdf (last visited Apr. 11, 2024).

14. 33 U.S.C. § 1344(q).

15. *Id.*

16. U.S. Env't Prot. Agency, CWA Section 404(q): Memorandum of Agreement between EPA and Department of the Army (Aug. 11, 1992), https://www.epa.gov/cwa-404/cwa-section-404q-memorandum-agreement-between-epa-and-department-army-text.

17. *See id.* at pt. IV(a).

18. *Id.*

19. *Id.* at pt. IV. (emphasis in original). An assessment of Aquatic Resources of National Importance, or ARNI, is a region-specific assessments that include

this threshold cannot be elevated even if EPA disagrees that the Corps has selected the least damaging practicable alternative, and EPA must file this notice within the specified comment period.[20] Second, within 25 days after the close of the comment period, the regional administrator must notify the district engineer that EPA has determined "the discharge *will* have a substantial and unacceptable impact on aquatic resources of national importance."[21]

The district engineer may respond to EPA's concerns either by proposing permit issuance notwithstanding EPA's objection or by proposing a permit modification in an effort to resolve EPA's objection. The latter requires the district engineer to provide a draft permit and decision document to EPA within five days of the decision to modify the proposed permit.[22] In the alternative, the district engineer may notify EPA that the project has been modified or conditioned so that there no longer are "substantial and unacceptable impacts to aquatic resources of national importance."[23] The MOA does not set a time limit for the district engineer to perform this step, so it may be a source of project delays.

If EPA remains dissatisfied, the relevant regional administrator has 15 days to recommend that the assistant administrator of the Office of Wetlands, Oceans and Watersheds request elevation of the permit decision from the assistant secretary of the Army for Civil Works.[24] The assistant administrator then has 20 days to make such a request

---

considerations like "economic importance of the aquatic resource, rarity or uniqueness, and/or importance of the aquatic resource to the protection, maintenance, or enhancement of the quality of the Nation's waters. Past 404(q) elevations have identified the Chesapeake Bay, vernal pools, bottomland hardwoods, sub-alpine fens, bogs, and coastal marshes as ARNIs." *Clean Water Act: Section 404(q) Dispute Resolution Process*, *supra* note 13. The term has a broad, flexible meaning that depends on its regional setting and the nature of the project. Sometimes it is not the aquatic resource proposed to be directly impacted but its regional watershed that is the basis for the ARNI designation. *See, e.g.*, F. Matthews & A. Savage, *Why Do Federal Agencies Rely on ARNI Designations in Environmental Permitting?*, 84 FLA. BAR J. 10, 56 (Dec. 2010) ("A review of multiple projects in which EPA has used the term ARNI reveals that ARNI is a broad term with almost limitless boundaries. The Chesapeake Bay, vernal pools, bottomland hardwoods, sub-alpine fens, bogs, coastal marshes, forested wetlands, priority habitat for migratory birds, essential fish habitat for federally managed fisheries, and seagrass have all been termed ARNIs.").

20. CWA Section 404(q): Memorandum of Agreement, *supra* note 16, at pt. IV.

21. *Id.* (emphasis in original).

22. *Id.*

23. *Id.*

24. Memorandum of Agreement, *supra* note 16, at pt. IV.

to the assistant secretary, during which time the Corps may not issue the disputed permit pending review at Corps headquarters.[25] Finally, the assistant secretary has 30 days to (1) direct the district engineer to continue processing of the permit notwithstanding EPA's objections, or (2) instruct the district engineer to proceed in a prescribed way, or (3) make the final permit decision.[26]

Although the Corps does not publish the documents associated with 404(q) elevation requests, other agencies have made some of these decisions available online. EPA publishes its elevation request letters, as well as Department of the Army responses to those letters.[27]

If EPA remains displeased with the final resolution of the permit application by the Corps following a Section 404(q) elevation process, it may move to veto the permit under Section 404(c). The next section discusses this process in detail.

C. EPA's Veto Authority under Section 404(c)

Section 404(c) grants EPA authority to "veto" Corps decisions to permit discharges or fill material in a defined area.[28] An EPA veto requires a determination that the proposed discharge "will have an unacceptable adverse effect on municipal water supplies, shellfish beds and fishery areas (including spawning and breeding areas), wildlife, or recreational areas. . . ."[29]

The veto process consists of three steps: (1) a proposed determination by the relevant regional administrator; (2) a recommended

25. *Id.*

26. *Id.* at pt. V. The MOA provides that "EPA reserves the right to proceed with Section 404(c). To assist EPA in reaching a decision on whether to exercise its Section 404(c) authority, the District Engineer will provide EPA a copy of the Statement of Findings/Record of Decision prepared in support of a permit decision after the ASA(CW) review. The permit shall not be issued during a period of 10 calendar days after such notice unless it contains a condition that no activity may take place pursuant to the permit until such 10th day, or if EPA has initiated a Section 404(c) proceeding during such 10 day period, until the Section 404(c) proceeding is concluded and subject to the final determination in such proceeding." *Id.*

27. U.S. Env't Prot. Agency, *Chronology of 404(q) Actions*, https://www.epa.gov/cwa-404/chronology-cwa-section-404c-actions (last updated Mar. 12, 2024).

28. 33 U.S.C. § 1344(c); 40 C.F.R. § 231.

29. 33 U.S.C. § 1344(c).

determination by that regional administrator; and (3) a final determination by the EPA administrator.[30]

The 404(c) veto process begins when the regional administrator notifies the applicant and the district engineer of EPA's intent to issue public notice of a proposed determination to prohibit or restrict the discharge.[31] In many cases, a 404(q) elevation will have preceded this process.[32] If, within 15 days after such notice, the regional administrator remains convinced that "unacceptable adverse effects" will occur, notice is issued in the *Federal Register*,[33] with a public comment period of between 30 and 60 days.[34]

Within 15 days after the close of the public comment period (or 30 days if there is a public hearing), the regional administrator must either issue a recommended determination or withdraw the proposed determination.[35] A recommended determination must be "promptly" forwarded to the EPA administrator in Washington D.C., along with the administrative record of EPA and, where possible, the administrative record of the Corps or, if applicable, the state, pertaining to the discharge in question.[36]

Receipt of the recommended determination and the administrative record triggers a 30-day deadline for EPA administrator to initiate consultation between "the Chief of Engineers, the owner of record, and, where applicable, the State and the applicant, if any."[37] These stakeholders have 15 days to notify the administrator if they will take corrective action to prevent the identified unacceptable adverse effects.[38] Receipt of the recommended determination and administrative record

---

30. 40 C.F.R. § 231.1(b).
31. *Id.* § 231.3(a)(1).
32. *Id.* at § 231.3 ("Comment: In cases involving a proposed disposal site for which a permit application is pending, it is anticipated that the procedures of the section 404 referral process will normally be exhausted prior to any final decision of whether to initiate a 404(c) proceeding.").
33. *Id.* § 231.3(a)(2).
34. A public hearing may be held on the proposed determination if the regional administrator determines that the public interest warrants one, and *must* be held if an affected landowner or the permit applicant requests one. *Id.* § 231.4(b). Any public hearing must occur at least 21 days after the public notice, and 15 days prior to the close of the public comment period. *Id.* § 231.4.
35. *Id.* § 231.5(a).
36. *Id.* § 231.5(b)–(e).
37. *Id.* § 231.6.
38. *Id.*

triggers a 60-day deadline for the final determination affirming, modifying, or rescinding the recommended determination.[39]

The regulatory timeframes are only aspirational. EPA may, "upon a showing of good cause, extend the time requirements in these regulations" via Federal Register notice.[40]

A Section 404(c) finding of "unacceptable adverse effect" focuses on specified resources; the term is defined as "impact on an aquatic or wetland ecosystem which is likely to result in significant degradation of municipal water supplies (including surface or groundwater) or significant loss of or damage to fisheries, shellfishing, or wildlife habitat or recreation areas," with due consideration to relevant portions of the Section 404(b)(1) Guidelines.[41]

The preamble to EPA's Section 404(c) regulations declares that the Section 404(b)(1) Guidelines establish not only the criteria for permit issuance by the Corps but also "the substantive criteria by which the acceptability of a proposed discharge is to be judged" for purposes of Section 404(c).[42] EPA may thus veto a Corps decision if, in its judgment, the Corps misapplied the Guidelines.[43]

Relative to the Guidelines, EPA has vetoed based on (1) potential significant degradation of an aquatic ecosystem,[44] (2) possible losses to wetland functions and values,[45] (3) availability of practicable alternatives to the proposed discharge with lesser adverse impacts to aquatic ecosystems,[46] and (4) failure to take "appropriate and practicable steps . . . to minimize potential adverse impacts . . . on the aquatic ecosystem."[47]

EPA has used its veto authority infrequently, vetoing only 14 disposal sites in more than 40 years, most recently in 2023. EPA need not

---

39. *Id.*

40. *Id.* § 231.8.

41. *Id.* § 231.2(e).

42. 44 Fed. Reg. 58,076 (Oct. 9, 1979).

43. As EPA stated in the preamble to the Section 404(b)(1) Guidelines issued after the 1979 Regulations, "if the Guidelines are properly applied [by the Corps], EPA will rarely have to use its 404(c) veto." 45 Fed. Reg. 85,337 (Dec. 24, 1980).

44. *See* 40 C.F.R. §§ 230.10(c), 230.22 & subpts C–G.

45. *See* 40 C.F.R. § 230.41(b). Nonetheless, none of these provisions describes what kinds of losses will be considered "unacceptable" for purposes of Section 404(c).

46. *See, e.g.*, James City Cnty., Va. v. U.S. Env't Prot. Agency, 955 F.2d 254 (4th Cir. 1992); Bersani v. U.S. Env't Prot. Agency, 674 F. Supp. 405 (N.D.N.Y. 1987), *aff'd*, 850 F.2d 36 (2d Cir. 1988), *cert. denied* 489 U.S. 1089 (1989).

47. *See James City Cnty.*, 955 F.2d 254.

veto all nonconforming permits, although some courts have held the decision not to veto a project is reviewable as final agency action under the Administrative Procedure Act.[48] And while the final 404(c) determination to veto a project is similarly reviewable, EPA's *initiation* of the Section 404(c) process is not, as it is not final agency action, as the court found in *City of Olmstead Falls v. U.S. Environmental Protection Agency.*

In *City of Olmstead Falls*, a federal district court held that because EPA's exercise of its veto authority is discretionary, federal courts lack jurisdiction to review the agency's failure to veto a Section 404 permit.[49] EPA's *initiation* of the Section 404(c) process is also not reviewable in court, as it is not a final agency action.[50] Plaintiffs must wait until the agency has vetoed a permit before they can sue.

Judicial review of final vetoes proceeds under the "arbitrary and capricious" standard of review.[51] Under this standard, a court cannot substitute its judgment for that of the agency.[52] To date, courts accordingly have shown little inclination to limit EPA's discretion to determine what kinds of impacts from discharges may be considered "unacceptable adverse effects" for purposes of Section 404(c), as the following case summaries demonstrate.

In *Bersani v. U.S. Environmental Protection Agency*, the court held that unacceptable adverse effects may properly include review of the Corps' application of the Section 404(b)(1) Guidelines, noting the Guidelines provide EPA with "a useful tool for evaluating discharges into the aquatic environment."[53] Likewise, the court held that EPA may also veto a permit if it disagrees with a Corps finding of no practicable

48. *See* notes 85 and 86 and accompanying text.

49. 266 F. Supp. 2d 718, 723 (N.D. Ohio 2003). The court also rejected the plaintiff's claim that the 404(b)(1) Guidelines create a nondiscretionary duty on EPA. *Id.* at 723–24. The court held that the Guidelines impose a duty on the Corps, but not on EPA. *Id.*

50. Newport Galleria Grp. v. Deland, 618 F. Supp. 1179 (D.C. 1985).

51. *See* James City Cnty., Va. v. U.S. Env't Prot. Agency, 12 F.3d 1330 (4th Cir. 1993) ("[t]he scope of review under the 'arbitrary and capricious' standard is narrow and a court is not to substitute its judgment for that of the agency"); Bersani v. U.S. Env't Prot. Agency, 674 F. Supp. 405 (N.D.N.Y. 1987); Alameda Water & Sanitation Dist. v. Reilly, 930 F. Supp. 486 (D. Colo. 1996); Russo Dev. Corp. v. Thomas, 735 F. Supp. 631 (D.N.Y. 1989).

52. *James City Cnty.*, 12 F. 3d at 1338.

53. *Bersani*, 674 F. Supp. at 414.

alternatives to the proposed discharge site.[54] Finally, the court concluded that nothing in Section 404(c) "indicates Congress' desire to limit EPA's role in assessing the environmental acceptability of a site."[55]

According to the Fourth Circuit,[56] Section 404(c) allows but cannot require EPA to consider "non-environmental" factors such as a city's need for a dependable supply of water,[57] and concluded that EPA's veto authority to protect the environment is broad, calling it "practically unadorned."[58]

In *Creppel v. U.S. Army Corps of Engineers*, the court concluded that "[S]ection 404(c) does *not* require a balancing of environmental concerns against 'the public interest,'" which in the *Creppel* case involved a project needed to protect the public against flood impacts.[59]

The veto process under Section 404(c) is very lengthy, with some determinations being modified decades after the original veto.[60] EPA proposed its first veto on August 1, 1980, which it finalized a year later.[61] To date, the agency had issued only 14 final vetoes, the most recent in 2023. EPA has a helpful website that provides all veto decisions in reverse chronological order, along with relevant background documents to provide context and detail.[62] Following is a reference

54. *Id.* at 415.

55. *Id.* at 417; *see also* Newport Galleria Grp. v. Deland, 618 F. Supp. 1179 (D.C. 1985) (noting in *dicta* that "it would be extraordinary if Congress granted EPA veto power over the Corps' permit decision, but precluded it from reconsidering those issues the Corps considered in granting the permit in the first place").

56. 955 F.2d 254 (4th Cir. 1992), *later proceeding after remand*, 12 F.3d 1330 (4th Cir. 1993).

57. *James City Cnty.*, 12 F.3d at 1335–36, and Alameda Water & Sanitation Dist. v. Reilly, 930 F. Supp. 486, 491 (D. Colo. 1996).

58. James City Cnty., Va. v. U.S. Env't Prot. Agency, 12 F.3d 1330 (4th Cir. 1993).

59. Creppel v. U.S. Army Corps of Eng'rs, 19 Env't L. Rep. 20,134, 20,136 (E.D. La. 1988) (this case concerns the Bayou aux Carpes Determination, discussed at notes 66–67 and accompanying text. *See also* City of Alma v. U.S. Env't Prot. Agency, 744 F. Supp. 1546 (S.D. Ga. 1990) (upholding a veto based on water quality and the loss of wetlands) and Alameda Water & Sanitation Dist. v. Reilly, 930 F. Supp. at 491 (upholding a veto based on water quality).

60. *See* note 64 and accompanying text (M.A. Norden Determination modified ten years after initial veto), and notes 66–67 and accompanying text (Bayou aux Carpes Determination, modified once at seven years and the second time 24 years after the initial veto in 1985).

61. 45 Fed. Reg. 51,275 (Aug. 1, 1980).

62. *Chronology of 404(c) Actions*, *supra* note 27.

list of the final vetoes (noting briefly the basis of each EPA veto for perspective):

1. 1981-Florida. North Miami Landfill Site in Dade County

EPA vetoed a permit involving a 103-acre fill using municipal solid waste, due to leachate after the project was initiated that was impacting fisheries and two endangered species.[63]

2. 1984-Alabama. M.A. Norden Co. Site in Mobile

EPA vetoed a 25-acre fill in tidal wetlands, highlighting issues with the practicable alternatives analysis.[64]

3. 1985-South Carolina. Jack Maybank Site, Charleston County

EPA vetoed a 900-acre permit seeking to impound riparian wetlands primarily for duck hunting, citing ecological services and public access of the potentially impacted wetlands.[65]

---

63. *See* Final Determination of the Administrator Concerning the North Miami Landfill Site Pursuant to Section 404(c) of the Clean Water Act, 46 Fed. Reg. 10,203 (Feb. 2, 1981). *See also* Proposed Determination to Prohibit, or Deny Specification, of an Area as a Disposal Site, 45 Fed. Reg. 51,275 (Aug. 1, 1980).

64. *See* Final Determination of the Administrator Concerning the M.A. Norden Site Pursuant to Section 404(c) of the Clean Water Act, 49 Fed. Reg. 29,142 (July 18, 1984). *See also* Proposed Determination to Prohibit, Deny, or Restrict the Specification, or the Use for Specification, of an Area as a Disposal Site; Public Hearing, 48 Fed. Reg. 51,732 (Nov. 10, 1983). The final determination of veto was modified in 1994 to allow the applicant to apply for a permit to build an access road across the wetlands in question, concluding that the road would not cause unacceptable adverse effects. M.A. Norden Company Site, AL: Modification of June 15, 1984, Clean Water Act Section 404(c) Final Determination, 59 Fed. Reg. 46,246 (Sept. 7, 1994).

65. *See* Final Determination Concerning the Jack Maybank Site on Jehossee Island, South Carolina, Pursuant to Section 404(c) of the Clean Water Act, 50 Fed. Reg. 20,291 (May 15, 1985). *See also* Notice of Public Hearing and Proposed Determination to Prohibit Specification of Area as a Disposal Site, 49 Fed. Reg. 30,112, 30,113 (July 26, 1984).

4. 1985-Louisiana. Bayou aux Carpes Site, Jefferson Parish

EPA vetoed a flood control project for unacceptable adverse effects under nearly every factor enumerated in Section 404(c).[66] The U.S. District Court for the Eastern District of Louisiana upheld the veto, holding that Section 404(c) does not require EPA to balance environmental effects against "the public interest."[67]

5. 1986-Massachusetts. Sweedens Swamp Site, Attleboro

EPA vetoed discharge into 32 acres of wetlands and alteration of an additional 13 acres due to non-water-dependent discharge, the use of mitigation to "buy-down" size, the public interest review, and issues regarding when the permit applicant "entered the marketplace."[68]

6. 1988-New Jersey. Russo Development Corporation, Carlstadt

EPA vetoed discharge into 8.5 acres in the Hackensack Meadowlands and required an after-the-fact permit for a previous discharge into 44 acres based on cumulative impacts to a rare wetland.[69] A court subsequently held the veto to be partially arbitrary and capricious because EPA improperly linked the new discharge to the prior discharge.[70]

---

66. *See* Final Determination of the U.S. Environmental Protection Agency's Assistant Administrator for External Affairs, Concerning the Bayou Aux Carpes Site in Jefferson Parish, Louisiana, Pursuant to Section 404(c) of the Clean Water Act, 50 Fed. Reg. 47,267 (Nov. 15, 1985). *See also* Proposed Determination to Prohibit, Deny, or Restrict the Specification, or the Use for Specification, of an Area as a Disposal Site; Notice and Public Hearing, 50 Fed. Reg. 20,602 (May 17, 1985). This Final Determination was modified twice, once in 1992 and again in 2009.

67. *See* Creppel v. U.S. Army Corps of Eng'rs, 19 Env't L. Rep. at 20,136 .

68. *See* Water Pollution Control; Final Determination of the Assistant Administrator for External Affairs Concerning the Sweedens Swamp Site, 51 Fed. Reg. 22,977 (June 24, 1986). *See also* Proposed Determination to Prohibit or Restrict the Specification of an Area for Use as a Disposal Site; Notice of Public Hearing, 50 Fed. Reg. 33,835, 33,836 (Aug. 21, 1985). Related litigation regarding market entry culminated in Bersani v. U.S. Env't Prot. Agency, 850 F.2d 36 (Court of Appeals 1988), *cert. denied* 489 U.S. 1089 (1989).

69. *See* Water Pollution Control; Final Determination of the Assistant Administrator for Water Concerning the Russo Development Corporation Site; Carlstadt, NJ, 53 Fed. Reg. 16,469 (May 9, 1988). *See also* Proposed Determination to Prohibit or Restrict the Specification of an Area for Use as a Disposal Site, 52 Fed. Reg. 29,431, 29,432 (Aug. 7, 1987).

70. *See* Russo Dev. Corp. v. Reilly, 21 Env't L. Rep. 21,345, 21,349 (D.N.J. 1991).

7. 1988-Florida. Henry Rem, Marion Becker et al., and Senior Corporation Sites, Dade County

EPA vetoed the proposed use of an agricultural technique known as "rock plowing" to create farmland out of wetlands in the Florida Everglades due to unacceptable adverse impacts to fish and wildlife habitat, food-chain production, recreation, and groundwater and surface water quality.[71]

8. 1989-Georgia. Lake Alma Impoundment, Bacon County.

EPA rejected creation of a recreational lake through damming a creek as having unacceptable adverse effects on wildlife, including secondary and cumulative effects.[72] The district court upheld the veto in 1990.[73]

9. 1989-Virginia. Ware Creek Supply Impoundment, James City County

EPA rejected the proposed impoundment of a creek to create a municipal water supply reservoir following a detailed environmental impact study, in which EPA found there would be unacceptable adverse effects to very high quality and probably irreplaceable resources despite the existence of less environmentally damaging practicable alternatives.[74] After a lengthy court battle, the Fourth Circuit Court of Appeals

---

71. *See* Final Determination of the U.S. Environmental Protection Agency's Assistant Administrator for Water Concerning Three Wetland Properties Owned by Henry Rem Estate, Marion Becker, et al. and Senior Corp., 53 Fed. Reg. 30,093 (Aug. 10, 1988). *See also* Proposed 404(c) Determination to Prohibit, Deny, or Restrict the Specification of Use of Three East Everglades Areas as Disposal Sites; Notice and Public Hearing Announcement, 52 Fed. Reg. 38,519 (Oct. 16, 1987).

72. *See* Water Pollution Control; Final Determination Concerning the Proposed Lake Alma Recreational Lake Project on Hurricane Creek, Alma, Bacon County, GA., 54 Fed. Reg. 6749 (Feb. 14, 1989). *See also* Proposed Determination to Prohibit, or Deny the Specification or the Use for Specification, of an Area as a Disposal Site: Ware Creek, James City County, VA, 53 Fed. Reg. 46,656, 46,657–58 (Nov. 18, 1988).

73. City of Alma v. U.S. Env't Prot. Agency, 744 F. Supp. 1546 (S.D. Ga. 1990).

74. *See* Water Pollution Control; Final Determination of the Assistant Administrator for Water Pursuant to Section 404(c) of the Clean Water Act Concerning the Proposed Ware Creek Water Supply Impoundment in James City Cnty., VA, 54 Fed. Reg. 33,608 (Aug. 15, 1989). *See also* Proposed Determination to Prohibit, or Deny the Specification or the Use for Specification, of an Area as a Disposal Site: Ware Creek, James City Cnty., VA, 53 Fed. Reg. 46,656, 46,657–58 (Nov. 18. 1988).

concluded that EPA was entitled to consider whether the environmental effects of the project were "unacceptable" given the absence of a practicable alternative and remanded.[75] A second round of veto attempts and court battles resulted in another Fourth Circuit decision holding that environmental impacts were an appropriate focus for a veto decision.[76]

10. 1990-Rhode Island. Big River Water Supply Impoundment, Kent County

EPA vetoed a dam intended to create a 3,400-acre municipal water supply reservoir based on negative environmental effects, including habitat and water quality impacts, and failure to explore all practicable alternatives.[77]

11. 1991-Colorado. Two Forks Water Supply Impoundments, Jefferson and Douglas Counties

EPA vetoed a dam and reservoir designed to support a regional water supply plan for Denver based on findings that the proposed project would have unacceptable environmental impacts on fisheries, wildlife, and recreation and that there were practicable, less damaging alternatives.[78] The district court upheld the veto in an opinion that approved a "sequencing" approach to analyzing alternatives, wherein alternatives are evaluated based on avoidance and minimization of wetland impacts, rather than on the effect of mitigation on ameliorating those impacts.[79]

---

75. *See* James City Cnty., Va. v. U.S. Env't Prot. Agency, 955 F.2d 254 (4th Cir. 1992). The Final Determination on Remand was issued in 1992. *See* James City Cnty., Va. v. U.S. Env't Prot. Agency, 12 F.3d 1330 (4th Cir. 1993).

76. James City Cnty., Va. v. U.S. Env't Prot. Agency, 12 F.3d 1330 (4th Cir. 1993).

77. *See* Water Pollution Control; Final Determination of Assistant Administrator for Water Pursuant to Section 404(c) of the Clean Water Act Concerning the Proposed Big River Water Supply Impoundment in Kent Cnty., RI, 55 Fed. Reg. 10,666 (Mar. 22, 1990). *See also* Proposed Determination to Prohibit the Use of Big River, Mishnock River, Their Tributaries and Adjacent Wetlands as Disposal Sites, RI, 54 Fed. Reg. 5133, 5134 (Feb. 1, 1989).

78. *See* Final Determination of the Assistant Administrator for Water Pursuant to Section 404(c) of the Clean Water Act Concerning the Two Forks Water Supply Impoundments in Jefferson and Douglas Cntys., Colo., 56 Fed. Reg. 76 (1991). *See also* Proposed Determination to Prohibit, Restrict, or Deny the Specification, or the Use for Specification, of an Area as a Disposal Site; South Platte River, 54 Fed. Reg. 36,862 (Sept. 5, 1989).

79. Alameda Water & Sanitation Dist. v. Reilly, 930 F. Supp. 486, 492 (D. Colo. 1996).

12. 2008-Mississippi. Yazoo Backwater Area Pumps Project, Issaquena County

EPA vetoed impacts of a pumping station on between 150,000 to 229,000 acres of wetlands, as well as an extensive network of streams, creeks, and other aquatic resources, to unacceptable adverse impacts including cumulative impacts and insufficient mitigation, notwithstanding the purpose of the project to protect residents from flooding.[80]

13. 2011-West Virginia. Spruce No. 1 Surface Mine in Logan County

EPA vetoed mountaintop coal mining that would have buried more than six miles of streams with mining waste, determining it would kill wildlife and harm downstream water quality.[81] This veto determination is discussed in further detail later in this section.

14. 2023-Alaska. Mining the Pebble Deposit in Bristol Bay, Alaska

EPA vetoed the use of Bristol Bay in southwest Alaska, as a disposal site for discharges associated with development of a mine at the Pebble Deposit, a large ore body in southwest Alaska, based on unacceptable adverse effects on salmon fishery areas.[82] This most recent veto determination by EPA is discussed in further detail later in this section and represents what may be the broadest application of EPA's veto powers to date.

---

80. *See* Final Determination of the Assistant Administrator for Water Pursuant to Section 404(c) of the Clean Water Act Concerning the Proposed Yazoo Backwater Area Pumps Project in Issaguena County, MS, 73 Fed. Reg. 54,398 (Sept. 19, 2008). *See also* Proposed Determination to Prohibit, Restrict, or Deny the Specification, or the Use for Specification, of an Area as a Disposal Site; Yazoo River Basin, Issaquena County, MS, 73 Fed. Reg. 14,806 (Mar. 19, 2008).

81. *See* Final Determination to Prohibit the Specification of and Restrict the Use for Specification of Certain Waters within Defined Areas as Disposal Sites; Spruce No. 1 Surface Mine, 76 Fed. Reg. 3,126 (Jan. 19, 2011). *See also* Proposed Determination to Prohibit and Restrict the Use of Certain Waters within Defined Areas as Disposal Sites; Spruce No. 1 Surface Mine, 75 Fed. Reg. 16,788 (Apr. 2, 2010).

82. *See* Final Determination to Prohibit the Specification of and Restrict the Use for Specification of Certain Waters within Defined Areas as Disposal Sites; Pebble Deposit Area, Southwest Alaska, 88 Fed. Reg. 7,441 (Feb. 3, 2023). *See also* Proposed Determination to Prohibit and Restrict the Use of Certain Waters within Defined Areas as Disposal Sites; Pebble Deposit Area, Southwest Alaska, 87 Fed. Reg. 32,021 (May 26, 2022).

Several courts explored the parameters of EPA's veto authority and the role of citizens in triggering a 404(c) veto process. The U.S. Supreme Court reaffirmed EPA's veto authority in *Coeur Alaska, Inc. v. Southeast Alaska Conservation*,[83] noting that "the Act gives EPA authority to 'prohibit' any decision by the Corps to issue a permit for a particular disposal site" referring to this authority as EPA's power to veto a permit.[84]

In 2007, the District Court for the District of Columbia allowed the plaintiffs to bring action against EPA under the Administrative Procedure Act, but not the Clean Water Act, for its decision not to veto a permit.[85] In contrast, the South Carolina District Court in 2008 did allow the plaintiffs to bring suit under the CWA citizen suit provision to assert that EPA should have asserted its Section 404(c) veto power with respect to a particular permit.[86]

The Yazoo Backwater Area Pumps Project veto process garnered much attention and subsequent litigation. In August 2008, EPA vetoed the discharge of dredged or fill material into wetlands in Issaquena, Mississippi, in connection with the construction of the proposed flood protection project.[87] The first Section 404(c) veto in 17 years, the EPA report authorizing the veto concluded "after extensive evaluation of the record for this project . . . that these large-scale hydrologic alterations would significantly degrade the critical ecological functions provided by approximately 67,000 acres of wetlands in the Yazoo Backwater Area, including those functions that support wildlife and fisheries

---

83. Coeur Alaska, Inc. v. Southeast Alaska Conservation, 557 U.S. 261 (2009).

84. *Id.* at 274.

85. All. to Save Mattaponi v. U.S. Army Corps of Eng'rs, 515 F. Supp. 2d 1 (D.C. 2007). However, the court held plaintiffs could not bring action under the Clean Water Act in this instance because EPA had used its discretion in deciding not to veto the permit. *Id.* at 4–5.

86. The court opted not to take the *All. to Save Mattaponi* court's stance in regard to the CWA citizen suit provision, and instead interpreted the Fourth Circuit's decision in Nat'l Wildlife Fed'n v. Hanson to mean citizens could sue EPA under the CWA for a failure to veto. S.C. Coastal Conservation League v. U.S. Army Corps of Eng'rs, 2008 U.S. Dist. LEXIS 69499, at *24–25 (D.S.C. Sept. 11, 2008) ("[A] plaintiff may maintain a citizen suit under Section 1365(a)(2) when the Administrator fails to exercise the duty of oversight imposed by Section 1344(c)." (quoting Nat'l Wildlife Fed'n v. Hanson, 859 F.2d 313, 316 (4th Cir. 1988))).

87. *See* Final Determination of the Assistant Administrator for Water Pursuant to Section 404(c) of the Clean Water Act Concerning the Proposed Yazoo Backwater Area Pumps Project in Issaquena County, *supra* note 80.

resources."[88] As described in a *Time Magazine* article on Earth Day 2008, the proposed project "would build the world's largest hydraulic pump to protect a sparsely populated area dominated by soybean fields from Yazoo River flooding, and it would drain or degrade enough wetlands to cover all five boroughs of New York City."[89] The primary component of the proposed project was a 14,000 cubic feet per second (cfs) pumping station that would pump surface water out of the Yazoo Backwater Area during high water events on the Mississippi River.[90] While EPA stated its support for improved flood protection for Mississippi Delta residents, EPA said it "believes that this vital objective can be accomplished consistent with ensuring effective protection for the area's valuable natural resources."[91] The Yazoo Backwater Area Pumps Project plan was subsequently proposed to be revised in 2020. In November 2020, the EPA under the Trump administration issued a letter to the Corps determining that the 2020 Proposed Plan was not covered by or subject to the 2008 404(c) determination. However, with the change in administrations, EPA superseded the prior administration's determination and instead confirmed that the final 2008 404(c) determination did apply to the 2020 proposed plan for the Yazoo Backwater Area Pumps Project Project and the Corps went back to the drawing board.[92]

---

88. *Id.*

89. Michael Grunwald, *A Green Day for Bush*, TIME (Feb. 2, 2008), https://content.time.com/time/nation/article/0,8599,1709351,00.html.

90. Press Release, U.S. Env't Prot. Agency, EPA Decision Protects 67,000 Acres of Mississippi Wetlands (Sept. 2, 2008), https://www.epa.gov/archive/epapages/newsroom_archive/newsreleases/8166182ff7d19b15852574b8005ffae1.html.

91. *See* Final Determination of the Assistant Administrator for Water Pursuant to Section 404(c) of the Clean Water Act Concerning the Proposed Yazoo Backwater Area Pumps Project in Issaquena County, *supra* note 80.

92. Letter from Assistant Administrator for Water to Acting Assistant Secretary of the Army (Civil Works), Nov. 17, 2021 (holding that the revised 2020 Plan for the Yazoo Pumps Project is prohibited by the 2008 Final Determination and reconsidering and reversing its November 30, 2020, letter, which held that the 2008 veto did not apply to the 2020 project), https://www.epa.gov/system/files/documents/2021-11/epa-reconsideration-of-november-30-2020-yazoo-letter.pdf. Thereafter, the Corps withdrew its Record of Decision and indicated it would work with EPA to determine the applicability of the 2008 veto to any future proposed flood plan. U.S. Army Corps of Eng'rs, Miss. Valley Div., Memorandum for the Record: Withdrawing Record of Decision for Final Supplement No. 2 to the 1982 Yazoo Area Pump Project Final Environmental Impact Statement (Dec. 15, 2021), *see* https://earthjustice.org/wp-content/uploads/18_-_feds._notice_of_withdrawal_of_rod.pdf.

The next veto garnering national attention was the veto of Spruce No. 1 Surface Mine in West Virginia in 2011.[93] EPA determined the proposed "mountaintop mining method"[94] would have buried more than six miles of streams with mining waste, killing wildlife and harming downstream water quality.[95] The veto of mountaintop mining was the first of its kind, because it served to withdraw a permit initially issued without objection in 2007 and thus was applied retroactively.[96] EPA nevertheless affirmed that its use of its veto authority would continue to be "extremely rare" and did not signal a change of policy.[97] EPA also raised questions as to the adequacy of stream creation as mitigation and the availability of practicable alternatives.[98]

In practice, the mere threat of an EPA veto can cause changes to the proposed discharge that ultimately avoids a veto.[99] Indeed, in 2013, EPA announced its intention to veto a surface coal mine in Kentucky

---

In 2023, the Corps decided it would try again and published notice of its intention to prepare an EIS for the project. U.S. Army Corps of Eng'rs, Notice of Intent to Prepare and Environmental Impact Statement for the Yazoo Backwater Area Water Management Project, 88 Fed. Reg. 43101 (July 6, 2023), https://earthjustice.org/wp-content/uploads/18_-_feds._notice_of_withdrawal_of_rod.pdf. At press-time, the final EIS had not yet been released.

93. The veto process was initiated in October 2009, with the proposed determination issued in April 2010 and the final veto issued in January 2011. Final Determination to Prohibit the Specification of and Restrict the Use for Specification of Certain Waters within Defined Areas as Disposal Sites; Spruce No. 1 Surface Mine, *supra* note 81. *See also* Amy Oxley, *No Longer Mine: An Extensive Look at the Environmental Protection Agency's Veto of the Section 404 Permit Held by the Spruce No. 1 Mine*, 36 S. Ill. U. L.J. 139 (2011).

94. Amy Oxley, 36 S. Ill. U. L.J. at 139 ("This style of mining removes the tops of mountains in order to recover coal and places the soil and rock from the top of the mountain, known as overburden, into valley fills.").

95. Although the Section 404(c) veto prevented discharge into two creeks, a third creek had already been impacted by the project at the time the determination was made. U.S. Env't Prot. Agency, *Questions & Answers—Spruce Mine Final Determination*, https://www.epa.gov/sites/default/files/2015-05/documents/final_spruce_404c_qa_011311.pdf (last visited Apr. 11, 2024).

96. *Id.*

97. *Id.*

98. *Id.*; *see also* Jason Rapp, *Coal and Water: Reclaiming the Clean Water Act for Environmental Protection*, 25 Tul. Env't L.J. 99, 133 (2011).

99. Frank E. Matthews & Amelia Savage, *Why Is ARNI an Environmental Permitting Stumbling Block?*, 41 No. 3 ABA Trends 1 (2010), https://www.stearnsweaver.com/blog/why-is-arni-an-environmental-permitting-stumbling-block/.

pursuant to Section 404(c).[100] EPA then coordinated with the project proponent, Revelation Energy, LLC, to substantially reduce the number of stream fills and the linear stream feet impacted thereby.[101] Considering these reductions sufficient to protect aquatic resources, EPA did not finalize the Section 404(c) veto for the project. This example demonstrates that cooperation during permit processing can avoid a potential veto. The Section 404(c) veto process, in other words, contains multiple opportunities for the Corps and project proponent to alter the project to address EPA's concerns, and it is likely in the interest of the project proponent to alter the project should EPA indicate its intention to initiate the Section 404(c) process.

EPA can take many years gathering data and fighting court battles to issue a final determination of permit veto, as the January 2023 veto of the Pebble Mine Permit demonstrates.[102] Since 2001, the Northern Dynasty Minerals Ltd. (NDM) and subsequently the Pebble Limited Partnership (PLP) had been collecting data and undertaking analysis in pursuit of permits to mine the Pebble deposit, a large mineral deposit containing copper, gold, and molybdenum located at the headwaters of the Bristol Bay watershed.[103] Subsistence, commercial and recreational fishing interests, conservation groups, indigenous groups, and others began requesting EPA use its veto authority to veto a permit prior to a permit application even being filed.[104] In response, EPA conducted an ecological risk assessment, which it released in January 2014 after three years of study.[105] In July 2014, EPA initiated review under 404(c) and subsequently released a Proposed Determination to veto the permit before the Corps even had a chance to review the project application.[106]

100. *See* Laura Kathryn Bomyea, *Dynamite, Disaster and Disappearing Options: How EPA Is Losing the Battle Against Destructive Mountaintop Removal Coal Mining Practices*, 6 Alb. Gov't. L. Rev. 224, 248–49 (2013).

101. Letter from Gwendolyn Keyes Fleming, Reg'l Adm'r, U.S. Env't Prot. Agency, to Colonel Peterson, Dist. Commander, U.S. Army Corps of Eng'rs, Huntington Dist. (May 31, 2012) (on file with U.S. Env't Prot. Agency).

102. EPA various decisions and notices in this convoluted case can be found at https://www.epa.gov/bristolbay/final-determination-pebble-deposit-area.

103. Env't Prot. Agency, Executive Summary of the Pebble Deposit Area 404(c) Final Determination, https://www.epa.gov/system/files/documents/2023-01/Pebble-Deposit-Area-404c-FD-Executive-Summary-Jan2023.pdf.

104. *Id.*

105. Bristol Bay Assessment—Final Report (2014), https://www.epa.gov/bristolbay/bristol-bay-assessment-final-report-2014 (last updated May 18, 2021).

106. 2014 Proposed Determination Pursuant to Section 404c of the Clean Water Act for Pebble Deposit Area, Southwest Alaska, https://www.epa.gov/bristolbay/2014

PLP brought suit challenging the Proposed Determination as arbitrary and capricious and contrary to the essential requirements of law, given that PLP had not yet applied for a permit, let alone had it denied. In November 2014, the District Court for the District of Alaska granted PLP's request for a preliminary injunction and halted the preemptive veto process.[107] On May 11, 2017, EPA and PLP settled the lawsuit, which the court accepted; the court subsequently dissolved the injunction and dismissed the case with prejudice. [108] Under the terms of the settlement, Region 10 agreed to "initiate a process to propose to withdraw the Proposed Determination" and to forbear sending a signed recommended determination to EPA Headquarters until May 11, 2021, or until notice of the Corps' final environmental impact statement (EIS) on PLP's CWA Section 404 permit application was published, whichever came first. In return, PLP agreed to submit its Section 404 permit application to the Corps within 30 months.[109]

In October 2019, a consortium of tribal, fishing, environmental, and conservation groups challenged EPA's withdrawal of the 2014 Proposed Determination in the U.S. District Court for the District of Alaska, asserting that withdrawal was not supported by the record and that EPA had failed to consider the relevant scientific and technical information. The district court dismissed the action, holding that EPA's decision to withdraw a proposed determination was unreviewable. On appeal, the Ninth Circuit in June 2021 reversed, finding that 40 C.F.R. § 231.5(a) provides the review standard and concluded that EPA is authorized to withdraw a proposed determination "only if the discharge of materials would be unlikely to have an unacceptable adverse effect."[110] The Ninth Circuit remanded the case to the district court for further proceedings.[111]

On October 29, 2021, following remand, the district court granted EPA's motion in the district court requesting that the court vacate EPA's

---

-proposed-determination-pursuant-section-404c-clean-water-act-pebble-deposit-area (last updated Sept. 8, 2023).

107. Order Granting Preliminary Injunction, Pebble Limited Partnership v. U.S. Env't Prot. Agency, No. 3:14–cv–00171 (D. Alaska Nov. 25, 2014).

108. *See* Env't Prot. Agency, Notice of Time Extension on Proposed Determination to Restrict the Use of an Area and a Disposal Site; Pebble Deposit Area, 86 Fed. Reg. 66548 (Nov. 23, 2021), https://www.govinfo.gov/content/pkg/FR-2021-11-23/pdf/2021-25515.pdf.

109. *Id.*

110. Trout Unlimited v. Pirzadeh, 1 F.4th 738, 757 (9th Cir. June 17, 2021).

111. *Id.*

decision to withdraw the 2014 Proposed Determination and remand the action to the EPA to reconsider its action. EPA had explained in its motion that, in making the withdrawal decision, EPA had not addressed the "unlikely to have an unacceptable adverse effect" standard in 40 C.F.R. § 231.5(a) that the Ninth Circuit subsequently held must be met when EPA withdraws a proposed determination and that such an omission "was serious and fundamental."[112] This effectively reinstated the 2014 Proposed Determination and reinitiated the 404(c) review process. On November 23, 2021, EPA Region 10 published notice extending the time requirement through May 31, 2022, to allow EPA to consider information that had become available since the 2014 Proposed Determination.[113]

Part of that new information included two actual 404 permit applications submitted by PLP, neither of which were available to EPA when it issued its 2014 Proposed Determination. In 2017, PLP actually submitted its initial Section 404 application, which triggering an Environmental Impact Study under NEPA,[114] which in turn resulted in PLP submitting a revised application in 2020. In the 2020 Mine Plan, PLP proposed to develop the Pebble deposit as a surface strip mine, to recover 1.3 billion tons of ore over a 20-year period.[115] On July 24, 2020, the Corps published notice of availability of the Final EIS, and on November 20, 2020, issued its Record of Decision denying the permit on the ground that it did not comply with the 404(b)(1) Guidelines and would be contrary to the public interest.[116] The Corps determined that, even with proposed mitigation, "the proposed discharge does not comply with the 404(b)(1) Guidelines because the proposed project will result in significant degradation of the aquatic ecosystem."[117]

On September 6, 2022, EPA Region 10 published notice of its 2022 Proposed 404(c) Determination to veto the permit on the ground that

---

112. *See* 86 Fed. Reg. at 66550.

113. 86 Fed. Reg. 66548 (Nov. 23, 2021).

114. For more information about the NEPA process, *see* Chapter 4.

115. Executive Summary of the Pebble Deposit Area 404(c), *supra* note 103.

116. U.S. Army Corps of Eng'rs, Alaska District, Pebble Project Final Environmental Impact Statement (July 2020), https://www.arlis.org/docs/vol1/Pebble/Final-EIS/index.html.

117. U.S. Army Corps of Eng'rs, Record of Decision for Application Submitted by Pebble Limited Partnership to the United States Army Corps of Engineers (Department of the Army Permit # POA-2017-00271) § 7.1 (Nov. 20, 2020).

the proposed discharges would cause unacceptable adverse impacts to important fishery areas.[118] On January 30, 2023, after two decades of analysis and decades of litigation from both project proponents and opponents, EPA issued a Final Determination under Section 404(c) to prohibit use of the headwaters of the Bristol Bay watershed in southwest Alaska as disposal sites for discharges of dredged or fill material associated with the Pebble Mine, and this determination was published in the Federal Register on February 3, 2023.[119] EPA's final determination broadly applies to future discharges from mining operations in the same waters and broadcasts a similar likely result for mining discharges in disposal areas in the vicinity that are not expressly covered by the Final Determination. Because it reflects the latest on EPA's interpretation of its authority under Section 404(c), EPA's final determination as published in the Federal Register is included in full here:

> Based on information in PLP's CWA Section 404 permit application, the FEIS, and the ROD, discharges of dredged or fill material to construct and operate the 2020 Mine Plan's proposed mine site would result in the permanent loss of approximately 8.5 miles (13.7 km) of anadromous fish streams, 91 miles (147 km) of additional streams that support anadromous fish streams, and approximately 2,108 acres (8.5 km^2) of wetlands and other waters in the same watersheds that support anadromous fish streams. These discharges would also result in streamflow alterations that would adversely affect approximately 29 miles (46.7 km) of additional anadromous fish streams downstream of the mine site due to greater than 20 percent changes in average monthly streamflow.
>
> The EPA has determined that the large-scale loss of and damage to headwater streams, wetlands, and other aquatic resources that support salmon populations in the SFK and NFK watersheds from the discharge of dredged or fill material

118. Env't. Prot. Agency, Proposed Determination to Prohibit and Restrict the Use of Certain Waters within Defined Areas as Disposal Sites; Pebble Deposit Area, Southwest Alaska, 87 Fed. Reg. 32,021 (May 26, 2022).

119. Env't Prot. Agency, Final Determination to Prohibit the Specification of and Restrict the Use for Specification of Certain Waters within Defined Areas as Disposal Sites; Pebble Deposit Area, Southwest Alaska, 88 Fed. Reg. 7441 (Feb. 3, 2023), https://www.federalregister.gov/documents/2023/02/03/2023-02287/final-determination-to-prohibit-the-specification-of-and-restrict-the-use-for-specification-of.

for the construction and routine operation of the 2020 Mine Plan will have unacceptable adverse effects on anadromous fishery areas in the SFK and NFK watersheds. The EPA has also determined that discharges of dredged or fill material for the construction and routine operation of a mine to develop the Pebble deposit anywhere in the mine site area that would result in the same or greater levels of loss or streamflow changes as the 2020 Mine Plan also will have unacceptable adverse effects on anadromous fishery areas in the SFK and NFK watersheds, because such discharges would involve the same aquatic resources characterized as part of the evaluation of the 2020 Mine Plan.

To prevent these unacceptable adverse effects, the Final Determination prohibits the specification of certain waters of the United States in the SFK and NFK watersheds as disposal sites for the discharge of dredged or fill material for the construction and routine operation of the 2020 Mine Plan, including future proposals to construct and operate a mine to develop the Pebble deposit with discharges of dredged or fill material into waters of the United States that would result in the same or greater levels of aquatic resource loss or streamflow changes as the 2020 Mine Plan. The Defined Area for Prohibition encompasses certain headwaters of the SFK and NFK watersheds and is delineated by the entirety of the Public Land Survey System (PLSS) quarter sections where mine site discharges were proposed in PLP's 2020 Mine Plan.

Separately, the EPA has also determined that discharges of dredged or fill material associated with future proposals to construct and operate a mine to develop the Pebble deposit will have unacceptable adverse effects on anadromous fishery areas (including spawning and breeding areas) anywhere in the SFK, NFK, and UTC watersheds if the adverse effects of such discharges are similar or greater in nature and magnitude to the adverse effects of the 2020 Mine Plan.

To prevent these unacceptable adverse effects, the Final Determination restricts the use for specification of certain waters of the United States in the SFK, NFK, and UTC watersheds as disposal sites for the discharge of dredged or fill material associated with future proposals to construct and operate a mine to develop the Pebble deposit with discharges of dredged or fill material into waters of the United States that would result in adverse effects similar or greater in nature and magnitude to the adverse effects of the 2020 Mine Plan. The Defined Area for Restriction encompasses certain headwaters of the SFK, NFK, and UTC watersheds where discharges associated with developing the Pebble deposit are likely. To the extent that future discharges are subject to the prohibition, the restriction will not apply.

The aquatic resources that would be lost or damaged by the discharges evaluated by the EPA play an important role in supporting salmon populations in the SFK, NFK, and UTC watersheds. Such resources are also integral components of a larger ecosystem, which helps support the health of the Bristol Bay watershed, an area of unparalleled ecological value, boasting salmon diversity and productivity unrivaled anywhere in North America. The watershed is made up of intact, connected habitats—from headwaters to ocean—that support abundant, genetically diverse wild Pacific salmon populations. The Bristol Bay watershed's Sockeye Salmon run is the world's largest, producing approximately half of the world's Sockeye Salmon. The watershed's Chinook, Coho, Chum, and Pink salmon populations are also significant. Bristol Bay's salmon populations support world-class, economically important commercial and sport fisheries, as well as a more than 4,000-year-old subsistence-based way of life for Alaska Natives.

Proposals to discharge dredged or fill material into waters of the United States associated with developing the Pebble deposit that are not subject to this final determination remain subject to all statutory and regulatory authorities and requirements under CWA Section 404.

Considering the immense and unique economic, social, cultural, and ecological value of the aquatic resources in the region, including the fishery areas in the SFK, NFK, and UTC watersheds and their susceptibility to damage, the EPA will carefully evaluate all future proposals to discharge dredged or fill material in the region.[120]

120. *Id.* at 7443.

In July 2023, in a rare move, the State of Alaska sought to challenge the veto in the U.S. Supreme Court pursuant to the Court's original jurisdiction and asked the Court to vacate EPA's January 2023 veto, arguing that the veto violated a 1976 land swap deal between the state of Alaska and an Alaska Native corporation known as the Cook Inlet Land Exchange. Alaska argued the veto deprived the state of the benefits of its bargain and violated principles of state sovereignty.[121] The Supreme Court denied Alaska's motion on January 8, 2024.[122]

On April 15, 2024, the Corps of Engineers issued another Record of Decision in light of EPA's January 2023 veto in which the Corps determined the entire mine site and portions of the transportation and pipline corridor fall within the areas EPA had either prohibited or restricted for disposal of dredged or fill material and, accordingly, there "are no available areas for disposal of dredged or fill material"[123] The Corps recognized the supremacy of EPA's veto power and ruled that "EPA's determination is a controlling factor that cannot be changed by a USACE decision maker and the application is hereby denied without prejudice."[124]

Typically, EPA prefers to collaborate with or exert pressure on the Corps to reach suitable outcomes if it finds a proposed discharge initially unacceptable; thus, EPA vetoes continue to be the exception, not the rule.[125] The Pebble Mine case notwithstanding, the threat of a permit veto can be a more effective and more practical bargaining tool than the actual veto itself.[126] However, some argue this arrangement may not effectively provide the protection for the environment

---

121. State of Alaska v. United States, Case No. 22O157 (Original), Motion for Leave to File Bill of Complaint (July 26, 2023), https://fingfx.thomsonreuters.com/gfx/legaldocs/zdpxroqrjpx/Alaska%20Pebble%20Mine%20SCOTUS.pdf.

122. The docket is available at https://www.supremecourt.gov/search.aspx?filename=/docket/docketfiles/html/public/22o157.html.

123. U.S. Army Corps of Eng'rs, Record of Decision: Review of the Application by Pebble Limited Partnership (POA-2017-00271) in light of the Prohibitions and Restrictions Imposed by the *Final Determination of the U.S. Environmental Protection Agency Pursuant to Section 404(c) of the Clean Water Act – Pebble Deposit Area, Southwest Alaska* (Jan. 2023), at 6, https://www.poa.usace.army.mil/Portals/34/docs/regulatory/specialpns/2024/POA-2017-00271.20240415.RecordofDecision.pdf?ver=QRA0ZnafUF28lJwzGqhnqA%3d%3d

124. *Id.* at 7.

125. Robert B. Moreno, Filling the Regulatory Gap: A Proposal for Restructuring the Clean Water Act's Two-Permit System, 37 Ecology L.Q. 285, 309 (2010).

126. Oxley, *supra* note 94, at 155–56.

intended by Congress because EPA has largely vacated its role as "gatekeeper of pollution discharges."[127] Nevertheless, EPA can—and will sparingly—use its veto authority to stop controversial projects that will have substantial adverse effects, as the Pebble Mine veto in 2023 and subsequent Corps Record of Decision demonstrate. And as the case law around EPA veto decisions shows, EPA's discretion to use its veto authority is very broad and can be exercised both preemptively before an application is even filed (Pebble Mine) and retroactively after the discharge activity is underway (Spruce Mine No. 1). It can also be used to strongly discourage, if not actually prevent, future applications featuring the same or similar disposal site (Pebble Mine 2023 Final Determination).

The recent heated wrangling over the Pebble Mine and Yazoo Backwater Area Pumps Project has shown how politicized the exercise of EPA's 401(c) veto authority has become in recent years, with the Trump administration seeking to "undo" or moderate veto determinations issued by previous administrations, only to have EPA emphasize its support for those prior determinations when the administration changed from Republican to Democrat. It remains to be seen whether future administrations will continue the flip-flopping, but EPA wields significant authority through this mechanism regardless of which party is in the White House.

D. 404(b)(1) Guidelines and Enforcement Issues

Permits are reviewed pursuant to particular criteria. As discussed in Chapter 4 of this book, the CWA requires the Corps to evaluate every wetland permit application under Section 404(b)(1) Guidelines that EPA promulgated in consultation with the Corps.[128] These Guidelines prohibit the Corps from issuing a wetland permit if there is a "practicable alternative" to the proposed activity that would have a less adverse

127. Moreno, *supra* note 125.

128. 33 U.S.C. § 1344(b)(1). *See also* 33 C.F.R. § 320.4(a)(1) ("[A] permit will be denied if the discharge authorized by such permit would not comply with the . . . 404(b)(1) Guidelines."); *id.* § 323.6(a). Although they are referred to as Guidelines, the 404(b)(1) Guidelines are binding regulations. The 404(b)(1) Guidelines do not, of course, apply to permits that are issued solely under Section 10 of the Rivers and Harbors Act.

impact on the aquatic ecosystem.[129] In addition, the Guidelines create a presumption that there are practicable alternatives to discharges of dredged or fill material into wetlands when the proposed activity is not water-dependent.[130]

The 404(b)(1) Guidelines also prohibit the issuance of a permit when the activity authorized by the permit causes or contributes to significant degradation of waters of the United States,[131] causes or contributes to a violation of state water quality standards, violates federal toxic pollution standards, jeopardizes endangered species or destroys or adversely modifies their critical habitat, or violates federal marine sanctuary protection requirements.[132] Further, the 404(b)(1) Guidelines form the basis for the mitigation requirements, which are discussed in greater detail in Chapter 6.

II. Section 404 Responsibilities of States and State-Level Regulation

A. Introduction

The United States is a cooperative federalism.[133] Congress acknowledged this at the outset of the Clean Water Act (CWA) by stating it is "the policy of the Congress to recognize, preserve, and protect the primary responsibilities and rights of States to prevent, reduce, and eliminate pollution, to plan the development and use (including restoration, preservation, and enhancement) of land and water resources,

---

129. 40 C.F.R. § 230.10(a). See generally Oliver Houck, Hard Choices: The Analysis of Alternatives Under Section 404 of the Clean Water Act and Similar Environmental Laws, 60 U. Colo. L. Rev. 773 (1989).

130. 40 C.F.R. § 230.10(a)(3).

131. *Id.* § 230.10(c). The Guidelines identify effects deemed to be "significant," and establish tests to be used in determining significance. *Id.* In addition, the Corps has clarified that the term "significant" under the 404(b)(1) Guidelines does not have exactly the same meaning as the term "significant" under NEPA. RGL 87-02, *Use of the Word "Significant" in Permit Documentation* (Mar. 30, 1987).

132. *Id.* at § 230.10(b).

133. *See* Robert L. Fischman, *Cooperative Federalism and Natural Resources Law*, 14 N.Y.U. Env't L.J. 179 (2005); Robert L. Glicksman, *From Cooperative to Inoperative Federalism: The Perverse Mutation of Environmental Law and Policy*, 41 Wake Forest L .Rev. 719 (2006); Jeanne Christie, *The Clean Water Act and Cooperative Federalism: Lessons of the Founding Fathers,* The Complete Wetlander (June 30, 2011).

and to consult with [EPA] in the exercise of [its] authority under [the CWA]."[134] Thus, although Congress gave the U.S. Environmental Protection Agency (EPA) and the U.S. Army Corps of Engineers (Corps) primary responsibility to jointly administer the CWA's Section 404 program,[135] it reserved vital roles for states.[136] Accordingly, under the broad non-preemption clauses of the CWA, states are free to adopt a regulatory or common law approach governing wetlands that is more stringent than those mandated by federal law.[137] While this chapter cannot cover detailed specifics of whether and how each state governs its wetlands,[138] it does provide a brief introduction to those issues. Moreover, it provides insights into the central role that states play in implementing the Section 404 program.

Congress enacted the CWA with a number of central roles for states.[139] First, states may assume the primary regulatory role through CWA Sections 404(g–h).[140] States may also issue State Programmatic General Permits (SPGPs) pursuant to CWA Section 404(e).[141] Furthermore, states are in a position to deny or condition permits pursuant to CWA Section 401[142] and, in the case of coastal states, pursuant to the Coastal Zone Management Act (CZMA).[143]

---

134. 33 U.S.C. § 1251(b).

135. *Id.* § 1344.

136. *See, e.g.*, Parts II.B–D of this chapter.

137. *See* 33 U.S.C. §§ 1365(e), 1370. It is important to note that some state laws preclude wetland regulation that exceeds federal requirements. *See* Jerome M. Organ, *Limitations on State Agency Authority to Adopt Environmental Standards More Stringent than Federal Standards: Policy Considerations and Interpretive Problems*, 54 Md. L. Rev. 1373 (1995), https://digitalcommons.law.umaryland.edu/mlr/vol54/iss4/9/. *Issue: "No More Stringent" Laws*, State Env't Res. Ctr. (Mar. 26, 2004), http://www.serconline.org/noMoreStringent.html.

138. For detailed evaluations of state wetland programs, *see* National Association of Wetland Managers, *State Wetland Programs*, https://www.nawm.org/wetland-programs/state-wetland-programs.

139. *See* Oliver Houck & Michael Rolland, *Federalism in Wetlands Regulation: A Consideration of Delegation of Clean Water Act Section 404 and Related Programs to the States*, 54 Md. L. Rev. 1242 (1995), https://digitalcommons.law.umaryland.edu/mlr/vol54/iss4/6/.

140. 33 U.S.C. § 1344(g); *see generally* Ass'n of State Wetland Managers, *Clean Water Act Section 404 Program Assumption* (Aug. 2011), https://www.nawm.org/pdf_lib/cwa_section_404_program_assumption.pdf.

141. 33 U.S.C. § 1344(e). *See* Chapter 5.

142. 33 U.S.C. § 1341.

143. 16 U.S.C. §§ 1451–1464. *See* 33 C.F.R. § 336.1(b)(9).

This section of this chapter is organized as follows: it opens with an exploration of the state assumption process, continues with a brief recap of the State Programmatic General Permit process (discussed in more detail in Chapter 5), goes on to discuss Section 401 certification and CZMA consistency determinations, and closes with a brief discussion of state laws in those states that have passed their own regulatory programs.

B. Assumption

The CWA allows states and tribes the option of assuming administration of the Clean Water Act Section 404 permit program in certain waters within state or tribal jurisdiction. CWA Section 404(g) allows for "assumption" of a wetland regulatory program by a state.[144] A state or tribe that has successfully proceeded through the assumption process becomes responsible for permitting, compliance, and enforcement of dredge and fill activities into certain waters of the United States within that state.[145] The Corps retains jurisdiction in tidal waters and their adjacent wetlands and waters used as a means to transport interstate or foreign commerce and their adjacent wetlands.[146] Further, Section 404 assumption has no effect on Corps authorities and responsibilities under Section 10 of the Rivers and Harbors Act.[147] EPA's rules setting forth the minimum requirements for a state to assumpt a Section 404 program are contained in 40 C.F.R. part 233.[148] All

144. 33 U.S.C. § 1344(g).

145. *Id.*

146. *Id.* States may not assume permitting authority over waters which "are presently used, or are susceptible to use in their natural condition or by reasonable improvement as a means to transport interstate or foreign commerce shoreward to their ordinary high water mark, including all waters which are subject to the ebb and flow of the tide shoreward to their mean high water mark, or mean higher high water mark on the west coast, including wetlands adjacent thereto."

147. Env't Prot. Agency, *State or Tribal Assumption of the CWA Section 404 Permit Program*; https://www.epa.gov/cwa-404/state-or-tribal-assumption-cwa-section-404-permit-program#:~:text=To%20be%20eligible%20to%20assume%20the%20Federal%20program%2C,permit%20decisions%2C%20and%205%20have%20adequate%20enforcement%20authority (last updated Oct. 31, 2023).

148. At press-time, EPA is in the process of overhauling its Section 404 Assumption Rules for the first time since 1988. Proposed rule amendments to the Clean Water Act Section 404 Tribal and State Program Regulations were published in the Federal Register on August 14, 2023. *See* 88 Fed. Reg. 55276 (Aug. 14, 2023). According

jurisdictional waters not retained by the Corps must be regulated when a state assumes a program: EPA will not approve a partial program.[149] To be eligible to assume the program, a state or tribe's program must have *at least* equivalent jurisdiction, regulate *at least* the same activities, provide for public participation, ensure compliance with the 404(b)(l) Guidelines, and have adequate enforcement authority. [150] States must have standards that are at least as stringent as those applicable to the federally administered program,[151] and if state law allows,[152] states may adopt even more stringent requirements, including a broader scope, than the federal program.[153]

The statute purports to give EPA little discretion in approving or denying a state or tribe's assumption application if the minimum program requirements are met.[154] The program must meet both the statutory requirements of Section 404(g) and (h), and EPA's detailed implementing regulations.[155]

Assumption does not eliminate federal oversight. This oversight comes from a variety of directions. CWA Section 404(j) mandates each

---

to the preamble, "The primary purpose of the proposed revision is to . . . clarify the requirements and processes for assumption and administration of a CWA section 404 permitting . . . [and] facilitate Tribal and State assumption of the section 404 program . . . by making the procedures and substantive requirements for assumption transparent and straightforward. It clarifies the minimum requirements for Tribal and State programs while allowing for flexibility in how these requirements are met. In addition, the proposed rule clarifies the criminal negligence standard for both the CWA section 402 and section 404 programs." Technical revisions to remove outdated references are also proposed.

149. 40 C.F.R. § 233.1(b).

150. 33 U.S.C. § 1344(h).

151. 40 C.F.R § 233.1(d).

152. *See* Organ, *supra* note 137.

153. 40 C.F.R. § 233.1(c). Because they are state-based, more stringent requirements or programs with broader jurisdiction are not subject to federal oversight or enforcement relative to those components. *Id.* For analysis of state wetland programs, *see* Nat'l Assoc. of Wetland Managers, State Wetland Programs, https://www.nawm.org/wetland-programs/state-wetland-programs (last visited Apr. 11, 2024).

154. 33 U.S.C. § 1344(h)(2)(a). Nevertheless, EPA's decision is subject to judicial review; EPA's approval of Florida's Section 404 assumption was vacated by the D.C. Circuit Court in Center for Biological Diversity, et al. v. Regan, et al., Case No. 21-119(RDM) (D.C. Cir. Feb. 15, 2024). Appeal of that decision was pending at press time. Center for Biological Diversity, et al., v. Regan, et al., Civil Action No. 21-119 (RDM) (D.C. Cir. Apr. 15, 2024).

155. *Id.*; 40 C.F.R. §§ 233.1, 233.10(a), (b), (c). The basic components of an approvable program include sufficient state authority:

administering state provide EPA notice and an opportunity to comment on each proposed individual or general permit.[156] EPA solicits comments from the Corps and the U.S. Fish and Wildlife Service or the National Marine Fisheries Services, as appropriate.[157] EPA may even

---

To issue permits that apply, and assure compliance with, any applicable requirements of Section 404, are for fixed terms not exceeding five years, and can be terminated or modified for cause;

To issue permits that apply to, and assure compliance with all applicable requirements for, inspection, monitoring, entering property, and requiring reports under the CWA;

To ensure that the public, and any other state the waters of which may be affected, receives notice of each application for a permit and an opportunity for public hearing before a ruling on each application;

To ensure that EPA receives notice of each application for a permit;

To ensure that any other state whose waters may be affected by the issuance of a permit may submit written recommendations to the permitting state and the EPA with respect to any permit application and that the permitting state will timely respond to the recommendations if rejected;

To ensure that no permit will be issued if anchorage and navigation of any of the navigable waters would be substantially impaired thereby;

To abate violations of the permit or the permit program, including civil and criminal penalties and other ways and means of enforcement;

To ensure continued coordination with federal and federal-state water related planning and review processes.

33 U.S.C. § 1344(h)(1). EPA's regulations governing program submissions and approval are set forth at 40 C.F.R. pt. 233, subpt. B. Along with a full and complete description of the program it intends to administer, the state must submit a statement from an appropriate state legal officer—e.g., attorney general or independent legal counsel for state agency—"that the laws of such State . . . provide adequate authority to carry out the described program." 33 U.S.C. § 1344(g). EPA regulations additionally require the state to submit a Memorandum of Agreement with the Regional Administrator of the EPA and a Memorandum of Agreement with the Secretary of the Army as well as copies of all applicable state statutes and regulations. 40 C.F.R. § 233.10(d), (e), (f). The Memorandum of Agreement between the regional administrator and the directors of any state agencies must set out the state and federal responsibilities for program administration and enforcement. *Id.* § 233.13. The Memorandum of Agreement between the Army Corps of Engineers and the directors of any state agencies in charge of administering the permit program must describe the waters over which the Corps retains jurisdiction, provide procedures for transferring existing permit applications to the state, and identify all general permits over which the state intends to assume authority. *Id.* § 233.14. Additionally, the U.S. Fish and Wildlife Service and the Army Corps of Engineers may submit comments to the EPA on the proposed program and statement. *Id.*

156. 33 U.S.C. § 1344(j); 40 C.F.R. § 233.50(a).

157. 33 U.S.C. § 1344(g).

object to any proposed permit.[158] Objections allow the state or any other interested party to request a hearing.[159] In the case of objections, until EPA's concerns are met or withdrawn, the state may not issue the proposed permit.[160] If the state does not revise the permit to meet EPA's concerns, the permit application is transferred to the Corps for standard processing,[161] and in such a case EPA may not a return the permit to the state by withdrawing objections that were not addressed by the state.[162]

Detailed oversight is not, in most cases, mandatory. Subject to certain exceptions,[163] EPA may waive its Section 404(j) oversight powers for certain categories of discharges.[164] For any such waiver, EPA must promulgate regulations establishing the categories of discharges that will not be subject to federal oversight.[165] EPA may terminate a waiver at any time and in specific cases.[166] While Corps-issued 404 permits

---

158. 40 C.F.R. § 233.50(b).

159. *Id.* § 233.50(g).

160. *Id.* § 233.50(f).

161. 33 U.S.C. § 1344(j); 40 C.F.R. § 233.50(j).

162. Friends of Crystal River v. U.S. Env't Prot. Agency, 35 F.3d 1073 (6th Cir. 1994). The time limits within which a state must act to address EPA objections are set forth in 33 U.S.C. § 1344(j). If a public hearing is conducted, the state must address remaining EPA objections within 30 days after completion of the hearing. If no hearing is conducted, the state must address EPA's objections within 90 days of receiving them. *Id.*

163. The following discharges are not eligible for a waiver from the Section 404(j) federal oversight provisions:

> Draft general permits,
>
> Discharges with reasonable potential for affecting endangered or threatened species as determined by the Fish and Wildlife Service,
>
> Discharges with reasonable potential for adverse impacts on waters of another state,
>
> Discharges known or suspected to contain toxic pollutants in toxic amounts or hazardous substances in reportable quantities,
>
> Discharges located in proximity of a public water supply intake,
>
> Discharges within critical areas established under state or federal law, including but not limited to national and state parks, fish and wildlife sanctuaries and refuges, national and historical monuments, wilderness areas and preserves, sites identified or proposed under the National Historic Preservation Act, and components of the National Wild and Scenic Rivers System.

40 C.F.R. § 233.51(b).

164. 33 U.S.C. § 1344(k).

165. *Id.* § 1344(l).

166. 40 C.F.R. § 233.51(c).

do not have a statutory expiration period, Section 404 permits issued by states or tribes are limited to a five-year duration.[167]

EPA may withdraw its approval of a state-run program if it determines that the state is not administering the program in accordance with federal requirements.[168] To initiate a withdrawal, EPA must first notify the state of its belief that the program is not being properly administered.[169] The state must then take appropriate corrective action within a reasonable amount of time but no more than 90 days after the state has been notified of its noncompliance.[170] Failure to take corrective action by the state allows approval to be withdrawn until the corrective action is taken and administration taken over by the Corps, who retains authority until EPA determines corrective action has been taken, after which the state can reassume the program.[171] States that have assumed authority may also voluntarily transfer program responsibilities required by federal law to the Corps, thus terminating state authority.[172]

To date, only two states—Michigan, and New Jersey[173]—and no tribes have assumed full permitting authority pursuant to Section 404(g). On February 15, 2024, the D.C. Circuit Court vacated the Florida program, holding that EPA's approval did not comport with the Endangered Species Act because it provided for programmatic take coverage.[174] Particularly after the D.C. Circuit Court's stinging rebuke of Florida's assumption program, states may be reluctant to administer such an extensive permitting program for a variety of reasons, including inadequate funding and administrative resources,

---

167. 33 U.S.C. § 1344(h)(1)(A)(ii).

168. *Id.* § 1344(i).

169. *Id.*

170. *Id.*

171. 33 U.S.C. § 1344(i).

172. 40 C.F.R. § 233.53.

173. *See id.* § 233.70 (Michigan 1984); § 233.71 (New Jersey 1994); EPA approved Florida's program in December 2020, 85 Fed. Reg. 57853 (Dec. 22, 2020), but the D.C. Circuit Court vacated that approval in February 2024 on the ground that the approval violated the Endangered Species Act, sending the program back to the Corps. Ctr. for Biological Diversity, et al. v. Regan, et al., Case No. 21-119(RDM) (D.C. Cir. Feb. 15, 2024). On April 12, the court denied Florida's request for a partial stay of the vacatur and entered partial final judgment, enabling Florida to take an appeal. Florida has appealed the decision to the D.C. Circuit Court of Appeals. *See supra* note 154.

174. Ctr. for Biological Diversity, et al. v. Regan, Case No. 21-119(RDM) (D.C. Cir. Feb. 15, 2024).

potential liability for "takings" under the Fourteenth Amendment to the Constitution of the United States, issues in adequately addressing Endangered Species Act take coverage, and perceived resistance by the Corps to cede its authority over the Section 404 program.[175] In the face of such obstacles, the trend is toward greater state involvement in the implementation of the Section 404 program pursuant to other authorities in the CWA—particularly State Programmatic General Permits and Section 401 certification—and in the CZMA.

As already detailed, EPA retains the authority to withdraw state administration,[176] and a 2008 review by the EPA revealed Michigan's program to be deficient.[177] In the face of recommended changes to continue assumption, Governor Jennifer Granholm initially proposed to eliminate funding for the state program, which in turn would have led to the transfer of the program back to the federal government, but input from multiple stakeholders (including both conservation organizations and industry groups) resulted in reconsideration,[178] and in 2013 the Michigan legislature enacted legislation to reform the state wetland program in order to continue its Section 404 assumption.[179]

The Environmental Council of the States (ECOS) issued a 2011 resolution supporting delegation of Section 404 administration to states committed to protecting wetlands.[180] The resolution called on the EPA to establish new, clearer guidelines for assumption, asks the U.S. Congress for funding, and states the importance of increased flexibility to help states assume responsibility for Section 404 administration.[181]

175. *See* Houck & Rolland, *supra* note 139.

176. 40 C.F.R. § 233.53(b).

177. The EPA expressed concern over several program weaknesses, including issues of jurisdiction, overly broad exemptions, and permitting authority. U.S. Env't Prot. Agency, Final Report Results of the U.S. Environmental Agency Region 5 Review of Michigan Department of Environmental Quality's Section 404 Program (2008).

178. Matthew D. Zimmerman, *Michigan's Wetland Statute Amended to Satisfy U.S. Environmental Protection Agency*, Nat'l Law Rev. (July 11, 2013), https://www.natlawreview.com/article/michigan-s-wetland-statute-amended-to-satisfy-us-environmental-protection-agency.

179. See *Senate Bill 0163 (2013)*, Michigan Legislature, http://www.legislature.mi.gov/(S(4caiu0l4ham12313ci442hwy))/mileg.aspx?page=GetObject&objectname=2013-SB-0163.

180. Env't Council of the States [ECOS], *State Assumption of Clean Water Act Section 404 Permit Program*, Res. 08-3 (Mar. 30, 2023), https://www.ecos.org/documents/resolution-08-3-state-delegation-of-clean-water-act-section-404-permit-program/.

181. *Id.*

The Association of State Wetlands Managers, Inc. (ASWM) (now the National Association of Wetland Managers, or NAWM) and ECOS collaborated to produce a handbook designed to help states and tribes in favor of assumption navigate the process.[182] Additionally, the handbook highlights the costs and benefits of assumption, helping states that may be considering assumption determine if taking over Section 404 responsibilities will be beneficial.[183] Nevertheless, most states and no tribes considering Section 404 assumption have not recently taken the leap, with the exception of Florida in 2020.[184] As discussed below, other states have been exploring assumption, but with the D.C. Circuit's strong rebuff of Florida's attempt,[185] they may be reluctant, notwithstanding EPA's proposed rule to streamline and clarify the process.[186]

Alaska has been exploring section 404 assumption for over a decade, and in the Fiscal Year 2023 budget, the Alaska legislature approved funding for DEC to evaluate assumption of Section 404 of the Clean Water Act and prepare a feasibility study. This report was completed in January 2023 and concluded that "[g]iven the benefits to the environment and economy of the state, DEC should take the necessary steps to assume the 404 Program from the Corps. Assuming the Corps' 404 permitting program will allow the State to issue approximately 75 percent of the 775 annual permit actions currently issued by the Corps (about 580 actions per year)."[187] In contrast, the state of Virginia also began weighing the costs and benefits of assumption over a decade ago, and in December 2012 the Virginia Department of Environmental Quality (DEQ) also produced a study on the matter

---

182. Ass'n of State Wetland Managers, Inc. & Env't Council of the States, Clean Water Act Section 404 Program Assumption: A Handbook for the States and Tribes (2011), https://www.nawm.org/pdf_lib/cwa_section_404_program_assumption.pdf. *See also* https://www.epa.gov/cwa404g (2022).

183. *Id.*

184. For the current status of Section 404 assumption efforts at the state and tribe level, *see* Env't Prot. Agency, *U.S. Interactive Map of State and Tribal Assumption under CWA Section 404*, https://www.epa.gov/cwa404g/us-interactive-map-state-and-tribal-assumption-under-cwa-section-404 (last updated Apr. 9, 2024).

185. Center for Biological Diversity, et al. v. Regan, et al., Case No. 21-119(RDM) (D.C. Cir. Feb. 15, 2024).

186. *See infra* note 148, *infra*, and accompanying text.

187. Jade North, LLC, Clean Water Act Section 404 Dredge and Fill Program Assumption Feasibility Report, prepared for Alaska Department of Environmental Conservation (Jan. 2023), https://dec.alaska.gov/media/yzwj4uni/dec-404-feasibility-study-1-26-23.pdf.

at the bequest of the Virginia legislature.[188] There, however, the DEQ concluded that assumption could yield increased efficiency in the permit process, but at the cost of "enter[ing] into a complex and lengthy process that could last up to two years with no certainty that EPA would approve the request."[189] Additionally, the Stakeholder Group[190] was generally in favor of maintaining the status quo, as it was generally pleased with the current system of federal and state permits.[191] Other states have also explored the costs and benefits of assuming the Section 404 program for assumable waters in their respective states.[192]

After many starts and stops, the state of Florida began exploring Section 404 assumption in earnest in 2017. In 2018, Florida's legislature passed a bill that gave the Florida Department of Environmental Protection (FDEP) authority to begin rulemaking and the application process to assume the Section 404 permitting program within those state waters where the Corps does not retain jurisdiction.[193] FDEP completed the rulemaking process on July 21, 2020.[194] Florida's "State 404 Program" combined the state's existing Environmental Resource Permitting (ERP) program with those components of the Section 404 program that are already not addressed by the ERP program, such as the requirement in the 404(b)(1) Guidelines to consider off-site alternatives and the no-action alternative and the mitigation hierarchy.[195]

188. Dep't of Env't Quality, Study of the Costs and Benefits of State Assumption of the Federal § 404 Clean Water Act Permitting Program 1 (2012), https://www.nawm.org/pdf_lib/va_study_state_assumption_2012.pdf.

189. *Id.* at 14.

190. *Id.* at 8.

191. *Id.* at 15.

192. For example, Oregon is still in the process of considering assumptions, but appears to be interested only in partial assumption, which is not allowable. *See* Eric Metz & Barbara Poage, SPGP's and 404 Assumption: Oregon's Experience, https://www.nawm.org/pdf_lib/assumption_webinar/spgps_and_404_assumption_oregons_experience_022621_metz_poage.pdf. In contrast, Arizona explored the concept and determined that assumption of the Section 404 program would not be beneficial. *See* https://azdeq.gov/node/4938.

193. Fla. Laws Ch. 2018-88, codified at Fla Stat. § 373.4146.

194. *See* State 404 Program, Florida Dep't of Environmental Protection, https://floridadep.gov/water/submerged-lands-environmental-resources-coordination/content/state-404-program (last updated Mar. 21, 2024).

195. *Id.* Florida's State 404 Program is codified at Fla. Admin. Code Ch. 62-331 and in the Florida Department of Environmental Protection, State 404 Program Applicant's Handbook, https://floridadep.gov/water/water/content/water-resource-management-rules#ERP (last updated Mar. 26, 2024). While Florida's ERP program requires

Florida submitted its assumption package to the EPA in August 2020, and EPA approved Florida's State 404 Program in December 2020.[196] EPA's approval of Florida's State 404 Program was challenged by various environmental groups, and on February 15, 2024, following a challenge by various environmental groups, the D.C. Circuit Court vacated EPA's approval of the Florida program on the ground that the unique approach taken to comply with the Endangered Species Act was too unique. The FWS had issued a programmatic biological opinion with a programmatic incidental take statement for the program that contemplated a technical assistance process between the state wildlife agency and FWS.[197] This technical assistance process required the state to incorporate all FWS avoidance and minimization measures into the State 404 permit as specific conditions, and FWS found that this process would prevent jeopardy to the continued existence of any listed species that might be affected by a given project.[198] The court held that this programmatic approach to compliance with the ESA did not meet the requirements of the ESA for either the preparation of biological opinions or incidental take statements

---

consideration of practicable design alternatives that will avoid or minimize wetland impacts, consideration of off-site alternatives or the no action alternative are not mandated. *See* Florida Department of Environmental Protection, Environmental Resource Permit Applicant's Handbook Volume I, § 10.2.1, https://www.flrules.org/gateway/reference.asp?No=Ref-12078 (last visited Apr. 11, 2024). For more information about the compensatory mitigation hierarchy, *see* Chapter 6.

196. 85 Fed. 83553 (Dec. 22, 2020), https://www.govinfo.gov/content/pkg/FR-2020-12-22/pdf/2020-28232.pdf.

197. U.S. Fish & Wildlife Serv., South-Atlantic Gulf & Mississippi Basin Interior Regions, Programmatic Biological Opinion for U.S. Environmental Protection Agency's Approval of FDEP's Assumption of the Administration of the Dredge and Fill Permitting Program under Section 404 of the Clean Water Act (Nov. 17, 2020), https://publicfiles.dep.state.fl.us/dwrm/404_Assumption_Application/USFWS_Biological_Opinion/FL404BiOp_Final_Signed.pdf.

198. Memorandum of Understanding Between the Florida Fish & Wildlife Conservation Commission, The United States Fish & Wildlife Service, & the Florida Department of Environmental Protection (Aug. 5, 2020), https://floridadep.gov/sites/default/files/Appendix_2_FDEP_FWC_FWS_404_MOU_Final_Full_Signatures.pdf; *see also* State 404 Program Applicant's Handbook, § 1.3.3 ("Compliance shall be required, as applicable, with any requirements resulting from consultation with, or technical assistance by, the Florida Fish & Wildlife Conservation Commission (FWC), the US Fish & Wildlife Service, and the National Marine Fisheries Services (NMFS) for permits reviewed under the State 404 Program."), https://www.flrules.org/gateway/reference.asp?No=Ref-12064.

and therefore vacated the approval.[199] Implementation of the State 404 Program was not enjoined pending the litigation, and the court's order is prospective only; the parties agreed it would not affect issued permits.[200] A key factor at play in the litigation is how consultation under the Endangered Species Act is handled under the program, since a federal agency does not issue the permit.[201] The court rejected the concept that FWS could "pre-approve" incidental take through a programmatic incidental take statement, but indicated it would entertain a motion for a limited stay as to pending or future State 404 applications that did not affect listed species.[202] However, on February 26, the FWS and EPA filed a supplemental brief declining to seek a limited stay. While reserving their right to appeal the decision, the federal defendants stated that a bifurcated program that federalized permit applications that "may affect" listed species would be impractical and inconsistent with the CWA, given EPA rules that disallow partial assumption.[203] On the same day, the state filed the expected motion for limited stay, on the ground that the court's ruling created chaos, with more than 1,000 pending permit applications currently stuck in limbo, and the Corps ill-equipped to deal with all of those pending applications. The state of Florida asked the court to grant a limited stay and suggested a procedure for wildlife agencies to review applications and make determinations as to whether the project would affect listed species and steps to be taken if a "may affect" determination is reached. In the alternative, the state asked the court to modify the state's Section 404 program to match New Jersey's approach to listed species, which was never challenged.[204] The court denied Florida's motion for stay on April 12[205], and Florida has appealed the court's decision to the D.C. Circuit Court of Appeals.

---

199. Center for Biological Diversity et al. v. U.S. Env't Prot. Agency et al., Case 21-119 (RDM) (D.D.C Feb. 15, 2024). Note that the Court has not yet ruled on the CWA count of the plaintiffs' complaint.

200. *Id.*

201. *Id.*

202. *Id.*

203. Federal Defendants' Supplemental Briefing Regarding Limited Stay, Case No. 21-119(RDM) (Feb. 26, 2024).

204. Florida Intervenors' Motion for Limited Stay of February 15, 2024 Vacatur Order, Case No. 21-119(RDM) (Feb. 26, 2024).

205. Memorandum Opinion, Case No. 21-119 (RDM) (Apr. 12, 2024).

The challenges of assuming the Section 404 program only over part of the jurisdictional waters in a state or on tribal lands have also proved daunting, so on August 14, 2023, EPA published proposed revisions to its assumption rules to "streamline and clarify" the assumption process.[206] It purports to harmonize requirements for program operation, compliance, and enforcement, set a clear procedure for determining the extent of waters the Corps would retain after assumption, allow a reasonable period of time between EPA approval and state or tribe implementation to facilitate a smoother transition and streamline the process for permitting dredge and fill activities that will take more than five years to complete. It also suggests a process for addressing the "no jeopardy" mandate of the Section 404(b)(1) Guidelines.[207] Uncertainty surrounding these and other issues have served as barriers to states and tribes in seeking to assume the program.[208]

C. State Programmatic General Permits

Even if a state doesn't fully assume the wetland permitting program, it can take on an increased role through CWA Section 404(e).[209] That section authorizes the Corps to issue state-level general permits known as state programmatic general permits (SPGPs).[210] Regulations state that programmatic permits are "a type of general permit founded on an existing state, local or other federal agency program and designed to avoid duplication with that program."[211] Programmatic general permits, like all general permits, can be issued only for activities that are "similar in nature, will cause only minimal adverse environmental effects when performed separately, and will have only minimal cumulative adverse effect on the environment."[212] The CWA limits the dura-

206. Proposed Rule, Clean Water Act Section 404 Tribal and State Program Regulation, 88 Fed. Reg. 55276 (Aug. 14, 2023), https://www.epa.gov/system/files/documents/2023-07/Pre-publication%20Version%20of%20the%20404%28g%29%20NPRM_508c_QC_1.pdf.

207. *Id.* at 55297.

208. *Id.* at 55282.

209. 33 U.S.C. § 1344(e).

210. For an example of an SPGP, see Dep't of the Army Programmatic General Permit State of Maryland, http://www.nab.usace.army.mil/Portals/63/docs/Regulatory/Permits/MDSPGP-4.pdf.

211. 33 C.F.R. § 325.5(c)(3).

212. 33 U.S.C. § 1344(e)(1).

tion of such permits to five years,[213] during which time the Corps may revoke or modify the SPGPs if the Corps "determines that the activities authorized by such general permit have an adverse effect on the environment or such activities are more appropriately authorized by individual permits."[214] Examples of states issuing SPGP include Pennsylvania, New Jersey, Delaware,[215] California,[216] and Florida.[217] More detail about SPGPs can be found in Chapter 5.[218]

D. Section 401 Certification

Even without assumption or an SPGP, states can play an important role in regulating wetlands under federal jurisdiction pursuant to Section 401(a) of the Clean Water Act. That section provides in part:

> Any applicant for a Federal license or permit to conduct any activity including, but not limited to, the construction or operation of facilities, which may result in any discharge into the navigable waters, shall provide the licensing or permitting agency a certification from the State in which the discharge originates or will originate, or, if appropriate, from the interstate water pollution control agency having jurisdiction over the navigable waters at the point where the discharge originates or will originate, that any such discharge will comply with [various provisions of the CWA dealing with effluent limitations and water quality standards]. . . . Such State or interstate agency shall establish procedures for public notice in the case of all applications for certification by it and, to the extent it deems appropriate, procedures for public hearings

213. *Id.* § 1344(e)(2).

214. *Id.*

215. U.S. Army Corps of Eng'rs, Philadelphia District Regulatory Program—State Programmatic General Permits, https://www.nap.usace.army.mil/Missions/Regulatory/Permits/SPGP.aspx.

216. U.S. Army Corps of Eng'rs, Sacramento District, Regional and Programmatic General Permits (army.mil), https://www.spk.usace.army.mil/Missions/Regulatory/Permitting/Regional-and-Programmatic-General-Permits/.

217. U.S. Army Corps of Eng's, Jacksonville District Regulatory Program—State Programmatic General Permits, https://www.saj.usace.army.mil/SPGP/.

218. For a good summary of state programmatic general permits, see Nat'l Ass'n of Wetland Managers, State Programmatic General Permits, https://www.nawm.org/wetland-programs/regulation/programmatic-general-permits.

> in connection with specific applications. In any case where a State or interstate agency has no authority to give such a certification, such certification shall be from the Administrator. If the State, interstate agency, or Administrator, as the case may be, fails or refuses to act on a request for certification, within a reasonable period of time (which shall not exceed one year) after receipt of such request, the certification requirements of this subsection shall be waived with respect to such Federal application. No license or permit shall be granted until the certification required by this section has been obtained or has been waived. . . . No license or permit shall be granted if certification has been denied by the State. . . .[219]

Often referred to as a "water quality certification,"[220] Section 401 provides states, territories, and authorized tribes[221] "with a powerful tool to protect the quality of their waters from adverse impacts resulting from the construction and/or operation of federally licensed or permitted projects."[222] Pursuant to Section 401, states have the opportunity to review proposed federal permits, including CWA Section 404 permits, and determine whether the activities authorized by such permits will violate applicable state effluent limits and water quality standards.[223] Under Section 401, states have the authority to (1) certify a Section 404 permit as being in compliance with state requirements; (2) require additional permit conditions as a condition of certification that ensure state requirements will be met, such as additional monitoring; (3) deny certification; or (4) waive their authority to certify

---

219. 33 U.S.C. § 1341(a)(1). *See* 33 C.F.R. § 320.4(d).

220. Env't Prot. Agency, *Overview of CWA Section 401 Certification* (Apr. 22, 2022), https://www.epa.gov/cwa-401/overview-cwa-section-401-certification.

221. Throughout this discussion of Section 401(c) certification, states, territories, and tribes that have been approved for treatment as states per 33 U.S.C. § 1377(e) will collectively be referred to as "states" for purposes of brevity, consistent with other portions of this book.

222. Env't Prot. Agency, Clean Water Act Section 401 Water Quality Certification Improvement Rule, 88 Fed. Reg. 66558, 66558 (Sept. 27, 2023)(to be codified at 40 C.F.R. pts. 121, 122, and 124, effective November 27, 2023).

223. States are authorized to require discharges associated with federally licensed or permitted activities to meet applicable effluent limitations pursuant to the state's administration of the permit program established under Section 402 of the CWA. In states having no authority to give such a certification, EPA certification is required. *See* 33 U.S.C. § 1341(a)(1).

the permit either affirmatively or through inaction.[224] If a state denies certification for a Section 404 nationwide or regional general permit, "the Corps allows specific projects to be covered by the Nationwide or Regional General Permit if the project proponent obtains certification from the certifying authority for that project. In that instance, a project proponent would submit a request for certification in accordance with final rule § 121.5 for individual Federal licenses or permits."[225] If a state attaches conditions to granting certification, a federal permit cannot be issued unless those conditions are incorporated in that permit.[226]

Certification authority—and the associated power to deny certification or impose conditions—is conferred only on the state, territory, or tribe in which a "discharge" from a permitted activity "originates or will originate."[227] Certifications are not required from downstream states whose waters may be affected by discharges originating in another state, although, as discussed later, Section 401(a)(2) provides procedures through which the water quality interests of downstream states may be considered. In its 2023 rulemaking, EPA has revised 40 C.F.R. § 121.13(c)(3) to provide greater clarity about the notice that must be provided to neighboring states and tribes and the timeframe in which neighboring jurisdictions may act.[228]

---

224. 33 U.S.C. § 1341(a)(1), (d). EPA revised its 401(c) rules in 2023; the preamble to the final rules states: Under CWA section 401, a federal agency may not issue a license or permit to conduct any activity that may result in any discharge into "waters of the United States" unless the state or authorized Tribe where the discharge would originate either issues a CWA section 401 water quality certification "that any such discharge will comply with the applicable provisions of Sections 301, 302, 303, 306, and 307" of the CWA, or waives certification. 33 U.S.C. 1341(a)(1). When granting a CWA section 401 certification, CWA section 401(d) directs states and authorized Tribes to include conditions, including "effluent limitations and other limitations, and monitoring requirements," necessary to assure that the applicant for a federal license or permit will comply with CWA sections 301, 302, 306, and 307, and with "any other appropriate requirement of State law." Env't Prot. Agency, Clean Water Act Section 401 Water Quality Certification Improvement Rule, 88 Fed. Reg. at 66558.

225. *See supra* note 222, 88 Fed. Reg. at 66571.

226. *See* 33 U.S.C. § 1341(d); *see also supra* note 222, 88 Fed. Reg. at 66561.

227. 33 U.S.C. § 1341(a)(1); *see* S.D. Warren Co. v. Bd. of Env't Prot., 868 A.2d 210, 215 (ME 2005), *aff'd on other grounds sub nom.* S.D. Warren Co. v. Maine Bd. of Env't Prot., 547 U.S. 370 (2006); North Carolina v. Fed. Energy Reg. Comm'n, 112 F.3d 1175, 1187 (D.C. Cir. 1997).

228. *See supra* note 222, 88 Fed. Reg. at 66635, to be codified at 40 C.F.R § 121.13(c)(3).

The Corps has promulgated regulations relating to state certification of discharges subject to Section 404. The basic procedures governing certifications for individual permits are found in 33 C.F.R § 325.2(b). Procedures governing certification of nationwide permits are found at 33 C.F.R. § 330.4(c).

For individual permits, if the district engineer determines that Section 401 certification is required because the activity may result in a discharge to navigable waters, the district engineer must notify the applicant of the requirement.[229] District engineers may issue a provisional permit on request, the validity of which is contingent upon the Corps' receipt of either state certification, conditional certification, or waiver.[230] The district engineer can obtain a copy of the state certification from the applicant or from the certifying agency.[231] State certification is a powerful tool for states to protect water quality because "[n]o permit will be granted until required certification has been obtained or has been waived."[232] If a state denies certification, the Corps will generally deny the application, stating the reason for denial is denial of certification. This does not prevent an applicant from resubmitting a permit application once the applicant has resolved the water quality certification issue with the state.[233]

1. Certifying State Procedures

Section 401(a) requires certifying states to "establish procedures for public notice in the case of all applications for certification by it and, to the extent it deems appropriate, procedures for public hearings in connection with specific applications."[234] State courts interpreting Section 401(a) have concluded that certifying agencies are not required, as a

229. 33 U.S.C. § 1341(a)(2).

230. *See* RGL 93-01, Provisional Permits, U.S. Army Corps of Eng'rs (Apr. 20, 1993), *reprinted at* 61 Fed. Reg. 30,994 (June 18, 1996), https://usace.contentdm.oclc.org/utils/getfile/collection/p16021coll9/id/1367. While this RGL is expired, Corps districts sometimes still follow this practice on request of the applicant, who may need the proof of permit issuance to mobilize contractors or obtain funding.

231. 33 C.F.R. § 325.2(b(1))(i).

232. *Id.* § 325.2(b)(1)(ii).

233. *Id.* § 325.2(b)(7).

234. 33 U.S.C. § 1341(a)(1).

matter of federal law, to conduct hearings on certification requests.[235] Those same courts have concluded that, as a matter of state law, neither the applicant nor other interested parties are necessarily entitled to a hearing on a certification request.[236] For some states, issuance of a state wetland permit for the same activity constitutes the necessary certification.[237] Attorneys should consult state law to determine what hearing procedures, if any, may be available or required in obtaining certification from the appropriate state agency.

2. Waiver of Certification

A state may waive certification. A waiver may occur in either of two ways: (1) the state provides a formal notice of waiver, or (2) the state fails or refuses to act on a request for certification within a reasonable period. The statute provides a "reasonable" period of *up to one year* after receipt of a request for certification for a state to act on the request.[238] Some federal agencies, including the Corps and EPA, "promulgated regulations describing a reasonable period of time for section 401 certification in relation to those agencies' licenses or permits prior to the 2020 Rule. . . . The Corps has routinely implemented a 60-day reasonable time period for section 401 decisions commencing when the certifying authority receives a section 401 certification request. See 33 CFR 325.2(b)(1)(ii).[239] EPA under the Trump administration revised its water quality certification rules in 2020, with the stated goal "to increase the predictability and timeliness of CWA

235. *See* Summit Hydropower P'ship v. Comm'r of Env't Prot., 629 A.2d 367, 372–75 (Conn. 1993); Triska v. Dep't of Health & Env't Control, 355 S.E.2d 531 (S.C. 1987).

236. *See* Summit Hydropower, 226 Conn. at 811–12, 629 A.2d at 376; *see also* Matter of Flax v. Ash, 142 Misc. 2d 828, 538 N.Y.S.2d 891 (Sup. Ct. 1988).

237. For example, issuance of the Environmental Resource Permit by the relevant state permitting agency in the state of Florida constitutes issuance of water quality certification for the activity in most cases. Operating Agreement between the Jacksonville Dist. of the U.S. Army Corps of Eng'rs, Fla. Dep't of Env't Prot., Northwest Fla. Water Mgmt. Dist., St. Johns River Water Mgmt. Dist., Southwest Fla. Water Mgmt. Dist. and Suwannee River Water Mgmt. Dist. Concerning Regulatory Programs for Activities in Wetlands and Other Surface Waters, Including Waters of the United States (Sept. 2012), Part II.A., https://floridadep.gov/sites/default/files/CorpsAgr-v79_9-4-12.pdf.

238. 33 U.S.C. § 1341(a)(1); 40 C.F.R. § 121.16(b).

239. 88 Fed. Reg. at 66585.

section 401 certification actions by clarifying timeframes for certification."[240] Under the Biden administration, EPA revised and replaced the 2020 rule in 2023,[241] "to be more consistent with the statutory text of the 1972 CWA and clarify elements of Section 401 certification practice that have evolved over the 50 years since the 1971 regulation was promulgated."[242] The 2020 rule provided that the federal agency could establish the reasonable period of time either categorically or on a case-by-case basis considering the complexity of the proposed project, nature of the discharge, and the "potential need for additional study or evaluation of water quality effects from the discharge."[243] The certifying authority (i.e., the state or tribe) was only authorized to request in writing that the reasonable period be extended and was not authorized to ask the project proponent to withdraw the certification request.[244] In contrast, the 2023 revisions allow the Federal agency and certifying authority to jointly agree in writing on the reasonable period of time for the certifying authority to act on the request, which could include categorical periods, and allow the certifying authority to extend the reasonable period merely by providing written notice.[245] The revisions also provide that "if the Federal agency and certifying authority do not agree upon a reasonable period of time, the default reasonable period of time will be six months from the date that the request for certification was received."[246] In no case, however, can the reasonable period exceed the statutory one-year period.[247]

The Corps regulations further limit the waiver period, stating that a waiver will be deemed to occur if the certifying agency fails or refuses to act on a request within 60 days after receipt of such a request unless the district engineer determines a shorter or longer period is reasonable for the state to act.[248] In determining whether a waiver period has

---

240. 85 Fed. Reg. 42,210 (July 13, 2020).

241. *See supra* note 222.

242. Press Release, Env't Prot. Agency, EPA Takes Action to Empower States, Territories, and Tribes to Protect Water Resources and Support Sustainable Development (June 2, 2022), https://www.epa.gov/newsreleases/epa-takes-action-empower-states-territories-and-tribes-protect-water-resources-and.

243. 88 Fed. Reg. at 42259.

244. 40 C.F.R. § 121.6 (2020).

245. 40 C.F.R. § 121.6 (2023); *supra* note 221, 88 Fed. Reg. at 66,662–663.

246. 40 C.F.R. § 121.6(c) (2023).

247. *Id.* § 121.6(b),(d).

248. 33 C.F.R. § 325.2(b)(1)(ii).

commenced or a waiver has occurred, the district engineer will verify that the certifying agency has received a valid request for certification.[249]

The waiver period begins to run only after a valid request for certification has been received by the state water quality agency.[250] Accordingly, it is generally advisable to seek a return receipt on the certification request. The "validity" of any request for certification is most likely to be determined by state law governing such requests—including, for example, filing requirements—although the case law is mixed on whether a federal agency may disregard state filing procedures for purposes of determining whether or when the waiver period has commenced.[251] The Corps regulations simply state that "[i]n determining whether or not a waiver period has commenced or waiver has occurred, the district engineer will verify that the certifying agency has received a valid request for certification."[252] It is, accordingly, advisable to consult state procedural requirements governing requests for certification.

3. Denial of Certification

In exercising their certification authority, states may determine that some effects of a federally permitted activity may violate applicable effluent limitations, water quality standards, or other appropriate requirements of state law. In such circumstances, the certifying agency may deny certification.[253] As noted earlier, if a state denies certification, the Corps will generally dismiss a permit application, usually allowing an applicant to re-submit the permit application when the state concerns have been addressed.

---

249. *Id.* § 325.2 (b)(1)(ii); *see also* Corps RGL No. 87-034, Section 401 Water Quality Certification, U.S. Army Corps of Eng'rs (Apr. 14, 1987) (expired), https://usace.contentdm.oclc.org/utils/getfile/collection/p16021coll9/id/1352.

250. North Carolina v. Fed. Energy Reg. Comm'n, 112 F.3d at 1184; City of Fredericksburg, Va. v. Fed. Energy Reg. Comm'n, 876 F.2d 1109 (4th Cir. 1989).

251. *Cf.* City of Fredericksburg, Va. v. Fed. Energy Reg. Comm'n, 876 F.2d 1109 (4th Cir. 1989) (concluding that under FERC regulations "a valid request for certification occurs only if the prospective licensee complies with the state agency's filing procedures"), *with* California v. Fed. Energy Reg. Comm'n, 966 F.2d 1541, 1552–54 (9th Cir. 1992) (deferring to FERC determination of when waiver period commenced over objection by state certifying agency).

252. 33 C.F.R. § 325.2(b)(1)(ii).

253. *See, e.g., 401 Water Quality Certification Fact Sheet*, Conn. Dep't of Env't Prot. (Apr. 2021), https://portal.ct.gov/DEEP/Permits-and-Licenses/Factsheets-Inland-Water/401-Water-Quality-Certification-Fact-Sheet.

4. Conditional Certification

A state agency's authority to impose conditions related to the state's water quality laws is found in Section 401(d) of the CWA, which provides:

> Any certification provided under this section shall set forth any effluent limitations and other limitations, and monitoring requirements necessary to assure that any applicant for a Federal license or permit will comply with any applicable effluent limitations and other limitations, under section 1311 or 1312 of this title, standard of performance under section 1316 of this title, or prohibition, effluent standard, or pretreatment standard under section 1317 of this title, and with any other appropriate requirement of State law set forth in such certification, and shall become a condition on any Federal license or permit subject to the provisions of this section.[254]

Prior to 2020, this ability to add certification conditions was left to the discretion of the state to determine what it deemed necessary to comply with the various CWA sections specifically enumerated in 401(d) as well as "any other appropriate requirement of State law."[255] In the 2020 Rule, however, EPA limited the phrase "other appropriate requirements of State law," to "state or tribal regulatory requirements for point source discharges into waters of the United States."[256] In the 2023 rule, EPA returned to the prior interpretation that it states "is more closely aligned with the statutory text and more environmentally protective."[257] Rather, states must simply include a "statement explaining why each of the included conditions is necessary to assure that the activity will comply with water quality requirements."[258] As a general matter, the Corps relies on state certifications to identify and consider any adverse effects that the proposed activity may have on water quality.[259]

In determining whether to certify, condition, or deny a request for certification, a state may consider effects beyond those caused by

---

254. 33 U.S.C. § 1341(d).
255. 88 Fed. Reg. at 66,593.
256. *Id.*; *see* 40 C.F.R. §§ 121.1(n), 121.3 (2020).
257. 88 Fed. Reg. at 66,593.
258. 40 C.F.R. § 121.7(d)(3).
259. 33 C.F.R. § 320.4(d).

the discharge(s) that confers jurisdiction on the Corps and provides a basis for certification. Corps regulations provide that "[a] certification obtained for the construction of any facility must also pertain to the subsequent operation of the facility."[260] EPA regulations provide that any certification must include a statement by the certifying agency that there is "a reasonable assurance that the activity will be conducted in a manner which will not violate applicable water quality standards" and must contain a statement of "any conditions which the certifying agency deems necessary or desirable with respect to the discharge *or the activity*."[261] The interpretation of the scope of state scrutiny was confirmed by the Supreme Court in *PUD No. 1 of Jefferson County v. Washington Deartment of Ecology*.[262] The Court held that Section 401(d) "is most reasonably read as authorizing additional conditions and limitations on the activity as a whole once the threshold condition, the existence of a discharge, is satisfied."[263] Accordingly, state authorities may consider any expected effects on water quality resulting from the continuing operation of the permitted activity and deny certification on the basis of such effects or impose conditions to minimize or eliminate them. The preamble to the 2023 certification rule recognizes *PUD No. 1*[264] and expressly extends the state's certification authority

260. *Id.* § 320.3(a). The regulation may reflect the provisions of §401(a)(3) of the CWA, which provides:

> The certification obtained pursuant to [Section 401(a)(1)] with respect to the construction of any facility shall fulfill the requirements of this section with respect to certification in connection with any other Federal license or permit required for the operation of such facility unless, after notice to the certifying State, . . . the State . . . notifies [the permitting or licensing] agency within sixty days after receipt of such notice that there is no longer reasonable assurance that there will be compliance with [various provisions of the CWA] because of changes since the construction license or permit certification was issued in (A) the construction or operation of the facility, (B) the characteristics of the waters into which the discharge is made, (C) the water quality criteria applicable to such waters or (D) applicable effluent limitations or other requirements.

33 U.S.C. § 1341(a)(3).

261. 40 C.F.R. § 121.2(a)(4) (2019); *see also* 33 C.F.R. § 121.2(a)(3)(2019) (emphasis added).

262. *PUD No. 1 of* Jefferson Cnty. v. Washington Dep't of Ecology, 511 U.S. 700, 114 S. Ct. 1900, 128 L. Ed. 2d 716 (1994).

263. *Id.* at 712.

264. 88 Fed. Reg. at 66,564.

over both construction and operation: "The certifying authority's evaluation is limited to the water quality-related impacts from the activity subject to the Federal license or permit, *including the activity's construction and operation*."[265] Thus, Section 401 of the CWA gives states and authorized tribes significant authority to condition activities occurring within their jurisdiction to protect water quality.

5. Judicial Review of Certification

Federal courts have exclusive jurisdiction to review state water quality certifications under CWA Section 401.[266] Whether or not a state's water quality certification is considered final agency action depends on the state's administrative appeal process and whether those processes guarantee parties the ability to appeal the decision or not.[267] In *Sierra Club v. West Virginia Department of Environmental Protection*, the state's water quality certification of a natural gas pipeline was subject to review as final agency action subject to the "arbitrary and capricious" review standard of that Administrative Procedure Act.[268] In that case, the court found West Virginia's water quality certification to be arbitrary and capricious where the state failed to provide a "reasoned explanation" why a company's past water quality violations would not continue in the future and vacated the certification.[269]

E. Coastal Zone Management Act (CZMA) Certification

Congress passed the Coastal Zone Management Act (CZMA) in 1972 to provide a mechanism for uniform management of the nation's coastal resources, including the Great Lakes.[270] Under a voluntary partnership with the federal government, coastal states develop Coastal

---

265. 40 C.F.R. § 121.3(a) (emphasis added).

266. Sierra Club v. West Virginia Dep't of Envtl Prot., 64 F.4th 487, 499 (4th Cir. 2023).

267. *Id.* at 500 (discretionary with state agency whether to grant review request); *cf.* Berkshire Environmental Action Team, Inc. v. Tennessee Gas Pipeline Company, LLC, 851 F.3d 105 (1st Cir. 2017) (Massachusetts certification letter not final because parties' right to administrative proceedings was guaranteed).

268. Sierra Club, 64 F.4th at 501.

269. *Id.* at 502–03.

270. Nat'l Oceanic & Atmospheric Admin., Office for Coastal Management | About the Office, https://coast.noaa.gov/czm/act/.

Management Programs (CMPs) to protect and administer their coastal resources.[271] Under CZMA Section 307(c)(3) and (d) applicants for federal license or permit activities that have reasonably foreseeable effects on any coastal use or resource of a state's coastal zone must certify to affected states that the proposed activities are consistent with the enforceable policies of the state's CMP.[272] States are responsible for providing consistency certifications for federal permits,[273] and their CMPs must provide public notice of the proposed activity and an opportunity for public participation.[274] All applicants for a Section 404 permit in a state with a CMP must provide in the application a certification that the proposed activity complies with and will be consistent with the CMP; the State agency must get a copy of the certification and any additional necessary information.[275] The state has six months from the date of receipt of all necessary data and information to review the applicant's consistency certification, unless the state and the applicant mutually agree to stay the review period.[276] Concurrence is presumed if the state has not acted within the six-month period if not stayed, and NOAA's regulations urge states and applicants to agree upon conditions during the review period that would allow the state to concur on consistency.[277] If a state CMP objects to the certification, the permit or license cannot be issued unless the state removes its objection or the applicant appeals the state's objection to the Secretary of Commerce.[278] The Secretary can override a state's objection if the national interest in approving the activity outweighs its adverse coastal effects both individually and cumulatively and no reasonable alternative is available that would allow the activity to be conducted in a manner consistent with the state's CMP.[279]

---

271. Nat'l Oceanic & Atmospheric Admin., Office for Coastal Management, The National Coastal Zone Management Program, https://coast.noaa.gov/czm/.

272. 16 U.S.C. § 1456(c).

273. 15 C.F.R. § 930.6. 15 C.F.R. pt. 930, subpt. D governs CZMA consistency determinations for activities requiring a federal permit.

274. 15 C.F.R. § 930.61.

275. *Id.* § 930.57.

276. *Id.* § 930.60.

277. *Id.* § 930.62.

278. 16 U.S.C. § 1456(3)(B)(iii); 15 C.F.R. § 930.64.

279. 15 C.F.R. § 930.121. 15 C.F.R. pt. 930, subpt. H governs the appeal process.

Currently, there are 35 federally approved state CMPs.[280] Since approval of the first CMP in 1978, thousands of federal license or permit activities have been reviewed for consistency.

III. Other Regulators and Obligations: The Role of Local and International Obligations in Regulating Wetlands

A. Introduction

In the realm of U.S. environmental law, most people think first of federal law,[281] then of state law. This is not without merit, as an elaborate web of federal laws apply to activities that impact wetlands, and in many states this web is interwoven with applicable state laws. In fact, many chapters of this book are dedicated to the intricacies of the federal wetland regulatory program, with reference to state involvement in some of those chapters.[282] Yet states and local governments often have wetland ordinances that may come into play with respect to proposed activities. Likewise, the United States is party to an international treaty, the Convention on Wetlands of International Importance especially as Waterfowl Habitat (referred to as the Ramsar Convention),[283] that provides obligations and opportunities from an international perspective.

This section is organized as follows: it opens with an exploration of local wetland regulation. It continues with an overview of the Ramsar Convention, particularly its designation process and wise use obligations. The chapter closes with a discussion of issues to watch in both areas.

---

280. The state CMPS can be accessed at https://coast.noaa.gov/czm/mystate/. The 35 approved CMPs include Puerto Rico, Guam, Northern Mariana Islands, and American Samoa. Alaska withdrew from the program in 2011. *Id.*

281. Federal Water Pollution Control Act, Pub. L. No. 92-500, 86 Stat. 816 (1972), *as codified in* 33 U.S.C. § 1344 (2018), further amended in Pub. L. No. 95-217, 91 Stat. 1567 (1977); Pub. L. No. 100-4, 101 Stat. 45 (1987). *See generally* Chapter 1.

282. For example, Chapter 5 discusses the important review role that states have in the Nationwide Permit process.

283. *Convention on Wetlands of International Importance Especially as Waterfowl Habitat* (Feb. 2, 1971), T.I.A.S. No. 1084, 996 U.N.T.S. 245 (amended 1982 & 1987) [hereinafter *Ramsar Convention*], https://en.unesco.org/about-us/legal-affairs/convention-wetlands-international-importance-especially-waterfowl-habitat.

B. State Wetland Laws

In addition to the role of the states discussed earlier in Part II of this chapter, states can and often do regulate wetlands independently of and sometimes more stringently than the federal government. The National Association of Wetland Managers conducted a review of state-level wetland regulation in all 50 states, completing its data collection in 2014 and issuing its report in 2015.[284] This report focused on four core elements of state and tribal wetland programs: wetland regulation, wetland monitoring and assessment, wetland water quality standards, and voluntary wetland restoration programs. The report found that 23 states have a wetland permitting program, six states additionally have a coastal permitting program, 31 states have regional or state programmatic general permit from the Corps, and 17 states have joint or parallel permitting programs with the Corps.[285] Twenty-five states have formal wetland mitigation programs that are independent from the Corps program.[286]

The state of Florida, for example, broadly defines waters of the state to include both isolated and connected wetlands; the state's environmental resource permitting program regulates activities in wetlands and surface waters as well as activities in uplands that may affect the flow of surface water and thereby impact water resources.[287] The state's program is separate from and in addition to the section 404 program; however, issuance of the environmental resource permit generally constitutes both Florida's water quality certification under Section 401(c)[288] and its certification of consistency with Florida's CMP.[289] While Florida regulates activities any non-exempt "project in, on, or over wetlands or other surface waters" regardless of whether

284. Nat'l Ass'n. of Wetland Managers, Status and Trends Report on State Wetland Programs in the United States (2015), https://www.nawm.org/pdf_lib/state_summaries/status_and_trends_report_on_state_wetland_programs_in_the_united_states_102015.pdf, (last updated Mar. 6, 2016).

285. *Id.* at 12.

286. *Id.* For more information concerning the federal wetland mitigation program, *see* Chapter 6.

287. Fla. Stat. ch. 373, Part IV.

288. *See* Part II.D of this chapter. *See* Florida Dep't of Env't Prot., Environmental Resource Permit Applicant's Handbook Vol. I, s. 1.3.1.1, https://www.flrules.org/gateway/reference.asp?No=Ref-12078.

289. *See* Part II.E of this chapter; Florida Dep't of Env't Prot., Environmental Resource Permit Applicant's Handbook Vol I., s. 1.3.1.1.

they are isolated or continuously connected to navigable waters,[290] the state regulatory program includes more exemptions than its federal counterpart.[291] It is important for practitioners to be familiar with the wetland programs specific to their geographic regions and to recognize that the programs can have significant differences in both scope and effect.[292]

C. Local Wetland Laws

Additionally, local regulation of wetlands through land use laws happens throughout the country. In fact, land use regulation is a province traditionally under the control of local governments, and as the opinion in the landmark 2001 U.S. Supreme Court case *SWANCC* noted, "[r]egulation of land use [is] a function traditionally performed by local governments."[293]

Local wetlands regulations come in all shapes and sizes.[294] Thousands of local governments nationwide already have ordinances or other local laws that govern activities in local wetlands.[295] Many go beyond federal or state requirements, and compliance with those local laws could add to both the cost and time investment required for particular projects.[296]

---

290. Fla. Admin. Code r. 62-330.020(2)(a).

291. *See, e.g.*, Fla. Admin. Code r. 62-330.051, 62-330.0511.

292. For the links the state wetland programs around the country, visit Nat'l. Ass'n of Wetland Managers, State Wetland Programs, https://www.nawm.org/wetland-programs/state-wetland-programs.html.

293. Solid Waste Agency of Northern Cook Cty. v. U.S. Army Corps of Engr's, 531 U.S. 159, 121 S. Ct. 675, 148 L. Ed. 2d 576 (2001), *citing* Hess v. Port Authority Trans-Hudson Corp., 513 U.S. 30, 115 S. Ct. 394, 130 L. Ed. 2d 245 (1994) (internal quotation marks omitted).

294. *See generally* Kim Diana Connolly, *Looking to Local Law: Can Local Ordinances Help Protect Isolated Wetlands?* 27 Nat'l Wetlands Newsl. 21 (May–June 2005), https://digitalcommons.law.buffalo.edu/cgi/viewcontent.cgi?article=1362&context=journal_articles.

295. A thorough review of all local ordinances governing wetlands is virtually impossible. However, many ordinances can be found at various compiled sources, including MuniCode, https://library.municode.com/, and State and Local Government on the Net, http://statelocalgov.net/index.cfm. Of course, a general internet search for local laws governing wetlands using any decent search engine will also yield a large number of results.

296. *See, e.g.*, Miami-Dade Code of Ordinances, Sec. 24-48, requiring a permit from the Miami-Dade Department of Environmental Resource Management "to fill,

As the Wisconsin Wetlands Association has remarked, there are several good reasons for localities to pass local wetland laws:

> 1) Home rule provides local governments with the authority and opportunity to improve wetland protection. . . . 2) Local ordinances can clarify and stabilize what wetlands are protected and how. . . . 3) Protecting local wetlands helps communities reduce costs on water-related services. . . . 4) Local governments are better positioned to consider and respond to wetland concerns at a watershed scale.[297]

Likewise, one scholar noted that a transition is happening in some local laws to a functionality based approach to regulating wetlands:

> Many local regulations are concerned with specific, discrete, and conceptually severable environmental units: common local environmental laws regulate the taking of a tree or pushing soil. However, some local governments have crested the fragmented perspective to regulate ecosystem function in a performance-based manner, where regulations are triggered by the significance and extent of an activity's impacts on ecosystem processes. In these instances, local governments provide more effective protection of ecosystem services by regulating ecosystem functionality.[298]

It is impossible to provide a detailed picture of all local wetlands laws, or even all the possible options, in this chapter. The next part of this section discusses selected approaches that existing local laws have taken to protect wetlands to help readers get a sense of what they might encounter. Readers are advised to research whether local laws might apply as they plan any projects or protective measures for wetlands in their areas.

---

dredge, or authorize, allow, suffer, or permit any type of work in, on, over, or upon tidal waters, submerged bay bottom lands, or wetlands anywhere in Miami-Dade County; flood hazard areas," https://library.municode.com/fl/miami_-_dade_county/codes/code_of_ordinances?nodeId=10620.

297. Wisc. Wetlands Ass'n, Land Use and Wetlands: Zoning Opportunities to Improve Wetland Protection 1 (2013), https://www.yumpu.com/en/document/read/50412306/land-use-and-wetlands-wisconsin-wetlands-association.

298. Keith H. Hirokawa, *Sustaining Ecosystem Services through Local Environmental Law*, 28 Pace Env't L. Rev. 760, 796–802 (Apr. 2011), http://digitalcommons.pace.edu/cgi/viewcontent.cgi?article=1676&context=pelr.

Some local laws build on a state system designed to encourage local action, such as Washington State's Growth Management Act.[299] For example, the wetlands ordinance in Port Angeles, Washington, echoes many of the values central to federal wetlands law.[300] That city declared it the policy of the City of Port Angeles

> . . . to require site planning to avoid or minimize damage to wetlands wherever possible; to require that activities not dependent upon a wetland location be located at upland sites; and to achieve no net loss of wetlands by requiring restoration or enhancement of degraded wetlands or creation of new wetlands to offset losses which are unavoidable. In addition, it is the intent of the City of Port Angeles that activities in or affecting wetlands not threaten public safety, cause nuisances, or destroy or degrade natural wetland functions and values. . . .[301]

In Port Angeles, wetland permit holders must undertake a wetland functional assessment,[302] must be regulated for all activities in wetlands including draining,[303] and may be required to post bond to guard against permit violations.[304] In a different approach taken by Washington's Walla Walla County, the local ordinance[305] designates all wetlands as "critical areas," triggering strict regulatory requirements, including extremely specific buffer zone requirements[306] and mitigation mandates.[307] Additionally, as the Environmental Law Institute observed in 2014, "all cities and counties with shorelines of the state must prepare a Shoreline Master Program aimed at designating 'preferred uses' of shoreline areas that are consistent with controlling

---

299. WASH. REV. CODE § 36.70A.010, https://app.leg.wa.gov/RCW/default.aspx?cite=36.70A.010&pdf=true; *see also* https://www.commerce.wa.gov/about-us/rulemaking/gma-laws-rules/.

300. *See* PORT ANGELES, WASH. CODE §§ 15.04 *et seq.* (2023), https://library.municode.com/wa/port_angeles/codes/code_of_ordinances.

301. *Id.* § 15.24.010(B).

302. *Id.* § 15.24.045.

303. *Id.* § 15.24.050.

304. *Id.* § 15.24.070(H)(2).

305. WALLA WALLA COUNTY, WASH. CODE § 18.08.300-675 (2023), https://library.municode.com/wa/walla_walla_county/codes/code_of_ordinances?nodeId=14868.

306. *Id.* § 18.08.340-45.

307. *Id.* § 18.18.346-47.

pollution and limiting environmental damage; these programs are supported, reviewed, and approved by the Department of Ecology."[308]

Likewise, in Michigan (one of the two states that has assumed state-level Section 404 authority),[309] many local governments have elected to enact wetlands regulations as allowed under Part 303 of the Natural Resources and Environmental Protection Act.[310] For example, in Michigan's Scio Township, under its Wetland and Watercourse Protection law,[311] a wetland administrator is appointed,[312] and a permit is required for most activities that could impact the township's wetlands.[313] If a permit is issued, it requires significant compensatory mitigation, and is only available in cases where

> . . . all feasible and prudent efforts have been made to avoid the loss of protected wetland. . . [and] all practical means have been considered to minimize protected wetland impacts . . . [and] it is practical to replace the protected wetland which will be unavoidably eliminated . . . [and] all alternatives for preserving protected wetlands and watercourses have been evaluated and found to be impractical, inappropriate, or ineffective.[314]

---

308. Env't Law Inst., State and Local Authority for Marine Protection—Washington (2014), https://www.eli.org/sites/default/files/files-pdf/state-local-mpas_washington.pdf.

309. *See State and Federal Wetland Regulations*, Michigan Dep't of Env't Quality , http://www.michigan.gov/deq/0,4561,7-135-3313_3687-10801--,00.html ("In 1984, Michigan received authorization from the federal government to administer Section 404 of the federal Clean Water Act in most areas of the state. A state administered 404 program must be consistent with the requirements of the federal Clean Water Act and associated regulations set forth in the Section 404(b)(1) Guidelines. Whereas in other states, where an applicant must apply to the U.S. Corps of Engineers and a state agency for wetland permits, applicants in Michigan generally submit only one wetland permit application to the DEQ."). *See also* Section II.B of this chapter.

310. Mich. Comp. Laws §§ 324.30301–324.30323; Mich. Admin. Code §§ 281.921–281.925. *See also* Nat'l Assoc. of Wetland Managers, State Wetland Programs, https://www.nawm.org/pdf_lib/state_summaries/michigan_state_wetland_program_summary_083115.pdf.

311. Scio Township, Mich. Code §§ 16-100 *et seq.* (2019), https://library.municode.com/mi/scio_township,_(washtenaw_co.)/codes/code_of_ordinances?nodeId=COOR_CH16EN_ARTVWEWAPR.

312. *Id.* § 16-134.

313. *Id.* § 16-156.

314. *Id.* § 16-247.

The township also has an environmental review board made up of five town residents (three of whom must have scientific experience) to review wetlands permit appeals and take other actions.[315] Michigan's Meridian Charter Township has declared that

> Preservation of the remaining township wetlands in a natural condition shall be and is necessary to maintain hydrological, economic, recreational, and aesthetic natural resource values for existing and future residents of the township, and, therefore, the township board declares a policy of no net loss of wetlands . . . [and] declares a long-term goal of net gain of wetlands to be accomplished through review of degraded or destroyed wetlands in the township and, through cooperative work with landowners, using incentives and voluntary agreements to restore wetlands.[316]

That township achieves those goals through a rigorous permitting and enforcement process.[317]

Massachusetts issues permits for its statewide Wetland Protections Act through local conservation commissions.[318] There are also additional local laws, such as that of Gloucester,[319] which claims very broad jurisdiction, including certain uplands and isolated wetlands,[320] and lays out a detailed regulatory approach.[321] In nearby Salem, Massachusetts,[322] local law requires, among other things, that a person

---

315. *Id.* § 16-278.

316. Meridian Charter Township, Mich. Code § 22-117(b) (2002), https://ecode360.com/28776402.

317. *Id.* § 22-119.

318. Mass. Gen. Laws ch. 131, § 40; 310 Mass.Code Regs. 10.00. *See also* Nat'l Assoc. of State Wetland Managers, Massachusetts State Wetland Program Summary, at 5, https://www.nawm.org/pdf_lib/state_summaries/massachusetts_state_wetland_program_summary_083115.pdf ("Massachusetts has a two-tiered structure for enforcement of wetlands protections. Local conservation commissions in each city and town are the first line of defense, both for wetlands permitting and for enforcement.") (2015).

319. *See* Gloucester, Mass. Code § 12, art. II (2023), https://library.municode.com/ma/gloucester/codes/code_of_ordinances?nodeId=PTIICOOR_CH12MA.

320. *Id.* § 12-11(b).

321. *Id.* §§ 12-25, *et seq.*

322. Salem, Mass. Code ch. 50.1-18 (2022), https://library.municode.com/MA/Salem/codes/code_of_ordinances?nodeId=PTIIICOOR_CH50WEPRCO.

who purchases, inherits, or otherwise acquires land with wetlands that faces a permit violation will be held accountable.[323]

Many other localities across the country have adopted a wide variety of local wetlands laws. Some are more protective than others, and a number are designed to support development. For example, given size thresholds at the time for regulating wetlands under the state Freshwater Wetlands Act in New York,[324] the city of White Plains set a significantly smaller size threshold than the then-applicable threshold of 12.4 acres to trigger local wetlands law.[325] In Norfolk, Virginia,[326] a seven-member city resident board issues permits in order to both "preserve and prevent the despoliation and destruction of wetlands within the city while accommodating necessary economic development in a manner consistent with wetlands preservation."[327] The city of Atlanta, Georgia, has its own wetlands law as well,[328] but it is primarily designed "to coordinate the City permitting process with the Corps of Engineers permitting process."[329]

In sum, not only can wetlands be regulated at the federal and state level, local governments may also impose additional restrictions. Practitioners must be aware of the multiple layers of regulations that may govern a particular activity in wetlands or surface waters.

323. *Id.* § 50-7.

324. The Freshwater Wetlands Act, N.Y. ENV'T CONSERV. art. 24 (1975). This act was amended in 2022 to make it increasingly more stringent over time; beginning in January 1, 2025, small wetlands of "unusual importance" will be regulated if they meet one of 11 new criteria in the amended legislation, and by January 1, 2028, the default size threshold of regulated wetlands will decrease from 12.4 acres to 7.4 acres. *See* https://dec.ny.gov/nature/waterbodies/wetlands/freshwater-wetlands-program.

325. WHITE PLAINS, N.Y. CODE § 3-5-3(b), https://library.municode.com/ny/white_plains/codes/code_of_ordinances?nodeId=TITIIIENCO_CH3-5STREPRPRENSESIFE_S3-5-3THCRME (setting a threshold of 1,000 square feet).

326. *See* NORFOLK, VA. CODE ch. 49 (2023), https://library.municode.com/va/norfolk/codes/code_of_ordinances?nodeId=COCI_CH49WECOPRSADU.

327. *Id.* § 49-5-1.

328. ATLANTA, GA. CODE art. VIII § 74-401 (Apr. 23, 2023), https://library.municode.com/ga/atlanta/codes/code_of_ordinances?nodeId=COORATGEVOII_CH74EN_ARTVIIIWEPRRE_S74-401PUIN.

329. *Id.* § 74-403.

D. International Opportunities and Obligations

Nations have adopted many differing approaches to regulating wetland resources across the world.[330] Although it does not directly regulate any wetland in the United States, obligations with respect to one particular international treaty apply to wetlands throughout our nation. The Ramsar Convention (formally known as the Convention on Wetlands of International Importance especially as Waterfowl Habitat)[331] is the only international environmental treaty that focuses on a specific ecosystem: wetlands. The Convention has a broad definition of wetlands, and includes "areas of marsh, fen, peatland or water, whether natural or artificial, permanent or temporary, with water that is static or flowing, fresh, brackish or salt, including areas of marine water the depth of which at low tide does not exceed six metres."[332] The treaty is designed to support national action and international cooperation for the conservation and wise use of wetlands and their resources.[333]

The treaty has been in place for more than 40 years. Following more than eight years of work by concerned nations and nongovernmental organizations,[334] the treaty was signed by representatives of 18 countries in Ramsar, Iran,[335] in February 1971,[336] and entered into

---

330. *See* Clare Shine & Cyrille de Klemm, IUCN Environmental Law Centre, Wetlands, Water and the Law: Using Law to Advance Wetland Conservation and Wise Use (1999), https://portals.iucn.org/library/efiles/documents/EPLP-038.pdf.

331. *Ramsar Convention*, *supra* note 283. A current copy of the Ramsar Convention text can be found at https://www.ramsar.org/sites/default/files/documents/library/current_convention_text_e.pdf.

332. *Ramsar Convention*, *supra* note 283, art. 1. This is much broader than the definitions of wetlands used under United States regulations and guidance, particularly in light of the recent U.S. Supreme Court decision in *Sackett v. Env't Prot. Agency*. *See* Chapter 2 herein.

333. *See* www.Ramsar.org.

334. G.V.T. Matthews, *The Ramsar Convention on Wetlands: Its History and Development* (1993) (recounting that "[i]t took just over eight years of conferences, technical meetings and behind the scenes discussions to develop a convention text"), https://leap.unep.org/sites/default/files/2020-09/Matthews-history.pdf.

335. The Convention's short name is not an acronym, but rather signifies the name of the city (Ramsar, Iran) where it was originally signed. For the signatory counties, *see* https://www.ramsar.org/countries.

336. The original 1971 version of the Convention can be found at https://www.ramsar.org/sites/default/files/documents/library/original_1971_convention_e.pdf.

force in 1975.[337] The convention represented a dramatic shift from historic perspectives throughout most of the world, where wetlands had been viewed as "disastrous realms, sources of disease, [and] obstacles to any form of positive development."[338] The convention[339] has been amended twice,[340] and signatories regularly come together in Conferences of the Parties to negotiate and agree to other important guidance documents.[341] The United States is an active participant in Ramsar activities.[342] Currently there are 172 contracting parties to the Ramsar Convention.[343]

Unaffiliated with the United Nations system of Multilateral Environmental Agreements,[344] the Convention Secretariat is headquartered in Switzerland,[345] and receives intercessional guidance from a Stand-

337. By its terms, the Ramsar Convention was to enter into force four months in 1975 after seven parties had ratified it. *Ramsar Convention*, *supra* note 283, at art. 10. Since then, almost 90 percent of UN member states across the world (172) have become "Contracting Parties" under the terms of the convention. For a current introduction to the history of the Convention, see *A Brief History of the Ramsar Convention*, https://www.ramsar.org/. The United States became a party in 1987 during the Reagan administration. *See* Contracting Parties to the Ramsar Convention (as of Aug. 24, 2023), https://www.ramsar.org/sites/default/files/documents/library/annotated_contracting_parties_list_e.pdf.

338. Matthews, *supra* note 334.

339. For a superb overview of the Convention, including its history and modern implementation, see THE RAMSAR CONVENTION MANUAL—A GUIDE TO THE CONVENTION ON WETLANDS (Ramsar, Iran, 1971) (2013) (hereinafter RAMSAR MANUAL), https://www.ramsar.org/sites/default/files/documents/library/manual6-2013-e.pdf.

340. The actual language of the incorporated amendments can be found at the official documents site: https://www.ramsar.org/search?search_api_views_fulltext=amendments&f%5B%5D=type%3Adocument.

341. The Guidelines adopted by the Conference of the Contracting Parties to the Ramsar Convention on Wetlands, https://www.ramsar.org/search?search_api_views_fulltext=guidelines. This website provides links to various guidance documents officially adopted during meetings of the Conference of the Contracting Parties.

342. *See* U.S. Fish and Wildlife Service, Ramsar Convention in the United States, https://www.fws.gov/partner/ramsar (last visited Apr. 11, 2024).

343. https://www.ramsar.org.

344. *See generally* Basic Information on Secretariats of Multilateral Environmental Agreements, Mission, Structure, Financing and Governance, https://www.ramsar.org/sites/default/files/documents/library/handbook1_5ed_introductiontoconvention_e.pdf.

345. *See* Ramsar, *The Ramsar Secretariat*, https://www.ramsar.org/about/the-secretariat (last visited Apr. 11, 2024).

ing Committee.[346] Under its current strategic plan, the Convention has four strategic goals: (1) "Addressing the Drivers of Wetland Loss And Degradation" . . . ; (2) "Effectively Conserving and Managing the Ramsar Site Network" . . . ; (3) "Wisely Using All Wetlands" . . . ; and (4) Enhancing Implementation." . . .[347] The strategic plan stresses the vision of the Ramsar Convention is that "Wetlands are conserved, wisely used, restored and their benefits are recognized and valued by all."[348] Thus, the mission is "[c]onservation and wise use of all wetlands through local and national actions and international cooperation, as a contribution towards achieving sustainable development throughout the world."[349]

The Secretariat and signatories also receive expert scientific and policy guidance from its Scientific and Technical Review Panel (STRP).[350] Member countries are encouraged to create National Ramsar Committees,[351] which tend to vary from country to country in terms of composition and role in meeting the convention's obligations.[352] In the United States, the U.S. National Ramsar Committee is made up of nonprofit, academic, and other parties with interests in wetlands, and federal governmental officials serve in an observer capacity.[353]

Under the Convention, each party must designate at least one site of international importance. Designation requires meeting official criteria, and completing a Ramsar Information Sheet (RIS) with

---

346. *See* Ramsar, *The Standing Committee*, https://www.ramsar.org/about/the-standing-committee (last visited Apr. 11, 2024).

347. The Fourth Ramsar Strategic Plan 2016–2024, https://www.ramsar.org/sites/default/files/hb2_5ed_strategic_plan_2016_24_e.pdf.

348. *Id.*

349. *Id.*

350. *See* Ramsar, *The Scientific and Technical Review Panel (STRP), Ramsar's Scientific Subsidiary Body*, https://www.ramsar.org/about/the-scientific-and-technical-review-panel (last visited Apr. 11, 2024).

351. *See* Ramsar, *Resolution 5.6: The Wise Use of Wetlands, Annex A*, https://www.ramsar.org/sites/default/files/documents/pdf/res/key_res_5.6e.pdf (suggesting that establishment of national wetland committees can assist with meeting "wise use" obligations).

352. *See* Marcela Bonells & Monica Zavagli, National Ramsar/Wetlands Committees across the Six Ramsar Regions: Diversity and Benefits (Sept. 2011), https://www.ramsar.org/sites/default/files/documents/pdf/strp/NRC_final_en.pdf.

353. *See* U.S. National Ramsar Committee, https://www.stetson.edu/law/international/biodiversity/us-ramsar-committee.php.

data on and support for the proposed site.[354] Once approved, sites join the List of Wetlands of International Importance.[355] After listing, a party is obliged "to promote the conservation of the wetlands included in the List, and as far as possible the wise use of wetlands in their territory."[356] However, the Convention provides that listing a site "does not prejudice [a party's] exclusive sovereign rights."[357] As of 2023, the Convention had designated 2,493 wetland sites of international importance totaling 256,759,538 hectares.[358] In the United States, there are 41 designated wetland sites of international importance.[359]

There are times that proposed projects in the United States may impact listed wetlands of international importance in this nation. The Convention has a process whereby Article 3.2 of the Convention provides that "each Contracting Party shall arrange to be informed at the earliest possible time if the ecological character of any wetland in its territory and included in the List has changed, is changing or is likely to change as the result of technological developments, pollution or other human interference. Information on such changes shall be passed without delay to the [Ramsar Secretariat]."[360] "Ecological character is the combination of the ecosystem components, processes and benefits/services that characterise the wetland at a given point in time"[361] and a "change in ecological character is the human-induced adverse alteration of any ecosystem component, process, and/or ecosystem benefit/service."[362] Accordingly, based on "informed,

354. *See* Ramsar, *Information Sheet on Ramsar Wetlands (RIS),* https://www.ramsar.org/sites/default/files/documents/library/key_ris_e.pdf. A new process for completing and updating future RIS's was approved in 2012. Resolution XI.8 Streamlining procedures for describing Ramsar Sites at the time of designation and subsequent updates, at https://www.ramsar.org/sites/default/files/documents/library/cop11-res08-e-anx2.pdf.

355. The current list of sites can be found here: https://www.ramsar.org/document/list-wetlands-international-importance-ramsar-list. The list as of April 18, 2024, is here: https://www.ramsar.org/sites/default/files/2023-08/sitelist.pdf.

356. *See* Ramsar Manual, *supra* note 339, at § 4.2.

357. *Id.* § 4.3.

358. *The List of Wetlands of International Importance* (May 9, 2023), https://www.ramsar.org/sites/default/files/documents/library/sitelist.pdf.

359. https://www.ramsar.org/country-profile/united-states-america.

360. *Ramsar Convention*, *supra* note 283, at art. 3.2.

361. Ramsar Manual, *supra* note 339, at 106.

362. *Id.* at 105.

authoritative or expert judgement,"[363] human-induced[364] changes (on-site or off-site)[365] can be brought to the attention to the Ramsar Secretariat and the authority within the nation that is responsible to the Secretariat.[366] In the United States, those considering such action should contact the U.S. Fish and Wildlife Service.[367] Upon receipt of the Article 3.2 report, the Secretariat may then inquire as to the status and request an update from the party[368] and will report back to the all parties at the next Conference of the Parties.[369]

Identifying the status of a wetland of international importance can elevate the profile of proposed actions that could impact that wetland and influence the outcome. For example, in 2011, concerned individuals and organizations got involved in an issue facing the smallest

---

363. COP10 Document 27 (2008), an information paper on "Background and rationale to the Framework for processes of detecting, reporting and responding to change in wetland ecological character," observes that: "[n]o guidance has been given on what degree of 'likelihood' or confidence is sufficient to require the triggering of the Article 3.2 process. Clearly it would defeat the aim of this provision if strict standards of evidence and substantiation were imposed. On the other hand, the system might be open to abuse (or at least ineffectiveness) if the merest suggestion or anxiety on the part of one person were enough to create the legal reporting obligation. The appropriate approach will lie somewhere in a middle ground of informed, authoritative or expert judgement." https://www.ramsar.org/sites/default/files/documents/pdf/cop10/cop10_dr27_e.pdf.

364. To trigger the Article 3.2 process, the change in ecological character must be human-induced and not the result of natural evolutionary change occurring in wetlands. Ramsar Manual, *supra* note 339, at 105. *See also* COP10 Document 27, which advises "There is, however, no guidance provided to Parties on how to distinguish human-caused changes from naturally-occurring changes. In practice this can be difficult, since, for example, an apparently natural change to a site may in practice be the consequence of a human-caused ex situ change, such as changes in the water management elsewhere in a river basin." https://www.ramsar.org/sites/default/files/documents/pdf/res/key_res_viii_08_e.pdf.

365. Resolution XI.9 (2012) recognized "that changes in the ecological character of wetlands may be due to in situ or ex situ activities," https://www.ramsar.org/sites/default/files/documents/library/cop11-res09-e.pdf.

366. *Id.*

367. U.S. Fish & Wildlife Service, *Ramsar*, https://www.fws.gov/partner/ramsar.

368. Once the Secretariat receives an Article 3.2 report from an NGO, the Secretariat will pass it along to the Party's Administrative Authority (AA), assuming that it comes from a reputable group and contains credible information. The AA is asked whether the Party is aware of the matter and requests the Party to advise the Secretariat on the status of the situation. Ramsar Manual, *supra* note 339, at § 4.3.7.

369. See Resolution XI.4 (2012) for an example of such a report. https://www.ramsar.org/sites/default/files/documents/pdf/cop11/res/cop11-res04-e.pdf.

Ramsar Wetland of International Importance in the United States, the Olentangy River Wetland Research Park,[370] located on the Ohio State University campus. That wetland was threatened by the potential placement of a gas pipeline under the site,[371] and local and state organizations like the Sierra Club were actively advocating for the site's protection.[372] More informally, a grassroots effort sprang up among Ohio State University students, alumni, and staff to avert the project.[373] During the consideration process, the U.S. National Ramsar Committee communicated directly with the university about obligations under the Ramsar Convention.[374] Ultimately, the parties involved reached an agreement to divert the pipeline around the wetlands, and the University touts the wetland's Ramsar status to this day.[375]

In addition to designating internationally important wetlands and attending to them, the Convention requires each party to employ the concept of "wise use" to all wetlands in a party's territory.[376] Viewed as predecessor of so-called "sustainability" concepts,[377] the wise use of wetlands is one of the Ramsar Convention's so-called three pillars.[378] "Wise use" requires Contracting Parties to develop plans to

370. *Information Sheet on Wilma H. Schiermeier Olentangy River Wetland Research Park* (Oct. 5, 2007), https://rsis.ramsar.org/RISapp/files/RISrep/US1779RIS.pdf.

371. Spencer Hunt, *Columbia Gas Won't Lay Pipeline under OSU Wetlands*, The Columbus Dispatch (Jan. 18, 2012), https://www.dispatch.com/story/news/environment/2012/01/18/columbia-gas-won-t-lay/23499270007/.

372. Spencer Hunt, *Columbia Gas Urged to Avoid OSU Wetlands in Gas Pipeline Route*, The Columbus Dispatch (Jan. 11, 2012), https://www.dispatch.com/story/news/environment/2012/01/11/columbia-gas-urged-to-avoid/23643031007/.

373. *Id.*

374. Letter from Kim Diana Connolly, 2011–2012 Chair, U.S. National Ramsar Committee, to Jay D. Kasey, Senior Vice President for Admin. and Planning, The Ohio State University (Oct. 3, 2011) (on file with K. Connolly); The Ohio State Univ., The Wilma H. Schiermeier Olentangy River Wetland Research Park: Ramsar Status—A Point of Pride, https://u.osu.edu/orwrpramsar/ramsar-background/.

375. Hunt, *supra* note 371.

376. *See* Ramsar Manual, *supra* note 339, at § 4.2.

377. *Id.*; *see also* Ramsar, *What Is the "Wise Use" of Wetlands?*, https://www.ramsar.org/about/the-wise-use-of-wetlands#:~:text=The%20Convention%20defines%20wise%20use,the%20context%20of%20sustainable%20development%E2%80%9D.

378. Royal C. Gardner & Kim Diana Connolly, *The Ramsar Convention on Wetlands: Assessment of International Designations Within the United States*, 37 Env't Law Reporter 10089 (Feb. 2007), https://digitalcommons.law.buffalo.edu/journal_articles/377/.

protect all wetlands in their territories, when possible.[379] "Wise use" includes maintaining the ecological character of the wetlands "within the context of sustainable development,"[380] which may be similar to the public interest review concept.[381] Always fundamental to the Convention, it serves as the vision for the Fourth Strategic Plan and the concept is repeated in the Plan's goals.[382]

Ramsar focuses modern concepts of wise use on the promotion of ecosystem services,[383] generally conceptualized as the benefits that flow to people and the nearby ecosystem through intact and healthy wetlands.[384] The Convention also calls for increased participation in the restoration and protection of wetlands at the local level.[385] This objective can be achieved by focusing on the economic and health benefits functioning wetlands provide for local populations.[386] The Strategic Plan lays out strategies for furthering the wise use of wetlands, primarily involving information gathering and development of protective national policies.[387]

Convention members are charged with cataloguing and assessing their wetlands,[388] then sharing these inventories via the Secretariat's website.[389] Knowledge sharing is viewed by the Convention as key to involving organizations and government entities not traditionally involved in wetland protection.[390] Recently, Contracting Parties have been encouraged to produce additional inventories of invasive alien

---

379. Convention on Wetlands of International Importance Especially as Waterfowl Habitat, Feb. 2, 1971, T.I.A.S No. 11084, 996 U.N.T.S. 245, https://treaties.un.org/doc/Publication/UNTS/Volume%20996/volume-996-I-14583-English.pdf.

380. *See* Ramsar Manual, *supra* note 339, at § 4.2.

381. 33 C.F.R. § 320.4(a). *See* Chapter 4.

382. Ramsar Resolution XII.2, The Strategic Plan 2016-2024, at 2 ("Wetlands are conserved, wisely used, restored and their benefits are recognized and valued by all."); *see also id.* at 6 (priority area of focus 29, 31), https://www.ramsar.org/sites/default/files/documents/library/4th_strategic_plan_2016_2024_e.pdf.

383. *See* Ramsar Manual, *supra* note 339, at § 1.3-1.4.

384. *Id.* For links to helpful resources about Ramsar's conception of ecosystem services provided by wetlands, see Ramsar, Wetland Ecosystem Services—an Introduction, https://www.ramsar.org/sites/default/files/documents/library/services_00_e.pdf.

385. Ramsar Resolution XII.2, *supra* note 339, at 6 (priority area of focus 31).

386. *Id* at 5 (priority areas of focus 24-25).

387. Ramsar Manual, *supra* note 339; *see also* Ramsar, *supra* note 377.

388. Ramsar Resolution XII.2, *supra* note 382.

389. *Id.*

390. *Id.*

species that are harming, or have the potential to harm, wetlands in their respective territories, especially listed Wetlands of International Importance.[391]

The Secretariat encourages use of intergovernmental cooperation, reporting and data-sharing among the parties to develop appropriate policies designed to satisfy wise use obligations.[392] The 4th Strategic Plan notes the importance of "preventing, stopping and reversing the loss and degradation of wetlands"[393] and supporting policies that acknowledge wetlands ecosystem services, such as the relationship of wetlands to ensuring the individual's right to water available for human use.[394] Parties are also obligated to assess the impact of individual projects that might compromise the character of wetlands.[395] Climate change is another important consideration in the latest Strategic Plan, with Contracting Parties charged with recognizing the "critical important of wetlands for climate change mitigation and adaptation."[396] The United States views Section 404 of the Clean Water Act (CWA) and the National Environmental Policy Act of 1969 (NEPA) as addressing these treaty requirements.[397]

One strategy for expanding wise use not identifiable as belonging to one of the two aforementioned classifications is wetland restoration.[398] Contracting Parties must identify and designate wetlands as Ramsar Sites and transboundary Ramsar Sites.[399] To provide Contracting Parties guidance on how to implement the wise use concept for all strategies, the Secretariat of the Convention has produced a series of handbooks, which can be found on the Convention's website and are intended to be used as a "toolkit" to promote wise use.[400]

---

391. *Id.* at 6 (priority area of focus 30).

392. *Id.* (priority area of focus 32).

393. *Id.* (priority area of focus 21).

394. *Id.* (priority area of focus 24).

395. *Id.* (priority area of focus 21).

396. *Id.* (priority area of focus 23).

397. Michael J. Podolsky, *U.S. Wetlands Policy, Legislation, and Case Law as Applied to the Wise Use Concept of the Ramsar Convention*, 52 Case W. Rsrv. L. Rev. 627, 644 (2001).

398. Ramsar Resolution XII.2, *supra* note 382.

399. *Id.*

400. *See, e.g.*, Ramsar Handbook 1: Wise Use of Wetlands (4th ed., 2010, Ramsar Convention), https://www.ramsar.org/sites/default/files/documents/library/hbk4-01.pdf; *see also* Ramsar Manual, *supra* note 339.

In summary, the Ramsar Convention imposes obligations as to existing designated wetlands of international importance and opportunities to designate additional wetlands that may come into play for some proposed activities in various U.S. wetlands now or in the future. Further, the concept of "wise use" can potentially add a layer of protection for non-Ramsar wetlands throughout the country.

8
CHAPTER

Navigating Appeals and Enforcement

I. Introduction

Conflicts are inevitable among those undertaking activities in wetlands, those seeking to govern them, and other stakeholders. Back in 2016, an article in Politico asked, ". . . how far up into the tributary network should protections go? And where's the line between land and water? Those basic questions have been the source of decades of legal brawls."[1] These brawls continue to this day, with little sign of letting up.[2] Meanwhile, the U.S. Army Corps of Engineers (Corps) is by

1. Annie Snider, *The Two Words That Rewrote American Water Policy: The Strange Tale of How a Supreme Court Justice Accidentally Triggered the Biggest New Water Rule in a Decade*, POLITICO (May 25, 2016), https://www.politico.com/agenda/story/2016/05/obama-wotus-wetlands-rule-supreme-court-000131. *See* Chapter 2 herein for more information.

2. See LAURA GATZ & KATE BOWERS, REDFINING WATERS OF THE UNITED STATES (WOTUS): RECENT DEVELOPMENTS (Cong. Research Serv., 2022), https://crsreports.congress.gov/product/pdf/R/R46927; *see also* Sackett v. Env't Prot. Agency, 598 U.S. 651 (2023); U.S. Army Corps of Eng'rs, Env't. Prot. Agency, Revised Definition of "Waters of the United States," Conforming Final Rule, 88 Fed. Reg 61964 (Sept. 8, 2023) (direct final rule conforming the Biden administration WOTUS rule published on January 18, 2023, to the U.S. Supreme Court's decision in *Sackett*). Those on the right say the amendments do not go far enough in narrowing the WOTUS definition,

design "charged with impartially balancing all aspects of the public interest."[3] although Section 404[4] and related laws have not changed for more than a generation, what one administration does to interpret the laws is often undone by the courts or a subsequent administration, as the nearly continuous judicial and executive efforts to define WOTUS since 2015 have made abundantly clear.[5]

The non-partisan Congressional Research Service identified several reasons for controversies about wetlands, including

> that they occur in a wide variety of physical forms, and the numerous values they provide, such as wildlife habitat, also vary widely. . . . The national policy goal of no net loss, endorsed by Administrations for the past two decades, had been reached by 2004, according to the Fish and Wildlife Service, as the rate of loss had been more than offset by net gains through expanded restoration efforts authorized in multiple

---

while those on the left believe legislation is needed to expand the definition to cover more waters. Many are also unhappy with the fact that the Agencies did not take any public comment on the amendments and made them immediately effective on publication. *See* Thomas Catenacci, Biden Admin Backs Down on Key Eco Regulations after Supreme Court Ruling: Top Republican Says EPA's Revision Tuesday Is Still in Violation of Federal Law (Aug. 29, 2023), https://www.foxnews.com/politics/biden-admin-backs-down-key-eco-regulations-supreme-court-ruling ("'Despite our warnings that the Biden WOTUS rule was clear regulatory overreach and the Supreme Court soundly rejecting its "waters of the United States" definition, the administration continues to take an unserious approach to issuing a durable rule that provides stability to millions of Americans,' said Sen. Shelley Moore Capito, R-W.Va., the ranking member of the Environment and Public Works Committee."); Biden Administration Finalizes Updated WOTUS Rule, JDSUPRA BLOG (Aug. 31, 2023), https://www.jdsupra.com/legalnews/biden-administration-finalizes-updated-2733799/ (". . . several Congressional Democratic leaders are increasingly vocal in their call for Congressional action to correct course on WOTUS and return historic protections").

3. Robert J. Pierce, U.S. *Army Corps of Eng'rs, The Corps, Section 404, and The Environment, in* WETLANDS AND REAL ESTATE TRANSACTIONS 128 (1988).

4. 33 U.S.C. § 1344.

5. *See* Chapter 2 for a discussion of the recent WOTUS iterations from the U.S. Supreme Court's decision in *Rapanos v. U.S.*, 547 U.S. 715, 126 S. Ct. 2208, 165 L. Ed. 2d 159 (2006) to the Obama administration's rule in 2015, 80 Fed. Reg. 37054 (June 29, 2015), repealed and replaced by the Trump administration in 2020 (*see* 84 Fed. Reg. 56,626 (Oct. 22, 2019) ("2019 Repeal Rule"), 85 Fed. Reg. 22,250 (Apr. 21, 2020) (replacement rule)), which in turn as replaced by the Biden administration in January 2023 (88 Fed. Reg. 3004 (Jan. 18, 2023), narrowed by the U.S. Supreme Court in *Sackett v. U.S.,* 598 U.S. 651 (2023) and by rule in September 2023 (88 Fed. Reg. 61964 (Sept. 8, 2023))).

laws. However, more recent data show wetlands losses of nearly 14,000 acres per year. Many protection advocates say that gains do not necessarily account for the changes in quality of the remaining wetlands, and many also view federal protection efforts as inadequate or uncoordinated. Others, who advocate the rights of property owners and development interests, characterize these efforts as too intrusive. Numerous state and local wetland programs add to the complexity of the protection effort.[6]

Stakeholders, in real life, can't and don't avoid either wetlands or problems . . . and disputes naturally ensue. Resolving those disputes may involve anything from internal agency reviews to judicial actions or criminal prosecutions (with potential incarceration). This chapter will walk through the various appeal options, enforcement possibilities, and judicial review mechanisms that may arise in the wetlands arena. This chapter explains the administrative appeals process and discusses three options for enforcement: (1) on an agency level by the U.S. Environmental Protection Agency (EPA) or the Corps, (2) in court with and through the Department of Justice, or (3) via citizen suit. It closes with options that various stakeholders have to seek judicial review of final decisions.

II. Administrative Appeals

The Corps created an internal administrative appeals process[7] to "promote and maintain a [process] that is independent, fair, prompt and efficient."[8] First implemented over a two-year period in 1999–2000,

6. Laura Gatz & Megan Stubbs, Wetlands: An Overview of Issues (Cong. Research Serv., 2017) Summary, https://www.everycrsreport.com/files/20170105_RL33483_740bd446f7ec4e3db28c47e468ee392cc2e00b93.pdf; *see also* Laura Gatz & Kate Bowers, Redefining Waters of the United States (WOTUS): Recent Developments (Cong. Research Serv., 2022), https://crsreports.congress.gov/product/pdf/R/R46927.

7. Final Rule Establishing an Administrative Appeal Process for the Regulatory Program of the Corps of Engineers, 64 Fed. Reg. 11,708 (Mar. 9, 1999); Final Rule Establishing an Administrative Appeal Process for the Regulatory Program of the Corps of Engineers, 65 Fed. Reg. 16,486 (Mar. 28, 2000) (amending 33 C.F.R. pts. 320, 326, and 331).

8. 33 C.F.R. § 331.1(a).

this process lets a Section 404 permit applicant[9] or recipient of a jurisdictional determination[10] bring an appeal[11] to a regional office if the applicant disagrees with a Corps District Office decision.[12] An administrative appeal may be required to exhaust administrative remedies before instituting legal action in federal court to challenge certain permitting or other Corps regulatory decisions.[13]

As discussed in other chapters, the Corps Regulatory Program[14] regulates several activities, including the discharge of dredged or fill material into WOTUS under Section 404.[15] The structure and design of Corps regulatory activities are deliberately decentralized.[16] In fact,

9. *See* Chapter 4 for a discussion of the Section 404 permit application process.

10. *See* Chapter 2 for more information on jurisdictional determinations.

11. The regulations define "appealable action" as "an approved [jurisdictional determination], a permit denial, or a declined permit." 33 C.F.R. § 331.2.

12. 33 C.F.R. part 331 sets out the administrative appeal process. For a list of the Corps district and division offices, *see* U.S. Army Corps of Eng'rs, *Where We Are U.S. Army Corps of Engineers*, http://www.usace.army.mil/Locations.aspx.

13. 33 C.F.R. § 331.10 ("The final Corps decision on a permit application is the initial decision to issue or deny a permit, unless the applicant submits an RFA, and the division engineer accepts the RFA, pursuant to this Part." If an action is appealed, the final Corps decision depends on the merit of the appeal: "(a) If the division engineer determines that the appeal is without merit, the final Corps decision is the district engineer's letter advising the applicant that the division engineer has decided that the appeal is without merit, confirming the district engineer's initial decision, and sending the permit denial or the proffered permit for signature to the appellant; or (b) If the division engineer determines that the appeal has merit, the final Corps decision is the district engineer's decision made pursuant to the division engineer's remand of the appealed action. These regulations provide that the Corps' initial decision to issue or deny a permit is the final decision on a permit application. For an appealed action, where the division engineer determines that the appeal has merit, the final Corps permit decision is the district engineer's decision pursuant to the division engineer's remand." *Id. See* Ozark Society v. Melcher, 229 F. Supp. 2d 896 (E.D. Ark. 2002); Bay-Houston Towing Co. v. United States, 58 Fed. Cl. 462 (2003).

14. The Corps Regulatory Program is explained at https://www.usace.army.mil/Missions/Civil-Works/Regulatory-Program-and-Permits/ and in the preceding chapters.

15. 33 U.S.C. § 1344. The Corps also issues permits for the obstruction of navigation under Section 10 of the Rivers and Harbors Act of 1899, 33 U.S.C. § 403, and permits for dumping of dredged material into the ocean pursuant to Section 103 of the Ocean Dumping Act. Marine Protection Research and Sanctuaries Act of 1972, 33 U.S.C. § 1413.

16. The Corps Regulatory Program: New Orleans District, U.S. ARMY CORPS OF ENG'RS, http://www.mvn.usace.army.mil/Missions/Regulatory/RegulatoryProgram.aspx (This delegation of authority recognizes the decentralized nature and management philosophy of the Corps of Engineers organization. Regulatory program

the primary work on each permit application is performed by one project manager, and usually approved by the leadership in a local district office.[17] While it has its advantages,[18] one obvious disadvantage of such a system is that it can lead to inconsistent decision making.[19] Prior to the implementation of an administrative appeals process, dissatisfied permit applicants were forced to seek initial redress for decisions with which they disagreed through the judicial process.[20]

In part as a response to that perceived complexity, the 1993 White House Wetlands Working Group developed a 40-point plan entitled *Protecting America's Wetlands: A Fair, Flexible, and Effective Approach*,[21] recommending that an administrative appeal process be established. The administrative appeal process was formally proposed by the Corps in 1995,[22] but took a number of years and several con-

management and administration is focused at the district office level, with policy oversight at higher levels.).

17. U.S. Army Corps of Engineers Permitting Process Information, U.S. ARMY CORPS OF ENG'RS, http://www.lrl.usace.army.mil/Portals/64/docs/regulatory/Permitting/PermittingProcessInformation.pdf ("Corps districts operate under what is called a project manager system, where one individual is responsible for handling an application from receipt to final decision. The project manager prepares a public notice, evaluates the impacts of the project and all comments received, negotiates necessary modifications of the project, and prepares appropriate documentation to support a recommended permit decision.").

18. As one recent National Academy of Sciences report put it, "[o]ne advantage of this structure is that district offices may have greater flexibility to pursue innovative efforts and novel actions tailored to local conditions and preferences." NAT'L RSCH. COUNCIL, ADAPTIVE MANAGEMENT FOR WATER RESOURCES PROJECT PLANNING 37 (2004), https://nap.nationalacademies.org/read/10972/chapter/1.

19. *See, e.g.*, U.S. GEN. ACCOUNTING OFFICE. WATERS AND WETLANDS—CORPS OF ENGINEERS NEEDS TO EVALUATE ITS DISTRICT OFFICE PRACTICES IN DETERMINING JURISDICTION (GAO-04-297, Feb. 2004) ("Corps districts differ in how they interpret and apply the federal regulations when determining which waters and wetlands are subject to federal jurisdiction."), https://www.gao.gov/products/gao-04-297.

20. Proposal to Establish an Administrative Appeal Process for the Regulatory Programs of the Corps of Engineers, 60 Fed. Reg. 37,280 (July 19, 1995) [hereinafter Proposal].

21. PROTECTING AMERICA'S WETLANDS: A FAIR, FLEXIBLE, AND EFFECTIVE APPROACH. WHITE HOUSE OFFICE ON ENV'T POL'Y, 2004 (An administrative appeals proposal was one of four proposals in the report to address landowner concerns, to allow for administrative appeals over decisions regarding jurisdiction, permit denials, and administrative penalties.), https://unioncounty-fl.gov/wp-content/uploads/47-Protecting-Americas-Wetlands.pdf.

22. Proposal, *supra* note 20, at 37,281 (The 1995 proposal involved a two-step process for appeals of a decision by the Corps that a particular area was subject to its

gressional directives to be finalized in 1999, only to be revised again a year later.[23]

For more than two decades now, permit applicants have been able to use the process set forth in 33 C.F.R. part 331 to "pursue an administrative appeal of certain Corps of Engineers decisions with which they disagree."[24] The decisions that can be appealed include "approved jurisdictional determinations (JDs), permit applications denied with prejudice, and declined permits."[25] Declined permits are permits offered to an applicant, which the applicant refuses to accept.[26]

---

jurisdiction, and a one-step process for appeals of denied permits or permits proffered with conditions to which an applicant objects.) (The initial proposed rule specifically noted that "[a]n ideal administrative appeal regulation for some people would be one that allows all third parties to request an administrative appeal of jurisdictional determinations and permit decisions.") *Id.* at 37,284.

23. Final Rule Establishing an Administrative Appeal Process for the Regulatory Programs of the Corps of Engineers, 64 Fed. Reg. 11,708 (Mar. 9, 1999); Final Rule Establishing an Administrative Appeal Process for the Regulatory Programs of the Corps of Engineers, 65 Fed. Reg. 16,486 (Mar. 28, 2000) (the revised rule created a one-step appeal process for jurisdictional determinations among other minor changes); for the congressional directives, see H.R. 2605 (introduced July 26, 1999) (A bill making appropriations for energy and water development for the fiscal year ending September 30, 2000, and for other purposes. This bill appropriated a total of $117 million dollars for the Corps Regulatory budget, "Provided, That the Secretary of the Army, acting through the Chief of Engineers, is directed to use $5,000,000 of funds appropriated herein to fully implement an administrative appeals process for the Corps of Engineers Regulatory Program, which administrative appeals process shall provide for a single-level appeal of jurisdictional determinations."). *See also* House Conference Report No. 106-336 (Sept. 27, 1999) (Noting that "[t]he conferees have provided $5,000,000 to fully implement an administrative appeals process for the Regulatory Program of the Corps of Engineers. This process shall provide for a single-level appeal of jurisdictional determinations, the results of which shall be considered final agency action under the Administrative Procedures Act. This language is not intended to create a new cause of action or legal mechanism that would result in additional litigation. The conference agreement deletes language proposed by the House providing that the results of a single-level appeal of jurisdictional determinations shall be considered final agency action under the Administrative Procedures Act.").

24. 33 C.F.R. § 331.1(a).

25. *Id.*

26. *Id.* § 331.2 ("Declined permit means a proffered individual permit, including a letter of permission, that an applicant has refused to accept, because he has objections to the terms and special conditions therein. A declined permit can also be an individual permit that the applicant originally accepted, but where such permit was subsequently modified . . . in such a manner that the resulting permit contains terms and special conditions that lead the applicant to decline the modified permit, provided

Administrative appeals are only available to an "affected party,"[27] defined as "a permit applicant, landowner, a lease, easement or option holder (i.e., an individual who has an identifiable and substantial legal interest in the property) who has received an approved JD, permit denial, or has declined a proffered individual permit,"[28] but not a third party. Affected parties may proceed *pro se* or through an attorney or agent.[29]

As set forth in the regulations, ultimate responsibility for deciding appeals rests with the division engineer (the senior employee at each of the Corps' nine Divisions).[30] The main players in the process, however, are the review officers (ROs)[31] designated for each Division.[32] This regionalized process departs from the centralized approach to internal appeals common in most other agencies, such as the EPA's Environmental Appeals Board (EAB).[33]

---

that the applicant has not started work in waters of the United States authorized by such permit. Where an applicant declines a permit (either initial or modified), the applicant does not have a valid permit to conduct regulated activities in waters of the United States, and must not begin construction of the work requiring a Corps permit unless and until the applicant receives and accepts a valid Corps permit.").

27. *Id.*

28. *Id.*

29. *Id.* § 331.7(e)(3).

30. *Id.* §§ 331.7, 331.3 ("The division engineer may act as the review officer (RO), or may delegate, either generically or on a case-by-case basis, any authority or responsibility described in this part as that of the RO. With the exception of JDs, as described in this paragraph (a)(1), the division engineer may not delegate any authority or responsibility described in this part as that of the division engineer. For approved JDs only, the division engineer may delegate any authority or responsibility described in this part as that of the division engineer, including the final appeal decision. In such cases, any delegated authority must be granted to an official that is at the same or higher grade level than the grade level of the official that signed the approved JD. Regardless of any delegation of authority or responsibility for ROs or for final appeal decisions for approved JDs, the division engineer retains overall responsibility for the administrative appeal process.").

31. *Id.*

32. *Id.*

33. Environmental Appeals Board, U.S. Env't Prot. Agency, https://yosemite.epa.gov/oa/eab_web_docket.nsf ("The U.S. Environmental Protection Agency's Environmental Appeals Board is an appellate tribunal established by regulation to hear administrative appeals under all major environmental statutes that EPA administers. Located in Washington, DC, the Board is an impartial tribunal independent for substantive purposes of all Agency components outside the Immediate Office of the Administrator. The Board's caseload consists primarily of appeals from permit decisions and administrative civil penalty decisions. . . .").

The actual appeal process can begin after an eligible decision is rendered by the Corps.[34] The Corps must provide notification of the available appeals process when rendering an eligible decision by including a Notice of Appeal (NAP) fact sheet[35] and a Request for Appeal (RFA) form,[36] as well as the relevant decision document.[37] In cases where an individual permit is proffered to the applicant for the first time, the Corps must also include a Notification of Applicant Options (NAO) fact sheet.[38] This initial proffer does not become an appealable action until the actual proffer is made.[39]

Applicants wishing to appeal must submit an RFA within 60 days of receiving an approved JD, permit denial, or declined permit.[40] When submitting an RFA, the appellant must grant a right of entry

---

34. 33 C.F.R. § 331.4.

35. 33 C.F.R. § 331.2 ("Notification of Appeal Process (NAP) means a fact sheet that explains the criteria and procedures of the administrative appeal process. Every approved JD, permit denial, and every proffered individual permit returned for reconsideration after review by the district engineer in accordance with Sec. 331.6(b) will have an NAP form attached.").

36. *Id.* ("Request for appeal (RFA) means the affected party's official request to initiate the appeal process. The RFA must include the name of the affected party, the Corps file number of the approved JD, denied permit, or declined permit, the reason(s) for the appeal, and any supporting data and information. No new information may be submitted. . . . The affected party initiates the administrative appeal process by providing an acceptable RFA to the appropriate Corps of Engineers division office. An acceptable RFA contains all the required information and provides reasons for appeal that meets the criteria identified in Sec. 331.5.").

37. *Id.* § 331.

38. *Id.* § 331.2 ("Notification of Applicant Options (NAO) means a fact sheet explaining an applicant's options with a proffered individual permit under the administrative appeal process.").

39. *Id.* (Defining a proffered permit as "a permit that is sent to an applicant that is in the proper format for the applicant to sign (for a standard permit) or accept (for a letter of permission). The term 'initial proffered permit' as used in this part refers to the first time a permit is sent to the applicant. The initial proffered permit is not an appealable action. However, the applicant may object to the terms or conditions of the initial proffered permit and, if so, a second reconsidered permit will be sent to the applicant. The term 'proffered permit' as used in this part refers to the second permit that is sent to the applicant. Such proffered permit is an appealable action.").

40. *Id.* § 331.6(a); *id.* § 331.2 ("Declined permit means a proffered individual permit, including a letter of permission, that an applicant has refused to accept, because he has objections to the terms and special conditions therein. A declined permit can also be an individual permit that the applicant originally accepted, but where such permit was subsequently modified by the district engineer, pursuant to 33 CFR 325.7, in such a manner that the resulting permit contains terms and special conditions that

for the Corps to the project site; such an entry can be made to allow the RO to clarify the record, or to conduct field tests/sampling directly related to the appeal.[41] The submitted RFA is reviewed by an RO, and a determination of acceptability (meaning completeness and meeting the criteria for appeal) must be issued within 30 days.[42] An RFA found to be incomplete or not meeting the criteria may be resubmitted within 30 days and reevaluated by the division office.[43] A decision will typically be issued within 90 days of receipt of an acceptable appeal, though site visits may delay a decision.[44]

Not surprisingly, RFAs must state the reasons for appeal.[45] The Corps offers some examples: procedural error; incorrect application of law, regulation, or officially promulgated policy; material fact omission; incorrect application of current regulatory criteria and associated guidance for identifying, delineating, and permitting activities in jurisdictional waters; or use of incorrect data.[46] Jurisdictional errors

---

lead the applicant to decline the modified permit, provided that the applicant has not started work in waters of the United States authorized by such permit.").

41. *Id.* § 331.2. *See also id.* § 331.7(c) (discussing specifics with respect to site investigations).

42. *Id.* § 331.7(b) ("If the RFA is acceptable, the RO will so notify the appellant in writing within 30 days of the receipt of the acceptable RFA. If the RO determines that the RFA is not complete the RO will so notify the appellant in writing within 30 days of the receipt of the RFA detailing the reason(s) why the RFA is not complete. If the RO believes that the RFA does not meet the criteria for appeal (see Sec. 331.5), the RO will make a recommendation on the RFA to the division engineer. If the division engineer determines that the RFA is not acceptable, the division engineer will notify the appellant of this determination by a certified letter detailing the reason(s) why the appeal failed to meet the criteria for appeal. No further administrative appeal is available, unless the appellant revises the RFA to correct the deficiencies noted in the division engineer's letter or the RO's letter.").

43. *Id.* ("The revised RFA must be received by the division engineer within 30 days of the date of the Corps letter indicating that the initial RFA is not acceptable. If the RO determines that the revised RFA is still not complete, the RO will again so notify the appellant in writing within 30 days of the receipt of the RFA detailing the reason(s) why the RFA is not complete. If the division engineer determines that the revised RFA is still not acceptable, the division engineer will notify the appellant of this determination by a certified letter within 30 days of the date of the receipt of the revised RFA, and will advise the appellant that the matter is not eligible for appeal. No further RFAs will be accepted after this point.").

44. *Id.* § 331.8.

45. *Id.* § 331.5(a).

46. *Id.*

may also be part of an appeal of a declined or denied permit—even if the original jurisdictional determination (JD) was not appealed.[47]

For appeals challenging a JD, the RO has the option to schedule an appeal meeting or a conference call, both of which are meant to be informal.[48] The appellant must bear her or his own costs to participate, and can bring an agent (such as a lawyer or engineer) to the meeting.[49] The meeting must be scheduled both at a location convenient to the appellant as well as near the site where the JD was conducted.[50]

For appeals of permit denials and declined permits, informal conferences allow participants to discuss openly the key issues and material facts associated with the appeal; these are normally scheduled within 60 days of an RFA filing.[51] Like other appeal events, conferences should be at a location reasonably convenient for the appellant and should include the RO, the appellant, the appellant's agent(s) as appropriate, and Corps District staff.[52] The conference is intended to be informal[53] and focus on the reasons for appeal contained in the RFA; new information cannot be raised.[54]

Not all actions are subject to appeal, including (1) where the applicant has waived appeal by signing the permit or jurisdictional determination, (2) a court has issued a decision on a site-specific matter, (3) a controlling factor is outside of Corps control, (4) an application has been modified or a jurisdictional determination has been superseded, (5) the 60-day deadline for filing an RFA has been missed, (6) the action is not final, and (7) most jurisidictional determinations

47. *Id.*
48. *Id.* § 331.7(d).
49. *Id.*
50. *Id.*
51. *Id.* § 331.7(e). (A delay beyond this 60-day window may be appropriate if "the RO determines that unforeseen or unusual circumstances require scheduling the conference for a later date.").
52. *Id.* § 331.7(e)(1–3).
53. *Id.* § 331.7(e)(7).
54. *Id.* § 331.7(e)(6) (2018) ("Any material in the administrative record may be discussed during the conference . . . [but i]ssues not identified in the administrative record by the date of the NAP for the application may not be raised or discussed, because substantive new information or project modifications would be treated as a new permit application. . . .").

associated with unauthorized activities unless the Corps accepts an after-the-fact permit application.[55]

In appeals through this process, the District's decisions should be upheld unless "the decision on some relevant matter was arbitrary, capricious, an abuse of discretion, not supported by substantial evidence in the administrative record, or plainly contrary to a requirement of law, regulation, Executive Order, or officially promulgated Corps policy guidance."[56] The record review is based on a substantial evidence standard,[57] and records are reviewed for both procedural and substantive analytical errors.[58] All decisions must be documented in writing.[59]

Administrative appeals may be filed for certain after-the-fact permit applications issued for unauthorized activities.[60] Initial corrective measures may be required before such an appeal can be heard,[61] and administrative penalties will still apply if the appeal is found to be without merit.[62] For appeals of decisions related to unauthorized activities, a signed tolling agreement must be included with the RFA, unless a signed tolling agreement has previously been furnished to the Corps district office.[63]

Based on the significant annual volume of Corps permit decisions and jurisdictional determinations, initial projections anticipated thousands of appeal requests annually.[64] As it turns out, however, the volume of appeals is very light. A review of tables published by Corps' Division offices showing appeals from 1999 through 2020 show a peak in 2008 with 22 appeals, but a steady decline in recent years to just a few per year.[65]

---

55. *Id.* § 331.5(b). Please refer to the regulation for the complete list of non-appealable actions.

56. *Id.* § 331.9(b).

57. *Id.*

58. *Id.*

59. *Id.*

60. *Id.* § 331.11.

61. *Id.* § 331.11(a).

62. *Id.* § 331.11(b).

63. *Id.* § 331.11(c).

64. *See* Federal Register, *Final Rule Establishing an Administrative Appeal Process for the Regulatory Program of the Corps of Engineers*, https://www.federalregister.gov/documents/2000/03/28/00-7439/final-rule-establishing-an-administrative-appeal-process-for-the-regulatory-program-of-the-corps-of.

65. *See, e.g.*, the South Atlantic full table of all appeals since 2000, https://www.sad.usace.army.mil/Missions/Regulatory/Regulatory-Appeals/Table-of-Appeals/

Reviews are focused on the matters at hand, and Corps administrative appeals regulations explicitly state that individual administrative appeals decisions have no precedential value.[66] The regulations direct that appeals decisions are not to be cited in other administrative appeals.[67] Nevertheless, copies of appeals are sent to Corps Headquarters, to be reviewed periodically for consistency.[68]

A list of final appeal decisions for the various divisions can be reviewed at their division websites, and some decision documents are hot-linked for review. The eight divisions are as follows: Great Lakes & Ohio River Division,[69] Mississippi Valley Division,[70] North Atlantic Division,[71] Northwestern Division,[72] Pacific Ocean Division,[73] South

---

(For example, there were four appeals brought in 2014, three in 2015, two in 2016, three in 2017, three in 2018, one in 2019, and one in 2020.).

66. 33 C.F.R. § 331.7(g) ("Because a decision to determine geographic jurisdiction, deny a permit, or condition a permit depends on the facts, circumstances, and physical conditions particular to the specific project and/or site being evaluated, appeal decisions would be of little or no precedential utility. Therefore, an appeal decision of the division engineer is applicable only to the instant appeal, and has no other precedential effect. Such a decision may not be cited in any other administrative appeal, and may not be used as precedent for the evaluation of any other jurisdictional determination or permit application.").

67. *Id.*

68. *Id.* ("While administrative appeal decisions lack precedential value and may not be cited by an appellant or a district engineer in any other appeal proceeding, the Corps goal is to have the Corps regulatory program operate as consistently as possible, particularly with respect to interpretations of law, regulation, an Executive Order, and officially-promulgated policy. Therefore, a copy of each appeal decision will be forwarded to Corps Headquarters; those decisions will be periodically reviewed at the headquarters level for consistency with law, Executive Orders, and policy.").

69. Administrative Appeals for Corps Decisions, U.S. Army Corps of Eng'rs Great Lakes & Ohio River Div., https://www.lrd.usace.army.mil/Wetlands-Permits/Decisions/.

70. Administrative Appeals, U.S. Army Corps of Eng'rs Miss. Valley Div., http://www.mvd.usace.army.mil/Missions/Regulatory/AppealedDecisions.aspx.

71. Administrative Appeals, U.S. Army Corps of Eng'rs N. Atl. Div., http://www.nad.usace.army.mil/Missions/CivilWorks/RegulatoryProgram/AppealedDecisions.aspx.

72. Appeal Decisions, U.S. Army Corps of Eng'rs NW. Div., http://www.nwd.usace.army.mil/Missions/CivilWorks/RegulatoryProgram/AppealDecisions.aspx.

73. Appeals, U.S. Army Corps of Eng'rs Pac. Ocean Div., http://www.pod.usace.army.mil/Missions/Regulatory/Appeals.aspx.

Atlantic Division,[74] South Pacific Division,[75] and Southwestern Division.[76] While administrative appeal decisions may not be precedential, they are certainly informative. Under the regulations, appeals decisions depend "on the facts, circumstances, and physical conditions particular to the specific project and/or site being evaluated."[77] The low number of appeals make meaningful comparisons among Divisions difficult. Nevertheless, potential appellants and their representatives would probably be well-served to review recent appeal decisions if they are available in their particular Division before initiating an appeal.

III. Enforcement

A. Overview

The EPA, the Corps, and the U.S. Department of Justice (DOJ) share responsibility for CWA Section 404 enforcement. EPA has civil and administrative enforcement authority under Section 309 of the CWA.[78] The Corps has such authority under Sections 309 and 404.[79] The U.S. attorneys at DOJ's Environment and Natural Resources Division provide civil representation in court and also prosecute activities made criminal under Section 309(c).[80] Among other penalties, this section establishes criminal penalties ranging from "a fine of not less than $2,500 nor more than $25,000 per day of violation, or by imprisonment

74. Table of Appeals, U.S. Army Corps of Eng'rs S. Atl. Div., http://www.sad.usace.army.mil/Missions/Regulatory/RegulatoryAppeals/TableofAppeals.aspx.

75. Appeal Decisions, U.S. Army Corps of Eng'rs S. Pac. Div., http://www.spd.usace.army.mil/Missions/Regulatory/RegulatoryAppeals/AdministrativeAppealsDecisions.aspx.

76. Table of Appeals, U.S. Army Corps of Eng'rs Sw. Div., http://www.swd.usace.army.mil/Missions/CivilWorks/Regulatory/RegulatoryAppeals/TableofAppeals.aspx.

77. 33 C.F.R. § 331.7(g).

78. 33 U.S.C. § 1319 (Although rarely invoked, EPA also has authority under Section 504 of the CWA to seek equitable judicial remedies "upon receipt of evidence that a pollution source or combination of sources is presenting an imminent and substantial endangerment to the health of persons or to the welfare of persons where such endangerment is to the livelihood of such persons, such as inability to market shellfish.)" *Id.* § 1364(a).

79. *Id.* § 1344(s).

80. *Id.* § 1319(c).

for not more than 1 year, or by both," for initial negligent violations, with monetary penalties doubling for knowing violations. Knowing endangerment can result in "a fine of not more than $250,000 or imprisonment of not more than 15 years, or both," although an organization convicted of knowing endangerment can be subject to a fine of not more than $1 million.[81] In some cases, discussed further later, citizen suits may provide an additional level of enforcement.

Section 404 violations that trigger enforcement actions almost always involve one of two situations: (1) discharges of dredged or fill material into wetlands without a valid Section 404 permit,[82] or (2) actions inconsistent with terms and conditions of a valid permit. Failing to comply with an order from the EPA or Corps is a third category that may result in substantial civil penalties.[83]

To find a violation, there must be (1) a "person" within the meaning of the CWA who (2) discharged pollutants (3) from a point source into (4) "waters of the United States" (5) without a valid permit, or not in accordance with the terms and conditions of a valid permit.[84] For successful civil actions, the government must prove each element by a preponderance of the evidence.[85] Intent is irrelevant: the CWA is based on strict administrative and civil liability, meaning good faith or other state of mind is no defense to civil enforcement actions.[86] However, as discussed later in this section, the CWA enumerates a variety of statutory factors that are taken into account in assessing the amount of the penalty to be imposed. In imposing civil penalties, the court must consider "the seriousness of the violation or violations,

81. *Id.* These amounts have been adjusted for inflation. *See infra* notes 113 and 114.

82. Unpermitted discharges violate CWA Section 301(a)'s directive that "[e]xcept as in compliance with . . . [Section 404], the discharge of any pollutant by any person shall be unlawful." *Id.* § 1311(a).

83. 33 U.S.C. §§ 1319(d), 1344(s)(4).

84. *See, e.g.,* U.S. v. Brace, 41 F.3d 117 (3d Cir. 1994) *cert. denied* 515 U.S. 1158 (U.S. 1995); *see* Smith v. Hankinson, No. 98-0451-P-S, 1999 U.S. Dist. LEXIS 5151, at 21 (S.D. Ala. Mar. 31, 1999), *per curiam aff'd,* 119 F. 3d 444 (11th Cir. 1999).

85. *See* Stoeco Dev. v. U.S. Army Corps of Eng'rs, 792 F. Supp. 339 (D.N.Y. 1992).

86. Kelly v. Env't Prot. Agency, 203 F.3d 519, 522–23 (7th Cir. 2000); Piney Run Preservation v. Com'rs, Carroll Cnty., 82 F. Supp. 2d 464 (D. Md. 2000) *vacated and remanded on other grounds*, 268 F.3d 255 (4th Cir. 2001); Stoddard v. W. Carolina Reg'l Sewer Auth., 784 F.2d 1200 (4th Cir. 1986); Pub. Interest Rsch. Grp. v. U.S. Metals Ref, 681 F. Supp. 237 (D.N.Y. 1987).

the economic benefit (if any) resulting from the violation, any history of such violations, any good-faith efforts to comply with the applicable requirements, the economic impact of the penalty on the violator, and such other matters as justice may require."[87] EPA and the Corps must consider similar factors in imposing administrative penalties.[88] A "person" for purposes of CWA enforcement is "an individual, corporation, partnership, association, state, municipality, commission, or political subdivision, or any interstate body."[89] Specific knowledge of a violation is not required.[90]

"Enforcement" can mean multiple things if a violation occurs, because EPA and the Corps have several options. In some situations, the agency may issue administrative orders (or, in the case of the Corps, cease and desist (C&D) letters) requiring compliance with Section 404 and related requirements.[91] In some cases, the agency may assess administrative penalties.[92] The agencies may also seek injunctive relief (including demands for restoration) and/or civil penalties.[93] If the agencies elect to commence civil actions, DOJ's Environment and Natural Resources Division represents the government.[94] Additionally, EPA and the Corps may refer particular violations to DOJ for possible criminal prosecution. The following subsections provide details as to how these various options unfold.[95]

---

87. 33 U.S.C. §1319(d).

88. *Id.* at §1319(g)(3) (administrative penalties).

89. 33 U.S.C. § 1362(5) (2018). *See also* 40 C.F.R. § 232.2 (2018); 33 U.S.C. § 1319(c)(6) (If criminal charges are sought, the definition expands to include responsible corporate officers.).

90. U.S. v. Bd. of Trustees of Fla. Keys Comm. College, 531 F. Supp. 267 (S.D. Fla. 1981).

91. 33 U.S.C. §§ 1319(a), 1344(s)(1).

92. *Id.* § 1319(g).

93. *Id.* §§ 1319(b), (d); 1344(s)(3)–(4).

94. Section 506 of the CWA mandates the EPA administrator to "request the Attorney General to appear and represent the United States in any civil or criminal action instituted under [the CWA] to which the Administrator is a party. Unless the Attorney General notifies the Administrator within a reasonable time, that he will appear in a civil action, attorneys who are officers or employees of the Environmental Protection Agency shall appear and represent the United States in such action." *Id.* § 1366.

95. *See generally* U.S. Env't Prot. Agency, *Enforcement under CWA Section 404*, https://www.epa.gov/cwa-404/enforcement-under-cwa-section-404.

B. Administrative Enforcement

The EPA and the Corps signed a Memorandum of Agreement (MOA) in 1989 that allocates Section 404 enforcement responsibilities.[96] Although it varies by case and has shifted some in recent years, in general the Corps takes lead on permit violations, while EPA takes lead on unpermitted discharges.[97] Either the Corps or EPA may initiate initial investigations, but the Corps generally performs more, in part because the Corps has more field staff.[98] For violations requiring immediate action, after investigating the matter, a notification letter or a C&D order issued to the alleged violator is typically the first step.[99] If time allows, initial corrective actions may be included in the notification.[100]

Many violations result in administrative orders pursuant to CWA Section 309(a) or 404(s)(1).[101] Congress directed that EPA administrative orders pursuant to Section 309 must "state with reasonable specificity the nature of the violation, and . . . specify a time for compliance not to exceed thirty days," though later compliance may be acceptable in some circumstances.[102] EPA's administrative orders generally require all continuing violations stop, and damaged wetlands be restored.[103]

If the Corps issues the order pursuant to Section 404, it triggers a more detailed process.[104] Because most Corps orders involve permit violations, the Corps is authorized to investigate.[105] Notice must be

96. *See* Memorandum of Agreement between the Department of the Army and the U.S. Env't. Prot. Agency Concerning Federal Enforcement for the Section 404 Program of the Clean Water Act 1–4 (Jan. 19, 1989) [hereinafter 1989 MOA], https://www.usace.army.mil/Missions/Civil-Works/Regulatory-Program-and-Permits/MOU-MOAs/.

97. *Id.* Please note the MOA creates no enforceable rights, and courts are precluded from blocking an enforcement action simply because it departs from the norms set forth in the MOA.

98. U.S. Army Corps of Eng'rs. Regulatory Contact Information, https://www.usace.army.mil/Missions/Civil-Works/Regulatory-Program-and-Permits/Regulatory-Contacts/.

99. 1989 MOA, *supra* footnote 96, at 3.

100. *Id.*

101. 33 U.S.C. §§ 1319(a), 1344(s)(1).

102. *Id.* § 1319(a)(5)(A).

103. Kelly v. U.S. Env't Prot. Agency, 203 F.3d 519 (7th Cir. 2000).

104. 33 C.F.R. § 326.

105. *Id.* § 326.3(a),(b).

given to the alleged violator personally, identifying the statutory basis, describing potential consequences for violations, and directing responsible parties to "submit any additional information that the district engineer may need at that time to determine what course of action he should pursue in resolving the violation."[106] The statute demands that the notice also provide "reasonable specificity," and "specify a time for compliance, not to exceed thirty days."[107] The Corps may order corrective measures if "serious jeopardy to life, property, or important public resources . . . may be reasonably anticipated to occur"[108] and wetland destruction may be considered serious jeopardy to important public resources.[109] Regulations also allow the Corps to conduct follow-up inspections and issue compliance orders.[110] EPA and Corps compliance orders can be challenged in a civil action as final agency action pursuant to the Administrative Procedure Act, although preliminary investigations or decisions not to pursue enforcement are generally not reviewable.[111]

EPA and the Corps can also impose administrative penalties in response to violations of wetland regulations.[112] Section 309(g) of the CWA authorizes the assessment of two classes of penalties in administrative enforcement actions:[113] Class I penalties (assessed after an informal hearing) or Class II penalties (some cases require a formal hearing pursuant to Administrative Procedure Act procedures governing on-the-record adjudications).[114] Class I penalties may not exceed $10,000 per

106. *Id.* § 326.3(c)(3).

107. *Id.* § 1344(3)(2).

108. *Id.* § 326. 3(d).

109. *See id.* § 320.4(b) (describing most wetlands as "productive" and "valuable").

110. *Id.* § 326.4.

111. Sackett v. Env't Prot. Agency, 566 U.S. 120 (2012). The Court held that landowners could challenge as final agency action pursuant to the Administrative Procedure Act compliance orders from the EPA for unauthorized filling of wetlands on their property; judicial review was not precluded by the CWA. *But see* Massachusetts v. Env't Prot. Agency, 549 U.S. 497, 527(2007) (holding that an agency's refusal to initiate enforcement proceedings is not ordinarily subject to judicial review) and Southern Ohio Coal Co. v. Office of Surface Min., 20 F.3d 1418 (6th Cir. 1994). (district courts lack jurisdiction to enjoin pre-enforcement EPA investigatory activities).

112. *See* 33 C.F.R. § 326.6(a)(2).

113. 33 U.S.C. § 1319(g)(2).

114. *Id.*

violation or a total of $25,000 for all violations, adjusted for inflation.[115] Class II penalties also may not exceed $10,000 per day, but the maximum penalty may reach up to $125,000, adjusted for inflation.[116]

In 2001, EPA issued a "Revised Clean Water Act Settlement Penalty Policy," which superseded the 1995 Interim Policy[117] as well as the 1986 Clean Water Act Penalty Policy and various guidance documents interpreting that policy.[118] EPA identified four goals for penalties in the Revised Settlement Policy: (1) penalties should be large enough to deter noncompliance; (2) they should help to ensure a level economic playing field by preventing the violator from gaining an unfair economic advantage over competitors by recouping any economic benefit of noncompliance plus an additional amount reflecting the seriousness of the violation; (3) penalties should be applied consistently across the country; and (4) EPA should use penalty formulas that allow prompt resolution of enforcement actions.[119] To that end, the Clean Water Act Settlement Policy incorporates the following formula: Penalty = Economic Benefit + Gravity +/– Gravity Adjustment Factors – Litigation Considerations – Ability to Pay – Supplemental Environmental Projects.[120] In theory, EPA's penalty policy allows violators to reach penalty settlements quickly that reflect the economic benefit and/or environmental harm attributable to their noncompliance. Although its

---

115. *Id.* Pursuant to the Federal Civil Penalties Inflation Adjustment Act of 1990, as amended (28 U.S.C. § 2461, *et seq.*) (FCPIAA), federal agencies must increase civil fines on a periodic basis. *See* U.S. Army Corps of Eng'rs, Civil Monetary Penalty Inflation Adjustment Rule, 88 Fed. Reg. 51234 (Aug. 3, 2023), https://www.govinfo.gov/content/pkg/FR-2023-08-03/pdf/2023-16025.pdf, amending 33 C.F.R. pt. 326. This amendment increased the penalties authorized for Class I penalties to $25,848 per violation with a maximum of $64,619, effective August 3, 2023. 33 C.F.R. § 326.6.

116. 33 U.S.C. § 1319(g)(2). Pursuant to the FCPIAA, EPA increased the Class II administrative penalties effective January 6, 2023. *See* Env't Prot. Agency, Civil Monetary Penalty Inflation Adjustment Rule, 88 Fed. Reg. 988 (Jan. 6, 2023), https://www.federalregister.gov/citation/88-FR-988, amending 40 C.F.R. § 19.4. This amendment increased the penalties authorized for Class II penalties to $25,847 per violation with a maximum of $323,081, effective January 6, 2023. 40 C.F.R. § 19.4.

117. Env't Prot. Agency, *Interim Clean Water Act Settlement Penalty Policy* (Mar. 1, 1995) [hereinafter 1995 CWA Penalty Policy], https://www.epa.gov/enforcement/interim-clean-water-act-settlement-penalty-policy.

118. *See* Env't Prot. Agency, *Water Enforcement Policy, Guidance and Publications* (Mar. 11, 2022), https://www.epa.gov/enforcement/water-enforcement-policy-guidance-and-publications.

119. 1995 CWA Penalty Policy, *supra* note 117, at 3.

120. *Id.* at 4.

intent is to have relatively even applied penalties across the country, actual penalties can vary with the facts of each case.

A separate, similar penalty policy specifically addressing wetland violations was issued in 2001.[121] In establishing this policy, EPA stressed that "the need to deter and remedy violations is especially evident with respect to the discharge of dredged or fill material into . . . wetlands."[122] Like the general Clean Water Act penalty policy, the Section 404 policy considers several elements in determining the appropriate amount of an administrative penalty: (1) the economic benefit derived; (2) the significance of the violation; and (3) relevant adjustment factors such as ability to pay, potential litigation costs, and the party's level of cooperation.[123] The severity of the violation and the benefit derived are combined with the several adjustment factors to determine the penalty amount. The Section 404 penalty policy encourages computer models to calculate the economic benefit gained from the violation in question.[124] A "bottom-line cash settlement penalty" is reached using detailed criteria for assessing the gravity of the violation; environmental significance, compliance significance, adjustments for recalcitrance or quick settlement, and other factors are assigned values and plotted in a settlement penalty calculation worksheet.[125]

The penalty policy encourages Supplemental Environmental Projects (SEPs); these are "environmentally beneficial projects that a violator agrees to undertake as part of a settlement, but is not otherwise legally obligated to perform."[126] Such projects may include purchase and dedicated use of buffers around wetland, and/or deeding over conservation easements in wetlands. Mitigation is never considered an appropriate SEP when it is designed to remedy violations because this type of remedial activity is not considered voluntary.[127] SEPs may

121. Env't Prot. Agency, *Clean Water Act Section 404 Settlement Penalty Policy* (Dec. 21, 2001) [hereinafter 2001 CWA Penalty Policy], https://www.epa.gov/enforcement/issuance-revised-clean-water-act-cwa-section-404-settlement-penalty-policy-december-21.

122. *Id.* at 3.

123. *Id.* at 6.

124. *Id.* at 9 (This model, known as the BEN model, and the 1993 BEN User's manual are available at https://nepis.epa.gov/Exe/ZyPURL.cgi?Dockey=P100F7TQ.txt).

125. 2001 CWA Penalty Policy, *supra* note 121, at 8 (Worksheet can be found in the policy as Attachment 1.).

126. *Id.* at 20.

127. *Id.*

result in "[f]avorable penalty consideration . . . because the SEP provides environmental benefit above and beyond what is required to remedy the violation(s) at issue in the enforcement action."[128]

Rules of practice govern the entry of penalty orders.[129] District engineers may propose and prepare penalty orders upon finding a permittee has violated a condition or limitation in that permit.[130] Orders must provide notice to the alleged violator, the public, and the relevant state agency in which the violation occurred.[131] A violator may request a hearing before a presiding officer, who is selected from the Corps' counsel staff or is an "other qualified person."[132] The right to a hearing will be deemed waived if the violator does not request a hearing in writing within 30 days of receiving notice of the proposed order.[133]

Hearings on proposed Class I penalties are informal and thus not governed by Sections 554 and 556 of the Administrative Procedure Act.[134] The Corps ensures certain formal procedural protections by regulation, including separation of adjudicative and prosecutorial functions,[135] prohibitions on ex parte communications,[136] and decisions based on evidence of record.[137] Based on recommendations from a presiding officer,[138] the district engineer may request additional information from parties to ensure a fair opportunity to be heard on such additional matters,[139] and may withdraw, modify, or issue the recommended decision based on the evidence of record.[140] The district engineer's decision becomes effective 30 days after issuance,[141] and constitutes final agency action for review purposes.[142]

EPA procedures governing Class I penalties are included in the agency's general consolidated rules of practice[143] and are substantially

128. *Id.*
129. *See* 33 C.F.R. pt. 326, 40 C.F.R. pt. 22.
130. 33 C.F.R. § 326.6(b)(1).
131. *Id.* § 326.6(b)(2)–(4).
132. *Id.* § 326.6(g), (h)(3).
133. *Id.* § 326.6(g)(2).
134. *See* 33 U.S.C. § 1319(g)(2)(A); 33 C.F.R. § 326.6(h)(1).
135. *See* 33 C.F.R. § 326.6(h)(4), (h)(5)(ii), (j)(3).
136. 33 C.F.R. § 326.6(h)(5).
137. *Id.* § 326.6(j)(1).
138. *Id.*
139. *Id.* § 326.6(j)(4).
140. *Id.* § 326.6(j)(5).
141. *Id.* § 326.69(k)(1).
142. *Id.* § 326.6(j)(5).
143. These are contained at 40 C.F.R. pt. 22.

similar to the procedures EPA employs in assessing Class II penalties, except the presiding officer need not be an administrative law judge but can be an EPA lawyer serving as a regional judicial officer. The presiding officer "shall conduct the hearing, and rule on all motions until an initial decision has become final or has been appealed.[144] Class I proceedings are subject to greater limitations on discovery[145] and allow for interlocutory appeals.[146]

Only EPA can bring Class II hearings, under regulations that generally incorporate and expand upon the procedural requirements governing Administrative Procedures Act on-the-record adjudications.[147] Hearings are before administrative law judges[148] authorized to rule on motions, order discovery, issue subpoenas, and generally perform "all . . . acts and take all measures necessary for the maintenance of order and for the efficient, fair and impartial adjudication of issues."[149] The presiding administrative law judge issues an initial decision with findings of fact and conclusions of law, along with a recommended penalty and a proposed final order.[150] If the recommended penalty differs from the penalty recommended in the complaint, the order must specify the reasons for departing from the recommended penalty,[151] and may not exceed that recommended in the complaint.[152] Class II initial decisions may be appealed to EPA's EAB.[153] Absent such an appeal, initial decisions are deemed to be final 45 days after service upon the parties.[154]

Administrative processes that could result in an assessment of penalties must provide opportunities for public participation, and any potential administrative penalties must allow for public notice and comment.[155] Interested parties who have submitted comments must be given notice of any hearing and provided "a reasonable opportunity to be heard and to present evidence."[156] If there is no hearing,

144. *See* 40 C.F.R. § 22.51.
145. *Id.* § 22.52.
146. *Id.* § 22.50(b).
147. *See* 5 U.S.C. §§ 554, 556–57; 40 C.F.R. pt. 22.
148. *See* 40 C.F.R. § 22.21(a).
149. 40 C.F.R. § 22.04(c).
150. *Id.* § 22.27(a).
151. *Id.* § 22.27(b).
152. *Id.*
153. *Id.* § 22.27(c); *see id.* §§ 22.29, 22.30.
154. *Id.* § 22.27(d).
155. 33 U.S.C. § 1319(g)(4)(A); 33 C.F.R. § 326.6(c); 40 C.F.R. § 22.38(d).
156. 33 U.S.C. § 1319(g)(4)(B); 33 C.F.R. § 326.6(c)(2); 40 C.F.R. § 22.38(d).

commenting parties may file a petition with EPA or the Corps seeking to set aside the order and have a hearing on the penalty,[157] which must be granted "[i]f the evidence presented by the petitioner in support of the petition is material and was not considered in the issuance of the order."[158] If such a petition is denied, the agency must "provide to the petitioner, and publish in the Federal Register, notice of and the reasons for such denial."[159]

A Class II administrative penalty allows the recipient (or any party who commented on a proposed penalty) to seek judicial review of a final order within 30 days in the United States Court of Appeals for the District of Columbia Circuit or in the court of appeals for the circuit in which that person resides or transacts business.[160] Class I penalty orders are reviewable in the U.S. District Court for the District of Columbia or the district in which the violation occurred.[161] Review must be sought within 30 days. The court must uphold the order "unless there is not substantial evidence in the record, taken as a whole, to support the finding of a violation" or the penalty assessment constitutes an abuse of discretion.[162] Class II penalties must be appealed to EPA's EAB and may be enforced in federal court if they are not paid.[163]

The Corps has the authority to issue "after-the-fact" permits to authorize fill as if it had been permitted at the outset and release the landowner from further enforcement liability.[164] An after-the-fact permit must be based on a formal permit application,[165] processed in accordance with the same procedures applicable to the processing of initial permits.[166] After-the-fact permits are deemed inappropriate "when restoration of the waters of the United States has been completed that eliminates current and future detrimental impacts."[167]

---

157. 33 U.S.C. § 1319(g)(4)(C); 33 C.F.R. § 326.6(c)(3); 40 C.F.R. § 22.38(f).
158. 33 U.S.C. § 1319(g)(4)(B); 33 C.F.R. § 326.6(c)(3); 40 C.F.R. § 22.38(f).
159. 33 U.S.C. § 1319(g)(4)(B); 33 C.F.R. § 326.6(c)(3); 40 C.F.R. § 22.38(f).
160. 33 U.S.C. § 1319(g)(8)(B).
161. *Id.* § 1319(g)(8)(A).
162. *Id.* § 1319(g)(8).
163. *Id.*
164. 33 C.F.R. § 326.3(e).
165. William W. Sapp, *Improving Wetlands Enforcement through Field Citation,* 1 Env't Law 747, 772 (1995).
166. 33 C.F.R. § 326.3(e)(1) (These applicable procedures are found at 33 C.F.R. pts 320–325.).
167. *Id.* § 326.3(e)(1)(i) .

After-the-fact permits are also not allowed if a district engineer determines that legal action is appropriate, or if litigation has already been initiated against the applicant by the appropriate federal, state, or local regulatory agencies.[168] After-the-fact permits are subject to a public interest review,[169] as well as EPA veto authority. The agencies may bring civil judicial actions to enforce Section 404 requirements for violations that are "willful, repeated, flagrant, or of substantial impact."[170] In such cases, temporary restraining orders and injunctions to prevent further damage, orders to require remediation of affected wetlands,[171] and civil penalties are all allowed.[172]

Civil actions can also be initiated by either the Corps or EPA to enjoin or seek other relief for any violation for which a compliance order could be issued.[173] Venue depends on the defendant's location, residence, or place of business.[174] Defendants are entitled to a jury trial on liability issues, but not on penalties.[175] Accordingly, the entire case may be tried before a jury, or may be split into jury and bench trial phases.[176] EPA has broad discretion in bringing enforcement actions, and may seek administrative orders,[177] penalties,[178] and/or temporary or permanent injunctions.[179] The penalties may be criminal or civil or both.[180]

Section 309(d) penalties can be quite substantial. Under the "continuing violation" theory, the original act constituting the violation and each day that the initial violation remains uncorrected are regarded as separate violations for purposes of calculating appropriate penalties.[181] A finding of a "continuing violation," as opposed to a discrete

168. *Id.* § 326.3(e)(1)(ii), (iv).
169. *Id.* § 326.3(e)(2).
170. *Id.* § 326.5(a).
171. 33 U.S.C. § 1319(b).
172. *Id* § 1319(d).
173. *Id.* § 1319(b).
174. *Id.*
175. Tull v. United States, 481 U.S. 412, 107 S. Ct. 1831, 95 L. Ed. 2d 365 (1987).
176. *See, e.g.*, U.S. v. Hobbs, 736 F. Supp. 1406 (E.D. Va. 1990).
177. 33 U.S.C. § 1319(a).
178. *Id.* § 1319(g).
179. *Id.* § 1319(b).
180. *Id.* § 1319(c), (d).
181. Benham v. Ozark Materials River Rock 17-5069 10th Cir 2018; 33 U.S.C. § 1319(d); Sasser v. Administrator, U.S. Env't Prot. Agency, 990 F.2d 127 (4th Cir. 1993); *see* United States v. Cumberland Farms of Connecticut, 647 F. Supp. 1166 (D. Mass. 1986); U.S. v. Ciampitti, 669 F. Supp. 684 (D.N.Y. 1987).

one-day violation, may subject a defendant to significant penalties.[182] Courts determine total civil penalties based on "the seriousness of the violation or violations, the economic benefit (if any) resulting from the violation, any history of such violations, any good-faith efforts to comply with the applicable requirements, the economic impact of the penalty on the violator, and such other matters as justice may require."[183] Courts impose the maximum penalty that could be assessed against the violator, or may reduce fines in accordance with the factors listed in Section 309(d).[184]

Most wetland enforcement actions are in a civil context. EPA's website notes that "[s]ince enactment of the Clean Water Act, EPA and the Corps have used their criminal enforcement authorities sparingly in response to Section 404 violations. . . . EPA and the Corps reserve their criminal enforcement authority for only the most flagrant and egregious Section 404 violations."[185]

The U.S. Sentencing Commission[186] promulgated[187] and updates Sentencing Guidelines used throughout all U.S. courts.[188] Pursuant to the CWA's criminal provisions,[189] a handful of cases involving criminal charges make it through to sentencing in the wetland arena.[190] EPA

182. Albert C. Lin, *Application of the Continuing Violations Doctrine to Environmental Law*, 23 Ecology L. Q. 723, 730 (1996), https://lawcat.berkeley.edu/record/1115656.

183. 33 U.S.C. § 1319(d).

184. *See, e.g.,* Weber v. Trinity Meadows Raceway, Inc., WL 477049 (1996) (A racetrack had been discharging pollutants into a river. Even though the raceway had committed twenty-three violations, the court imposed a significantly reduced penalty to reflect the fact that the discharges were mainly of natural materials, such as wood shavings, and posed no harm to human health.).

185. Section 404 Enforcement U.S. Env't Prot. Agency, http://water.epa.gov/type/wetlands/outreach/fact15.cfm.

186. *See generally* United States Sentencing Commission, http://www.ussc.gov/.

187. 28 U.S.C. §§ 991-98; 52 Fed. Reg. 18,046 (1987).

188. The 2021 version of the United States Sentencing Commission Guidelines Manual is available at https://www.ussc.gov/guidelines/2021-guidelines-manual-annotated.

189. 33 U.S.C. § 1319(c).

190. A search of EPA's Summary of Criminal Prosecutions website for prosecutions involving 33 U.S.C. § 1344 yielded six prosecutions between 1993 and 2019. There were two prosecutions during the Clinton Administration. In 1993, two individuals and their company were convicted of illegally dredging a channel and disposing of the dredged material in San Franscisco Bay; the company was sentenced to 36 months' probation and a $10,000 fine; one individual was sentenced to 24 months

maintains a summary of criminal prosecutions on its website, through which users can search for prosecutions under the CWA cases by year or subject matter, and understand more about facts and judgments in various cases involving wetlands.[191]

Potential criminal penalties under the CWA are substantial. For negligent violations, fines of up to $25,000 per day of violation and imprisonment for up to one year are possible, adjusted for inflation.[192] For knowing violations, fines may range up to $50,000 per day of violation and imprisonment for three years.[193] For knowing endangerment violations, fines up to $250,000 per day of violation and imprisonment for up to 15 years are authorized.[194] In all cases, repeat offenders are

---

incarceration and a $5,000 fine, while the other received six months and a $2,000 fine. In 1997, an individual was found guilty of negligent excavation of a ditch draining a wetland in Minnesota without a permit and sentenced to 12 months of probation, four community service projects, donation of 13.5 acres of land to the state, and a $65,000 fine. Jumping ahead to the George W. Bush Administration, in 2003, an individual and his company were convicted of knowingly dumping mixed solid wastes into wetlands in Florida; the company was sentenced to 60 months' probation, court costs and restitution, and a $25,000 fine, while the owner himself was sentenced to 36 months incarceration, following by 36 months' probation and ordered to pay court costs and $25,000. During the Obama Administration, there were convictions in 2012 and 2013. In 2012, one man was convicted of dumping soil materials into and around Gales Creek in Oregon in order to divert the creek; he was sentenced to 60 months' probation and ordered to pay $1,250 in fines. 2013 saw the largest criminal penalty; Hancock County Land, LLC was convicted of knowingly ditching, draining, and filling wetlands on property it had acquired for development in Mississippi and sentenced to 24 months' probation and $1,000,000 in fines. The last reported conviction came during the Trump Administration in 2019, where a "dirt broker" was convicted of charging a fee in exchange for providing an open space to dump approximately 1,800 truckloads of construction debris and fill material on private property that included wetlands and other WOTUS. He was sentenced to 30 months incarceration, followed by 12 months' probation. See Summary of Criminal Prosecutions, U.S Env't Prot. Agency, https://cfpub.epa.gov/compliance/criminal_prosecution/index.cfm (last visited May 27, 2024).

191. Summary of Criminal Prosecutions, U.S. ENV'T PROT. AGENCY, https://www.epa.gov/enforcement/summary-criminal-prosecutions-u-s-district-courts.

192. 33 U.S.C. § 1319(c). *See also* 28 U.S.C. § 2461, *et seq.*

193. *Id.*

194. *Id.*

subject to a doubling of maximum fines and prison terms.[195] EPA and the Corps guidance on enforcement priorities has identified situations in which criminal actions are appropriate.[196]

Section 309(c)(6) defines "person" to mean "any responsible corporate officer,"[197] and under the responsible corporate officer doctrine, an officer may be convicted even if not directly involved in or without direct knowledge of the violation. Corporations may also be subject to criminal prosecution for wetland violations.[198]

Absent governmental action, in certain situations, CWA Section 505 authorizes enforcement through citizens' suits.[199] Citizens may bring suit (1) against "any person . . . alleged to be in violation of . . . an effluent standard or limitation under [the CWA]";[200] or (2) against the Corps or EPA alleging agency failure to perform a nondiscretionary act or duty.[201] District courts are authorized "to enforce such an effluent standard or limitation . . . or to order [EPA] to perform such act or duty, as the case may be, and to apply any appropriate civil penalties under [Section 309(d) of the CWA]."[202] However, plaintiffs are

195. *Id.*

196. U.S. Env't Prot. Agency, *U.S. Army Corps of Eng'rs, Guidance on Civil and Criminal Enforcement Priorities* (Dec. 1990), https://www.epa.gov/cwa-404/1990-epa-and-army-corps-engineers-enforcement-priorities-guidance-under-cwa-section-404 (considering the environmental harm inflicted, the violator's culpability, deterrence value of a high penalty, and any economic benefit received); *see also* U.S. Env't Prot. Agency, Enforcement under CWA Section 404 | US EPA, https://www.epa.gov/cwa-404/enforcement-under-cwa-section-404.

197. 33 U.S.C. § 1319(c)(6).

198. U.S. v. Marathon Dev. Corp., 867 F.2d 96 (1st Cir. 1989) (Corporation indicted for wetland violations); Stillwater of Crown Point Homeowner's Ass'n, Inc. v. Stiglich, 999 F. Supp. 2d 1111 (N.D. Ind. 2014) (holding principal was personally liable for CWA violations pursuant to responsible corporate officer doctrine).

199. 33 U.S.C. § 1365; *see also* Jim May, *Now More Than Ever: Trends in Environmental Citizen Suits at 30*, 10 Widener L. Rev. 1 (2003), https://papers.ssrn.com/sol3/papers.cfm?abstract_id=1334221.

200. 33 U.S.C. § 1365(a)(1). *See* Northwest Env't Advocates v. Portland, 56 F.3d 979 (9th Cir. 1995) (listing types of permit conditions that citizens may enforce); Committee to Save Mokelumne River v. East Bay Util., 13 F.3d 305 (9th Cir. 1993), *cert. denied*, 115 S. Ct. 198 (1994) (citizen suit may compel an alleged violator to obtain a permit); *see also* City & Cnty. of San Francisco v. U.S. Env't Prot. Agency, 75 F.4th 1074, 1090 (9th Cir. 2023).

201. 33 U.S.C. § 1365(a)(2).

202. *Id.* § 1365(a).

still required to meet traditional constitutional standing requirements in bringing such suits.[203]

A citizen suit must allege violation of an "effluent standard or limitation, that the plaintiff has complied with the notice requirements of Section 505(b),"[204] and that neither EPA nor a state "has commenced and is diligently prosecuting" either a civil or criminal action in federal or state court regarding the alleged violation.[205] Such suits can be brought "against any person (including (i) the United States and (ii) any other governmental instrumentality or agency to the extent permitted by the eleventh amendment to the Constitution). . . ."[206] A potential plaintiff must first send a "60-Day Notice Letter" that provides official and detailed notice of the alleged violation to the agencies, to the state in which the alleged violation occurs, and to the alleged violator.[207]

No citizen suit can be brought if a governmental entity "has commenced and is diligently prosecuting a civil or criminal action in a court of the United States, or a State to require compliance with the standard, limitation, or order."[208] However, if prosecution is underway, "any citizen may intervene as a matter of right."[209] Those seeking to bring a citizen suit have the burden to prove that the state has failed to diligently prosecute an action.[210] Citizen suits may seek both injunctive relief and civil penalties (paid to the government), but cannot recover damages.[211] However, the court has discretion to award litigation costs to a prevailing (or substantially prevailing) party.[212]

203. *See generally* James Robert May, Principles of Constitutional Environmental Law (Am. Bar Ass'n 2011).

204. 33 U.S.C. § 1365(b).

205. *Id.* § 1365(b)(1)(B).

206. *Id.* § 1365(a)(1).

207. *Id.* § 1365(b)(1); 40 C.F.R. §§ 135.1–.3.

208. 33 U.S.C. § 1365(b)(1)(B).

209. *Id.*

210. Piney Run Pres. Ass'n v. Cnty. Comm'rs of Carroll Cnty., Md., 523 F.3d 453, 459 (4th Cir. 2008) (Piney Run II) (quoting Karr v. Hefner, 475 F.3d 1192, 1198 (10th Cir. 2007); Supporters to Oppose Pollution v. Heritage Grp., 973 F.2d 1320 (7th Cir. 1992); North & South Rivers Watershed Ass'n v. Scituate, 949 F.2d 552 (1st Cir. 1991); Ohio Valley Env't Coal., Inc. v. Maple Coal Co., 808 F. Supp. 2d 868, (S.D.W. Va. 2011); Arkansas Wildlife Fed'n v. The ICI Americas, Inc., 842 F. Supp. 1140 (E.D. Ark. 1993), *aff'd*, 29 F.3d 376 (8th Cir. 1994).

211. Walls v. Waste Res. Corp., 761 F.2d 311 (6th Cir. 1985); StarLink Logistics Inc. v. ACC, LLC, 642 F. Supp. 3d 652, 686 (M.D. Tenn. 2022).

212. 33 U.S.C. § 1365(d).

9
CHAPTER

Conclusion: Managing Controversies and Succeeding in Traversing the World of Wetlands Law and Regulation

I. Introduction

It is generally accepted that wetlands are a vital resource on many levels.[1] Yet throughout the nation and world, these vital resources

1. *See* Nat'l Park Serv., *Why Are Wetlands Important?,* https://www.nps.gov/subjects/wetlands/why.htm (last updated May 5, 2016) ("wetlands are increasingly seen as productive and valuable resources worthy of protection and restoration"); Earthtalk, *Why Are Wetlands So Important to Preserve?*, Sci. Am. (June 19, 2013), https://www.scientificamerican.com/article/why-are-wetlands-so-important-to-preserve/. As the U.S. Fish and Wildlife Service explained in 2011: "Wetlands are transitional from true aquatic habitats to dry land (upland) and as a result, their abundance, type, and condition are directly reflected in the health and abundance of many species. In 1986, the United States Congress enacted the Emergency Wetlands Resources Act (Public Law 99-645) recognizing that wetlands are nationally important resources and that these resources have been affected by human activities. Under the provisions of this Act, the Service is required to update wetland status and trends studies of the Nation's wetlands at 10 year intervals. To date, there have been five national reports on wetland status with this study being the latest. Recently, Congress has considered a number

frequently face potential degradation or destruction.[2] As Wetlands International observes, "[t]he pressure on wetlands is likely to intensify in the coming decades due to increased global demand for land and water, as well as climate change."[3]

The previous chapters of this book explain the various ways that Congress, Corps and EPA, other federal agencies, most states, and many local governments regulate activities in wetlands—and at the same time these chapters explore the controversies those regulatory approaches frequently encounter. As far back as the early 1990s, "the whole issue of regulation of wetlands [has been] in constant flux."[4] This remains true today—wetlands law and policy is an ever-changing area of practice. Perhaps the most controversial development is the ping-pong match that has evolved between the Democratic and Republican

---

of policy issues that involve wetlands. Some of these reflect long-standing interests of the Federal government and influence a number of incentive and disincentive measures to conserve wetlands and if possible increase both the extent and improve the environmental quality aspects wetlands provide (Copeland 2010). *See* T.E. Dahl, U.S. Fish & Wildlife Service, *Status and Trends of Wetlands in the Conterminous United States 2004 to 2009*, at 17, https://www.fws.gov/media/status-and-trends-wetlands-conterminous-united-states-2004-2009 (the latest iteration of this report, Status and Trends of Wetlands in the Conterminous United States 2009 to 2019, can be accessed at https://www.fws.gov/media/status-and-trends-wetlands-conterminous-united-states-2009-2019; the library of all the reports can be found at https://www.fws.gov/library/collections/wetlands-status-and-trends); Jane Madgwick, Wetlands International, *Why Wetlands Are a Versatile Climate and Biodiversity Hack* (Mar. 24, 2022), https://www.weforum.org/agenda/2022/03/wetlands-climate-change/.

2. *See* Gordon Meeks Jr. & L. Cheryl Runyon, National Conference of State Legislatures, Wetland Protection and the States (Apr. 1990) ("Until recently, the nation's wetlands were considered virtual wastelands to be filled famed, dredges and/or drained for what were perceived to be more 'useful' economic purposes such as farming, water supplies, construction and waterfront development. The intrinsic values of wetlands were not fully recognized until their loss started to reveal problems. Sportsmen gradually began to notice a decline in the numbers of wildlife and fish. Commercial fur trappers found dwindling catches in their traps. Rural homeowners discovered contamination in their well water and also found that they had to drill much deeper to find adequate water. Flooding along rivers and shorelines increased over historic levels. Timber companies in the south grew concerned over the declining number of bald cypress trees that grow only in freshwater swamps. The public recognized that flood control, groundwater recharge, water pollution control, and wildlife habitat were direct benefits of wetland preservation.").

3. *Why Wetlands Matter*, Wetlands Int'l, https://www.wetlands.org/wetlands/why-wetlands-matter/ (last visited Apr. 12, 2024).

4. Steven M. Silverberg & Mark S. Dennison, Wetlands and Coastal Zone Regulation and Compliance 1 (1993).

parties in this arena, with major rule rewrites seeming to occur with each shift in the political party holding the office of President.[5]

Yet, for the most part, the issues that regulators and other stakeholders grapple with in the wetlands regulatory arena are not new. The only "hot" issue that has not been discussed in depth among most wetland experts for decades is regulating in the context of climate change. Yet, even that area received some discussion before this millennium, and a significant amount in the past decade.[6] Research on the interplay of wetlands and climate change and how wetlands can ameliorate the effects of climate change has been on the rise.[7]

This chapter highlights some of the key unresolved issues, first looking back at recommendations from others over the years regarding wetland policy, then examining current and unresolved issues starting with climate change and followed by a list of some unresolved issues about which those interested in or practicing wetlands should be aware.

II. Historic and Modern Recommendations on Wetlands Law and Policy

Over the years, recommendations have abounded regarding national wetlands law and policy. This section explores some of these

5. As examples of the recent rancor, see Chapter 2 of this book for the ongoing dispute about the definition of "waters of the United States", Chapter 5 for the 2020, 2021 and 2024 overhauls of the NEPA rules, and Chapter 7 about the two administration-based major overhauls of the water quality certification rule.

6. *See, e.g.*, John S. Hoffman et al., *U.S. Environmental Protection Agency, Projecting Future Sea Level Rise: Methodology, Estimates to the Year 2100, & Research Needs* 38 (2d ed. 1983); Report of the Louisiana Wetland Protection Panel, Convened by Louisiana Geological Survey and the United States EPA, Saving Louisiana's Coastal Wetlands: The Need for a Long-Term Plan of Action (EPA-230-02-87-026) (1987); U.S. Env't Prot. Agency, America's Wetlands: Our Vital Link Between Land And Water 12 (1988).

7. *See, e.g.*, Shokoufeh Salimi, Suhad A.A.A.N. Almuktar & Miklas Scholz, *Impact of Climate Change on Wetland Ecosystems: A Critical Review of Experimental Wetlands,* J. Env't Mgmt. (May 15, 2021), https://pubmed.ncbi.nlm.nih.gov/33611067/; William R. Moomaw et al., Wetlands in a Changing Climate: Science, Policy and Management (USGS 2018). The 2024 NEPA rule revisions also mandate consideration of climate change and environmental justice. See Chapter 5 at notes 75 and 76.

suggestions since the 1980s, reflecting on their similarities and how they might inform those currently working on wetlands issues.

In the late 1980s, a diverse group of wetland experts joined together to develop recommendations for wetland policy. This National Wetlands Policy Forum published a final report that began by noting that Forum members "firmly believe the nation cannot afford to allow the present situation—with its inadequate wetlands protection, its unacceptable delays and confusion, its costs, and frustrations—to continue"[8] and issuing several consensus suggestions. First, the Forum suggested committing to "a national wetlands protection policy to achieve no overall net loss of the nation's remaining wetlands base, as defined by acreage and function, and to restore and create wetlands, where feasible, to increase the quality and quantity of the nation's wetlands resource base."[9] It recommended moving toward these goals not in a way that prevents all activities in wetlands but rather by:

- Provid[ing] better incentives to private wetlands owners to protect permanently these resources for the public benefit. We recommend the creation of a system of National Wetlands Preservation Trusts, an Agricultural Wetlands Reserve Program, and several other initiatives to provide the incentives we believe are necessary.
- Expand[ing] and improve[ing] both government and nongovernment wetlands acquisition and preservation programs.
- Reduc[ing] wetlands losses resulting from government programs that either affect wetlands directly or encourage private landowners to alter them.
- Institut[ing] more effective and evenhanded regulatory programs to ensure than no types of wetlands conversions—including those resulting from drainage, excavation, the destruction of vegetation, and other such causes—are

8. Conservation Found., National Wetlands Policy Forum, Protecting America's Wetlands: An Action Agenda (1988).

9. *Id.* ("Although calling for a stable and eventually increasing inventory of wetlands, the goal does not imply that individual wetlands will in every instance be untouchable or that the no-net-loss standard should be applied on an individual permit basis—only that the nation's overall wetlands base reach equilibrium between losses and gains in the short run and increase in the long term. The public must share with the private sector the costs of restoring and creating wetlands to achieve this goal.").

allowed to escape unreviewed because of peculiarities in the wetlands protection laws and regulations.[10]

Forum members also recommended increased efforts at restoring altered wetlands by:

- Implement[ing] stronger mitigation requirements within the regulatory programs so that, taken as a whole, permitted conversions are fully offset by wetlands restoration or creation.
- Requir[ing] that all government agencies provide full compensation for any wetlands altered by facilities they construct or support.
- Establish[ing] a cooperative public-private National Wetlands Restoration Initiative to search out opportunities for restoration of wetlands. This initiative should particularly focus on government-owned lands and areas that have been altered by the construction of facilities undertaken or sponsored by government [, and]
- Implement[ing] an Agricultural Wetlands Reserve Program that, in addition to protecting existing wetlands, will fund the restoration of 2.5 million acres of former agricultural wetlands over the next 10 years.[11]

In terms of improving both protection and management efficiency, many Forum recommendations focused "on making the full set of wetlands protection and management programs operate more efficiently and effectively than at present, providing better protection with less delay, frustration, and cost."[12] They proposed achieving this through advance planning (including State Wetlands Conservation Plans), education "about wetlands values and how best to undertake protection and management efforts," and expansion of the "information base used to justify and design protection and management programs" to overcome information gaps through "substantial research by both the public and private sectors," including making that information "more widely available to those involved in wetlands protection and management."[13]

10. *Id.*
11. *Id.*
12. *Id.*
13. *Id.*

Stating that the "Forum's proposals encouraging voluntary protection of wetlands should reduce the need for regulation,"[14] the Final Report nevertheless recognized that "regulatory programs will continue to have an important role in wetlands protection"[15] and recommended they be made more effective and efficient by:

- Delegat[ing] primary responsibility for all wetlands regulation to qualified states, so long as they have the authority and capability necessary to achieve the proposed wetlands protection goal and have undertaken State Wetlands Conservation Plans indicating how they will do so.
- Provid[ing] financial and technical assistance, allow[ing] partial delegation of responsibilities, allow[ing] states to assume permitting authorities under Section 404 of the Clean Water Act over all wetlands; and requir[ing] federal activities to be consistent with approved State Wetlands Conservation Plans, in order to encourage the assumption of wetland regulatory responsibilities by the states.
- Work[ing] toward adopting a single regulatory definition of wetlands.
- Consider[ing] regulating small conversions of less valuable wetlands through regional general permits that provide for expedited processing as long as full advance or concurrent compensation is provided for any wetlands that are altered.
- Allocat[ing] more funding to state and federal regulatory agencies for wetlands permitting activities.
- Expand[ing] the monitoring and enforcement activities of the agencies responsible for implementing regulatory programs.
- Ensur[ing] that regulatory agencies do not make inappropriate use of maps prepared for the purpose of inventorying the nation's wetlands resources.[16]

Forum members recommended quick implementation and several immediate steps to avoid "both [] lost public benefits as wetlands continue to be converted and [] costs of the economic inefficiencies

14. *Id.*
15. *Id.*
16. *Id.*

created by current regulatory programs."[17] Furthermore, recognizing limits in existing law at the time, the Final Report recommended the following legislative changes on both the federal and state levels:

- Establish[ing] the recommended goal as national policy.
- Encourag[ing] delegation of federal wetlands regulatory responsibilities to qualified states.
- Establish[ing] such initiatives as Wetlands Preservation Trusts and an Agricultural Wetlands Reserve Program.
- Requir[ing] the president to report to Congress every five years on the nation's success in achieving the national wetlands protection goal.
- [And,] recommend[ing] states immediately begin the process of assuming primary regulatory responsibility for undertaking the preparation of State Wetlands Conservation Plans, administratively consolidating their wetlands regulation activities, and enacting any legislation they need to provide full protection to their wetlands and qualify for the delegation of federal regulatory responsibilities.

While acknowledging the resource investment (both fiscal and other) needed to move forward on the recommendations, Forum members noted that "every day of delay in implementing the Forum's recommendations will cause continued diminution of the nation's often irreplaceable wetlands endowment and perpetuate the current unacceptable situation. Wetlands will continue to be altered at excessive rates and the regulated community will continue to suffer the inefficiencies of current protection programs" and concluded, by consensus, that "as stewards of these resources, all of us in the public, private, and nonprofit sectors must work together to protect them for the use and benefit of future generations."[18]

Shortly before, focusing on local wetlands law, recommendations by a group of experts in the early 1980s making wetlands policy recommendations on local law touched on themes mirroring discussions on a national level such as those just set forth.[19] That group recommended the following:

---

17. *Id.*

18. *Id.*

19. Jon A. Kusler, Corbin C. Harwood & Richard B. Newton, Our National Wetland Heritage: A Protection Guidebook, Env't Law Inst.

1. Adopt a general wetland protection policy.
2. Educat[e] the public.
3. Identify and map wetland areas.
4. Acquir[e] wetlands requiring total protection.
5. Regulate wetlands activities.
6. Reduce property tax assessment.
7. Undertak[e] rehabilitation efforts.

The next decade, an Interagency Working Group on Federal Wetlands Policy convened by the President William Jefferson Clinton's White House Office on Environmental Policy issued a 1993 report entitled *Protecting America's Wetlands: A Fair, Flexible, and Effective Approach.*[20] Stating boldly that the report offered a "comprehensive package of improvements to the Federal wetlands program that reflects a new broad-based consensus among Federal agencies," the introduction noted that

> [f]or years, many have argued that the Federal government badly needed to improve its wetlands program to make it fairer and more effective. But for too long, contradictory policies from feuding Federal agencies have blocked progress, creating uncertainty and confusion. This wetlands package reflects a sharp break through the past gridlock caused by warring Federal agencies and contains a balanced, common sense, workable set of improvements that will make the program simpler, fairer, better coordinated with state and local efforts and more effective at protecting wetlands.[21]

PUBLICATION (1983) ("Chapters 1 and 2 discuss the need to protect and manage wetlands, threats to wetlands, and wetland origins and characteristics. Chapters 3, 4 and 5 identify management principles and standards, wetland protection techniques, and procedures for evaluation of development proposals. Chapters 6, 7 and 8 consider Federal, State and local regulatory efforts. Chapter 9 addresses legal issues in wetland regulation. Chapters 10 and 11 consider nonregulatory management techniques and the role of the private sector in wetland protection. The Appendices include a draft wetland protection ordinance, examples of wetland protection ordinances, a guide to federal programs which affect wetlands, a list of endangered animal species dependent on wetlands, and examples of deed restrictions.").

20. *See* White House Office on Environmental Policy, *Protecting America's Wetlands: A Fair, Flexible, And Effective Approach* (Aug. 24, 1993), https://unioncounty-fl.gov/wp-content/uploads/47-Protecting-Americas-Wetlands.pdf.

21. *Id.*

Protecting America's Wetlands: A Fair, Flexible, and Effective Approach called for many areas of reform:

- To address "landowner concerns" seeking a regulatory process that is more efficient, responsive, and fair, the report set forth proposed reforms calling for Deadlines for Permit Action, the Adoption of an Appeals Process, Delineation Training and Certification, and Voluntary, Cooperative Programs;
- To limit permit-by-permit decisions and allow for advanced planning and watershed-based management, the report set forth proposed reforms calling for: Incentives for States/Locals to Integrate Watershed and Wetlands Planning; State/Tribal Wetlands Conservation Plan Endorsement; Greater Integration of Advance Planning Into the Section 404 Regulatory Program; increased use of Programmatic General Permits; review of Nationwide Permit 26 (NWP 26); endorsement of Mitigation Banking; Promotion of Voluntary, Cooperative Programs; a Revised Executive Order on Wetlands, and Better and Coordinated Information and Technical Assistance on Wetland Issues;
- To ensure that Federal wetlands programs do not place unnecessary restrictions or burdens on farmers and other landowners, while providing necessary environmental safeguards, the report set forth proposed reforms calling for a Prior Converted Cropland Rulemaking, a Package to Eliminate Duplication and Inconsistency among what was then called the Soil Conservation Service (SCS), EPA, the Corps, and FWS by making the SCS the Lead Agency on Agricultural Lands, Guaranteeing Consistency in Delineations on Agricultural Lands, Greatly Increase Farmers' Certainty in Agency Decisions, Clarifying that Certain Man-Made Wetlands Are Not Jurisdictional, and increasing support to the Wetlands Reserve Program;
- To address issues that having "all wetlands . . . treated the same" is inefficient from a regulatory perspective, and that it would instead be better to rank wetlands based upon their relative function and importance to society, the report set forth proposed reforms calling for Section 404(b)(1) Guidelines Flexibility Guidance, Improved Analytical Tools for Wetlands Functional Assessment, Advance Planning Efforts, and Regionalized General Permits for Activities in Defined Categories of Waters;

- To address issues regarding which waters fall within Section 404's jurisdiction, the report set forth proposed reforms regarding the 1987 Wetlands Delineation Manual, examination of the definition of "waters of the United States," "wetlands," "isolated waters," and examples of artificial wetlands;
- To address issues regarding mitigation under Section 404, the report set forth proposed reforms that supported a sequential approach to mitigation involving Issuing Mitigation Planning Guidance, Endorsing the Use of Mitigation Banking Under the Section 404 Regulatory Program and Issuing Mitigation Banking Guidance, and Developing Improved Analytical Tools to perform wetland functional assessments that would help determine appropriate and effective mitigation measures;
- To address issues regarding restoration of the nearly half of the wetland acreage that existed in the lower 48 States prior to European settlement, the report set forth proposed reforms that involved an expanded Wetlands Reserve Program, Promotion of Wetlands Restoration through Voluntary, Cooperative Programs and Outreach Activities, and Revisions to the Executive Order on Wetlands to establish wetlands restoration as an essential vehicle for Federal and quasi-Federal agencies to achieve no-net-loss goals through a voluntary approach;
- To address issues regarding federal agency programs contributing to confusion, delays, overlap, and a general sense that no single agency is "in charge" regarding wetlands policy, the report set forth proposed reforms that called for Continued Implementation of the 1992 Interagency Section 404(q) MOAs;
- To address the appropriate role of State, Tribal, or local governments, the report set forth proposed reforms that would Assist States, Tribes, and Local Governments in Taking a Stronger Role in Wetlands Protection, Provide Incentives for States, Tribes, and Regional and Local Governments to Integrate Watershed and Wetlands Planning, Increase Deference to State, Tribal, Regional, and Local Wetlands Decision-making, Endorse State/Tribal Wetlands Conservation Plans, Encourage State/Tribal Assumption of Section 404, and Provide States/Tribes with Access to Wetlands Delineation Training;
- To address debate about the scope of regulated activities, the report set forth proposed reforms that would close regulatory

loopholes by clarifying the types of activities that involve discharges of dredged or fill material subject to Section 404 by Clarifying the Definition of "Discharge of Dredged Material," Clarifying the Definition of "Discharge of Fill Material," and seeking Legislative Clarification of Scope of Activities Regulated Under Section 404;

- To address the unique climatological and physiographic conditions in Alaska and resolve debates about the proposed "Alaska 1 percent rule," which would have exempted wetlands in Alaska from mitigation requirements until one percent of Alaska's wetland resources had been developed, the report promised to initiate meetings with the Federal resource agencies, Alaska state and local government agencies, representatives of native villages, industry groups including oil and fishing interests, and environmental groups, to consider other environmentally appropriate means to assure regulatory flexibility and the feasibility of alternative permitting procedures in Alaska;[22] and
- To address issues related to regulatory "takings" under the Fifth Amendment of the U.S. Constitution and support private property rights, the report declared that due to the unique nature of each situation, issues must be considered on a case-by-case basis to make the program as efficient, predictable, consistent, and equitable as possible.[23]

In 1995, two years after the initial report, the Clinton administration suggested progress had been made on many of the reforms suggested in this report. It pointed to Section 404 exemptions for "prior converted croplands"; the proposal for an administrative appeals program; more flexibility for farmers with wetlands on their property; changes to the Nationwide Permit Program; permitting process streamlining to increase efficiency; working with state, local, and tribal governments to take a greater role in protecting and managing wetland resources; a focus on mitigation banking on a larger scale; Wetlands Reserve Program (WRP) expansion; clarification of the definition of "discharge" to limit continuing damage, but explicitly excluding activities with only inconsequential environmental effects;

22. The "Alaska 1% rule" was proposed by the George H.W. Bush Administration and withdrawn by the Clinton Administration. *Id.* at 22.
23. *Id.*

reduced wetland loss rates; expanded public outreach; and work by "[n]onprofit organizations, States, local agencies, and landowners" to address the needs of private landowners.[24] Yet, despite those declarations of progress, many of these very issues remain under debate nearly three decades later.

Many of these themes were picked up well over a decade later in a 2009 book written not by lawyers or by regulators, but instead by two reporters after four years spent researching wetlands regulation in Florida.[25] These journalists concluded with one thought: "if nothing else, the government would do well to be honest about how things really work" and proposed what they called "a 12-step program toward making a more honest system":[26]

> 1) Substituting for "'no net loss' . . . a focus on policies that would encourage developers, road-builders, miners, and everyone else to avoid dredging or filling swamps and marshes [to avoid] spending millions in tax dollars trying to fix the problems that result: flooding, water pollution, and so on" and asking whether it isn't "more conservative to conserve the natural processes that are already there rather than spending government money on a man-made fix."
>
> 2) Avoiding what they labeled "accounting tricks," and urging governments to abandon the practice of counting wetland preservation "as if it were new acreage that never existed before" or other methods of trading or managing loss creatively that "cook the books and allow for continued destruction";[27]
>
> 3) Emphasizing restoration, noting that "a wetland that's been filled in and paved may never be a wetland again, but one that's been converted by agriculture can be restored" and observing that while "[p]reservation is nice—an admirable goal outside of no net loss—[]it should not count toward any sort of ratio that allegedly makes up for destruction";[28]

---

24. Off. Env't Pol'y, Exec. Off. of the President, *Two Years of Progress, Meeting Our Commitment for Wetlands Reform—Protecting America's Wetlands: A Fair, Flexible and Effective Approach, August 1993–August 1995* (Aug. 1995).

25. Craig Pittman & Matthew Waite, Paving Paradise: Florida's Vanishing Wetlands and the Failure of No Net Loss (2009).

26. *Id.*

27. *Id.*

28. *Id.*

4) Instituting a pay-as-you-go system that requires the federal permitting program pay for itself, similar to the program under Florida state law;[29]

5) Setting a deadline for the Corps permit review based on the size of the project and whether it involves wiping out the habitat of any endangered species—another way to encourage a smaller impact;[30]

6) Providing the public with better access to information about how each agency is doing its job;[31]

7) Mapping important wetland habitat;[32]

8) Assessing where the "tipping point" for allowing more wetlands permits lies;[33]

9) Saving priority areas;[34]

10) Considering the approach in Ontario, Canada, that provides landowners an incentive to leave mapped wetlands alone by offering tax breaks for property that keeps its marshes and swamps in a natural state;[35]

11) Increasing monitoring and imposing fines, bans on doing business with government agencies, requirements that a project cease, threats that future permits will be denied or at least delayed, or other consequences for permit applicant failure or dishonesty;[36] and

12) Increasing the ability of local governments to stringently regulate their wetlands and eliminate the federal "elevation" policy.[37]

These journalists admitted their 12 recommendations were challenging, and that

> [c]hanging the way we protect wetlands won't be easy. It will require making some hard choices between private property rights, which benefit the owners of wetlands only when those

29. *Id.*
30. *Id.*
31. *Id.*
32. *Id.*
33. *Id.*
34. *Id.*
35. *Id.*
36. *Id.*
37. *Id.*

> wetlands can be developed, and the rights of the population at large to flood protection and clean water and abundant fishing and duck-hunting, things that are available only when we leave wetlands alone. It will require action by Congress and the legislature, two bodies that so far have shown more interest in making it easier to wipe out wetlands than in trying to save them. But remember, wetlands protection affects more than just our quality of life and our survival on the planet. As taxpayers, we're footing the multi-million-dollar bill for this program.[38]

In 2011, a former regulator-turned-environmental-law-professor added a series of recommendations in the conclusion to his book[39] that echoed many of these now-familiar themes:

- Congress should pass the Clean Water Restoration Act to remove doubts about federal jurisdiction over wetlands by deleting the reference to "navigable waters" in the Clean Water Act.
- The Corps should reorient its regulatory philosophy. Although the Corps should strive to make its procedures "user friendly," the Corps should remember that the public is the ultimate customer. The Corps' primary obligation ought to be the goals of the Clean Water Act: to restore and maintain the chemical, physical, and biological integrity of the nation's waters.
- The Corps needs to emphasize avoidance of wetland impacts and deny more permits. Avoidance especially ought to be invoked with respect to wetlands that are difficult to restore. Furthermore, these permit decisions should be based on ecological factors, not concerns about regulatory takings.
- The EPA should maintain its veto authority and not hesitate to unsheathe it.
- The Corps should eliminate NWP 21, governing surface coal mining operations.
- The Corps should make permit decisions on a watershed basis, taking into account cumulative impacts.

38. *Id.*

39. Royal C. Gardner, Lawyers, Swamps, and Money, U.S. Wetland Law, Policy, and Politics (2011).

- The Corps and the EPA should identify minimization best practices.
- The Corps should implement the regulatory preference for compensation from mitigations banks; at the same time, the Corps should tighten up on early credit releases.
- Congress should discontinue perverse incentives that contribute to wetland destruction.
- The Corps and the EPA should increase enforcement efforts and use technology to do so.
- The Corps should provide more transparency in the section 404 program.

Reviewing the foregoing recommendations shows many common themes persist. Accordingly, the emerging and unresolved issues identified in the next section of this chapter are far from unique. While wetland law and policy continues to evolve, to be sure, many of the pressures on the system have existed for decades and will continue to inform the way forward.

III. Emerging and Unresolved Issues

The issue of climate change and the role of wetlands in addressing it presents both obstacles and opportunities for wetland regulation. The first part of this section thus explores climate-related issues in some depth. Other unresolved issues listed here are presented in a very brief fashion, both because they have been touched on by various experts over the past several decades, as set forth in the previous section and discussed elsewhere in more depth in previous chapters of the book.

A. Climate Change and Wetlands

Wetlands and climate change have been discussed for decades but are now becoming part of the legal and regulatory discourse. One increasingly recognized function for many wetlands is carbon sequestration,[40]

---

40. *See* David Were et al., *Carbon Sequestration by Wetlands: A Critical Review of Enhancement Measures for Climate Change Mitigation,* Earth Systems & Env't 3 (Apr. 24, 2019), https://link.springer.com/article/10.1007/s41748-019-00094-0 ("Wetlands are among the most important ecosystems in the response strategy to climate change, through carbon sequestration."); Junyu Zou et al., *Rewetting Global*

a vital service as we consider how to mitigate for and adapt to climate change.[41] As complex biogeochemical systems,[42] wetlands have been susceptible to human-induced[43] (and non-human-induced)[44] impacts

---

Wetlands Effectively Reduces Major Greenhouse Gas Emissions, NATURE GEOSCIENCE 15 (July 28, 2022), https://www.nature.com/articles/s41561-022-00989-0.

41. Watchwords of climate change policy are "adaptation" and "mitigation." In short, these terms are used to describe dealing with and planning for climate change impacts. *See generally* KIRSTIN DOW & THOMAS E. DOWNING, THE ATLAS OF CLIMATE CHANGE: MAPPING THE WORLD'S GREATEST CHALLENGE (Univ. of Calif., 2d ed. 2007).

42. 9th INTECOL International Wetland Conference, Wetlands in a Complex World (2012), https://conference.ifas.ufl.edu/intecol/ (last visited Nov. 5, 2023) ("Wetlands are sources, sinks, and transformers of materials and habitats for diverse life forms. They are a source of food, fiber, and clean water for humans, a carbon sink and source, may reduce flood damage, be a site for groundwater reservoirs, be a sink for pollutants, an agent of chemical transformation, a buffer for climate change, and a corridor for migrating animals. Wetlands are complex ecosystems because they are driven by many physical, chemical, and biological processes. This complexity means that understanding wetland ecosystems requires an interdisciplinary approach that engages many specializations, including biology, chemistry, biogeochemistry, ecology, hydrology, pedology, to mention a few.").

43. Royal C. Gardner, *Rehabilitating Nature: A Comparative Review of Legal Mechanisms That Encourage Wetland Restoration Efforts*, 52 CATH. U.L. REV. 573 (2003) ("In many parts of the world, people have long drained, filled, and otherwise destroyed vast areas of wetlands."); R. Kolka et al., *Chapter 13: Terrestrial Wetlands*, U.S. GLOBAL CHANGE RESEARCH PROGRAM, SECOND STATE OF THE CARBON CYCLE REPORT (2018), HTTPS://CARBON2018.GLOBALCHANGE.GOV/CHAPTER/13/ ("Competing land uses and economic development will continue to threaten wetlands in North America. Multiple policies have been designed to protect against, and mitigate for, wetland loss. However, while losses are greatly stemmed, the United States continues to experience net losses of wetlands in terms of absolute acreage in spite of the no net-loss policy. Canada and Mexico currently have no nationwide wetlands inventory, limiting the ability to estimate wetland conversion or function, including carbon fluxes and pools. It is important to remember that no net-loss policies do not protect against reduced functionality in restored versus natural wetlands.").

44. *See, e.g.*, Statement by Dr. Musonda Mumba, Secretary General of the Convention on Wetlands for World Wetlands Day, February 2, 2022 ("To date, nearly 90 percent of the world's wetlands have been degraded or lost. We are losing wetlands three times faster than forests. There is an urgency to raise global awareness on wetlands to arrest and reverse their rapid loss and encourage actions to restore and conserve these vital ecosystems"), https://icriforum.org/events/world-wetlands-day-2022/; Maya Buchanan et al., Resilience of U.S. Coastal Wetlands to Accelerating Sea Level Rise, 4 ENV'T RSCH. COMMC'NS 6 (June 8, 2022), https://iopscience.iop.org/article/10.1088/2515-7620/ac6eef ("Coastal wetlands provide a wide array of ecosystem services, valued at trillions of dollars per year globally. Although accelerating sea level rise (SLR) poses the long-term threat of inundation to coastal

for many years. Most human-induced impacts threaten ecosystems by decreasing their associated functions, values, and services.[45] Climate change exacerbates these threats.[46] As *Wetlands*, a wetlands science text, explains: "[w]etlands have significant yet generally under-appreciated roles in the global carbon cycle. They are also positioned in the landscape where climate change could affect them more than most other ecosystems."[47] Planning for climate change when dealing with wetlands thus requires us to acknowledge the roles of wetlands "both as players in and recipients of climate change. . . ."[48] Managers and policymakers must develop scientifically sound and workable plans for adapting to and mitigating for change to wetland ecosystems.[49] Likewise, scientific experts confirm that climate change[50] will affect wetlands.[51] Though the precise manner and extent of the effects

---

areas, wetlands may be sustained in two ways: by positive net surface-elevation change (SEC) from sediment and organic matter buildup and by accumulation, or horizontal migration into refugia—low-lying, undeveloped upland areas that become inundated.").

45. For a discussion of a summary of the functions and values of wetlands, *see* Env't Prot. Agency Office of Wetland, Office of Wetlands, Oceans and Watersheds, *Functions and Values of Wetlands* (Mar. 2002) https://www.epa.gov/sites/default/files/2021-01/documents/functions_values_of_wetlands.pdf.

46. *See* Deborah Zabarenko, *Wetlands Could Unleash "Carbon Bomb,"* Reuters UK (July 20, 2008), https://blog.nwf.org/2008/07/reuters-wetlands-could-unleash-carbon-bomb/ ("The world's wetlands, threatened by development, dehydration and climate change, could release a planet-warming 'carbon bomb' if they are destroyed, ecological scientists said on Sunday.").

47. William J. Mitsch & James G. Gosselink, Wetlands 313 (4th ed. 2007).

48. *Id.*

49. For a terrific portal into research on climate change and wetlands, *see* Nat'l Ass'n of State Wetland Managers, *Wetlands and Climate Change*, https://www.nawm.org/science/wetlands-and-climate-change (last visited Mar. 6, 2023).

50. For links to many excellent websites that address climate change generally, see NASA, *Global Climate Change*, https://climate.nasa.gov/ (last visited Mar. 6, 2023).

51. *See supra* notes 39–46 and accompanying text; *see also* A.E. Altor & W.J. Mitsch, *Pulsing Hydrology, Methane Missions, and Carbon Dioxide Fluxes in Created Marshes: A 2-Year Ecosystem Study,* 28 Wetlands 423 (2008); A.E. Altor & W.J. Mitsch, *Methane Emissions and Carbon Dioxide Fluxes in Created Wetland Mesocosms: Effects of Hydrologic Regime and Hydric Soils*, 18 Ecological Applications 1307 (2008); *Destruction of Wetlands Worsens Global Warming*, Mongabay (July 20, 2008), https://news.mongabay.com/2008/07/destruction-of-wetlands-worsens-global-warming/ ("Destruction of wetland ecosystems will generate massive greenhouse gas emissions in coming years, warn experts convening at an international wetlands conference in Brazil."); U.S. Climate Change Technology

are as yet unknown, scientists have presented compelling data regarding a number of areas of impact. As seen from the preceding citations, these include sea level rise, varying effects on coastal wetlands, unintended effects from biofuel production, hurricane-related effects, methane issuance, and ecosystem alteration.

As the United Nations recognized on World Wetlands Day in 2023, international support and action is key, and "there is an urgent need to raise global awareness on wetlands to reverse their rapid loss and to encourage the restoration and conservation of these vital ecosystems."[52] Likewise, the International Union for Conservation of Nature (IUCN) concluded over a decade ago that "there is a growing scientific understanding that the conservation and wise use of wetlands can no longer be achieved without taking climate change into account."[53] This scientific consensus continues to grow.[54]

In addition to being impacted negatively by climate change, scientific research also shows that wetlands themselves may contribute to climate change. Wetlands emit large amounts of the greenhouse gas methane.[55] EPA estimates that "[n]atural wetlands are responsible for approximately 76% of global methane emissions from natural sources. . . . Wetlands provide a habitat conducive to methane-producing (methanogenic) bacteria that produce methane during the decomposition of organic material."[56] Some scientists point to wetland disturbance as a reason for the sharp 2008 increase in methane

---

Program, Technology Options for the Near and Long Term 3.2.1.6 (Nov. 2003), https://permanent.fdlp.gov/lps60383/nov_cctp_report.pdf ("Climatic condition is the single most important factor in determining success in protecting carbon stored in existing wetlands. Fire, permafrost melt, sea-level rise, and more frequent droughts will affect wetlands.").

52. Statement by Dr. Musonda Mumba, Secretary General of the Convention on Wetlands for World Wetlands Day, February 2, 2023, https://www.ramsar.org/sites/default/files/2023-09/Statement%20by%20Dr%20Musonda%20Mumba_%20English.pdf.

53. Ger Berkamp & Brett Orlando, *Wetlands and Climate Change, Exploring Collaboration between the Convention on Wetlands (Ramsar, Iran, 1971) and the UN Framework Convention on Climate Change* (Oct. 1999), https://www.ramsar.org/sites/default/files/documents/library/dn1999-9papere.pdf.

54. *See supra* footnotes 39–49 and accompanying text.

55. U.S. Env't Prot. Agency, *Methane, Sources and Emissions*, http://www.energybc.ca/cache/naturalgas/www.epa.gov/methane/sources.html.

56. *Id.*

emissions worldwide, the first increase for more than a decade.[57] "According to the NOAA researchers, the dramatic increase in methane emissions in the Northern Hemisphere "may be a result of very warm conditions over Siberia throughout 2007, potentially leading to increased bacterial emissions from wetland areas."[58] Researchers continue to work to determine "embattled ecosystems that will become even more important as a buffer against the storms and sea-level rise that are predicted to accompany global warming.[59]

---

57. Annual Greenhouse Gas Index (AGGI) Indicates Sharp Rise in Carbon Dioxide and Methane in 2007 (Apr. 23, 2008), https://www.sustainablebusiness.com/2008/10/methane-levels-surged-in-2007-43798/ ("Methane levels in the atmosphere have more than tripled since pre-industrial times, accounting for around one-fifth of the human contribution to greenhouse gas-driven global warming. Until recently, the leveling off of methane levels had suggested that the rate of its emission from Earth's surface was being approximately balanced by the rate of its destruction in the atmosphere. However, the balance has been upset since early 2007, according to research published this week in the American Geophysical Union's 'Geophysical Review Letters.' The paper's lead authors, Matthew Rigby and Ronald Prinn of the Massachusetts Institute of Technology, say this imbalance has resulted in several million metric tons of additional methane in the atmosphere. Methane is produced by wetlands, rice paddies, cattle, and the gas and coal industries. It is destroyed in the atmosphere by reaction with the hydroxyl free radical, often referred to as the atmosphere's 'cleanser.' 'This increase in methane is worrisome because the recent stability of methane levels was helping to compensate for the unexpectedly fast growth of carbon dioxide emissions,' said climate modeler Drew Shindell at NASA's Goddard Institute for Space Studies in New York. 'If methane continues to increase rapidly, we'll lose that offsetting effect. We will use NASA's climate modeling capability to improve our understanding of what is causing the increase and project future methane levels.'" In its update to the AGGI in spring 2023, NOAA reported that "[t]he atmospheric burden of methane has increased more rapidly over the past few years than at any other point in the on-going measurement record, which began in 1983." AGGI (updated spring 2023), https://gml.noaa.gov/aggi/aggi.html.

58. *Id. See also* Stephen Leahy, *Climate Change: Wetlands Loss Fuelling CO2 Feedback Loop*. Interpress Serv. (July 22, 2008), https://stephenleahy.net/2008/07/25/wetlands-loss-fuelling-co2-feedback-loop/ ("Without substantial reductions in emissions of fossil fuels, up to 85 percent of wetlands will be lost in the future. That loss is far more than a loss of important bird habitat—it would also release enough carbon and methane to almost certainly tip the climate into an era of extreme and rapid change, experts believe.").

59. *See supra* footnotes 39–49 and accompanying text; *see also* Joseph Stromberg, *How Will the Wetlands Respond to Climate Change*? Smithsonian (Jan. 2013), https://www.smithsonianmag.com/science-nature/how-will-the-wetlands-respond-to-climate-change-164048534/.

The Corps has incorporated sea-level change into its planning activities since 1986,[60] and has incorporated climate change discussions into its recent reissuance of the Nationwide Permits.[61] EPA also incorporates climate change considerations into the CWA regulatory program "as they relate to permit reviews and compensatory mitigation."[62] Stakeholders would be well advised to pay close attention to how the regulatory program views climate change in coming years. In April 22, 2021, President Biden set ambitious greenhouse gas pollution reduction targets, seeking to achieve a 50-52% reduction from 2005 levels in net greenhouse gas emissions by 2030.[63]

Then in November 2022, the White House under President Biden announced its "Roadmap for Nature-Based Solutions to Fight Climate Change, Strengthen Communities, and Support Local Economies."[64] This roadmap has informed how the federal regulatory agencies

60. U.S. Army Corps. of Eng'rs, *Responses to Climate Change Program, Sea-Level Change Adaptation*, https://www.usace.army.mil/corpsclimate/Responses-to-Climate-Change-Program/ (last visited Apr. 12, 2024).

61. The Corps recognizes the importance of climate change resiliency and both mitigation and adaptation efforts to address climate change. The Corps discusses climate change in the context of the NWP reissuance in each of the national decision documents for the 41 NWPs. Some activities authorized by various NWPs may be associated with energy production (including the energy production through solar, wind, and other renewable resources), distribution, and use, while other activities authorized by the NWPs may contribute to adaptation to climate change and help increase the resilience of communities to the adverse effects of climate change. Reissuance and Modification of Nationwide Permits, 86 Fed. Reg. 73,522, 73,527 (Dec. 27, 2021).

62. U.S. Env't Prot. Agency, *Water as a Climate Change Solution*, http://water.epa.gov/scitech/climatechange/Watersheds-and-Wetlands.cfm.

63. White House Briefing Room, FACT SHEET:President Biden Sets 2030 Greenhouse Gas Pollution Reduction Target Aimed at Creating Good-Paying Union Jobs and Securing U.S. Leadership on Clean Energy Technologies (Apr. 22, 2021), https://www.whitehouse.gov/briefing-room/statements-releases/2021/04/22/fact-sheet-president-biden-sets-2030-greenhouse-gas-pollution-reduction-target-aimed-at-creating-good-paying-union-jobs-and-securing-u-s-leadership-on-clean-energy-technologies/.

64. The White House, *FACT SHEET: Biden-Harris Administration Announces Roadmap for Nature-Based Solutions to Fight Climate Change, Strengthen Communities, and Support Local Economies* (Nov. 8, 2022), https://www.whitehouse.gov/briefing-room/statements-releases/2022/11/08/fact-sheet-biden-%e2%81%a0harris-administration-announces-roadmap-for-nature-based-solutions-to-fight-climate-change-strengthen-communities-and-support-local-economies/.

consider such topics.[65] As a part of that process, the Federal Emergency Management Agency (FEMA) is revising its floodplain management rules "to require consideration of nature-based solutions as alternatives for all projects that have the potential to affect floodplains or wetlands."[66] Executive Order 14008, issued in 2021, requires federal agencies to address "climate-related and other cumulative impacts on disadvantaged communities, as well as the accompanying economic challenges of such impacts."[67] Federal agencies face increasing pressure to consider the effects of climate change in reviewing federal permits.

In accordance with these directives, the 2024 NEPA rules now explicitly recognize climate change as an environmental effect, defining the "effects" of the action that must be considered in a NEPA evaluation to include "climate change-related effects, including the contribution of a proposed action and its alternatives to climate change, and the reasonably foreseeable effects of climate change on the proposed action and its alternatives."[68] Further, the 2024 NEPA rules now declare the policy to use the NEPA process to identify reasonable alternatives that will "reduce climate change-related effects."[69]

This assertedly "bipartisan" rulemaking[70] may and likely will be challenged, but represents a growing awareness of the effect of climate change and the need to incorporate an analysis of its effects

---

65. The Roadmap outlines five focus areas for federal agencies to combat the effects of climate change: "(1) updating policies, (2) unlocking funding, (3) leading with federal facilities and assets, (4) training the nature-based solutions workforce, and (5) prioritizing research, innovation, knowledge, and adaptive learning that will advance nature-based solutions."

66. *Id.* FEMA's interim program policies can be found here: Partial Implementation of the Federal Flood Risk Management Standard for Public Assistance (Interim), FEMA Policy 104-22-0003, https://www.fema.gov/sites/default/files/documents/fema_fp-104-22-0003-partial-implemetnation-ffrms-pa-interim.pdf.

67. Executive Order 14008—Tackling the Climate Crisis at Home and Abroad, 86 Fed. Reg. 7,619 (Feb. 1, 2021).

68. 89 Fed. Reg. at 35442-43, 35575 (to be codified at 40 C.F.R. §1508.1(i)).

69. 89 Fed. Reg. at 35554-55 (to be codified at 40 C.F.R. §1500.2(e)).

70. Press Release, Biden-Harris Administration Finalizes Reforms to Modernize Environmental Reviews, Accelerate America's Clean Energy Future, Simplify the Process to Rebuild our Nation's Infrastructure, and Strengthen Public Engagement, The White House (Apr. 30, 2024), https://www.whitehouse.gov/ceq/news-updates/2024/04/30/biden-harris-administration-finalizes-reforms-to-modernize-environmental-reviews-accelerate-americas-clean-energy-future-simplify-the-process-to-rebuild-our-nations-infrastructure/.

into all major federal decision-making, including permitting decisions by the Corps.

On May 29, 2024, the U.S. Department of Agriculture (USDA) announced that it "will invest up to $50 million in fiscal year 2024 through the Wetland Reserve Enhancement Partnership (WREP) to support conservation partners with local projects that help protect, restore and enhance critical wetlands on agricultural lands and help mitigate climate change as part of President Biden's Investing in America agenda. With funding from the 2018 Farm Bill and the Inflation Reduction Act—the largest climate investment in history, including historic funding for conservation easements and other conservation programs—WREP empowers eligible conservation partners to work with local agriculture producers to protect, restore and enhance high-priority wetlands on agricultural lands."[71].

The program is expected to further both the climate change and environmental justice goals of the Biden Administration as part of his Justice40 Initiative. WREP is part of the USDA's Agricultural Conservation Easement Program; through the program, private landowners voluntarily place eligible land under conservation easements.

Most significantly perhaps, in April 2024, the Biden White House announced "The America the Beautiful Freshwater Challenge," recognizing the importance of wetlands in the "fight against climate change" based on their function of absorbing and storing carbon.[72]

B. New Wetland and Waters Restoration Goals

Hearkening back to familiar themes of prior administrations, the Biden Administration's American the Beautiful Freshwater Challenge also establishes two new national goals to "build upon and improve out country's long-standing policy of no net loss of wetlands" with "bold, new national goals" to help recover lost wetland acres:

---

71. USDA Nat. Res. Cons. Serv., Press Release: Biden-Harris Administration to Invest $50 Million in Projects that Restore Natural Functions and Values of Wetlands As Part of Investing in America Agenda (May 29, 2024), https://www.nrcs.usda.gov/news/biden-harris-administration-to-invest-50-million-in-projects-that-restore-natural-functions.

72. White House, The America the Beautiful Freshwater Challenge: A Partnership to Conserve and Restore America's Rivers, Lakes, Streams, and Wetlands (April 2024), at 1, https://www.whitehouse.gov/wp-content/uploads/2024/04/America-the-Beautiful-Freshwater-Challenge.pdf.

1) Reconnect, restore, and protect 8 million acres of wetlands by 2030, with an emphasis on forested, vegetated, peat soil, brackish, and tidal wetlands; and
2) Reconnect, restore, and protect 100,000 miles of our nations' rivers and streams by 2030, using approaches like removal of impediments and stream bank restoration."[73] This national challenge dovetails with a similar global Freshwater Challenge, which aims to restore 850 million acres of wetlands globally by 2030.[74] The Freshwater Challenge has three principal purposes: (1) integrate restoration and conservation of freshwater ecosystems into "relevant global, regional, and national processes to tackle the climate and nature crisis and achieve sustainable development"; (2) quantify the restoration and conservation effort; and (3) fast-track existing restoration and conservation commitments by increasing overall investment into that effort.[75]

In addition to the national numeric goals, the America the Beautiful Freshwater Challenge calls on all states, tribes, and local governments to develop and advance their own policies and strategies to protect freshwater ecosystems, with the following additional goals:

- Protect our sources of clean drinking water, including groundwater aquifers to ensure that we are safeguarding these from

73. *Id.*

74. *Id.* The global Freshwater Challenge was launched in March 2023 at the UN Water Conference in New York by Colombia, DR Congo, Ecuador, Gabon, Mexico and Zambia; 38 more countries joined the Freshwater Challenge at a COP28 event in Dubai on December 20, 2023.The World's Freshwater Challenge, https://www.freshwaterchallenge.org/. The 46 current member counties participating in the Freshwater Challenge include the United States as well as Botswana, Brazil, Burkina Faso, Cambodia, Canada, Chad, Chile, Colombia, DR Congo, Dominican Republic, Ecuador, El Salvador, Fiji, France, Finland, Gabon, Gambia, Germany, Guinea, Iraq, Kenya, Liberia, Malawi, Mali, Mauritania, Mexico, Moldova, Mozambique, Nepal, Netherlands, Niger, Norway, Pakistan, Peru, Republic of Congo, Senegal, Slovenia, Spain, Tajikistan, Tanzania, the United Arab Emirates, Uganda, the United Kingdom, Zambia and Zimbabwe. https://www.freshwaterchallenge.org/joining.

75. The World's Freshwater Challenge, Purpose of the Freshwater Challenge, https://www.freshwaterchallenge.org/about-the-challenge. The Freshwater Challenge does require each member country to specify national targets for restoring and conserving rivers and wetlands by 2030 and the implement plans to achieve these targets. The World's Freshwater Challenge, Frequently Asked Questions, https://www.freshwaterchallenge.org/q-a.

contamination and helping to recharge these important resources;

- Support achieving and maintaining fishable and swimmable waterways;
- Enhance the natural climate resilience provided by healthy and functional freshwater and estuary resources, including protection from floods, wildfires, aquifer depletion, intense heat, soil health degradation, nutrient loading and drought;
- Support aquatic ecosystem biodiversity, including addressing threats from invasive species;
- Honor Tribal trust and treaty obligations and ways of life, and incorporate Indigenous Knowledge into restoration approaches;
- Ensure that freshwater resources and estuaries continue to support regional and rural economies, including clean manufacturing, global supply chain, outdoor recreational industries, farmers, ranchers, and forest owners;
- Harness and protect the national security, supply chain, and drinking water benefits of freshwater and estuary resources; and
- Protect clean, safe access to our freshwater and estuary resources, especially for communities with environmental justice concerns."[76]

Many of these themes are familiar. How these ambitious numeric and qualitative goals will be achieved—and whether they will survive the next presidential election—remains to be seen.

C. Federal Jurisdiction

As explored at length in Chapter 2, the issue of which wetlands and other waters are under federal control has been subject to a shifting set of regulatory and judicial interpretation since Section 404 became law. This lack of clarity and resulting close attention by many wetlands stakeholders is likely to continue for some time to come.

---

76. https://www.whitehouse.gov/wp-content/uploads/2024/04/America-the-Beautiful-Freshwater-Challenge.pdf.

D. Regulatory Efficacy, Efficiency, Equity, and Transparency

As explored at length in Chapters 2–8, various issues related to wetlands regulation trigger concerns regarding fairness, efficiency, and transparency. These debates, as reflected in the previous section, have been interwoven throughout the fabric of wetland regulation since the 1970s. Such issues will continue to receive attention from many stakeholders, and differing opinions as to how to proceed will result in regulatory and legislative proposals, and various lawsuits, for decades to come. The Council on Environmental Quality's rules implementing NEPA require "consideration of principles of environmental justice" in every federal permitting decision.[77] In April 2023, the Biden Administration issued Executive Order 14096, requiring federal agencies to consider the effects of permitting actions on environmental justice, recognizing that "every person must have clean air to breathe; clean water to drink; safe and healthy foods to eat; and an environment that is healthy, sustainable, climate-resilient, and free from harmful pollution and chemical exposure."[78] Implementing Executive Order 14096, the 2024 amendments to the NEPA rules also incorporate concerns about environmental justice into the NEPA analysis; they expressly define the "effects" of the action that must be considered in a NEPA evaluation to include "disproportionate and adverse effects on communities with environmental justice concerns, whether direct, indirect, or cumulative," and "effects on Tribal resources."[79] It is further CEQ policy to use the NEPA process to identify reasonable alternatives that will "address adverse health and environmental effects that disproportionately affect communities with environmental justice concerns."[80] EPA promotes the use of its EJSCREEN program, a mapping and screening tool, to compile nationally consistent data and an approve that combines both environmental and demographic indicators into a single mapping database. EPA uses EJScreen as a preliminary step when considering environmental justice, including

77. The CEQ has issued additional guidance that requires consideration of principles of environmental justice during NEPA reviews. https://www.epa.gov/environmentaljustice/environmental-justice-and-national-environmental-policy-act.

78. Executive Order 14096—Revitalizing Our Nation's Commitment to Environmental Justice for All, 88 Fed. Reg. 25251 (Apr. 26, 2023) (taking a "government-wide approach to environmental justice" for any federal activity "that affects or has the potential to affect human health and the environment." *Id.*).

79. 89 Fed. Reg. at 35442-43, 35575 (to be codified at 40 C.F.R. §1508.1(i)).

80. 89 Fed. Reg. at 35554-55 (to be codified at 40 C.F.R. §1500.2(e)).

in carrying out its responsibilities in permitting programs, such as its authority under Section 404(q), which is discussed in Chapter 7 of this book.[81] The tool helps EPA overlay areas where people of color and/or low-income live with proposed permitting activities and environmental quality issues (such as flooding) associated with the activity to determine whether there is a "combination of environmental and demographic indicators that is greater than usual."[82]

E. Mitigation

The "new" mitigation rules from 2008 have been in place for more than 15 years at this point,[83] but still are controversial. As explored in Chapter 6, particularly in light of recent takings jurisprudence,[84] this will be an area of continued controversy, particularly to the extent that credits from wetland mitigation banks continue to be scarce in certain jurisdictions, and permitting of new banks continues to lag.[85]

IV. Conclusion

As the discussions in this book have demonstrated, regulating activities in wetlands ecosystems is both scientifically and politically complicated. As one scientist explained in 2001, the definition of wetlands became "troublesome" when "the federal government began regulating them."[86] That remains very true today.

Opinions abound about how the regulatory program should be changed. As stated more than three decades ago in the White House Office on Environmental Policy's *Protecting America's Wetlands: A Fair, Flexible, and Effective Approach*, "critics of the wetlands

81. U.S. Envtl Prot. Agency, How Does EPS Use EJScreen?, https://www.epa.gov/ejscreen/how-does-epa-use-ejscreen (last visited May 27, 2024).

82. U.S. Envtl Prot. Agency,Purposes and Uses of EJScreen, https://www.epa.gov/ejscreen/purposes-and-uses-ejscreen (last visited May 27, 2024).

83. Compensatory Mitigation for Losses of Aquatic Resources, 73 Fed. Reg. 19,594, 19,672 (Apr. 10, 2008) (codified at 33 C.F.R. pts. 325, 332 and 40 C.F.R. pt. 230).

84. *See* Koontz v. St. Johns River Water Mgmt. Dist., 570 U.S. 595 (2013) (applying regulatory takings analysis to wetland permit denial when denial was based on applicant refusal to concede to agency mitigation requests).

85. *See* Chapter 6, notes 146–149 thereof, and accompanying text.

86. William M. Lewis, Wetlands Explained: Wetland Science, Policy, and Politics in America (Oxford Press, 2001).

regulatory program have performed a service to the country by highlighting the need for meaningful reform in the administration of wetland regulatory programs."[87] Today, critics remain, and that statement still rings true. As discussed above, 2021–2024 saw the White House set extremely ambitious goals for the restoration and conservation of wetlands, which correspond with similar goals set by a number of countries around the world. These goals, if realized, would restore and protect 8 million acres of wetlands nationally and 850 million acres globally.[88] While we can likely never fully restore the estimated 391 million acres of wetlands present during Colonial America,[89] these ambitious goals may give hope to the critics. Whether these goals will translate into regulatory reform—and whether they will even survive the next presidential administration—are unknown at this time, but the space bears close watching.

Wetlands regulation will remain an important, yet controversial area of environmental and natural resources law, particularly in the era of climate change. Those who practice law or consult in the area work to represent stakeholders who usually hold strong, and divergent, views. It is always exciting to practice wetlands law and work on wetlands policy issues in this constantly shifting landscape.

87. *See Protecting America's Wetlands: A Fair, Flexible, And Effective Approach, supra* note 20.

88. White House, The America the Beautiful Freshwater Challenge: A Partnership to Conserve and Restore America's Rivers, Lakes, Streams, and Wetlands (April 2024), at 1, https://www.whitehouse.gov/wp-content/uploads/2024/04/America-the-Beautiful-Freshwater-Challenge.pdf.

89. See Chapter 1, note 20, Executive Summary ("At the time of Colonial America, the area that now constitutes the 50 United States contained an estimated 392 million acres of wetlands."

TABLE OF CASES